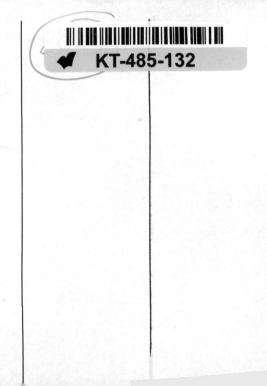

Moscow

"All you've got to do is decide to go
and the hardest part is over.

So go!"

TONY WHEELER, COFOUNDER – LONELY PLANET

Contents

Left: Russian man

Above: Moscow skyline

Right: Georgian *khachapuri* pastry (p43)

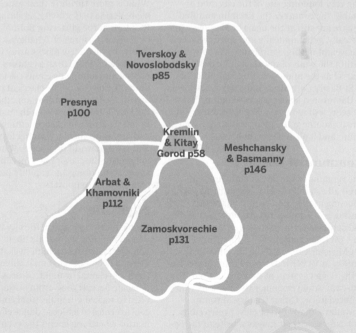

Welcome to Moscow

During any season, any hour of the day, Moscow thrills visitors with its artistry, history and majesty.

Kremlin & Red Square

The very founding site of the city (and arguably, the country), the Kremlin and Red Square are still at the heart of Moscow – historically, geographically and spiritually. Feel the weight of this significance as you wander within the walls of the ancient fortress, marvel at the mind-boggling magnificence of St Basil's Cathedral, and pay your respects to the revered leader of a now-defunct state. Moscow will move you. She'll tantalise your senses, soothe your spirit, and boggle your mind; and it all starts right here.

Communist History

The remains of the Soviet state are scattered all around the city. Monuments remember fallen heroes and victorious battles, while museums attempt to analyse and synthesise the past. See Lenin and Stalin – off their pedestals – at the whimsical Art Muzeon. Step into the Socialist Realist fantasy at VDNKh. Descend into the depths of the Soviet system at Bunker-42 Cold War Museum. And remember the millions who suffered at the Gulag History Museum. Nowadays, many fun or clever retro clubs and cafes give their guests a taste of the Soviet experience. You can even try your hand at Soviet-era arcade games (beyond Tetris).

Performing Arts

What is more thrilling than watching a nimble ballerina defy gravity, as she spins across the stage at the glittering Bolshoi Theatre? Or feeling the force of Tchaikovsky's *1812 Overture,* just a few blocks away from where it premiered more than a century ago? Or oohing and aahing as circus performers soar under the big tent? The classical performing arts in Moscow are still among the best in the world. Nowadays, even the most traditional theatres are experimenting with innovative arrangements, reviving lost favourites and hosting world premieres. Whether you appreciate the classics or experiment with the contemporary, the capital's performing arts are sure to impress.

Nightlife

People like to talk about 'the city that never sleeps', but they should talk about Moscow. You don't have to be a high-heeled glamour girl or a deep-pocketed man about town to enjoy the capital by night. Moscow has a club or a cafe for everyone, from nostalgia-rich retro to rocked-out indie, from contemporary-cool art cafes to let-loose dance clubs. And no matter where you spend the evening, all are invited to gather in the wee hours to watch the sunrise over Moscow's golden domes and silver skyscrapers.

Why I Love Moscow

By Mara Vorhees, Author

The Russian capital never ceases to inspire, confound, disgust or delight me in some unexpected way. This time I was thrilled to discover the capital's new obsession with 'park life'. Not just summer cafes – I've always appreciated that – but also bike paths, ping-pong clubs, outdoor theatres and dance parties. It's hip to be outside and active; and the city has accommodated with gorgeous green spaces. The Park of Culture and Leisure (aka Gorky Park) has finally come into its own – along with a new generation of health-conscious, hopeful Muscovites.

For more about our authors, see p272.

Top: Dancers at the Cathedral of Christ the Saviour

Moscow's
Top 10

The Kremlin (p60)

1 This ancient fortress is the founding site of Moscow and the ultimate symbol of political power in Russia. Within its ancient walls you can admire the artistry of Russia's greatest icon painters, shed a tear for Russia's great and tragic rulers, peer down the barrel of the gargantuan Tsar Cannon and gawk at the treasure trove that fuelled a revolution. On your way out, admire the bouquets left by newlyweds and scrutinise the perfect synchronicity of the guards at the Tomb of the Unknown Soldier.

⊙ *Kremlin & Kitay Gorod*

Red Square (p75)

2 Stepping onto Red Square never ceases to inspire: the tall towers and imposing walls of the Kremlin, the playful jumble of patterns and colours adorning St Basil's Cathedral, the majestic red bricks of the State History Museum and the elaborate edifice of GUM, all encircling a vast stretch of cobblestones. Individually they are impressive, but the ensemble is electrifying. Come at night to see the square empty of crowds and the buildings awash in lights. BELOW: ST BASIL'S CATHEDRAL (P77)

⊙ *Kremlin & Kitay Gorod*

JEROEN P│WILLBEHOMESOON.COM / GETTY IMAGES ©

TIM MAKINS / GETTY IMAGES ©

Ballet at the Bolshoi (p87)

3 An evening at the Bolshoi Theatre is the ultimate 'special occasion' in the capital. Ever since its opening in 1824, the theatre has offered a magical setting for a spectacle. Nowadays, the recently renovated main stage sparkles even brighter than before, with expanded theatre space draped in rich red velour and glittering with newly gilded mouldings. The historic theatre is the premier place to see the Bolshoi Ballet – one of the leading ballet companies in the country (and the world). BELOW: DANCERS PERFORMING *SERENADE*, CHOREOGRAPHY BY GEORGE BALANCHINE © THE GEORGE BALANCHINE TRUST

☆ *Tverskoy & Novoslobodsky*

Gorky Park (p133)

4 The revamp of Gorky Park has turned a decrepit theme park – famed setting for spy novels – into Moscow's hippest, most happening hot spot. From morning (when runners ply the riverside path) to night (when dancers move to sultry music), the hipsters have taken over. In fact, the whole length of the Krymskyaya nab – from Red October to Vorobyovy Gory – has been redesigned into a chain of sparkling fountains, sport courts, outdoor art exhibits and summer cafes. From May to September, there's no better place to be.

◉ *Zamoskvorechie*

5

Suzdal *(p168)*

5 Gently winding waterways, flower-drenched meadows and a dome-spotted skyline make this medieval capital a perfect fairy-tale setting. Under Muscovite rule, Suzdal was a wealthy monastic centre; in the late 17th and 18th centuries, wealthy merchants paid for the construction of 30 charming churches. Suzdal was bypassed by the railway and later protected by the Soviet government, all of which limited development in the area. These days, its main features are its abundance of ancient architectural gems and its decidedly rural atmosphere. LEFT: MUSEUM OF MODERN ARCHITECTURE & PEASANT LIFE (P171)

⊙ *Day Trips from Moscow*

Banya at Sanduny Baths *(p99)*

6 What better way to cope with big-city stress than to have it steamed, washed and beaten out of you? The *banya* is a uniquely Russian experience that will leave you feeling clean, refreshed and relaxed. Even in winter, the tension of constant cold is released by the hot, steamy bath, while a beating with birch branches helps to improve circulation. Sanduny is Moscow's oldest bathhouse – a luxurious setting in which to indulge in this national pastime.

🏃 *Tverskoy & Novoslobodsky*

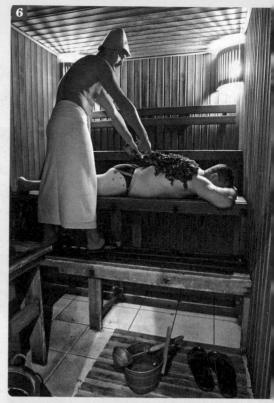

Tretyakov Gallery (p135)

7 The memorable Russian Revival building on Lavrushinsky per is Moscow's largest art museum, covering the span of Russian art history from ancient icons to avant-garde. (Indeed, the Tretyakov's second building on Krymsky val continues further into the 20th century with Supremetism, constructivism and, of course, socialist realism.) The Tretyakov is famed for its impressive collection of wonderful realist paintings by the Peredvizhniki. But the museum also contains show-stopping examples of Russian Revival and art nouveau artwork.

◉ *Zamoskvorechie*

Shopping at Izmaylovsky Market (p150)

8 It's a fine line between shopping and fun at the kremlin Win Izmailovo. Cross the footbridge and walk through the tent-roofed gate to enter a Disney-like medieval village, complete with wooden church, whitewashed walls and plenty of souvenir shops. Just as in times of yore, the best shopping is in the trade rows outside the kremlin walls. Wander among the stalls of the sprawling market to find an endless array of traditional handicrafts, as well as art and antiques, Central Asian carpets, Soviet paraphernalia and more.

🔒 *Meshchansky & Basmanny*

Moscow Metro *(p37)*

9 The Moscow metro is at once a history lesson and an art museum (not to mention a pretty efficient form of transportation). Construction started in the 1930s and it continues today. The design of the stations and the direction of the expansion tell a story about Moscow in the 20th and 21st centuries. Even more intriguing is the amazing artwork and architectural design that characterises the stations, many of which are constructed from granite and marble, and are adorned with mosaics, bas-reliefs and other detailing.

⊙ *Tour of the Metro*

Moscow River Boat Tours *(p33)*

10 Avoid traffic jams, feel the breeze on your face and get a new perspective on the city's most famous sights when you see them from one of the ferry boats that ply the Moscow River. The 90-minute tour provides a wonderful overview of the city, cruising past Novodevichy Convent, Gorky Park, the Cathedral of Christ the Saviour, the Kremlin and Novospassky Monastery. Incidentally, the ferry can also be a useful form of transport from one sight to another.

🏃 *Guided Tours*

What's New

Park Life

Moscow's major green spaces – namely **Gorky Park** (p133) and **Hermitage Garden** (p88) – have been revamped into vibrant centres of sport and culture. Gone (mostly) are the kiddie rides and unkempt areas. In their place are sport clubs, bike trails, music festivals, art exhibits, dance parties – and, of course, plenty of summer cafes. Young, active 'hipsters' are digging park life in these new-found urban oases.

Jewish Museum & Centre for Tolerance

The excellent, interactive multimedia presentations encourage visitors to ask challenging questions at this brand new, ground-breaking museum. (p89)

Moscow Museum

This city museum has a new location and a new mission. Visit the cool post-industrial space (formerly a Defence Ministry warehouse) for artistic, thought-provoking exhibits on contemporary issues. (p125)

Krymskaya naberezhnaya

This embankment is now closed to traffic and filled with fountains and art. The fantastic urban space also provides a perfect pedestrian route from Red October to Gorky Park. (p137)

Flakon

This former glassworks has been turned over to artists and designers. Besides the business offices and design studios, there are a slew of cool boutiques selling truly original stuff. (p92)

Street Food

Moscow's parks and plazas are dotted with cafes, kiosks and food trucks, serving up cheap tasties. Sample the best of Moscow's street food around Gorky Park and Hermitage Garden. (p44)

War of 1812 Museum

The war got a new museum for its 100-year anniversary. What better use for the former Central Lenin Museum building? (p79)

Author Cuisine

The dining scene in Moscow keeps getting better and better, as creative chefs offer their own interpretations of international cuisine. The focus is on freshness, flavour and – above all – innovation. (p43)

Road Manners

Big cars are no longer above the law, it seems. Not only are parking restrictions enforced (no more footpath parking), but drivers actually stop for pedestrians on the crosswalk. (p186)

Velo Bike

Launched in 2013, Moscow's bike-share program has hundreds of bikes available at a few dozen stations around town. Anyone with a credit card can use one. (p231)

Summer Music Festivals

City dwellers rock the summer away at big-name music festivals, held at the VDNKh, Gorky Park, Kolomenskoe and Art Muzeon.

For more recommendations and reviews, see **lonelyplanet.com/Moscow**

Need to Know

For more information, see Survival Guide (p227)

Currency
Roubles (₽)

Language
Russian

Visas
Nearly all foreigners visiting Russia need a visa to enter. Details of the application process vary depending on where you apply and what kind of visa you need. See p30.

Money
ATMs widely available. Credit cards accepted by most hotels and restaurants.

Mobile Phones
Local SIM cards can be used in European and Australian phones; other phones must be set to roaming.

Time
Moscow Time (GMT/USC plus three hours)

Daily Costs

Budget less than ₽1500
➡ Dorm beds: from ₽500

➡ Cheap, filling meals at cafeterias: less than ₽300

➡ Use student ID (if available) or take advantage of free sights and activities

Midrange ₽1500-8000
➡ Double rooms: from ₽2500 at hostels, from ₽3500 at minihotels

➡ *Prix-fixe* lunch menus: ₽200–500

➡ Two-course dinner with a glass of wine: ₽600–1000

➡ Tickets to the theatre: from ₽500

Top End more than ₽8000
➡ Double rooms: start at ₽8000 and go all the way up

➡ Two-course meals: from ₽1000

➡ Bolshoi Theatre tickets: from ₽1000

Advance Planning

Two months before Apply for your visa.

One month before Reserve accommodations. Reserve tickets for the Bolshoi and other theatres.

One week before Book any guided tours that you intend to take.

One day before Book a taxi from the airport, if necessary.

Useful Websites

Lonely Planet (www.lonelyplanet.com/moscow) Destination information, hotel booking, traveller forum and more.

Calvert Journal (www.calvertjournal.com) Excellent articles on Russia's contemporary creative culture.

Moscow Times (www.themoscowtimes.com) Leading English-language newspaper in Moscow.

Expat.ru (www.expat.ru) Run by and for English-speaking expats living in Moscow.

Art Guide (www.artguide.ru) Listings for exhibits and other arty events, as well as museum listings.

Moscow is My Oyster (http://moscowismyoyster.tumblr.com) Fun blog about eating, drinking, shopping and people-watching in Moscow.

WHEN TO GO

Standout seasons to visit are late spring and early autumn. Summer is also pleasant, and long hours of sunlight bring out revellers.

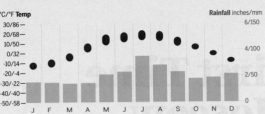

Arriving in Moscow

Airports All three airports are accessible by the convenient Aeroexpress train (p228) from the city centre. If you wish to take a taxi, book an official airport taxi through the dispatcher counter (₽2000 to ₽2500).

Train stations Rail riders will arrive at one of the central train stations. All of the train stations are located in the city centre, with easy access to the metro. Alternatively, most taxi companies offer a fixed rate of ₽400 to ₽600 for a train-station transfer.

For much more on **arrival** see p228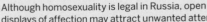

Etiquette

Russians are sticklers for formality. Follow these tips to avoid faux pas.

➡ **Visiting Homes** Remove your shoes and coat on entering a house. Always bring a gift. If you give anyone flowers, make sure it's an odd number – even numbers of blooms are for funerals.

➡ **Religion** Women should cover their heads and shoulders when entering a church. Some monasteries and churches also require skirts. Men should remove their hats and avoid wearing shorts.

➡ **Eating & Drinking** Russians eat resting their wrists on the table edge, with fork in left hand and knife in the right.

Sleeping

Advance reservations are highly recommended, especially if you intend to stay at a minihotel or hostel, most of which only have a handful of rooms, which are often booked out. Weekdays (Sunday to Thursday nights) are especially busy – and more expensive – due to business travellers. Moscow has some of the world's highest average hotel rates (though this situation has improved). Five-star hotels offer fabulous service and amenities, but you will pay for them. Don't expect much value for your money at midrange hotels. Hostels, on the other hand, often offer friendly faces and loads of services for the price of a dorm bed.

Useful Websites

➡ **Booking.com** (www. booking.com) Often offers the best deals on rooms.

➡ **Moscow Hotels** (www. moscow-hotels.com) Descriptions of rooms and services, plus online booking.

➡ **Moscow Hotels** (www. moscow-hotels.net) Room descriptions, plus online booking.

For much more on **sleeping** see p174

LGBT TRAVELLERS

Although homosexuality is legal in Russia, open displays of affection may attract unwanted attention. Watchdog groups have reported an increase in violence since 2011 legislation banning 'gay propaganda'. There have also been reports of police harassment around gay clubs and cruising areas in Moscow. Exercise extra caution around LGBT-specific venues (or avoid them) and you are unlikely to experience any problems. For more information, see p233.

First Time Moscow

For more information, see Survival Guide (p227)

Check List

➡ Make sure your passport is valid for at least six months beyond the expiry date of your visa.

➡ Arrange your visa (p30).

➡ Check airline baggage restrictions.

➡ Check travel advisory websites.

➡ Tell banks and credit-card providers your travel dates.

➡ Organise travel insurance.

What to Pack

➡ Good walking shoes – Russian cities are best explored on foot.

➡ A phrasebook or translation app.

➡ Earplugs and eye mask for noisy hotels and bright White Nights.

➡ A good supply of Ibuprofin (or pain killer of you choice) for the morning after.

➡ Sense of humour and a bucketful of patience.

Top Tips for Your Trip

➡ Consider using a specialist travel agency to arrange visas.

➡ Treat yourself to a stay at a business or luxury hotel at the weekend, when rates drop substantially.

➡ Fixed-price lunches – common in Moscow – are a great deal and an ideal way to sample the cuisine at fancier restaurants.

➡ Schedule some time out of the capital at rural or off-the-beaten track destinations to fully appreciate what is special about Russia.

What to Wear

Muscovites are style mavens. They are not always successful, but most Muscovites make an effort to look good – not only for the theatre or a posh restaurant, but also for an outing to the park or a stroll around town. If you want to go out on the town, plan to 'dress up' – that means dresses and heels for women, and collared shirts and leather shoes for men. Sneakers, sandals and jeans are not acceptable.

For sightseeing, a comfortable pair of waterproof walking shoes will come in handy, as will an umbrella or rain jacket.

In winter, bundle up with several layers and wear a long, windproof coat to stay nicely warm. Hats and coats are always removed on entering a museum or restaurant and left in the cloakroom.

Be Forewarned

Moscow is a mostly safe city, with relatively little street crime and no dangerous 'bad' parts of town. Some precautionary measures:

➡ Be extra alert about pickpockets at train stations and metro stations.

➡ Avoid unofficial taxi cabs late at night, especially those waiting outside clubs and bars.

➡ Never get in a taxi that already has two or more people in it.

➡ Always carry a copy of your passport, visa and registration. Dark-skinned people, in particular, may be targets for police harassment.

Money

➡ Even if prices are listed in US dollars or euros, you will be presented with a final bill in roubles.

➡ ATMs, linked to international networks are all over Moscow – look for signs that say 'bankomat' (банкомат).

➡ Credit cards are commonly accepted, but Americans may have some difficulty if they do not have a 'chip and pin' credit card. This is more of a problem at shops than at hotels and restaurants.

➡ Inform your bank or credit-card provider of the dates you'll be travelling in Russia, to avoid a situation where the card is blocked.

Bargaining

Prices are fixed in shops, but at souvenir markets, such as Izmaylovsky, polite haggling over prices is expected. You'll get 5% off with little effort, but vendors rarely budge past 10%.

Tipping

➡ **Restaurants** Leave small change or 10%, if the service warrants it.

➡ **Guides** Around 10% of their daily rate; a small gift will also be appreciated.

➡ **Taxis** No need to tip as the fare is either agreed to before you get in or metered.

➡ **Hotels** Only in the most luxurious hotels need you tip bellboys etc, and only if service is good.

Language

English is becoming more common, especially among younger folks. All hotels are likely to have English-speaking staff, while restaurant and museum staff might have more limited skills. In recent years, English signs have appeared in metro stations and at major attractions. Most restaurants offer menus in English. Still, learning Cyrillic and a few key phrases will help you decode street signs and timetables.

Phrases to Learn Before You Go

 Is this Moscow or local time?
Это московское или местное время?
e·ta ma·skof·ska·ye i·li myes·na·ye vryem·ya

Russia has 11 time zones but the entire country's rail and air networks run on Moscow time. Ask if you're not certain what time zone your transport is running on.

 I live in Moscow, I won't pay that much.
Я живу в Москве, я не буду платить так много.
ya zhih·vu v mask·vye ya nye bu·du pla·tit' tak mno·ga

Taxi drivers and market sellers sometimes try to charge foreigners more, so you may want to bargain in Russian.

 Are you serving?
Вы обслуживаете? vih aps·lu·zhih·va·it·ye

It may be hard to attract the attention of workers in the service industry – if you want to get served, use this polite expression.

 I don't drink alcohol.
Я не пью спиртного.
ya nye pyu spirt·no·va

Refusing a drink from generous locals can be very difficult, so if you're really not in the mood you'll need a firm, clear excuse.

 May I have an official receipt, please?
Дайте мне официальную расписку, пожалуйста.
deyt·ye mnye a·fi·tsi·yal'·nu·yu ras·pis·ku pa·zhal·sta

Russian authorities might expect an unofficial payment to expedite their service, so always ask for an official receipt.

Street Names

We use the transliteration of Russian names of streets and squares to help you when deciphering Cyrillic signs and asking locals the way. See Language (p237) for more.

➡ al – alleya (аллея; alley)

➡ bul – bulvar (бульвар; boulevard)

➡ nab – naberezhnaya (набережная; embankment)

➡ per – pereulok (переулок; lane or side street)

➡ pl – ploshchad (площадь; square)

➡ pr – prospekt (проспект; avenue)

➡ sh – shosse (шоссе; highway)

➡ ul – ulitsa (улица; street)

Getting Around

For more information, see Transport (p228)

Metro

The Moscow metro is cheap, efficient, interesting to look at, and easy to use. The downside is that it's uncomfortably crowded during peak periods.

Taxi

Well-marked 'official' taxi cabs do not roam the streets looking for fares. Catch a cab by flagging down a car (but be prepared for an unofficial unmarked cab) or by booking through a licensed agency.

Walking

Distances can be vast, but Moscow is a surprisingly walkable city, especially in the centre. Use the underground crosswalk when crossing busy streets.

Bicycle

Cycling on the streets is dangerous but it's a pleasant way to get around if you stick to the cycling routes along the river and in the city parks. Bikes are available from VeloBike and various rental stations around town.

Other Transport

A network of buses, trolleybuses, trams and *marshrutki* (fixed-route minibuses) transport Muscovites around town, but they are difficult to navigate without knowing the routes. They will not be useful for most visitors.

Key Phrases

Poezdka (Поездка) Metro ride. When purchasing tickets, ask for 'one ride' *(odnu poezdku)* or 'five rides' *(pyat poezdok)*, etc.

Vy seychas vykhodite? (Вы сейчас выходите?) Literally 'Are you exiting now?' used when trying to reach the door to exit the train. (The implication is, 'If not, get out of the way.')

Perekhod (Переход) Transfer from one line to another.

Vykhod v gorod (Выход в город) Exit to the city.

How to Hail a Taxi

In lively nightlife areas or outside hotels you might find taxi cabs waiting for a fare, but normally they are few and far between. Unofficial cabs are common and relatively safe:

➡ Go out to the street, stick out your hand and flag down a passing car.

➡ Do not get into a car that already has a passenger. If you are not comfortable with the car or driver for any reason, wave him on.

➡ Otherwise, state your destination. The driver might name a price, in which case you should feel free to negotiate.

➡ If the driver does not state a price, it's at your discretion. Normally, you can travel anywhere in the city centre for ₽200 to ₽300. During heavy traffic or late at night, you should offer more.

➡ Alternatively, you can call a taxi company and schedule a pick-up (or ask your hotel to do so). It's also possible to book taxis online. See p229.

TOP TIPS

➡ Moscow traffic can be brutal, especially during peak travel periods. Go metro!

➡ Buy multiple-ride tickets (five, 11 or 20 rides) to avoid queuing to buy tickets each time.

➡ Transfers from one metro line to another require long walks and extra time. Study your metro map before you set out to avoid or minimise changing lines.

➡ If you want to use the Moscow River ferries as transportation, purchase an all-day pass, which allows you to get on and off at any stop along the route.

When to Travel

➡ The metro runs from 5.30am to 1.30am.

➡ On working days (Monday through Friday), street traffic is almost always heavy, and the metro is almost always busy. But during rush hours (8am to 10am, 5pm to 7pm), it's jam-packed.

➡ If you can't avoid travelling during these hours, keep your elbows out and eyes alert. You probably won't encounter any problems, but you will have to queue to ride the escalator and fight for your space on the train.

➡ For more leisurely travel, ride the metro on weekends or during the week after 8pm.

Metro Etiquette

➡ Have your ticket ready before you approach the turnstyle.

➡ On the escalator, stand on the right and walk on the left.

➡ When the train pulls up to the platform and doors open, let riders exit the train before you get on.

➡ Offer your seat to elderly riders, children and pregnant women.

➡ When preparing to exit, position yourself near the door as the train approaches your station. If somebody is in your way, you can ask 'Vy seychas vykhodite?' (Are you exiting now?) to indicate your intention to get off.

➡ When making transfers between lines, walk on the left side of the perekhod (walkway).

Tickets

➡ The Moscow metro is still the capital's best bargain. One ride is ₽40, but you will save time and money if you buy multiple-ride tickets (five rides for ₽160, 11 rides for ₽320, 20 rides for ₽540).

➡ Buy your ticket at the window or at the automated machine.

➡ You will receive a paper card, which you tap on the reader (a circle light) before going through the turnstyle.

➡ When you tap your ticket, the reader will turn green to indicate that you should pass. It also displays a number to inform you how many rides you have left.

For much more on **getting around** see p229 ➡

LP MAGAZINE / GETTY IMAGES ©

Moscow metro (p37)

Top Itineraries

Day One

Kremlin & Kitay Gorod (p58)

 Arrive at the Kremlin ticket office at 9.30am sharp to reserve your time to enter the **Armoury**. Dedicate your morning to inspecting the ancient icons and gawking at the gold and gems in the Kremlin. Afterwards, stroll through **Alexander Garden** and catch the changing of the guard at the **Tomb of the Unknown Soldier**. Exiting Alexander Garden, jump right into the queue on Red Square for **Lenin's Tomb** before it closes at 1pm.

> **Lunch** Have lunch at Bosco Cafe (p81) or Stolovaya 57 (p81).

Kremlin & Kitay Gorod (p58)

 Linger over lunch as long as you like, ogling the Kremlin spires and St Basil's domes. If you wish to see the interior of the **cathedral**, you can do so after lunch. Otherwise, stroll through **Kitay Gorod**, discovering the countless **17th-century churches**.

> **Dinner** Dine at a restaurant on ul Petrovka, such as Lavka-Lavka (p94).

Tverskoy (p85)

Get tickets in advance to see a show at the world-famous **Bolshoi Theatre**. Afterwards, enjoy a late evening drink at **3205 in Hermitage Garden**.

Day Two

Khamovniki (p112)

 A beautiful 17th-century bell tower is the beacon that will guide you to the historic fortress of **Novodevichy Convent**, which contains nearly five centuries of history. After admiring the art and architecture, head next door to the eponymous cemetery, where many famous political and cultural figures are laid to rest.

> **Lunch** Indulge in a traditional lunch at Golubka (p127) or Stolle (p128).

Arbat (p112)

Make your way into the Arbat district for an afternoon of art appreciation. Peruse the collections of the world-famous **Pushkin Museum of Fine Arts**, or investigate one of the smaller niche galleries, such as whimsical **Burganov House** or the provocative **Multimedia Art Museum**.

> **Dinner** Sample scrumptious Georgian cuisine at Elardzhi (p127).

Arbat (p112)

After dinner you can stroll along Moscow's most famous street – **the Arbat** – enjoying the talents of buskers and the atmosphere of old Moscow. If you prefer a more formal setting for your entertainment, catch a concert at **Rhythm Blues Cafe**.

DANITA DELIMONT / GETTY IMAGES ©

Tomb of the Unknown Soldier (p74)

Day Three

Zamoskvorechie (p131)

 Get an early start to beat the crowds to the **Tretyakov Gallery**. Take your time inspecting the icons, examining the Peredvizhniki, marvelling at the Russian Revival and ogling the avant-garde.

> **Lunch** Grab lunch at Produkty (p140) or Mizandari (p140) at Red October.

Zamoskvorechie (p131)

After lunch, stroll along the **Krymskaya naberezhnaya**, where you can frolic in fountains and explore the outdoor art gallery at **Art Muzeon**. Then head across the street to **Gorky Park** for an afternoon of bicycle riding or boat paddling. Stay into the evening for outdoor cinema, sundowners, and drinking and dancing under the stars.

> **Dinner** Dine at a summer cafe, such as AC/DC in Tbilisi (p140).

Zamoskvorechie (p131)

It's easy to wile away a summer evening in Gorky Park. But if you're up for something more, the former **Red October** factory is now the city's hottest nightlife spot, jam-packed with eating, drinking and entertainment venues. Let yourself wander, stopping here for dessert, there for drinks, and somewhere else for dancing. Explore the galleries. Rock the bar scene. Have fun.

Day Four

Izmailovo (p150)

Reserve the morning for shopping at the **Izmaylovsky Market**, crammed with souvenir stalls selling everything from silver samovars to Soviet propaganda posters to modern pop-culture *matryoshki*.

> **Lunch** Izmaylovsky market is famous for the grilled shashlyk (kebabs).

Basmanny (p146)

On your way back to the centre, make a stop at **Flakon** or **Winzavod Center for Contemporary Art** and nearby **ArtPlay** to see what's happening in Moscow's former industrial spaces. These contemporary art centres now undertake a different kind of production – art, fashion and design – where you can continue your souvenir shopping.

> **Dinner** Reserve your table for an *hauterusse* feast at Café Pushkin (p107).

Presnya (p100)

 Dinner at the Café Pushkin is a multicourse medley of old-fashioned Russian cuisine (accompanied by plenty of vodka shots). If you're still standing afterwards, head to Jagger (p110) or Manon Club (p110) for sunset drinks and dancing the night away.

If You Like...

Architecture

Ascension Church at Kolomenskoe The first building with a tent roof on a brick structure, creating a uniquely Russian style. (p141)

Hotel Metropol An art nouveau masterpiece, replete with mosaics, stained glass and wrought iron. (p177)

VDNKh Exuberant fountains and Socialist Realist architecture galore. (p90)

Ostankino TV Tower Still one of the tallest free-standing structures in the world. (p90)

Narkomfin and **Melnikov House** Two quintessential examples of Constructivist architecture, now in states of disrepair. (p103) (p123)

Ryabushinsky Mansion Shekhtel's whimsical fusion of Russian Revival and art nouveau. (p102)

Church of the Trinity in Nikitniki An exquisite example of Russian baroque, concealed by hulking grey edifices. (p80)

Moscow State University One of Stalin's Seven Sisters, the ultimate in Stalinist grandiosity. (p126)

Contemporary Art

Garage Museum of Contemporary Art An exciting contemporary art venue housed in a paper pavilion at Gorky Park. (p137)

Winzavod Center for Contemporary Art A former wine-bottling facility that's home Moscow's most prestigious art galleries. (p148)

Lenin's Mausoleum (p75)

Multimedia Art Museum
Excellent photography and other multimedia exhibits in a newly revamped building. (p125)

Red October A former chocolate factory, now home to bars, cafes and a handful of galleries. (p137)

Burganov House A working studio that displays the artist's creations as well as some examples from his private collection. (p123)

Tsereteli Studio-Museum A classical mansion filled with enamel artistry and a courtyard crammed with sculptures. (p104)

Moscow Museum of Modern Art An eclectic collection of works by artists from the 20th and 21st centuries. (p88)

Soviet History

Lenin's Mausoleum Pay your respects to the founder of the Soviet state. (p75)

Art Muzeon Soviet heroes put out to pasture. (p137)

Bunker-42 Cold War Museum A secret underground Cold War communications centre that's now open for exploration. (p149)

Moscow metro A monument to socialism and populism. (p37)

VDNKh Also known as the USSR Economic Achievements Exhibition. (p90)

Gulag History Museum A memorial to the victims of the harsh Soviet justice system. (p88)

Contemporary History Museum Features an excellent selection of propaganda posters, amid other Soviet nostalgia. (p89)

Charming Churches

Ul Varvarka in Kitay Gorod A tiny street lined with 17th-century churches. (p82)

Upper St Peter Monastery Home of the lovely Cathedral of Metropolitan Pyotr. (p88)

Church of the Small Ascension A 17th-century beauty with whitewashed walls and carved detailing. (p102)

Church of the Nativity of the Virgin in Putinki An elaborate concoction of tent roofs and onion domes. (p89)

Church of St Nicholas in Khamovniki Colourful church of the weavers' guild, which was also the home church of Leo Tolstoy. (p125)

Church of St John the Warrior An 18th-century example of Moscow baroque. (p139)

Iconography

Tretyakov Gallery The world's best collection of icons, including the revered *Holy Trinity* by Andrei Rublyov. (p135)

Annunciation Cathedral in the Kremlin Iconostasis featuring work by Andrei Rublyov, Theo-phanes the Greek and Prokhor of Gorodets. (p71)

Museum of the Russian Icon Thousands of examples from the private collection of a Russian businessman. (p149)

Rublyov Museum of Early Russian Culture & Art A small museum on the grounds of the monastery where Rublyov was a monk. (p151)

For more top Moscow spots, see the following:

➡ Museums & Galleries (p35)

➡ Tour of the Metro (p37)

➡ Eating (p41)

➡ Drinking & Nightlife (p45)

➡ Entertainment (p48)

➡ Shopping (p52)

PLAN YOUR TRIP IF YOU LIKE...

Parks & Gardens

Gorky Park Moscow's most famous green space is now an ideal spot for riverside strolls and bike rides. (p133)

Hermitage Garden Summer cafes and outdoor theaters dot this inner-city oasis. (p88)

Alexander Garden A flower-filled space just outside the Kremlin walls. (p74)

Aptekarsky Ogorod An urban botanical garden with species from three climate zones. (p150)

Vorobyovy Gory Nature Preserve The wooded hillocks overlooking a picturesque bend in the Moscow River. (p126)

Russian Literature

Tolstoy Estate-Museum The Moscow residence of Russia's greatest realist novelist. (p125)

Bulgakov House-Museum Long a pilgrimage site; now a cool literary hang-out. (p103)

Gogol House The abode where Gogol spent his final tortured months. (p102)

Pushkin House-Museum A short-term home for the national bard and his new bride. (p123)

Month by Month

January

Though January represents the deepest, darkest days of winter, it is a festive month, kicked off by New Year's celebrations in the grandest tradition.

☆ Winter Festival

An outdoor fun-fest for two weeks in December and January for those with antifreeze in their veins. Admire the ice sculptures on Red Square, stand in a crowd of snowmen on ul Arbat and ride the troika at Izmaylovsky Park.

☆ Winter Holidays

Locals ring in the New Year with friends, with a city-wide celebration on Red Square. For the faithful, all-night church services take place on Christmas (7 January), while the Epiphany (mid-January) is marked with a plunge into icy water at designated spots around town.

February

Maslenitsa marks the end of winter, but it seems premature. Temperatures are cold, hovering around -10°C for weeks. The city still sparkles with snow, and sledders and skiers are in heaven.

☆ Maslenitsa

This fete kicks off Orthodox Lent. Besides bingeing on *bliny* (crêpes), the week-long festival features horse-drawn sledges and storytelling clowns. The festival culminates with the burning of an effigy to welcome spring.

March

The spring thaw starts at the end of March, when everything turns to mud and slush. It is Moscow's dreariest month: tourists tend to stay away.

☆ International Women's Day

Russia's favourite holiday was founded on 8 March to honour the women's movement. On this day men buy champagne, flowers and chocolates for their better halves – and for all the women in their lives.

April

The days are blustery but spring is in the air. Moscow residents flock to sights and museums during this season, since there are not too many tourists.

☆ Golden Mask Festival

The Golden Mask festival (www.goldenmask.ru) involves two months of performances by Russia's premier drama, opera, dance and musical performers, culminating in a prestigious awards ceremony in April.

May

Spring arrives! Many places have limited hours during the first half of May, due to the public

holidays. Nonetheless, flowers are blooming and people are celebrating.

☆ May Holidays

From May Day (1 May) to Victory Day (9 May), the first half of the month is a nonstop holiday. The city hosts parades on Red Square, as well as fireworks and other events at Park Pobedy.

🎭 Chekhov International Theatre Festival

In odd-numbered years, theatre troupes descend on Moscow from all corners of the world for this renowned biannual festival (www.chekhovfest.ru). Drama and musical theatre performances are held at participating venues around town, from mid-May to mid-June.

June

June is the most welcoming month. Temperatures are mild and the days are long and sunny. The markets are filled with wild berries, and girls wear white bows in their hair to celebrate the end of the school year.

🎭 Moscow International Film Festival

This week-long event (www.moscowfilmfestival.ru) attracts filmmakers from the US and Europe, as well as the most promising Russian artists. Films are shown at theatres around the city.

♟ White Nights

Moscow does not have an official White Nights festival, but the capital still enjoys some 18 hours of daylight in June. Revellers stay out late to stroll in the parks and drink at the many summer terraces and beer gardens.

🎭 Park Live

The biggest concert event of the summer, this three-day open-air music festival (www.parklive.pro) takes place at VDNKh during the last weekend in June.

July

Many Muscovites retreat to their *dachas* to escape summer in the city. The weather is hot and humid. Hotel prices are down in July and August.

☆ Outdoor Concerts

Though many theatres are closed, the concert calendar is packed. Summer is the time for outdoor music festivals, such as Subbotnik (www.subbotnikfestival.ru) in Gorky Park and Afisha Picnic (picnic.afisha.ru) at Kolomenskoe. Estates such as Ostankino and Tsaritsyno host classical concerts on their grounds.

September

Early autumn is a standout time to be in the capital. The heat subsides and the foliage turns the city splendid oranges, reds and yellows.

🎭 City Day

Den goroda (City Day) celebrates Moscow's birthday on the first weekend in September. The day kicks off with a festive parade, followed by live music on Red Square and plenty of food, fireworks and fun.

October

The mild weather and colourful foliage continue in October, though this month usually sees the first snow of the season.

🎭 Moscow Biennale of Contemporary Art

This month-long festival (www.moscowbiennale.ru), held in odd-numbered years (and sometimes in different months), aims to establish the capital as an international centre for contemporary art. Venues across the city exhibit works by artists from around the world.

☆ Kremlin Cup

An international tennis tournament (www.kremlincup.ru) is held every October at the Olympic Stadium. Not surprisingly, Russian players dominate this event.

December

Short days and long nights keep people inside for much of the month. But many bundle up to admire the city sparkling in the snow and partake of one of the city's premier cultural events.

🎭 December Nights Festival

Perhaps Moscow's most prestigious music event, this annual festival (www.artsmuseum.ru) is hosted by the Pushkin Museum of Fine Arts, with a month of performances by high-profile musicians and accompanying art exhibits.

With Kids

Filled with icons and onion domes, the Russian capital might not seem like an appealing destination for kids, but you'd be surprised. In Moscow, little people will find museums, parks, theatres and even restaurants that cater especially to them.

Japanese macaque at Moscow Zoo (p104)

ALEXEY BUBRYAK / GETTY IMAGES ©

Museums

Most sights and museums offer reduced-rate tickets for children up to 12 or 18 years of age. Kids younger than five are often free of charge. Look out for family tickets.

Art Museums

The Pushkin Museum of Fine Arts (p117) and the Museum of Decorative & Folk Art (p91) both have educational centres that allow kids aged five to 13 years to create their own art. Garage Museum of Contemporary Art (p137) also has programs for kids.

Moscow Planetarium

The planetarium (p105) has interactive exhibits that allow kids to perform science experiments, taste freeze-dried space food and run around on the surface of the moon.

Central Museum of the Armed Forces

You might not let your children play with guns, but how about climbing around on tanks, trucks and missiles (p91)?

Experimentanium

A place for children to discover for themselves the answer to the endless 'Why?' (p91).

Soviet Arcade Games Museum

Find out what it was like to be a kid in the Soviet Union (p149).

Outdoor Fun

Even in winter, there are plenty of chances to get outside for fresh air and exercise.

Parks

With over 100 parks and gardens, Moscow has plenty of space for kids to let off steam – many parks include playgrounds. Larger spaces such as Gorky Park (p133), Vorobyovy Gory Nature Preserve (p126) and Izmaylovsky Park (p150) rent bicycles, paddle boats and such.

River Cruises

Most little ones love a boat ride. It's also the perfect way for kids to see the city's historic sights, as there's no need to fight the crowds or linger too long in one place.

Moscow Zoo

Even toddlers will get a kick out of the *detsky zoopark* (children's zoo; p104), with close-up encounters with their favourite animals.

Eating

Many restaurants host 'children's parties' on Saturday and Sunday afternoons, offering toys, games, entertainment and supervision for kids while their parents chow down.

Diners

Classics such as Starlite Diner (p94 and p142) are family favourites, especially on weekends.

Pizza

Pizza guarantees good reception, but several outlets of Akademiya also offer children's programming on weekends.

Play Areas

Restaurants such as Anderson for Pop (p108) and Cafe Schisliva (p127) have dedicated play areas for children. At Elardzhi (p127), kids frolic in the courtyard with playground and petting zoo.

Entertainment

Little ones have never had such a range of entertainment choices.

Musical Theatre

Local legend Natalya Sats founded the Moscow Children's Musical Theatre (p129) to entertain and educate kids with song and dance.

Puppet Theatre

Kids will see hundreds of puppets at the Obraztsov Puppet Museum (p97), then see them come to life at the attached theatre.

Animal Theatre

Kuklachev's cats (p129) and Durov's animals (p98) put on a good show for kids of all ages.

Circus

The acrobatics will astound and amaze, while clowns and animal tricks will leave them laughing. Choose between two acclaimed circuses: Bolshoi Circus on Vernadskogo (p129) and Nikulin Circus on Tsvetnoy Bulvar (p97).

Transport

The metro might be fun for kids, but be careful during rush hour, when trains and platforms are packed. Detskoe Taxi will look out for your kids, and offers smoke-free cars and child seats upon request.

PLAN YOUR TRIP WITH KIDS

For Free

The good news is that Moscow is no longer the most expensive city in the world; the bad news is that it's still pretty darn close. However, budget-minded travellers can find a few bargains if they know where to look.

Festival-goers at Kolomenskoe Museum-Reserve (p141)

Art Centres

Most of Moscow's post-industrial art centres are free to enter (though you may pay for individual galleries or special exhibits). Spend an afternoon browsing the galleries and admiring the architectural repurposing.

Churches

Many of Moscow's churches contain amazing iconography and eye-popping frescoes. The Cathedral of Christ the Saviour (p121), in particular, feels more like a museum than a church.

Parks

Maybe it's no surprise that a park does not charge an admission fee: the surprise is what you'll find inside. Gorky Park (p133) has an open-air cinema and an observatory, which are free of charge. Hermitage Garden (p88) has ping-pong tables, yoga classes and dance lessons – all free.

Estates

At Kolomenskoe Museum-Reserve (p141) and Tsaritsyno Palace (p144) you pay to enter the museums, but seeing the beautiful grounds and churches costs nothing.

Lenin's Tomb

Don't pay money, just pay your respects. This is one of Moscow's wacky and wonderful things to do (p75).

Moscow Metro

So it's not quite free. But it only costs P40 to ride the metro, which is an amazing amalgamation of art museum, history lesson and mass-transit system.

VDNKh

Replete with fountains and socialist realist splendour, this vast complex (p90) is a curious vestige of communist paradise gone awry. Capitalism has taken hold here, but it's still free to enter.

Izmaylovsky Market

Perhaps it goes without saying that you don't have to pay to shop, but this souvenir market (p150) is still a fun, practically free way to spend a day.

Free Museums

Look out for Moscow's 'Night at the Museum', when museums around town waive their entry fees. This occurs annually, usually in May. Some museums are always free.

Jewish Museum & Centre of Tolerance

This is a thought-provoking, barrier-breaking multimedia gem (p89), addressing a challenging but worthy subject.

Ryabushinsky Mansion

Sometimes you do get something for nothing, namely an interesting literary museum and architectural masterpiece (also known as the Gorky House-Museum) (p102).

Museum of the Russian Icon

This is the private collection (p149) of a Russian businessman, who has put it on display – for free – in hopes of reigniting interest in this under-appreciated art form.

Sakharov Centre

Free political and artistic exhibits, as well as information about the life and times of the dissident (p151).

Free Tours

Moscow Free Tour

This highly rated outfit (p32) offers a free daily walking tour, led by knowledgeable and extremely enthusiastic guides.

Moscow Greeter

Volunteer 'greeters' – local residents – show visitors their favourite places in the city. Donations accepted.

Moscow 360

An ambitious tour company (p32) offering four free walking tours.

Free Wi-Fi

At hotels, restaurants and cafes all over Moscow, wi-fi is almost always free.

Visas

Save for a handful of exceptions, everyone needs a visa to visit Russia. Arranging one is straightforward but time-consuming, bureaucratic and – depending on how quickly you need the visa – costly. Start the application process at least a month before your trip.

Tourist at St Basil's Cathedral

ANNA BRYUKHANOVA / GETTY IMAGES ©

Types of Visas

For most travellers a tourist visa (single- or double-entry, valid for a maximum of 30 days) will be sufficient. If you plan to stay longer than a month, you can apply for a business visa or – if you are a US citizen – a three-year multi-entry visa.

Tourist Visa

These are the most straightforward Russian visas available, but they are also the most inflexible. They allow a stay of up to 30 days in the country, with one or two entries within that time period. It is not possible to extend a tourist visa. In addition to the standard documents required for all Russian visas, you'll need a voucher issued by the hotel or travel agency that provided your invitation. Note that Russian consulates also reserve the right to see your return ticket or some other proof of onward travel, but this is rarely requested.

Business Visa

A single-entry business visa is valid for up to three months, while a multiple-entry visa may be valid for up to 12 months. Both of these allow complete freedom of movement once you arrive in Russia. In addition to the standard documents required for all Russian visas, you'll need to include a cover letter stating all details about the traveller, and the date and purpose of the trip.

Three-Year Visa

As of 2012, US citizens are eligible to apply for a three-year multi-entry visa – tourist or business – which is good for stays up to six months at a time. This is a major breakthrough for regular visitors! The application process is essentially the same as that of other visas, although the fee is slightly higher.

Transit Visa

For transit by air, this visa is usually good for up to three days. For a nonstop Trans-Siberian Railway journey it's valid for 10 days, giving westbound passengers a few days in Moscow; those heading east, however, are not allowed to linger. To obtain a transit visa, you will need to show the itinerary for your entire trip, as well as any visa needed for your onward journey.

Application Process

Invitation

To obtain a visa, everyone needs an invitation, also known as 'visa support'. Hotels and hostels provide this service for their guests. If you are not staying in a hotel or hostel, you will need to buy an invitation from a travel agent or via a specialist visa agency. Some companies offering visa support include the following:

➡ **Visa House** (www.visahouse.ru)

➡ **Visa to Russia** (www.visatorussia.com)

➡ **Way to Russia** (www.waytorussia.net)

Application

If at all possible, it's advisable to apply for your visa in your home country; some consulates may decline applications from non-residents.

Start by entering your details in the online form of the Consular Department of the **Russian Ministry of Foreign Affairs** (http://visa.kdmid.ru) and assembling the required documents.

Different consular offices apply different fees and processing rules, so be sure to check the requirements of the specific consulate where you will be applying. Russian embassies in the UK and US have contracted agencies to process the submission of visa applications (for an additional fee, of course):

➡ **VFS.Global** (http://ru.vfsglobal.co.uk) In the UK.

➡ **Invisa Logistic Services** (http://ils-usa.com) In the US.

Other consulates receive applications directly. In addition to the standard documents required for Russian visas, you may be required to provide pay stubs, bank statements, proof of insurance, or proof of property ownership.

If you are travelling with children, you will probably need copies of their birth certificates. The charge for the visa will also vary, depending on the type of visa applied

PLAN YOUR TRIP VISAS

for and how quickly you need it. Avoid potential hassles by checking requirements well in advance.

Registration

Every visitor to Russia is obligated to have their visa registered within seven business days of arrival. If you are in Moscow for less than seven business days, you are exempt. If you leave Moscow, you must register again in any city where you stay seven days or longer.

When you check in at a hotel or hostel, you surrender your passport and visa so the hotel can register you with the local visa office. You'll get your documents back the next day.

If you are staying in a homestay or rental apartment, your landlord can register your visa through the local post office. But this is a big hassle that most landlords don't care to undertake. An easier alternative is to get registered through the agency that issued your invitation (though you'll probably pay an extra fee).

Extensions

Extensions are time consuming and difficult; tourist visas can't be extended at all. Note that many trains out of St Petersburg and Moscow to Eastern Europe cross the border after midnight, so make sure your visa is valid up to and including this day.

Guided Tours

Moscow is a big, overwhelming city with a strange alphabet. Letting the locals show you around is a good way to get your bearings and learn something new. Tipping your guide (₽200 to ₽500) is an accepted practice. Small gifts from home are also appropriate and appreciated.

Moscow River boat tour

Walking Tours

Moscow Free Tour

Every day, these enthusiastic ladies offer an informative, inspired, two-hour guided walk around Red Square and Kitay Gorod – and it's completely free. It's so good, that (they think) you'll sign up for one of their excellent **paid tours** (Map p255; ☑495-222 3466; http://moscowfreetour.com; Nikolskaya ul 4/5; paid tours ₽950-1550), covering the Kremlin, the Arbat and the Metro, or their more thematic tours such as communist Moscow or mystical Moscow.

Moscow 360

This ambitious **company** (☑8-915-205 8360; www.moscow360.org) FREE offers four – count 'em, four! – different walking tours, all of which are free of charge. They include tours of Red Square, the Cathedral of Christ the Saviour and the Metro, as well as – the most unusual – an AK-47 Tour (the guiding and transport are free, but you'll pay to shoot). Tips are gratefully accepted – obviously.

Moscow Mania

This team of historians (with PhDs and everything) are passionate about their city and their subject. They have designed some 50 **tours** (www.mosmania.com; 2hr tours ₽2500-3500) on specialised topics – or they will customise one for you. Private tours for up to eight people.

Patriarshy Dom Tours

Provides a changing schedule of special-ised **tours** (Map p264; ☑495-795 0927; www. toursinrussia.com; Vspolny per 6, Moscow school No 1239; Moscow tours ₽700-900, day trips from ₽1500; Ⓜ Barrikadnaya) of local museums, specific neighbourhoods, and unusual themes, as well as out-of-town trips to the Golden Ring towns and other day-trip destinations. Occasionally takes groups inside the Great Kremlin Palace, which is otherwise closed to the public. Pick up the monthly schedule at upscale hotels or view it online.

Capital Tours

Capital Tours (Map p255; ☑495-232 2442; www.capitaltours.ru; Gostiny Dvor, ul Ilynka 4, entry 6; Kremlin tours ₽1600, other tours ₽900;

⊗10am Fri-Wed; MKitay-Gorod), a spin-off of Patriarshy Dom, offers a daily Kremlin tour, as well as regularly scheduled tours of the metro and Moscow by night. The guides are well informed but not super engaging. Also on offer: a daily four-hour tour of Jewish Moscow, which goes by vehicle to two synagogues and other sites of note.

Boat Tours

Both boat-tour companies follow essentially the same route, from Kievsky vokzal or the Radisson Royal in Dorogomilovo, to Novospassky Monastery in Taganka. Highlights of the trip are Novodevichy Convent, MGU, Gorky Park, the Cathedral of Christ the Saviour and the Kremlin.

Capital Shipping Co

Ferries (ССК, Столичная Судоходная Компания; ☑495-225 6070; www.cck-ship. ru; 90min tour adult/child ₽500/300, 24hr pass ₽800/400) ply the Moscow River from May to September (every 20 minutes); board at any dock along the route. Originally, this was simply a form of transportation, but visitors realised that riding the entire route (1½ hours) was a great way to see the city. Alternatively, buy a full-day pass, which allows you to get on and off at will. CCK also offers boat excursions out of central Moscow, such as to the Nikolo-Ugreshsky Monastery in the eastern suburb of Dzerzhinsky.

Radisson River Cruises

The Radisson operates **big river boats** (www.radisson-cruise.ru; 2½hr cruise adult/child ₽900/650, 1½hr cruise ₽650/450; ⊗1-9pm; MKievskaya) that cart 140 people up and down the Moscow River from the dock in front of the hotel and from the dock in

Gorky Park. In summer, there are five or six daily departures from each location. Boats are enclosed (and equipped with ice cutters), so the cruises run year-round, albeit less frequently in winter.

Bike Tours

Cover more ground and see more sites, while getting fresh air and a bit of exercise: that's a win-win-win!

Moscow Bike Tours (☑8-916-970 1419; www.moscowbiketours.com; 3hr tour ₽1800) runs recommended bike tours, on which you'll enjoy magnificent views of Moscow from Krymskaya embankment, riding through Gorky Park and all the way down to Sparrow Hills, before crossing into Khamovniki. Day and evening rides offered, with an extended tour available on weekends.

Bus Tours

Moscow 360

See the sights of Moscow from the comfort of an air-conditioned **minivan** (☑8-915-205 8360; www.moscow360.org; 3hr tour ₽600; ⊗3.30pm), with an informative, entertaining guide telling tales along the way. The tour covers Tverskaya, Prechistenka, Novodevichy, Sparrow Hills, Park Pobedy and more.

Hop On, Hop Off

Affiliated with Capital Tours, this **colourful bus** (www.hoponhopoff.ru; adult/child ₽600/400; ⊗10am-5pm) circulates around the city centre, stopping at 13 designated points. As the name implies, you can hop on and off as many times as you like within a 24-hour period. Buses are supposed to run every 30 minutes.

Travelling to St Petersburg

Travel between Moscow and St Petersburg has never been easier. If you plan to include the second capital in your itinerary, you're sure to find a transportation option to fit your mood and budget.

Train

All trains to St Petersburg depart from Leningradsky vokzal. Book your tickets at any train station or through your hotel. Alternatively, buy your tickets online at www.tutu.ru (in Russian) or the official site of the Russian railway (www.rzd.ru).

Overnight

There are about 10 overnight trains travelling between Moscow and St Petersburg. Most services depart between 10pm and midnight, arriving the following morning between 6am and 8am.

On the more comfortable *firmeny* trains, a 1st-class *lyuks* ticket (two-person cabin) costs ₽5500 to ₽6000, while a 2nd-class *kupe* (four-person cabin) is ₽3000 to ₽4000.

Sample departure times and fares:

➡ **2 Krasnaya Strela** 11.55pm, eight hours, 1st/2nd class ₽5800/3600

➡ **4 Ekspress** 11.30pm, nine hours, 1st/2nd class ₽5500/3400

➡ **20 Tversk** 12.56am, eight hours, 1st/2nd class ₽6000/4000

➡ **54 Grand Express** 11.40pm, nine hours, 1st/2nd class ₽7600/3600

Sapsan

These high-speed trains travel at 200km/h to make the journey in about four hours. Trains depart throughout the day. Comfortable seats are ₽3100 to ₽3400, except in the early morning, when you'll pay ₽10,000 and up. Sample departure time and fares:

➡ **752 Sapsan** 6.45am, four hours, ₽11,800

➡ **758 Sapsan** 1.30pm, 4½ hours, ₽3400

➡ **762 Sapsan** 4.30pm, four hours, ₽3200

➡ **764 Sapsan** 7.25pm, four hours, ₽3200

Air

All airlines fly into Pulkovo Airport in St Petersburg (75 to 90 minutes). Book flights through the airline websites in advance and you can get tickets as cheap as ₽2200 one way, although normally prices are between ₽3000 and ₽3600.

➡ **Aeroflot** (www.aeroflot.ru) Flies out of Sheremetyevo up to 10 times a day.

➡ **Rossiya Airlines** (www.rossiya-airlines.com) Flies out of Domodedovo about eight times a day.

➡ **S7 Airlines** (www.s7.ru) Flies out of Domodedovo five times a day.

Boat

There are numerous cruise boats plying the routes between Moscow and St Petersburg, most stopping at Uglich, Yaroslavl, Goritsky Monastery, Kizhi and Mondrogy (near Lake Ladoga). Ships are similar in quality and size, carrying about 250 passengers.

➡ **Mosturflot** (www.mosturflot.ru, in Russian) Cruises from seven to 10 days.

➡ **Orthodox Cruise Company** (www.cruise.ru) The *Anton Chekhov* spends 11 days cruising between the cities.

➡ **Rechturflot** (www.rechturflot.ru) The quickest trip is a six-day cruise on the *Ryleev*.

➡ **Vodohod** (www.bestrussiancruises.com) Cruises range from 10 to 13 days.

State History Museum (p79)

Museums & Galleries

Moscow's rich history and dynamic culture are highlights of this cosmopolitan capital, as showcased by the ever-expanding array of museums and galleries. Once a cornerstone of conservatism, these venues are now experimenting with new technologies and subject matter, in an attempt to entertain and educate.

Museums

Moscow is packed with museums. History museums remember every era of Russia's past; countless country estates are now architectural museums; military museums commemorate the nation's wartime heroics; and anybody who was anybody has a 'house-museum' in their honour. There are two space museums, two Jewish museums, and two chocolate museums. Whatever you're into, Moscow has a museum for you.

Galleries

Moscow is home to two world-class art museums: the Tretyakov Gallery, exhibiting Russian art, and the Pushkin Museum of Fine Arts, a showcase mainly for European art. They are both spectacular venues – well worth a day (or more) to admire their wide-ranging collections. In addition to these standard bearers, the capital contains countless smaller niche galleries dedicated to particular artists or genres.

NEED TO KNOW

Opening Hours

Most museums are open from about 10am to 6pm, though hours often fluctuate from day to day. Be aware that most museums are completely closed at least one day a week – often Monday. Look for late evening hours on at least one day a week.

Sanitary Day

Many museums close for cleaning one day per month, usually during the last week of the month.

Admission Prices

Many museums still maintain a dual pricing system, where foreign visitors pay a higher entry fee than Russian residents. Even student prices are often reserved for students of local universities, but it's still worth inquiring.

Lonely Planet's Top Choices

Armoury (p74) Russia's storehouse of priceless treasures and historic artefacts.

Tretyakov Gallery (p135) The crème de la crème of Russian art, from ancient icons to exquisite modernism.

Jewish Museum & Centre of Tolerance (p89) Genii and outcasts, dissidents and revolutionaries – the history of Jews in Russia at a glance.

Best History Museums

The Kremlin (p60) Recounting nearly a thousand years of history, starting from the founding of Moscow.

Bunker-42 Cold War Museum (p149) Descend to the underground – literally – to see this secret Cold War bunker.

Gulag History Museum (p88) Stalin's slaughterhouse – the history of one of the world's cruellest prison systems.

Jewish Museum & Centre of Tolerance (p89) Explores a history that was long overlooked.

State History Museum (p79) A massive collection covering Russian history from the Stone Age to Soviets.

Best Literary Museums

Bulgakov House-Museum (p103) The censored writer's former flat offers a calendar of lively cultural events.

Tolstoy Estate-Museum (p125) See where Russia's most celebrated novelist lived and worked.

Ryabushinsky Mansion (p102) This architectural landmark was also the home of Soviet writer Maxim Gorky.

Gogol House (p102) Gaze into the fireplace where Gogol famously tossed his *Dead Souls* manuscript.

Best Art Galleries

Tretyakov Gallery (p135) The first stop for art-lovers: the world's premier venue for Russian art.

Garage Museum of Contemporary Art (p137) Unusual, thought-provoking art in a gallery made of paper in Gorky Park.

New Tretyakov Gallery (p138) All of the 20th century: socialist realism versus avant-guarde and non-conformist art.

Gallery of European & American Art (p118) The Pushkin's collection of Impressionist and post-Impressionist paintings is unparalleled.

Burganov House (p123) A sprawling maze of buildings and courtyards, filled with whimsical sculpture and art.

Best for Offbeat

Soviet Arcade Games Museum (p149) Arcade games as history lesson and sociological study.

Moscow Design Museum (p79) Catch an exhibit in the big, bold, black-and-white bus.

Moscow Museum (p125) The medieval history is fine, but the rotating temporary exhibits are provocative and perplexing.

Best Contemporary Art Centres

Winzavod Center for Contemporary Art (p148) The original post-industrial art complex, in a former wine-bottling factory.

Red October (p137) Once a chocolate factory, now an art and entertainment hot spot.

Flakon (p92) This former glassworks is packed with boutiques selling designer stuff.

ArtPlay on Yauza (p148) A design centre housed in the former Manometer factory.

Ploshchad Revolyutsii metro station (p39)

👁 Tour of the Metro

Every day, as many as nine million people ride the Moscow metro – that's more than in New York and London combined. What's more, this transport system marries function and form: many of the stations are marble-faced, frescoed, gilded works of art. Take this tour for an overview of Moscow's most interesting and impressive metro stations.

NEED TO KNOW

→ **Start** Komsomolskaya

→ **End** Park Pobedy

→ **Distance** 18km, one to two hours

→ **Time** The Moscow metro operates every day from 5.30am until 1am. The metro is often uncomfortably crowded during peak commuter times, so the best time to take a tour is on a Saturday or Sunday morning, or any evening after 8pm.

→ **Price** One ride costs ₽40, which will allow you to tour any number of stations as long as you don't exit the metro. If you intend to use the metro for transportation during your stay in Moscow, you can purchase a card with multiple rides at discounted rates (eg, five rides for ₽160 or 11 rides for ₽320).

Komsomolskaya

At Komsomolskaya the red line (Sokol-nicheskaya liniya) intersects with the Ring line (Koltsevaya liniya). Both stations are named for the youth workers who helped with early construction. In the red-line station, look for the Komsomol emblem at the top of the limestone pillars and the majolica-tile panel showing the volunteers hard at work. The Ring-line station has a huge stuccoed hall, the ceiling featuring mosaics of past Russian military heroes.

From Komsomolskaya, proceed anti-clockwise around the Ring line, getting off at each stop along the way.

Prospekt Mira

Originally named for the nearby MGU Botanical Garden, Prospekt Mira features elegant, white-porcelain depictions of figures planting trees, bringing in the harvest and generally living in harmony.

Novoslobodskaya

Thirty-two stained-glass panels envelop this station in art nouveau artistry. Six windows depict the so-called intellectual professions: architect, geographer, agronomist, engineer, artist and musician.

At one end of the central hall is the mosaic *Peace in the Whole World*. The pair of white doves was a later addition to the mosaic, replacing a portrait of Stalin.

Belorusskaya

The ceiling mosaics celebrate the culture, economy and history of Russia's neighbour to the west. The 12 ceiling panels illustrate different aspects of their culture, while the floor pattern reproduces traditional Belarusian ornamentation.

Switch here to the green Zamoskvoretskaya line (where the Belarusian theme continues) and travel south.

Mayakovskaya

This is the pièce de résistance of the Moscow metro. This grand-prize winner at the 1938 World's Fair in New York has an art-deco central hall that's all pink

HISTORY OF THE MOSCOW METRO

When Stalin announced plans for *Metrostroy* (construction of the metro) in the 1930s, loyal communists turned out in droves to lend a hand. Thousands of people toiled around the clock in dire conditions, using pickaxes and spades and hand-pulled trolleys. Some 10,000 members of the Moscow Komsomol (Soviet youth league) contributed their time to building the communist dream.

The first metro line opened on 16 May 1935 at 7am. Thousands of people spent the night at the doors of the station so they might ride the first train on the red line (between Park Kultury in the south and Sokolniki in the north). Two additional lines opened in 1938.

Construction continued during the Great Patriotic War, with the opening of two additional lines. Several stations actually served as air-raid shelters during the Siege of Moscow in 1941. The Ring line (Koltsevaya line) opened in the early 1950s.

Khrushchev's tastes were not as extravagant as Stalin's, so later stations employ a uniform, utilitarian design. But the metro continued to expand, and still continues today (as does Moscow itself).

rhodonite, with slender, steel columns. The inspiring, upward-looking mosaics on the ceiling depict *24 Hours in the Land of the Soviets*.

This is also one of the deepest stations (33m), which allowed it to serve as an air-raid shelter during WWII.

Teatralnaya

This station was formerly called Ploshchad Sverdlova in honour of Lenin's right-hand man (whose bust was in the hall). Nonetheless, the station's decor follows a theatrical theme. The porcelain figures represent seven of the Soviet republics by wearing national dress and playing musical instruments from their homeland.

Change here to Ploshchad Revolyutsii station on the dark blue line (Arbatsko-Pokrovskaya liniya).

Ploshchad Revolyutsii

This dramatic station is basically an underground sculpture gallery. The life-sized bronze statues represent the roles played by the people during the revolution and in the 'new world' that comes after. Heading up

the escalators, the themes are: revolution, industry, agriculture, hunting, education, sport and child rearing. Touch the nose of the border guard's dog for good luck on exams.

Take the dark blue line heading west.

Arbatskaya

This shallow station was damaged by a German bomb in 1941. The station was closed (supposedly permanently) and a parallel line was built much deeper. Service was restored on this line the following decade, which explains the existence of two Arbatskaya stations (and two Smolenskaya stations, for that matter) on two different lines.

At 250m, Arbatskaya is one of the longest stations. A braided moulding emphasises the arched ceiling, while red marble and detailed ornamentation give the whole station a baroque atmosphere.

Kievskaya

This elegant white-marble hall is adorned with a Kyivan-style ornamental frieze, while the frescoed panels depict farmers in folk

Mayakovskaya metro station

Tour of the Metro

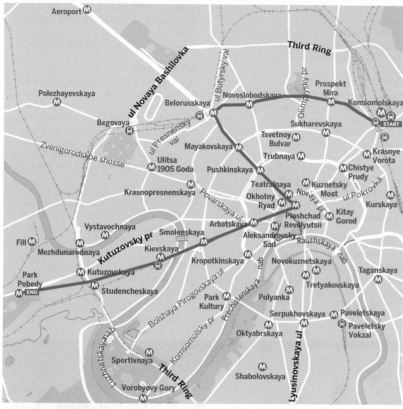

Komsomolskaya metro station (p38)

costume, giant vegetables and other aspects of the idyllic Ukrainian existence.

The fresco at the end of the hall celebrates 300 years of Russian-Ukrainian cooperation.

Park Pobedy

This newer station opened after the complex at Poklonnaya Gora, which commemorated the 50th anniversary of the victory in the Great Patriotic War.

Park Pobedy is the deepest Moscow metro station, and it has the longest escalators in the world. The enamel panels at either end of the hall (created by Zurab Tsereteli) depict the victories of 1812 and 1945.

From here you can return to the centre by retracing your ride on the dark blue line.

Shchi (cabbage soup)

Eating

In recent years Moscow has blossomed into a culinary capital. Foodies will be thrilled by the dining options, from old-fashioned haute russe *to 'author cuisine'. Daring chefs are breaking down stereotypes and showing the world how creative they can be. They're importing exotic ingredients, rediscovering ancient cooking techniques and inventing new ones. And Moscow diners are eating it up. Literally.*

Local Specialities

Russian cuisine is strongly influenced by climate and class. Long winters and short growing seasons mean the cuisine is dependent on root vegetables such as potatoes and beets. Fresh produce has always been a rarity, so vegetables are often served pickled; fruit is frequently served in the form of compote.

According to an old Russian proverb, '*shchi* (cabbage soup) and *kasha* (porridge) is our nourishment'. This saying emphasises the important role played by soups and grains in sustaining generations of peasants through cold, dark winters.

BREAKFAST

Russians rarely skip breakfast (*zavtrak*). Russian cuisine includes half-a-dozen kinds of *kasha*, including buckwheat, millet, oat and semolina. *Bliny* are thin, crêpe-like pancakes with sweet or savoury fillings.

At the very least, you'll get bread (*khleb*) with butter and jam, alongside your cup of tea.

NEED TO KNOW

Opening Hours

Many eateries are open noon to midnight daily, often with later hours on Friday and Saturday.

Price Guide

The following prices are for a main dish.

€	under ₽500
€€	₽500-1500
€€€	over ₽1500

Business Lunch

Discounts of up to 25% are sometimes available for dining before 4pm or 5pm. Alternatively, many places offer a fixed-price 'business lunch' during this time, which is is a great way to sample some of the pricier restaurants around town.

Booking Tables

Most of the fancier places require booking in advance for dinner, as well as for lunch or brunch on weekends.

Tipping

The standard for tipping in Moscow is 10%, while a slightly smaller percentage is acceptable at more casual restaurants. The service charge is occasionally included in the bill, in which case an additional tip isn't necessary.

Websites

➡ **Restoran.ru** (www.restoran.ru) Restaurant reviews, recipes and other news about food stuff in Moscow.

➡ **Moscow Times** (www.themoscow-times/guides/dining) Publishes a dining guide that is searchable by cuisine, metro station and other features.

➡ **Menu.ru** (www.menu.ru) Listings (in Russian) of menus, maps and other logistical info for hundreds of restaurants, bars and clubs.

APPETISERS & SALADS

Whether as the preamble to a meal, or something to snack on between vodka shots, *zakuski* (appetisers) are an important part of Russian cuisine. Back in the day, a good host always had a spread of *zakuski* ready on the table to welcome unexpected guests.

Most famously, *ikra* (caviar) is the snack of tsars and New Russians. The best caviar is black caviar, from *osetra* (beluga sturgeon). However, due to overfishing, sturgeon populations have declined drastically in recent years, driving up prices and threatening the fish with extinction. The much cheaper and saltier option is red salmon caviar. Russians spread it on buttered bread and wash it down with a slug of vodka or a toast of champagne.

Most traditional menus offer a multitude of salads, many with names that will leave you scratching your head. The universal favourite is *salat olivye* (Olivier salad), which is chopped chicken or ham, mixed with potatoes, eggs, peas and mayonnaise. Another classic is *seld pod shuby* ('herring in a fur coat'), a colourful conglomeration of herring, beets and potatoes.

SOUPS

Soups are perhaps the pinnacle of Russian cooking, with both hot and cold varieties turning up on menus and in local kitchens. The most famous is borsch (beetroot soup), but other favourites include *solyanka,* a meat broth with salty vegetables and a hint of lemon, and *okroshka,* a cold soup made from *kvas* (fermented rye-bread water).

Soups are served as the first course of a Russian meal. As such, they often appear on the menu under the heading *Pervaya,* which means 'first'.

MAIN COURSES

Traditional Russian main courses are usually heavy, meat-based dishes. Fried cutlets *(kotlet)* and grilled kebabs *(shashlyk)* are popular preparations that often show up on the menu, listed under *Glavnaya* (main) or *Vtoraya* (second).

Especially satisfying in winter, *zharkoye* (hot pot) is an appropriately named meat stew served piping hot in a single-serving ceramic pot.

Pelmeni (dumplings) are the ultimate Russian comfort food. Traditionally from Siberia but now served everywhere, these bite-size dumplings are usually stuffed with pork or beef, then topped with sour cream. Variations such as salmon or mushroom *pelmeni* are also on the menus of modern Moscow restaurants.

Moscow Trends
FOREIGN CUISINES

A decade ago, Moscow was mad for sushi. You'll still see it on many menus, but the raw fish craze is finally starting to peter out. What is not going anywhere is the more general interest in international flavours. When you tire of beetroot soup and beef stroganoff, you'll be able to find excellent French, Italian and American restaurants, not to mention Chinese, Lebanese, Thai, Turkish and more.

Also popular – and perhaps more interesting for visitors to Moscow – are the rich cuisines from former Soviet republics of Central Asia and the Caucasus. The capital is littered with restaurants representing the best of Armenian, Azeri, Georgian and Uzbek cuisines – usually with natives manning the kitchen.

CREATIVE CUISINE

Nowadays, the most exciting trend in Moscow cuisine is the emergence of *avtorskaya kukhnya* ('author cuisine'. As the name implies, young chefs are creating their own brands of cooking, incorporating the best of local and international elements. Seasonal menus highlight local ingredients. But cooking techniques, food preparations and flavours are adapted from all over the world, resulting in menus that are innovative, unique – and delightfully delicious.

This fresh take on cooking is on full display at the annual **Omnivore Festival** (www.omnivore-moscow.ru), which is held over five days in March, with master classes, taste testing, eating and drinking, culminating with a giant dinner party.

VEGETARIANS

The culinary revolution has opened up some new options for vegetarians and vegans. Most restaurants now offer at least one vegetarian choice. Additionally, there is no shortage of Indian and Italian restaurants offering meat-free options.

During the 40 days before Orthodox Easter (*post,* in Russian), many restaurants offer a Lenten menu that is happily animal-free.

Cook Like a Local

If you love Russian food, you can learn to make it yourself. **Taste of Russia** (Map p270; 8-906-717 8290; www.tasterussia.ru; bldg 4, Kazarmenny per 3; 3hr course ₽3500, market tour ₽1500; MKurskaya) offers courses in English, as well as market tours, wine tastings and special children's classes. Courses take place in the evening, when you prepare the meal, then eat it together.

TABLE SCRAPS FROM HEAVEN

Writer Darra Goldstein describes the former Soviet republic of Georgia as 'a land blessed by Heaven's table scraps'. Short of Heaven itself, Moscow is the best place outside the Caucasus to sample this rich, spicy cuisine.

The fertile region – wedged between the East and the West – has long been the beneficiary and victim of merchants and raiders passing through. These influences are evident in Georgian cooking, which shows glimpses of Mediterranean and Middle Eastern flavours. But the truly Georgian elements – the important differences – are what make this cuisine so delectable. Most meat and vegetable dishes use ground walnuts or walnut oil as an integral ingredient, yielding a distinctive, nutty flavour. Also characteristic of Georgian cuisine is the spice mixture *khmeli-suneli,* which combines coriander, garlic, chillies, pepper and other spices with a saffron substitute made from dried marigold petals.

Georgian chefs love to prepare food over an open flame, and grilled meats are among the tastiest items on any Georgian menu. Herbs such as coriander, dill and parsley are often served fresh, with no preparation or sauce, as a palate-cleansing counterpoint to rich dishes. Grapes and pomegranates show up not only as desserts, but also as tart complements to roasted meats. The most beloved item on the Georgian menu is undoubtedly *khachapuri,* a rich, cheesy bread that is made with circles of fresh dough cooked with sour, salty *suluguni* cheese. Sometimes it is topped with a raw egg in the crater.

Around Moscow, there are scores of Georgian restaurants covering all price ranges. Sample this delicious cuisine now; you may not have another chance until you get to Tbilisi.

Lonely Planet's Top Choices

Delicatessen (p94) Eat, drink and chat at Moscow's smartest and friendliest gastropub.

Café Pushkin (p107) Moscow's long-standing favourite for traditional Russian food delights in an aristocratic mansion.

Khachapuri (p105) A casual, contemporary place for the eponymous Georgian speciality.

As Eat Is (p105) No fancy stuff, just fresh, local and truly innovative cooking.

Kitayskaya Gramota (p152) A very serious take on Cantonese cooking in a playful, ironic environment.

Lavka-Lavka (p94) Delicacies straight from local farms cooked by a creative chef.

Best by Budget

€

Varenichnaya No 1 (p126) A friendly, family place for dumplings and other old-fashioned Russian cooking.

Shawarma Republic (p92) A very special 'united nations' shawarma for consumption in a pretty garden.

Dukhan Chito-Ra (p153) Possibly the best khinkali dumplings this side of the Caucasus range.

Zupperia (p91) Casual lunchtime joint run by a celebrity chef; it's just about soups.

Stolle (p108) A friendly cafe serving fresh-baked pies with your favourite fillings.

€€

Ragout (p108) A rare combination of inventive cuisine, trendy crowd and affordable prices.

Favorite (p107) Beloved by locals and expats alike, for burgers, steaks and beer.

€€€

Café Pushkin (p107) Still the best splurge in Moscow.

Ugolyok (p107) Food and design that's edgy, artistic and elegant, all at once.

Brasserie Most (p94) A luxury gastrotour from Bretagne to Alsace and down to Corsica.

Best by Cuisine

Russian

Café Pushkin (p107) Dine in *haute russe* style, just like the aristocrats of old.

Chemodan (p128) Get a taste of the wilds of Siberia.

Caucasian

Khachapuri (p105) Refreshingly affordable, but still delicious Georgian fare.

Barashka (p95) Sample exotic Azeri fare in a restaurant reminiscent of a Baku courtyard.

Elardzhi (p127) Traditional Georgian fare, served in a comfortable but cool courtyard setting.

Central Asian

Vostochny Kvartal (p127) This is a wonderfully exotic setting for *plov* and other eastern fare.

Vegetarian

Fresh (p92) Not only fresh, but diverse, nutritious and mouthwatering.

Moscow-Delhi (p153) A secret Indian village kitchen in the middle of Moscow.

Best Chefs

Delicatessen (p94) Ivan Shishkin can claim responsibility for the capital's first food-centric gastropub.

Lavka-Lavka (p94) Boris Akimov launched the farm-to-table movement in Moscow.

As Eat Is (p105) Sergei Berezutsky brings his own modern signature style to Russian cooking.

Uilliam's (p107) This is chef Uilliam Lamberti's flagship restaurant, where he 'cooks from the heart'.

Best Street Food

Shawarma Republic (p92) A very special 'united nations' shawarma.

AC/DC in Tbilisi (p140) Burgers with a strong Caucasian accent.

Passion fruit cocktails

Drinking & Nightlife

Back in the day, the local pub was the ryumochnaya, *which comes from the word* ryumka, *meaning 'shot'. This was a grim place, serving up 100g shots, but nothing else. Moscow's drinking possibilities have expanded exponentially (although there are still a few old-school* ryumochnye *around). Now, drinkers can choose from wine bars, whisky bars, cocktail bars, sports bars, microbreweries and more.*

What to Drink

VODKA

The word 'vodka' is the diminutive of the Russian word for water, *voda,* so it means something like 'a wee drop'. Most often vodka is tipped down in swift shots, often followed by a pickle.

In recent years, drinking cocktails has become more fashionable, meaning that women at least can get away with mixing their vodka.

BEER

Many visitors are surprised to learn that *pivo* (beer) is the city's most popular alcoholic drink. The market leader is Baltika, which makes no fewer than 12 excellent brews. If you prefer your beer straight from the tap, head to one of the fine microbreweries.

WINE

Russians traditionally drink *Sovietskoe shampanskoe (*sparkling wine) to toast special occasions and to sip during intermission

NEED TO KNOW

Opening Hours

Most bars and pubs have the same opening hours as eating venues (from noon to midnight). Some hot spots stay open for drinking until 5am or 6am, especially on Friday and Saturday nights.

How Much?

Prices for alcohol vary widely, depending on where you are drinking. Expect to pay anywhere from ₽100 to ₽400 for a pint of beer or 50g of vodka. At upmarket clubs, cocktails can cost ₽500 and up.

How to Get Past Face Control

➡ Dress up: skirts and heels for women, dress pants and leather shoes for men.

➡ Arrive in a small group, preferably with more men than women.

➡ Speak English. Foreigners are not as special as they used to be, but they're still sort of special.

➡ Smile. Show the bouncer that you are going to enhance the atmosphere inside.

➡ Book a table. At more elite clubs this requires a sometimes hefty 'table deposit'.

at the theatre. It tends to be sickeningly sweet: look for the label that says *sukhoe* (dry). Nowadays, the capital has a few sweet wine bars, where Muscovites drink fine vintages, mostly from Europe.

KVAS

Kvas is a mildly alcoholic, fermented, rye-bread water. Cool, refreshing and slightly sweet, it is a popular summer drink that tastes something like ginger beer.

In the olden days it was dispensed on the street from big, wheeled tanks. Nowadays, the kegs are smaller, but they still set up in parks and outside metro stations to serve thirsty passers-by. This cool, tasty treat is also commonly served in restaurants.

Where to Drink

Drinking is a favourite national pastime in Russia, and modern Moscow offers venues for every occasion, mood and season. Former factories have been converted into nightclubs; leafy courtyards contain beer gardens; and communal apartments now serve as cosy cafes. Pedestrian streets such as ul Arbat and Kamergersky per are hot spots for strollers and drinkers. The former Red October chocolate factory in Zamoskvorechie is now packed with diverse drinking establishments.

NIGHTCLUBS

Moscow nightclubs are notorious for their fast pace and over-the-top excesses. New wild clubs each outdo the last with glitz and glamour. To ensure the clientele enhances the atmosphere, many clubs exercise 'face control', allowing in only a select few patrons. Fortunately, for the rest of us, there are a slew of less discriminating clubs that also have great music, strong drinks and cool vibes. Most clubs start hopping after midnight and keep going until dawn.

PUB CRAWLS

Solo traveller looking for drinking buddies? Freaked out by face control? An organised pub crawl is a guaranteed way to meet fine folks from around the world, get into some cool clubs and discover Moscow's nightlife:

➡ **City Pub Crawl** (www.citypubcrawl.ru; ₽1500) Five clubs. Five drinks. And one band of very merry Moscow travellers.

➡ **Moscow Pub Crawl** (www.moscowpubcrawl. com; ₽600) Your fee gets you into four hot drinking venues, with a welcome drink at each one. The evening culminates at a local nightclub, where you can let loose on the dance floor.

SUMMER CAFES

Summer doesn't last very long in Moscow, so locals know they need to take advantage of the warm weather. That's why every restaurant worth going to opens a *letnoe kafe* (summer cafe). They take over the courtyard, or the sidewalk, or the rooftop – because they know that people want to be outside.

Lonely Planet's Top Choices

Enthusiast (p96) A bar disguised as a scooter repair shop.

3205 (p95) An extensive and innovative bar menu, served in a delightful garden setting.

Noor (p96) A little hippy, a little hipster, totally cool.

Time-Out Bar (p109) Cool cocktails and fabulous views.

Best by Drink

Beer

Favorite (p107) Serving Brickstone Beer, brewed in Moscow.

Cafe Vokzal (p96) A mammoth-size pub with cheapish beer and a student crowd.

Edward's (p155) A local in a non-conventional location at a redeveloped factory.

Wine

Gavroche Wine Bar (p128) Warm up with a glass of vino in these cosy quarters.

3205 (p95) A garden setting begging for a glass of Bordeaux.

Jean-Jacques (p107) Moscow's original wine bar now has outlets all over town.

Cocktails

Jagger (p110) A hot-to-trot nightclub and bar in the midst of the Trekhgornaya complex.

Time-Out Bar (p109) Speciality cocktails for any time of day.

Delicatessen (p94) This gastropub mixes a killer cocktail.

WT4 (p142) Mingle with Moscow's trendiest in a cool post-industrial environment.

Coffee

OMG! Coffee (p154) An encyclopedia of coffee brewing in one long menu.

Coffee Bean (p155) It was the first coffee chain in Moscow – it's still the best.

Art Lebedev Cafe Studio (p109) An art-filled nook for stylish coffee drinkers.

Conversation (p109) This Brooklyn-style coffee place encourages lingering.

Gogol-Mogol (p128) A perfect pitstop when you want something sweet with your joe.

Best Summer Cafes

Manon Club (p110) Featuring a lovely wide terrace overlooking the Moscow River.

Le Boule (p142) Proof that alcohol and sports are compatible – cider and pétanque at Gorky Park.

3205 (p95) A perfectly lovely place in Hermitage Garden.

Best for Gays & Lesbians

12 Volts (p97) Friendly and cosy – a shelter as much as a good-time place.

Secret (p155) Against the political odds, people keep sharing the Secret.

Best for Dancing

Gipsy (p142) A modern nomads' gathering on the roof of a former chocolate factory.

Manon Club (p110) Dance until dawn – then watch the sun rise over Moscow.

Best for Watching Sport

Zhiguli Beer Hall (p128) Locally brewed beer and big-screen sports – Amen.

Nikulin Circus on Tsvetnoy Bulvar (p97)

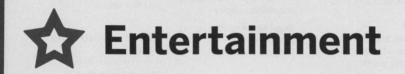

☆ Entertainment

Moscow's performing arts are a major drawcard: classical ballet, music and theatre are at the heart of Russian culture. For so long, that's all there was. Happily, times have changed, as directors, conductors and choreographers are unleashing their creative spirits. If you have your heart set on Tchaikovsky, you won't be disappointed, but if you're yearning for something experimental, you'll find that too.

Performing Arts

The classical performing arts are one of Moscow's biggest attractions. Highly acclaimed, professional artists stage productions in elegant theatres around the city, most of which have been recently revamped and look marvellous.

OPERA & BALLET

Nobody has ever complained about a shortage of Russian classics at the opera and ballet. Take your pick from Tchaikovsky,

Prokofiev, Rimsky-Korsakov or one of the other great Russian composers, and you are guaranteed to find him on the playbill at one of the major theatres. The choreography and staging of these classics is usually pretty traditional (some might even say uninventive), but then again, that's why they're classics. If you tire of the traditional, keep your eye out for more modern productions and premieres that are also staged by some local companies.

The largest opera and ballet company in the city – and the most celebrated – is the Bolshoi. The repertoire of this world-famous company is mostly classical, with choreography in the style of Balanchine and Petipa. In recent years, the Bolshoi has premiered many new works. After an extensive five-year renovation, the historic stage at the Bolshoi Theatre reopened in 2011 to much fanfare.

A sort of rival to the Bolshoi is the Stanislavsky & Nemirovich-Danchenko Musical Theatre, which is approaching its centennial in 2019. In addition to its classical repertoire, this prominent company has staged ground-breaking ballets and avant-garde operas in recent years.

There are a slew of younger opera and ballet companies around the city. For experimental, contemporary fare, check out the ground-breaking New Ballet, performing in a small theatre in Basmanny.

CLASSICAL MUSIC

It's not unusual to see highly talented musicians working the crowds inside the metro stations, often violinists single-handedly performing Vivaldi's *Four Seasons* and flautists whistling away at Mozart or Bach. While it's possible to hear a good show in the metro station, a visit to one of the local orchestra halls is highly recommended.

Founded in 1922, the city's oldest and most prestigious symphony orchestra is Moscow Philharmonic Society, which performs at the Tchaikovsky Concert Hall, as well as the Great Hall of the Moscow Conservatory. Giving hundreds of concerts a year, the orchestra is still the standard bearer for orchestral music in the capital, if not in the country.

Across town at the International House of Music, the National Philharmonic Orchestra of Russia was the country's first private symphony orchestra when it was founded in 1990. Also around that time, the feisty Levine sisters founded the Moscow Symphony Orchestra (MSO), an upstart assemblage that still operates on a relatively small budget, under the direction of the young Vladimir Ziva. The MSO performs at the Moscow Tchaikovsky Conservatory.

CONTEMPORARY MUSIC

Live bands and DJs travel from other parts of Russia and all over Europe to perform in Moscow's many clubs and theatres. Summer is an especially busy concert season, with several big outdoor music festivals. Check the schedules of local clubs or look for signs advertising the biggest names.

NEED TO KNOW

Tickets

Nowadays, most theatres sell tickets online. Or, you can do it the old-fashioned way and buy tickets directly from the theatre box office or from a *teatralnaya kassa* (theatre kiosk), several of which are scattered about the city.

Prices

The classical performing arts remain an incredible bargain in Moscow, especially if you go anywhere other than the Bolshoi Theatre. Generally speaking, only the most expensive tickets, in front of the orchestra, can compare to what you would pay in the West for a similar performance. Happily, Moscow venues do not charge higher prices for foreigners. Tickets start around ₽500, with prices for the best seats ranging from ₽2000 to ₽4000.

Theatre Seasons

Unfortunately for summer visitors, many venues are closed between late June and early September.

THEATRE

Due to the language barrier, drama and comedy are less alluring prospects for non-Russian speakers than are music and dance. Nonetheless, Moscow has a long theatre tradition, which remains vibrant today. The capital has around 40 professional theatres and countless amateur theatres, staging a wide range of plays.

CIRCUS

The circus has long been a favourite form of entertainment for Russians young and old. There are two highly lauded, permanent circuses in Moscow, putting on glittering shows for Muscovites of all ages. Near the centre of town, Tsvetnoy bulvar has been the site of the Moscow circus since 1880. This so-called 'Old' Circus – now named for the famous clown Yury Nikulin – had always set the standard by which all other circuses were measured. Until 1971, that is, when the new Bolshoi Circus on Vernadskogo was built. This state-of-the-art facility was bigger and better, with five replaceable arenas (water, ice, equestrian, etc) and room for 3500 spectators.

EASY STEAMING

The dos and don'ts of the *banya:*

➡ **Do** take advantage of the plunge pool (or at least the cold shower, if there is no pool on site). It's important to bring your body temperature back down after being in the *banya*.

➡ **Don't** bother with a bathing suit. Most public *bani* are segregated by gender, in which case bathers steam naked. In mixed company, wrap yourself in a sheet (provided at the *banya*).

➡ **Do** rehydrate in between steams. Tea or even beer are common, but it is also important to drink water or juice.

➡ **Don't** stop at one! Most bathers will return to the *parilka* (steam room) several times over the course of an hour or two.

The shows performed by both companies feature acrobatics and animals, as well as dance, cabaret and clowns. The displays of daring-do are truly amazing, especially the aerial arts. Only the Nikulin Circus features big cats in their performances, but both venues have monkeys, bears and sea lions. The animals are apparently not mistreated – though their very involvement in the show might make you cringe.

Spectator Sports

Russia's international reputation in sport is well founded, with athletes earning international fame and glory for their success in ice hockey, gymnastics and figure skating.

FOOTBALL

The most popular spectator sport in Russia is football (soccer), and five Moscow teams play in Russia's premier league (Vysshaya Liga). Currently, football is enjoying a boom, with several state-of-the-art stadiums being built for the upcoming World Cup in 2018.

Moscow's most successful team is **FC Spartak** (www.spartak.com). The team's nickname is Myaso, or 'Meat', because it was sponsored by the collective farm association during the Soviet era. Nowadays, Spartak plays at the brand spanking new Spartak Stadium (also known as Otkrytie Arena), north of centre near Tushino Airfield.

Meanwhile, their rivals, **FC Dynamo** (www.fcdynamo.ru) are looking forward to the new ultra-modern VTB Arena – a 45,000-seat stadium complete with its own shopping and entertainment complex – expected to open in 2016.

Other Moscow teams in the league are two-time winner **FC Lokomotiv** (www.fclm.ru) and three-time winner **Central Sports Club of the Army** (CSKA; www.pfc-cska.com).

ICE HOCKEY

Moscow's main entrant in the Continental Hockey League (KHL) is **HC CSKA** (www.cska-hockey.ru), or the Red Army team. HC CSKA has won more Soviet championships and European cups than any other team in history. They play at the CSKA Arena.

BASKETBALL

Men's basketball has dropped in popularity since its days of Olympic glory in the 1980s, but Moscow's top basketball team, **CSKA** (www.cskabasket.com), still does well in the European league. They play at the CSKA Arena, but they'll move to VTB Arena when it's complete.

Banya

Nothing beats winter like the *banya*. Less hot but more humid than a sauna, the Russian bath sweats out all impurity.

Enter the steam room *(parilka)* naked (yes, the *banya* is normally segregated by gender). Bathers can control the temperature – or at least increase it – by ladling water onto the hot rocks. You might add a few drops of eucalyptus to infuse the steam with scent. Then sit back and watch the mercury rise.

To eliminate toxins and improve circulation, bathers beat each other with a bundle of birch branches, known as *veniki* (or you might want to have a professional do this for you).

When you can't take the heat, retreat. A public *banya* allows access to a plunge pool, usually filled with ice-cold water. The contrast in temperature is invigorating, energising and purifying.

A *banya* is not complete without a table spread with snacks, or at least a thermos of tea. And just when you think you have recovered, it's time to repeat the process. As they say in Russia, '*s lyokum parom*' (easy steaming).

Lonely Planet's Top Choices

Bolshoi Theatre (p87) Russia's ultimate theatre experience and one of the world's most opulent and sophisticated theatre venues.

Masterskaya (p97) A convivial bar with a live-music line-up that's eclectic, like Moscow itself.

Sanduny Baths (p99) Sweat your stress away at this luxurious *banya*.

Moscow International House of Music (p145) This contemporary riverside concert hall is an atmospheric place for some musical magic.

Best Opera & Ballet

Bolshoi Theatre (p87) Watch the dancers glide across the stage in Moscow's most famous and most historic theatre.

Stanislavsky & Nemirovich-Danchenko Musical Theatre (p97) A long-standing opera and ballet company with a tendency towards innovation.

New Ballet (p156) Breaking down barriers (physically and culturally) in dance.

Novaya Opera (p97) Re-creating the classics in a beautiful setting in the Hermitage Gardens.

Best Classical Music

Tchaikovsky Concert Hall (p110) A huge auditorium that is home to the city's oldest philharmonic.

Moscow International House of Music (p145) An impressive venue for the National Philharmonic of Russia.

Moscow Tchaikovsky Conservatory (p110) Hosts several different professional orchestras, as well as student recitals.

Best Contemporary Music

Masterskaya (p97) The capital's hottest indie rock spot, tucked into a hidden corner behind the Bolshoi.

Sixteen Tons (p110) A long-standing venue for local acts and national names.

Rhythm Blues Cafe (p129) Good old-fashioned jazz and blues music in a cool, casual setting.

Art Garbage (p156) Local bands and DJs keep the tunes coming, seven nights a week.

Best Banyi

Sanduny Baths (p99) The tsar of Russian *banyi* – a historic and opulently decorated bathhouse.

Bersenevskiye Bany (p145) The original Smirnov vodka distillery, now turned newish bathhouse at Moscow's hipster mile.

Krasnopresnkiye Banyi (p111) A popular, public *banya* with excellent, clean facilities.

Best Spectator Sports

Spartak Stadium (p110) A state-of-the-art facility for Moscow's most successful football team.

Luzhniki Stadium (p130) Still the capital's largest and most storied stadium.

CSKA Arena (p98) Home of the capital's most successful basketball and hockey teams – but not for long.

Shopping

News flash: Moscow is an expensive city. So don't come looking for bargains. Do come looking for creative and classy clothing and jewellery by local designers; an innovative art scene; high-quality handicrafts, linens, glassware and folk art; and unusual souvenirs that you won't find anywhere else.

Fashion

Beware of sticker shock when you check out the up-and-coming fashion industry in Moscow. A few local designers have blazed a trail, inventing sophisticated and stylish fashions, which you can try on at boutiques around town.

EVENTS

Moscow hosts two major fashion events:

➡ **Moscow Fashion Week** (www.mfw.ru) Held at Gostiny Dvor at the end of March.

➡ **Mercedes Benz Fashion Week Russia** (www.mercedesbenzfashionweek.ru) Held at the World Trade Centre in April and October.

FUR

Winter brings out the best or the worst of Russian style (depending on your perspective). Muscovites still see fur as the most effective and fashionable way to stay warm. Some advice from a local fashion connoisseur: 'Your protests that fur is cruel are likely to be met by blank stares and an uncomfortable shifting of feet. Don't come in winter if this offends you.' If you think you might want to do as the Muscovites do when in Moscow, stop by Yekaterina and pick out a fur hat.

Arts & Crafts

Moscow's prolific craftspeople display their knick-knacks and bric-a-brac at souvenir shops around town, as well as at Izmaylovo market. Feel free to haggle, but don't expect prices to decrease more than 5% or 10%.

The speciality of Russian craftsmen is painted wooden knick-knacks. Traditional wooden nesting dolls, dishes and utensils are painted in decorative floral patterns, known as *khokhloma*. Painted lacquer boxes (*palekh* boxes)– are usually black with a colourful, detailed scene.

The village of Gzhel, situated about 50km southeast of Moscow, has been renowned for its pottery since the 14th century, and nobody will leave Russia without forming a decisive opinion about *gzhel* porcelain – those curly white pieces with cobalt blue floral design.

Textiles

Welcome to Calico Moscow. Once famed for its textile industry, the capital still offers bargains on soft, rich linens and woollens. Russia's cool, moist summers and fertile soil are ideal for producing flax, the fibre used to manufacture linen. This elegant, durable fabric is respectfully known in Russia as 'His Majesty Linen'.

High-quality linen products, including tablecloths, napkins, bed covers and even clothing, are still manufactured in Russia – and prices are lower than their Western counterparts.

Lonely Planet's Top Choices

Izmaylovsky market (p150) A sprawling souvenir market, now in fancy 'kremlin' digs.

Khokhlovka Original (p156) Unusual and controversial clothes from a co-op of young Russian designers.

Podarki vMeste s Vorovski (p98) Designer gifts – from felt boots to stylish ceramics inspired by folklore.

Best for Art

Winzavod Center for Contemporary Art (p148) The city's first post-industrial contemporary art centre now plays host to its highest-profile art galleries.

Artefact Gallery Centre (p130) This cluster of high-end galleries has a wide variety of paintings and artwork for sale.

Best for Handicrafts

Izmaylovsky Market (p150) By far, Moscow's biggest selection of traditional handmade items.

Ochevidnoyeneveroyatnoye (p157) Surreal, provocative, ironic, hilarious and all sorts of other unusual gifts available at Winzavod Center for Contemporary Art.

Podarki vMeste s Vorovski (p98) New forms for Russian folklore – great for gifts and souvenirs.

Association of Artists of the Decorative Arts (p130) A trove of tiny shops, packed with handcrafted treasures.

Russian Embroidery & Lace (p130) Handmade sweaters, dresses, linens and other lovelies.

Best Fashion

Khokhlovka Original (p156) See the best and boldest new Russian designers at this hidden showroom.

Flakon (p92) A redeveloped factory occupied by shops selling all kinds of designer items and clothing.

Razu Mikhina Workshop (p157) Ethno-futurist clothes and stylish jewellery at Darya Razumikhina's workshop inside Winzavod Center for Contemporary Art.

Chapurin Boutique (p130) Designer Igor Chapurin's flagship store on the banks of the Moscow River.

Alena Akhmadullina Boutique (p84) A showcase of this romantic designer's work on one of Moscow's best shopping strips.

Best for the Home

Depst (p98) Homewares, clothes and loads of other useful items from a co-op of Russian designers.

PLAN YOUR TRIP SHOPPING

NEED TO KNOW

Opening Hours

Most shops are open from 10am until 8pm. Large shopping centres stay open until 10pm or later. Hours are shorter on Sunday, from about noon to 8pm.

Customs Regulations

Items more than 100 years old cannot be taken out of the country. Anything vaguely 'arty', such as art, musical instruments, antiques or antiquarian books (meaning those published before 1975) must be assessed by the **Expert Collegium** (p232). Bring two photographs of your item, your receipt and your passport. The bureaucrats will issue a receipt for tax paid, which you show to customs officers on your way out of the country.

ArtPlay (p148) A post-industrial space largely dedicated to interior design, with many shops in the premises.

Russian Embroidery & Lace (p130) Handmade linens and lovelies.

Trekhgornaya Manufaktura Factory Outlet (p111) High-quality fabrics from one of the country's oldest textile factories.

Explore Moscow

MOSCOW'S TOP SIGHTS

Neighbourhoods at a Glance

❶ Kremlin & Kitay Gorod p58

Red Square and the Kremlin are the historical, geographic and spiritual heart of Moscow, as they have been for nearly 900 years. The mighty fortress, the iconic onion domes of St Basil's Cathedral and the granite mausoleum of Vladimir Lenin are among the city's most important historical sights. The surrounding streets of Kitay Gorod are crammed with churches and old architecture. The starting point for any visit to Moscow.

❷ Tverskoy & Novoslobodsky p85

The streets around Tverskaya ul comprise the vibrant Tverskoy district, which is char-

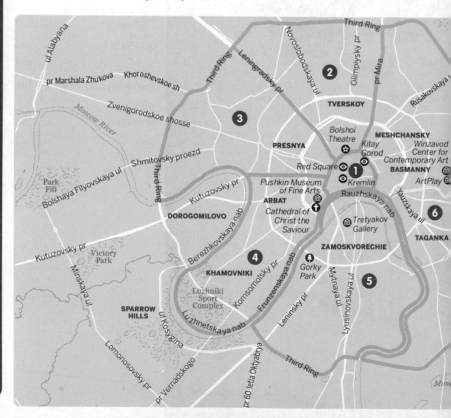

acterised by old architecture and new commerce. Aside from being a cultural centre (it's home to 20-plus theatres and concert halls, including the world-famous Bolshoi Theatre), Tverskoy is also the city's liveliest commercial district, its streets lined with restaurants, shops and other venues, such as the Sanduny Baths.

❸ Presnya p100

The vast, diverse Presnya district spans the centuries, taking in development from the last three. The district's diverse attractions include its impressive and varied architecture, several noteworthy literary sites, and more-traditional venues, such as the zoo and planetarium. Presnya is also home to many of Moscow's top restaurants, including the highly lauded Café Pushkin. The former textile factory at Trekhgornaya is fast becoming a centre for nightlife and dining.

❹ Arbat & Khamovniki p112

The side-by-side districts of Arbat and Khamovniki are rich with culture. Moscow's most famous street, ul Arbat, is something of an art market, complete with portrait painters and soapbox poets, while the nearby streets are lined with museums and galleries, including the world-class Pushkin Museum of Fine Arts. Khamovniki is home to the ancient Novodevichy Convent & Cemetery, as well as several unique newer museums. Further out, it's worth a trip to the south side of the Moscow River for certain key destinations, such as triumphant Park Pobedy.

❺ Zamoskvorechie p131

Zamoskvorechie – which means 'Beyond Moscow River' – stretches south from the bank opposite the Kremlin. This district is the site of Moscow's traditional art museum, the Tretyakov, as well as the capital's most exciting contemporary art and entertainment complex, in the former Red October chocolate factory. Green Gorky Park lies further south along the Moscow River, while two ancient fortress-monasteries guard the city's southern flank.

❻ Meshchansky & Basmanny p146

The Meshchansky and Basmanny districts flank the little Yauza River in the eastern part of the city. The former is a bustling neighbourhood that retains its quaint 19th-century outlook. The latter is largely comprised of old factories, now taken over by hipsters, and housing innovative postmodern galleries and clubs. South of the Yauza, Taganskaya pl is a monster intersection that can be difficult to navigate, but the district is home to a few unusual sights such as Bunker-42 and the Museum of the Russian Icon.

NEIGHBOURHOODS AT A GLANCE

Kremlin & Kitay Gorod

KREMLIN | KITAY GOROD

Neighbourhood Top Five

1 Wandering around the grounds of the **Kremlin** (p60); exploring 500 years of artistic mastery, political power and spiritual devotion; and gawking at the royal treasures in the Armoury.

2 Marvelling at the multicoloured, multidomed spectacle of **St Basil's Cathedral** (p77).

3 Paying your respects to Vladimir Ilych Ulyanov and other communist leaders at **Lenin's Mausoleum** (p75).

4 Discovering the ancient churches hidden among the narrow streets of **Kitay Gorod** (Map p255).

5 Watching ballerinas spin across the stage at the **Kremlin Ballet** (p84).

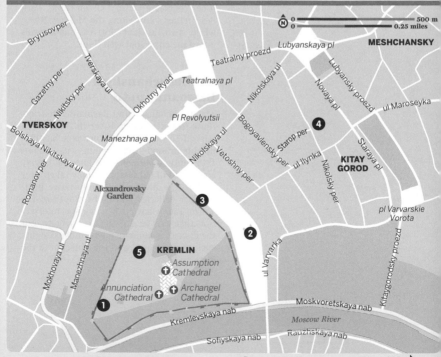

For more detail of this area see Map p255 ➡

Explore: Kremlin & Kitay Gorod

If you have only one day in Moscow, you will probably spend it here. With more time, you might spend more than one day here, exploring the churches and museums, and viewing the trappings of power.

The neighbourhood's key attractions are clustered around Red Square and within the walls of the Kremlin. It doesn't matter which of these two you take in first, but try to leave time for both. Your visit to the Kremlin should be planned around admission to the Armoury: it requires advance purchase of tickets, which specify the admission times.

Besides being a major tourist attraction, Red Square hosts concerts, festivals, parades and other official events. As a result, the place is sometimes closed to the public and it's almost always packed with people. Come early in the morning or late in the evening to catch a glimpse of the square when it is sparsely populated, vast and majestic.

Travellers with some extra time will enjoy wandering the medieval streets of Kitay Gorod, discovering ancient hidden churches and popping into shops and cafes. It is a welcome change from the hustle and bustle that characterises the Kremlin and Red Square.

Local Life

➡ **Parks** Muscovites don't often hang out on Red Square, but they do enjoy Alexander Garden, where they stroll among the flower beds, snap photos and (gasp) lounge on the grass.

➡ **Wedding Parties** The Tomb of the Unknown Soldier is Moscow's top destination for wedding parties, who snap photos and drink champagne while the bride and groom pay their respects by laying flowers on the grave site.

➡ **Shopping Malls** It may be too expensive for most Muscovites to shop at the stores in GUM, but it's not too expensive to eat at Solovaya 57 – as evidenced by the lines of locals out the door at lunchtime.

Getting There & Away

➡ **Metro** Three metro lines converge at Red Square. Teatralnaya station is on the green line; Okhotny Ryad station is on the red line; and Ploshchad Revolyutsii is on the dark blue line.

➡ **Metro** The orange line and the purple line intersect in Kitay Gorod, with both stations sharing the name of the neighbourhood. The red line has an eponymous station at Lubyanka, which is also useful for Kitay Gorod.

Lonely Planet's Top Tip

If you think Red Square is impressive by day, come back at night, when the crowds are gone and the lights cast a magical glow on the historic buildings.

KREMLIN & KITAY GOROD

✖ Best Places to Eat

➡ Loft Café (p81)
➡ Friends Forever Cafe (p81)
➡ Coffee Mania (p81)
➡ Bosco Cafe (p81)

For reviews, see p81 ➡

♟ Best Places to Drink

➡ Cafe Tantsy (p82)
➡ Dissident Vinoteca (p82)
➡ Mandarin Combustible (p82)

For reviews, see p82 ➡

◉ Best Soviet Relics

➡ Lenin's Mausoleum (p75)
➡ Stolovaya 57 (p81)
➡ Lubyanka Prison (p149)
➡ Four Seasons Moscow (p177)

For reviews, see p79 ➡

TOP SIGHT
THE KREMLIN

The apex of Russian political power and once the centre of the Orthodox Church, the Kremlin (Кремль) is the kernel not only of Moscow but of the whole country. It's from here autocratic tsars, communist dictators and modern-day presidents have done their best – and worst – for Russia. These red-brick walls and tent-roof towers enclose some 800 years of artistic accomplishment, religious ceremony and political power.

Entrance Towers

Kutafya Tower

The **Kutafya Tower** (Кутафья башня; Map p255), which forms the main visitors' entrance today, stands apart from the Kremlin's west wall, at the end of a ramp over the Alexander Garden. The ramp was once a bridge over the Neglinnaya River and used to be part of the Kremlin's defences; this river has been diverted underground, beneath the Alexander Garden, since the early 19th century. The Kutafya Tower is the last of a number of outer bridge towers that once stood on this side of the Kremlin.

Trinity Gate Tower

From the Kutafya Tower, walk up the ramp and pass through the Kremlin walls beneath the 1495 **Trinity Gate Tower** (Троицкая башня255). At 80m it's the tallest of the Kremlin's towers. Right below your feet were the cells for prisoners in the 16th century.

DON'T MISS...

➡ The frescoed interior of Assumption Cathedral

➡ The gilded cover of the coffin of Tsarevitch Dmitry in Archangel Cathedral

➡ Icons by Theophanes and Rublyev in the Annunciation Cathedral

➡ The Crown of Monomakh in the Armoury

PRACTICALITIES

➡ Map p255

➡ www.kreml.ru

➡ adult/student ₽350/100

➡ ⊘10am-5pm Fri-Wed, ticket office 9.30am-4.30pm

➡ Ⓜ Aleksandrovsky Sad

Government Buildings

Poteshny Palace

Immediately inside the Trinity Gate Tower, the lane to the right (south) passes the 17th-century **Poteshny Palace** (Потешный дворец), where Stalin lived. The yellow palace was built by Tsar Alexey Mikhailovich and housed the first Russian theatre. Here, Tsar Alexey enjoyed various comedic performances. In keeping with conservative Russian Orthodox tradition, however, after the shows he would go to the *banya* (Russian bathhouse), then attend a church service to repent his sins. The bombastic marble, glass and concrete **State Kremlin Palace** (Государственный кремлёвский дворец), built between 1960 and 1961 for Communist Party congresses, is now home to the Kremlin Ballet (p84).

Arsenal

To the north of the State Kremlin Palace is the 18th-century **Arsenal** (Арсенал), commissioned by Peter the Great to house workshops and depots for guns and weaponry. An unrealised plan at the end of the 19th century was to open a museum of the Napoleonic Wars in the Arsenal. Now housing the Kremlin Guard, the building is ringed with 800 captured Napoleonic cannons.

Senate

The offices of the president of Russia, the ultimate seat of power in the modern Kremlin, are in the yellow, triangular former **Senate** (Сенат) building, a fine 18th-century neoclassical edifice, east of the Arsenal. Built in 1785 by architect Matvei Kazakov, it was noted for its huge cupola. In the 16th and 17th centuries this area was where the boyars (high-ranking Russian nobles) lived. Next to the Senate is the 1930s **Supreme Soviet** (Верховный Совет) building.

Patriarch's Palace

Patriarch's Palace (Патриарший дворец) was mostly built in the middle of the 17th century for Patriarch Nikon, whose reforms sparked the break with the Old Believers. Now quiet, the palace in its heyday was a busy place. Apart from the Patriarch's living quarters, it had huge kitchens, warehouses and cellars stocked with food, workshops, a school for highborn children, offices for scribes, dormitories for those waiting to be baptised, stables and carriage houses.

The palace now contains an exhibit of 17th-century household items, including jewellery, hunting equipment and furniture. Patriarch's Palace

NO BAGS ALLOWED

Before entering the Kremlin, deposit bags at the **left-luggage office** (Map p255; per bag ₽60; ☺9am-6.30pm Fri-Wed), beneath the Kutafya Tower in Alexander Garden.

The Kremlin has been open to tourists since 1955.

TICKETS

The **main ticket office** (Кассы музеев Кремля; Map p255; ☺9.30am-4pm Fri-Wed; ⓂAleksandrovsky Sad) is in Alexander Garden, next to the Kremlin wall. The ticket to the 'Architectural Ensemble of Sobornaya pl' covers entry to all five church-museums, as well as Patriarch's Palace. It does not include the Armoury or the Diamond Fund Exhibition, but you can and should buy tickets for the Armoury and any special exhibits here. You can also order tickets on the Kremlin website, but you still have to pick them up at the ticket office in Alexander Garden.

The Kremlin

A DAY AT THE KREMLIN

Only at the Kremlin can you see 800 years of Russian history and artistry in one day. Enter the ancient fortress through the Trinity Gate Tower and walk past the impressive Arsenal, ringed with cannons. Past the Patriarch's Palace, you'll find yourself surrounded by white-washed walls and golden domes. Your first stop is **Assumption Cathedral** ❶ with the solemn fresco over the doorway. As the most important church in prerevolutionary Russia, this 15th-century beauty was the burial site of the patriarchs. The **Ivan the Great Bell Tower** ❷ now contains a nifty multimedia exhibit on the architectural history of the Kremlin. The view from the top is worth the price of admission. The tower is flanked by the massive **Tsar Cannon & Bell** ❸.

In the southeast corner, **Archangel Cathedral** ❹ has an elaborate interior, where three centuries of tsars and tsarinas are laid to rest. Your final stop on Sobornaya pl is **Annunciation Cathedral** ❺, rich with frescoes and iconography.

Walk along the Great Kremlin Palace and enter the **Armoury** ❻ at the time designated on your ticket. After gawking at the goods, exit the Kremlin through Borovitsky Gate and stroll through the Alexander Garden to the **Tomb of the Unknown Soldier** ❼.

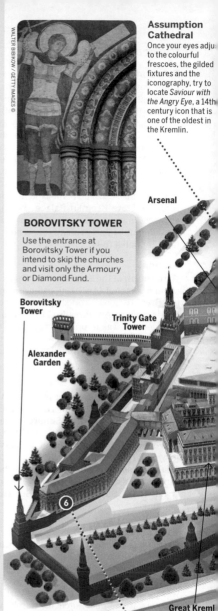

Assumption Cathedral
Once your eyes adjust to the colourful frescoes, the gilded fixtures and the iconography, try to locate *Saviour with the Angry Eye*, a 14th century icon that is one of the oldest in the Kremlin.

Arsenal

BOROVITSKY TOWER
Use the entrance at Borovitsky Tower if you intend to skip the churches and visit only the Armoury or Diamond Fund.

Borovitsky Tower

Trinity Gate Tower

Alexander Garden

Great Kremlin Palace

Armoury
Take advantage of the free audio guide to direct you to the most intriguing treasures of the Armoury which is chock-full of precious metalworks and jewellery, armour and weapons, gowns and crowns, carriages and sledges.

TOP TIPS

» **Lunch** There are no eating options. Plan to eat before you arrive or stash a snack.

» **Lookout** After ogling the sights around Sobornaya pl, take a break in the park across the street, which offers wonderful views of the Moscow River and points south.

AVOID CONFUSION

Regular admission to the Kremlin does not include Ivan the Great Bell Tower. But admission to the bell tower does include the churches on the Kremlin grounds.

mb of the Unknown Soldier
t the Tomb of the Unknown Soldier honouring
heroes of the Great Patriotic War. Come
he top of the hour to see the solemn
chronicity of the changing of the guard.

Patriarch's Palace

Ivan the Great Bell Tower
Check out the artistic electronic renderings
of the Kremlin's history, then climb 137 steps
to the belfry's upper gallery, where you will
be rewarded with super, sweeping vistas of
Sobornaya pl and beyond.

Moscow River

Tsar Cannon & Bell
Peer down the barrel of the monstrous Tsar Cannon and pose for a picture
beside the oversized Tsar Bell, both of which are too big to serve their
intended purpose.

Sobornaya pl

nunciation thedral
nire the artistic
stery of Russia's
atest icon painters –
ophanes the Greek
Andrei Rublyov –
are responsible for
ny of the icons in the
sis and festival rows
e iconostasis.

Archangel Cathedral
See the final resting
place of princes and
emperors who ruled
Russia for more than
300 years, including
the visionary Ivan the
Great, the tortured
Ivan theTerrible
and the tragic
Tsarevitch Dmitry.

KREMLIN & RED SQUARE

Ploshchad Revolyutsii

Ploshchad Revolyutsii

Four Seasons Hotel Moskva

pl Revolyutsii

Okhotny Ryad

Museum of the War of 1812

Kazan Cathedral

Manezhnaya pl

Resurection Gate

State History Museum

GUM

Corner Arsenal Tower

Tomb of the Unknown Soldier

Lenin's Mausoleum

Red Square

Place of Sculls

Senate

Arsenal

Saviour Gate Tower

St Basil's Cathedral

Alexander Garden

Supreme Soviet

Tsar Tower

Alarm Tower

Kutafya Tower (Main Entrance)

Kremlin Ticket Offices

Patriarch's Palace

Tsar Cannon

Konstantin & Yelena Tower

Trinity Gate Tower

Left-luggage Office

State Kremlin Palace

Ivan the Great Bell Tower

Assumption Cathedral

Tsar Bell

Kremlin Ticket Office

Poteshny Palace

Church of the Deposition of the Robe

Sobornaya pl

Terem Palace

Hall of Facets

Archangel Cathedral

Annunciation Cathedral

Great Kremlin Palace

Armoury & Diamond Fund Exhibition

Manezhnaya

Borovitskaya Tower (Alternative Entrance)

Kremlevskaya

MOSCOW RIVER

ssumption Cathedral

STAND ON CEREMONY

Every Saturday at noon from April to October, the Presidential Regiment shows up on Sobornaya pl for a ceremonial procession, featuring some very official-looking prancing and dancing, both on foot and on horseback. The price of admission to the Kremlin allows access to the demonstration.

The director of the Kremlin museums is Elena Gagarina, the daughter of pilot and cosmonaut Yury Gagarin.

often holds **special exhibits**, which can be visited individually, without access to the other buildings on Sobornaya pl.

Church of the Twelve Apostles

From inside the Patriarch's Palace, you can access the five-domed **Church of the Twelve Apostles** (Церковь двенадцати апостолов). The pretty little chapel contains a gilded wooden iconostasis and a collection of icons by leading 17th-century icon painters.

Cross Hall

The highlight of the Patriarch's Palace is perhaps the ceremonial **Cross Hall** (Крестовая палата), where feasts for the tsars and ambassadors were held. From the 18th century the room was used to produce *miro* (a holy oil used during church services, which contains over 30 herbal components); the oven and huge pans from the production process are on display.

Assumption Cathedral

On the northern side of Sobornaya pl, with five golden helmet domes and four semicircular gables facing the square, the **Assumption Cathedral** (Успенский собор) was the focal church of prerevolutionary Russia and the burial place of most of the heads of the Russian Orthodox Church from the 1320s to 1700. A striking 1660s fresco of the Virgin Mary faces Sobornaya pl, above the door once used for royal processions. If you have limited time in the Kremlin, come straight here. The visitors' entrance is at the western end.

In 1470 Russian architects Krivtsov and Myshkin were commissioned by Ivan the Great to replace the old dilapidated cathedral, which dated from 1326. As soon as the ceiling was put up, one of the walls collapsed. During Soviet times, history books said this calamity was the result of bad handiwork, but today revisionist history indicates that an earthquake caused the collapse. Either way, Krivtsov and Myshkin lost their jobs, and Italian architect Aristotle Fioravanti was given a crack at it. After the foundation was completed, Fioravanti toured Novgorod, Suzdal and Vladimir to acquaint himself with Russian architecture. His design is a more spacious version of the Assumption Cathedral at Vladimir, with a Renaissance twist.

The church closed in 1918. According to some accounts, in 1941, when the Nazis were on the outskirts of Moscow, Stalin secretly ordered a service in the cathedral to protect the city from the enemy. The cathedral was officially returned to the Church in 1989, but it now operates as a museum.

Frescoes

The interior of the Assumption Cathedral is unusually bright and spacious, full of frescoes painted in warm golds, reds and blues. The west wall features a scene of the Apocalypse, a favourite theme of the Russian Church in the Middle Ages. The pillars have pictures of martyrs, considered to be the pillars of faith. Above the southern gates there are frescoes of Yelena and Constantine, who brought Christianity to Greece and the south of Russia. The space above the northern gate depicts Olga and Vladimir, who brought Christianity to the north.

Most of the existing images on the cathedral walls were painted on a gilt base in the 1640s, with the exception of three grouped together on the south wall: *The Apocalypse* (Апокалипсис), *The Life of Metropolitan Pyotr* (Житие Митрополита Петра) and *All Creatures Rejoice in Thee* (О тебе радуется). These are attributed to Dionysius and his followers, the cathedral's original 15th-century mural painters.

Patriarchs' Tombs

The tombs of many leaders of the Russian Church (metropolitans up to 1590, patriarchs from 1590 to 1700) are against the north, west and south walls of Assumption Cathedral. Near the west wall there is a shrine with holy relics of Patriarch Hermogen, who instigated an uprising during the Time of Troubles in 1612.

HISTORY OF THE KREMLIN

A *kremlin* (fortified stronghold) has existed on this site since Moscow's earliest years. In 1147 Yury Dolgoruky summoned his allies to this spot, which would have been occupied by a wooden fort. When the city became the capital of medieval Rus in the 1320s, the Kremlin served as the headquarters of the Russian Orthodox Church and the seat of the prince.

The ambition of Ivan III (the Great) was to build a capital that would equal the fallen Constantinople in grandeur, power, achievements and architecture. In an effort to build the 'Third Rome', Ivan brought from Italy stonemasons and architects, who built new walls, three great cathedrals and other structures. Most of the present-day buildings date from this period.

Although Peter I (the Great) shifted the capital to St Petersburg, the tsars still showed up here for coronations and other celebrations. The fortress was captured by Napoleon, who inflicted serious damage before making his retreat in 1812. But still the ancient symbol endured. The citadel wouldn't be breached again until the Bolsheviks stormed the place in November 1917.

Also a supporter of Minin and Pozharsky's revolt against the Polish occupation, the martyr was later arrested, beaten and starved to death.

Throne of Monomakh

Near the south wall of Assumption Cathedral is a tent-roofed wooden throne made in 1551 for Ivan the Terrible, known as the Throne of Monomakh. Its carved scenes highlight the career of 12th-century Grand Prince Vladimir Monomakh of Kiev – considered to be Ivan's direct predecessor.

Iconostasis

Assumption Cathedral's iconostasis dates from 1652, but its lowest level contains some older icons. The 1340s *Saviour with the Angry Eye* (Спас Ярое око) is second from the right. On the left of the central door is the *Virgin of Vladimir* (Владимирская Богоматерь), an early-15th-century Rublyov school copy of Russia's most revered image, the *Vladimir Icon of the Mother of God* (Владимирская икона Богоматери). The 12th-century original, now in the Tretyakov Gallery, stood in the Assumption Cathedral from the 1480s to 1930. One of the oldest Russian icons, the 12th-century red-clothed *St George* (Святой Георгий) from Novgorod, is by the north wall.

The original icons of the lower, local tier are symbols of victory brought from Vladimir, Smolensk, Veliky Ustyug and other places. The south door was brought from the Nativity of the Virgin Cathedral in Suzdal.

Church of the Deposition of the Robe

The delicate single-domed **Church of the Deposition of the Robe** (Церковь Ризположения), beside the west door of the Assumption Cathedral, was built between 1484 and 1486 in exclusively Russian style. It was the private chapel of the heads of the Church, who tended to be highly suspicious of such people as Italian architects. The interior walls, ceilings and pillars are covered with 17th-century frescoes. It houses an exhibition of 15th- to 17th-century woodcarvings.

Ivan the Great Bell Tower

With its two golden domes rising above the eastern side of Sobornaya pl, the **Ivan the Great Bell Tower** (Колокольня Ивана Великого) is the Kremlin's tallest structure – a landmark visible from 30km away. Before the 20th century it was forbidden to build any higher than this tower in Moscow.

Its history dates back to the Church of Ioann Lestvichnik Under the Bells, built on this site in 1329 by Ivan I (and later destroyed). In 1505, Italian Marco Bono designed a new belfry, originally with

The first stone structures in the Kremlin were built in the 1330s at the behest of Ivan 'Moneybags' Kalita. Only the Church of the Saviour's Transfiguration survived into the 20th century, but it was demolished by Stalin approximately 600 years after it was built.

SPECIAL EXHIBITS

Temporary exhibits from the Kremlin collections are held on the ground floor of the Assumption Belfry and in Patriarch's Palace.

In 1812 French troops used the Assumption Cathedral as a stable; they also looted 295kg of gold and over five tonnes of silver from here, but much of it was recovered.

GET INSIDE THE GREAT KREMLIN PALACE

The Great Kremlin Palace is not open to the public, but Patriarshy Dom Tours (p32) sometimes arranges tours inside this grandiose building.

only two octagonal tiers beneath a drum and a dome. In 1600 Boris Godunov raised it to 81m.

The building's central section, with a gilded single dome and a 65-tonne bell, dates from between 1532 and 1542. The tent-roofed annexe, next to the belfry, was commissioned by Patriarch Filaret about 100 years later.

Architectural Exhibit

Ivan the Great houses the **Museum of the History of Moscow Kremlin Architecture** (Музей истории архитектуры Московского кремля; Map p255; admission ₽500), a multimedia presentation of the architectural history of the Kremlin complex. Using architectural fragments and electronic projections, the exhibit illustrates how the Kremlin has changed since the 12th century. Special attention is given to individual churches within the complex, including several churches that no longer exist. The 45-minute tour ends with a 137-step climb to the top of the tall tower, yielding an amazing (and unique!) view of Sobornaya pl, with the Church of Christ the Saviour and the Moskva-City skyscrapers in the distance.

That said, at the time of research, the bell tower was closed for no apparent reason, with no indication of when it might reopen. If it is open, the price of a ticket to Ivan the Great is supposed to include admission to the other churches (not the Armoury), so you don't have to buy an additional ticket to the Kremlin grounds.

Tsar Bell

Beside (not inside) the Ivan the Great Bell Tower stands the world's biggest bell, a 202-tonne monster that has never rung. An earlier version, weighing 130 tonnes, fell from its belfry during a fire in 1701 and shattered. Using these remains, the

---

TOWERS OF POWER

The present Kremlin walls were built between 1485 and 1495, replacing the limestone walls from the 14th century. The walls are 6m to 17m tall, depending on the landscape, and 2m to 5m thick. They stretch for 2235m. Originally, a 32m-wide moat encircled the northern end of the Kremlin, connecting the Moscow and Neglinnaya Rivers.

The 20 distinctive towers were built between 1485 and 1500, with tent roofs added in the 17th century. Originally, the towers had lookout posts and were equipped for heavy fighting. Most were designed by Italian masons.

The most prominent tower is the Saviour Gate Tower (p76), the clock tower soaring above Red Square. Right next to it is the **Tsar Tower**, (Царская башня), a later addition (1680), which sits on top of the Kremlin wall. Legend has it that Ivan the Terrible watched executions and other Red Square activities from the old wooden tower that previously stood on this site. Next along is the **Alarm Tower** (Набатная башня), which used to house the Spassky Alarm Bell, used to warn of enemy attacks and to spur popular uprisings. After quashing one such uprising, Catherine the Great was so outraged that she had the clapper removed from the bell, so it could sound no more.

The two towers anchoring the northern and southern ends of this eastern wall played important roles in the Kremlin's defenses. At the corner of Alexander Garden, **St Nicholas Tower** (Никольская башня) was previously a gated defensive tower on the northeastern flank. Through this gate, Dmitry Pozharsky and Kuzma Minin (as depicted in the statue in front of St Basil's Cathedral) led a civilian army and drove out the Polish occupiers. At the southern end of Red Square, **Konstantin & Yelena Tower** (Константино-Еленинская башня) was built to protect the settlements outside the city. It is complete with firing platforms and a drawbridge over the moat.

Annunciation Cathedral (p71)

In 1600, Boris Godunov increased the height of the Ivan the Great Bell Tower from 60m to 81m. Local legend says that this was a public works project designed to employ the thousands of people who had come to Moscow during a famine, but historical documents contradict the story, as the construction apparently did not coincide with a famine. The height was probably increased so that the belfry could also serve as a watch tower.

current **Tsar Bell** (Царь-колокол) was cast in the 1730s for Empress Anna Ivanovna. The bell was cooling off in the foundry casting pit in 1737 when it came into contact with water, causing an 11-tonne chunk to break off. One hundred years later, the architect Montferrand took the damaged bell out of the pit and put it on a pedestal. The bas-reliefs of Empress Anna and Tsar Alexey, as well as some icons, were etched on its sides.

CAMERA SHY

Photography is not permitted inside the Armoury or in any of the buildings on Sobornaya pl (Cathedral Sq).

Tsar Cannon
North of the Ivan the Great Bell Tower is the 40-tonne **Tsar Cannon** (Царь-пушка). It was cast in 1586 by the blacksmith Ivan Chokhov for Fyodor I, whose portrait is on the barrel. No shot has ever sullied its 89cm bore – certainly not the cannonballs beside it, which are too big even for this elephantine firearm.

Under Orthodox law, the fourth marriage of Ivan the Terrible disqualified him from entering the church proper, so he had the southern gallery of the Annunciation Cathedral converted into the Archangel Gabriel Chapel, from where he could watch services through a grille.

Archangel Cathedral
The **Archangel Cathedral** (Архангельский собор), at the southeastern corner of Sobornaya pl, was for centuries the coronation, wedding and burial church of tsars. It was built by Ivan Kalita in 1333 to commemorate the end of the great famine, and dedicated to Archangel Michael, guardian of the Moscow princes. By the turn of the 16th century it had fallen into disrepair and was rebuilt between 1505 and 1508 by the Italian architect Alevisio Novi. Like the Assumption Cathedral, it has five domes and is essentially Byzantine-Russian in

style. However, the exterior has many Venetian Renaissance features, notably the distinctive scallop-shell gables and porticoes.

Tsarist Tombs

The tombs of almost all Muscovy's rulers from the 1320s to the 1690s are here. The only absentee is Boris Godunov, whose body was taken out of the grave on the order of a 'False Dmitry' and buried at Sergiev Posad in 1606. The bodies are buried underground, beneath the 17th-century sarcophagi and 19th-century copper covers. Tsarevitch Dmitry (a son of Ivan the Terrible), who died mysteriously in 1591, lies beneath a painted stone canopy. It was Dmitry's death that sparked the appearance of a string of impersonators, known as False Dmitrys, during the Time of Troubles. Ivan's own tomb is out of sight behind the iconostasis, along with those of his other sons, Ivan (whom he killed) and Fyodor I (who succeeded him). From Peter the Great onwards, emperors and empresses were buried in St Petersburg, the exception being Peter II, who died in Moscow and is here.

Murals

Some 17th-century murals were uncovered during restorations of the Archangel Cathedral in the 1950s. The south wall depicts many of the rulers buried here; on the pillars are some of their predecessors, including Andrei Bogolyubsky, Prince Daniil and Alexander Nevsky.

Hall of Facets & Terem Palace

Hall of Facets

Named for its Italian Renaissance stone facing, the **Hall of Facets** (Грановитая палата) was designed and built by Marco Ruffo and Pietro Solario between 1487 and 1491, during the reign of Ivan the Great. Its upper floor housed the tsars' throne room, the scene of banquets and ceremonies. Access to the Hall of Facets was via an outside staircase from the square below. During the Streltsy Rebellion of 1682, several of Peter the Great's relatives were tossed down the exterior **Red Staircase**, so called because it ran red with their blood. (It's no wonder that Peter hated Moscow and decided to start afresh with a new capital in St Petersburg.) Stalin destroyed the staircase, but it was rebuilt in 1994.

The hall is 500 sq metres, with a supporting pillar in the centre. The walls are decorated with gorgeous murals of biblical and historical themes, although none are original. Alas, the building is closed to the public.

Terem Palace

The 16th- and 17th-century **Terem Palace** (Теремной дворец) is the most splendid of the Kremlin palaces. Made of stone and built by Vasily III, the palace's living

---

KREMLIN TOURS

Let the professionals show you around the Kremlin:

Kremlin Excursion Office (Map p255; ☑495-697 0349; www.kremlin.museum .ru; Alexander Garden; 90min tour ₽2500; ⓂAlexandrovsky Sad) Offers 'official' tours of the Kremlin grounds, churches and exhibits.

Capital Tours (p32) Departing from the tour office in Gostinny Dvor every day that the Kremlin is open. Price includes admission; book at least two days in advance.

Kremlin Tour with Diana (☑916-333 2555; www.kremlintour.com) Diana Zalenskaya offers private tours of the Kremlin, with or without the Armoury included (US$110 to US$140, plus guiding fee).

quarters include a dining room, living room, study, bedroom and small chapel. Unfortunately, the palace is closed to the public, but you can glimpse its cluster of 11 golden domes and chequered roof behind and above the Church of the Deposition of the Robe.

Annunciation Cathedral

The **Annunciation Cathedral** (Благовещенский собор; Map p255; Blagoveshchensky sobor), at the southwest corner of Sobornaya pl, contains the celebrated icons of master painter Theophanes the Greek (Feofan Grek in Russian).

Vasily I built the first wooden church on this site in 1397. Between 1484 and 1489, Ivan the Great had the Annunciation Cathedral rebuilt to serve as the royal family's private chapel. Originally the cathedral had just three domes and an open gallery around three sides. Ivan the Terrible, whose tastes were more elaborate, added six more domes and chapels at each corner, enclosed the gallery and gilded the roof.

Frescoes

Many murals in the Annunciation Cathedral's gallery date from the 1560s. Among them are *Capture of Jericho* in the northern porch, *Jonah and the Whale* in the northern arm of the gallery, and the *Tree of Jesus* on its ceiling. Other frescoes feature ancient philosophers such as Aristotle, Plutarch, Plato and Socrates holding scrolls inscribed with their own wise words. Socrates' scroll reads: 'No harm will ever come to a good man. Our soul is immortal. After death the good shall be rewarded and the evil punished'. Plato's says: 'We must hope God shall send us a heavenly Teacher and a Guide'.

In the small central part of the cathedral, the 16th-century frescoes include Russian princes on the north pillar and Byzantine emperors on the south, both with Apocalypse scenes above them.

Iconostasis

The real treasure of Annunciation Cathedral is the iconostasis, where in the 1920s restorers uncovered early-15th-century icons by three of the greatest medieval Russian artists. It was most likely Theophanes who painted the six icons at the right-hand end of the biggest row of the six tiers of the iconostasis. From left to right, these are the *Virgin Mary, Christ Enthroned, St John the Baptist,* the *Archangel Gabriel,* the *Apostle Paul* and *St John Chrysostom.* Theophanes was a master of portraying pathos in the facial expressions of his subjects, setting these icons apart from most others.

The obelisk in Alexander Garden was originally a monument to commemorate the House of Romanovs. In 1918 it had a dramatic change in mission when it was redesignated the Monument to Revolutionary Thinkers (Map p255), in honour of those responsible for the spread of communism in Russia.

CHANGING OF THE GUARD

Every hour on the hour, the guards of the Tomb of the Unknown Soldier perform a perfectly synchronised ceremony to change the guards on duty.

The Tomb of the Unknown Soldier contains the remains of one soldier who died in December 1941 at Km 41 of Leningradskoe sh – the nearest the Nazis came to Moscow.

ARMOURY

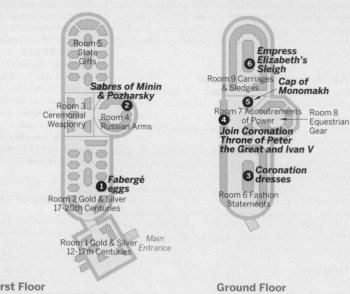

First Floor

Ground Floor

Room 5 State Gifts

Sabres of Minin & Pozharsky
❷

Room 3 Ceremonial Weaponry

Room 4 Russian Arms

❶ **Fabergé eggs**

Room 2 Gold & Silver 17-20th Centuries

Room 1 Gold & Silver 12-17th Centuries

Main Entrance

Empress Elizabeth's Sleigh
❻

Room 9 Carriages & Sledges

Cap of Monomakh

❺

Room 7 Accoutrements of Power
❹

Room 8 Equestrian Gear

Join Coronation Throne of Peter the Great and Ivan V

❸ **Coronation dresses**

Room 6 Fashion Statements

🏃 Museum Tour
Armoury

LENGTH ONE HOUR
SEE ARMOURY (P74)

Your tour starts upstairs, where the first two rooms house gold and silver from the 12th to 20th centuries, many of which were crafted in the Kremlin workshops. In Room 2, you'll find the renowned ❶**Easter eggs** made by St Petersburg jeweller Fabergé. The tsar and tsarina traditionally exchanged these gifts each year at Easter. Most famous is the Grand Siberian Railway egg, with gold train, platinum locomotive and ruby headlamp, created to commemorate the Moscow–Vladivostok line.

The following rooms display armour, weapons and more armour and more weapons. Don't miss the helmet of Prince Yaroslav, the chainmail of Boris Godunov, and the ❷**sabres of Minin and Pozharsky**.

Downstairs in Room 6, you can see the ❸**coronation dresses** of 18th-century empresses (Empress Elizabeth, we're told, had 15,000 other dresses). Other 'secular' dress is also on display, including an impressive pair of boots that belonged to Peter the Great. The following room contains the ❹**joint coronation throne** of boy tsars Peter the Great and his half-brother Ivan V (with a secret compartment from which Regent Sofia prompted them), as well as the 800-diamond throne of Tsar Alexey, Peter's father. The gold ❺**Cap of Monomakh**, jewel-studded and sable-trimmed, was used for two centuries at coronations.

End your tour in Room 9, which houses centuries' worth of royal carriages and sledges. Look for the ❻**sleigh** in which Elizabeth rode from St Petersburg to Moscow for her coronation, pulled by 23 horses at a time – about 800 in all for the trip.

Crown display, the Armoury (p74)

The third icon from the left, *Archangel Michael,* is ascribed to Andrei Rublyov, who may also have painted the adjacent *St Peter.* Rublyov is also reckoned to be the artist of the first, second, sixth and seventh (and probably the third and fifth) icons from the left of the festival row, above the *deesis* (biggest) row. The seven icons at the right-hand end are attributed to Prokhor of Gorodets.

Archaeology Exhibit

The basement of Annunciation Cathedral holds a permanent exhibit on the archaeology of the Kremlin – an appropriate place, as this is actually a remnant of the 14th-century church that previously occupied this site.

On display are hundreds of artefacts – glassware, ceramics, tools and woodworks – that were excavated from Borovitsky Hill in the 1960s and 1970s. Archaeologists found around 30 'treasure troves', which included silver jewellery and coins dating to medieval times.

Great Kremlin Palace

Housing the Armoury and much more, the 700-room **Great Kremlin Palace** (Большой Кремлёвский дворец; Map p255) was built between 1838 and 1849 by architect Konstantin Thon as an imperial residence for Nicholas I. It is now an official residence of the Russian president, used for state visits and receptions. However, unlike Russian tsars, the president doesn't have living quarters here.

GETTING TICKETS TO THE ARMOURY

Visitors are allowed to enter the Armoury only at specified times (10am, noon, 2.30pm and 4.30pm). Tickets go on sale 45 minutes prior to each session. Try to be at the ticket window when the sales begin, as they sell a limited number of tickets for each entry time.

The Diamond Fund is managed by the Ministry of Finance, which retains a monopoly on the mining and sale of precious stones. As such, the collection includes many magnificent raw diamonds, some in excess of 300 carats.

GETTING TICKETS TO THE DIAMOND FUND

Purchase tickets to the Diamond Fund in the lobby of the exhibit.

The huge palace incorporates some of the earlier buildings such as the Hall of Facets, Terem Palace and several chapels. Although vast, the building has never received great praise, being criticised as 'barrack-like' and 'pretentious'. Several ceremonial halls are named after saints, including St George, St Vladimir, St Andrew, St Catherine and St Alexander. St George's Hall is mainly used for state awards ceremonies, while major international treaties are signed in St Vladimir's Hall. The Great Kremlin Palace (apart from the Armoury) is closed to tourists.

Armoury

The **Armoury** (Оружейная палата; Map p255; adult/student ₽700/250; ⊘10am, noon, 2.30pm & 4.30pm; MAleksandrovsky Sad) dates back to 1511, when it was founded under Vasily III to manufacture and store weapons, imperial arms and regalia for the royal court. Later it also produced jewellery, icon frames and embroidery. During the reign of Peter the Great all craftspeople, goldsmiths and silversmiths were sent to St Petersburg, and the Armoury became a mere museum storing the royal treasures. To this day, the Armoury still contains plenty of treasures for ogling, and remains a highlight of any visit to the Kremlin.

If possible, buy your ticket to the Armoury when you buy your ticket to the Kremlin. Your ticket will specify a time of entry. A one-hour audio guide is also available to point out some of the highlights of the collection.

Diamond Fund of Russia

If the Armoury hasn't sated your lust for diamonds, there are more in the separate **Diamond Fund Exhibition** (Алмазный фонд России; Map p255; www.almazi.net; admission ₽500; ⊘10am-1pm, 2-5pm Fri-Wed). The fund dates back to 1719, when Peter the Great established the Russian Crown treasury.

The bulk of the exhibit is gemstones and jewellery garnered by tsars and empresses, including the 190-carat diamond given to Catherine the Great by her lover Grigory Orlov. The Great Imperial Crown, encrusted with 4936 diamonds, was the coronation crown of Catherine the Great and successive rulers. Security is super tight and you are not allowed to bring cameras, phones or bags of any sort.

Alexander Garden

The first public park in Moscow, **Alexander Garden** (Александровский сад; Map p255; MAleksandrovsky Sad) sits along the Kremlin's western wall. Colourful flower beds and impressive Kremlin views make it a favourite strolling spot for Muscovites and tourists alike. Back in the 17th century, the Neglinnaya River ran through the present gardens, with dams and mills along its banks. When the river was diverted underground, the garden was founded by architect Osip Bove, in 1821.

Tomb of the Unknown Soldier

The **Tomb of the Unknown Soldier** (Могила неизвестного солдата; Map p255) at the north end of Alexander Garden is a kind of national pilgrimage spot, where newlyweds bring flowers and have their pictures taken. The inscription reads: 'Your name is unknown, your deeds immortal.' There's an eternal flame, and other inscriptions listing the Soviet hero cities of WWII – those that withstood the heaviest fighting – and honouring 'those who fell for the motherland' between 1941 and 1945. South of the tomb, a row of red urns contains earth from the 'hero cities'.

TOP SIGHT
RED SQUARE

Setting foot on Red Square (Красная площадь) for the first time is a guaranteed awe-striker. The vast rectangular stretch of cobblestones, surrounded by architectural marvels, is gasp-inducing gorgeous. In old Russian *krasny* meant 'beautiful', and 'Krasnaya Ploshchad' lives up to its name. It evokes an incredible sense of import to stroll the place where so much of Russian history has unfolded.

Lenin's Mausoleum

Although Vladimir Ilych requested that he be buried beside his mum in St Petersburg, he still lies in state at the foot of the Kremlin wall, receiving visitors who come to pay their respects to the founder of the Soviet Union. Line up at the western corner of the square (near the entrance to Alexander Garden) to see the **embalmed leader** (Мавзолей Ленина; Map p255; www.lenin.ru; ⊙10am-1pm Tue-Thu, Sat & Sun; ⓂPloshchad Revolyutsii) **FREE**, who has been here since 1924. Photography is not allowed, and stern guards ensure visitors remain respectful and silent.

After trouping past the embalmed figure, emerge from the mausoleum and inspect the Kremlin wall, where other communist heavy hitters are buried, including the following:
➡**Josef Stalin** The second general secretary, successor to Lenin.
➡**Leonid Brezhnev** The fourth general secretary, successor to Khrushchev.
➡**Felix Dzerzhinsky** The founder of the Cheka (forerunner of the KGB).
➡**Yakov Sverdlov** Key organiser of the revolution and first official head of the Soviet state.
➡**Andrei Zhdanov** Stalin's cultural chief and the second most powerful person in the USSR immediately after WWII.
➡**Mikhail Frunze** The Red Army leader who secured Central Asia for the Soviet Union in the 1920s.

DON'T MISS...

➡ Lenin's Mausoleum
➡ Spassky Tower
➡ Resurrection Gate
➡ Kazan Cathedral

PRACTICALITIES

➡ Map p255
➡ Krasnaya pl
➡ ⓂPloshchad Revolyutsii

From 1953 to 1961, Lenin shared his tomb with Stalin. During the 22nd Party Congress, the esteemed and ancient Bolshevik Madame Spiridonova announced that Vladimir Ilych had appeared to her in a dream, insisting that he did not like spending eternity with his successor. With that, Stalin was removed and given a place of honour immediately behind the mausoleum.

PLACE OF SKULLS

The 13m circular stone platform in front of St Basil's Cathedral is known as the **Place of Skulls** (Лобное место; Map p255). Legend has it that it was the site of executions; in reality, it was a stage for tsarist decrees and religious ceremonies.

➜**Inessa Armand** Lenin's rumoured lover. The director of Zhenotdel, an organisation fighting for equality for women within the Communist Party.

Resurrection Gate

At the northwestern corner of Red Square, **Resurrection Gate** (Map p255) provides a great vantage point for your first glimpse of Red Square. With its twin red towers topped by green tent spires, the original 1680 gateway was destroyed because Stalin thought it an impediment to the parades and demonstrations held in Red Square. This exact replica was built in 1995. Just outside the gateway is the bright **Chapel of the Iverian Virgin**, originally built in the late 18th century to house the icon of the same name.

Kazan Cathedral

The original **Kazan Cathedral** (Казанский собор; Map p255; Nikolskaya ul 3; ◷8am-7pm; ⓜOkhotny Ryad) FREE was founded on this site at the northern end of Red Square in 1636 in thanks for the 1612 expulsion of Polish invaders. Three hundred years later, the cathedral was completely demolished, allegedly because it impeded the flow of celebrating workers in May Day and Revolution Day parades. The little church that occupies the site today is a 1993 replica.

GUM

The elaborate 240m facade on the northeastern side of Red Square, **GUM** (ГУМ; Map p255; www.gum.ru; Krasnaya pl 3; ◷10am-10pm; ⓜPloshchad Revolyutsii) is a bright, bustling shopping mall with hundreds of fancy stores and restaurants. With a skylight roof and three-level arcades, the spectacular interior was a revolutionary design when it was built in the 1890s, replacing the Upper Trading Rows that previously occupied this site. Pronounced *goom*, the initials GUM originally stood for the Russian words for 'State Department Store'. When it was privatised in 2005, the name was officially changed to 'Main Department Store'. Fortunately, the words for 'state' and 'main' both start with a Russian 'G'.

Saviour Gate Tower

The Kremlin's 'official' exit onto Red Square is the stately red-brick **Saviour Gate Tower** (Спасская башня; Map p255). This gate – considered sacred – has been used for processions since tsarist times. The two white-stone plaques above the gate commemorate the tower's construction in 1491. The current clock was installed in the gate tower in the 1850s. Hauling 3m-long hands and weighing 25 tonnes, the clock takes up three of the tower's 10 levels. Its melodic chime sounds every 15 minutes across Red Square.

MIHAI SIMOCA /GETTY IMAGES ©

TOP SIGHT
ST BASIL'S CATHEDRAL

At the southern end of Red Square stands the icon of Russia: St Basil's Cathedral (Покровский собор, Храм Василия Блаженного). This crazy confusion of colours, patterns and shapes is the culmination of a style that is unique to Russian architecture. In 1552 Ivan the Terrible captured the Tatar stronghold of Kazan on the Feast of Intercession. He commissioned this landmark church, officially the Intercession Cathedral, to commemorate the victory.

Exterior
The cathedral's apparent anarchy of shapes hides a comprehensible plan of nine main chapels. The tall, tent-roofed tower in the centre houses the namesake Church of the Intercession of the Holy Mother of God. The four biggest domes top four large octagonal-towered chapels, and there are four smaller chapels in between. Each was consecrated in honour of an event or battle in the struggle against Kazan.

The onion domes were originally green, most likely acquiring their characteristic colours and patterns during an 18th-century restoration. But the church has always been a spectacle. Dutch tiles and gilded rings embellish the tent roof. Approximately 300 multicoloured, semicircular gables adorn the upper tiers of the churches, while pink and white columns and coffers decorate the lower tiers.

Church of St Vasily the Blessed
The Church of St Vasily the Blessed, the northeastern chapel on the first floor, contains the canopy-covered crypt of its namesake saint, one of the most revered in Moscow. Vasily (Basil) the Blessed was known as a 'holy fool', sometimes going naked and purposefully

DON'T MISS
→ Church of St Vasily the Blessed
→ Portals from the vestry to the central church
→ Icon of the Old Testament Trinity
→ Icon of the Life of St Alexander Nevsky

PRACTICALITIES
→ Map p255
→ www.saintbasil.ru
→ adult/student ₽250/50, audio guide ₽200
→ ⊙11am-5pm
→ Ⓜ Ploshchad Revolyutsii

The official name of St Basil's Cathedral is the Intercession Cathedral. The misnomer 'St Basil's' refers to the extra northeastern chapel, which was built over the grave of Vasily (Basil) the Blessed.

AUDIO GUIDE

An audio guide to the history and architecture of St Basil's is available for ₽200.

According to legend, Ivan the Terrible had the architects of St Basil's blinded, so that they could never build anything comparable. However, records show that they were actually employed a quarter of a century later to add an additional chapel to the structure.

MININ & POZHARSKY

Out front of St Basil's is a statue of **Kuzma Minin and Dmitry Pozharsky** (Памятник Минина и Пожарского; Map p255), one a butcher and the other a prince, who together raised and led the army that ejected occupying Poles from the Kremlin in 1612.

humiliating himself for the greater glory of God. He was believed to be a seer and miracle-maker, and even Ivan the Terrible revered and feared him. This tenth chapel – the only one at ground level – was added in 1588, after the saint's death. Look for the icon depicting St Vasily himself, with Red Square and the Kremlin in the background.

Church of the Intercession of the Holy Mother of God

The tall, tent-roofed tower in the centre of the cathedral houses the Church of the Intercession of the Holy Mother of God. The ceiling soars to nearly 47m. Some of the walls have been restored to their original appearance (a painted red-brick pattern), while others show off fragments from oil murals that were painted later. From the vestry, the doorways into this central chapel are among the most elaborate architectural elements in the cathedral, gorgeously embellished with tile and brick work.

Church of Saints Cyprian & Justina

The colourful Church of Saints Cyprian & Justina is adorned with oil paintings depicting the lives of the 4th-century saints, as well as Biblical stories. At 20m, the vault in the dome depicts the *Mother of God of the Burning Bush*. The paintings and the iconostasis date to the end of the 18th century.

Church of the Holy Trinity

With white-washed walls and a spiralling symbol of eternity painted in the vault, the light-filled Church of the Holy Trinity is a favourite. A gorgeous 16th-century chandelier is suspended from the 20m ceiling. But the gem of the room is the unusual iconostasis. The 16th-century *Icon of the Old Testament Trinity* in the third tier is among the oldest and most esteemed pieces of artwork in the cathedral.

Church of the Entry of the Lord into Jerusalem

This chapel is dedicated to the Entry of the Lord into Jerusalem, also known in Orthodoxy as Willow Sunday. At 23m, this is one of the tallest towers in the cathedral. White-washed walls (as originally painted) show off the architectural elements. Above the northern entrance, you can see the scar left by a shell that hit the wall in October 1917. The iconostasis was moved from the Cathedral of St Alexander Nevsky in the Kremlin in 1770. One of the most sacred and revered pieces in the cathedral is the 17th-century icon of the *Life of St Alexander Nevsky*, which depicts 33 scenes from the saint's life.

⊙ SIGHTS

KREMLIN   MUSEUM
See p60.

LENIN'S MAUSOLEUM   MAUSOLEUM
See p75.

ST BASIL'S CATHEDRAL   CHURCH
See p77.

RED SQUARE   HISTORIC SITE
See p75.

STATE HISTORY MUSEUM   MUSEUM
Map p255 (Государственный исторический музей; www.shm.ru; Krasnaya pl 1; adult/student ₽300/100, audio guide ₽300; ⊗10am-6pm Wed & Fri-Mon, 11am-9pm Thu; ⓂOkhotny Ryad) At the northern end of Red Square, the State History Museum has an enormous collection covering the whole Russian empire from the time of the Stone Age. The building, dating from the late 19th century, is itself an attraction – each room is in the style of a different period or region, some with highly decorated walls echoing old Russian churches.

The exhibits about medieval Rus are excellent, with several rooms covering the Mongol invasions and the consolidation of the Russian state. The 2nd floor covers the Imperial period, with exhibits featuring personal items of the royals, furnishings and decoration from the palace interiors and various artworks and documents from the era. Specific rooms are dedicated to the rule of various tsars. An unexpected highlight is an exhibit addressing the expansion of the Russian Empire by examining the growing network of roads and how people travelled.

ARCHAEOLOGICAL MUSEUM   MUSEUM
Map p255 (Музей археологии Москвы; www.mosmuseum.ru; Manezhnaya pl 1; ⓂOkhotny Ryad) An excavation of Voskresensky Bridge (which used to span the Neglinnaya River at the foot of Tverskaya ul) uncovered coins, clothing and other artefacts from old Moscow. The museum displaying these treasures is situated in a 7m-deep underground pavilion that was formed during the excavation itself. The entrance is at the base of the Four Seasons Hotel Moskva. It was closed for renovation at the time of research.

WAR OF 1812 MUSEUM   MUSEUM
Map p255 (Музей отечественной войны 1812 года; www.1812shm.ru; pl Revolyutsii 2; adult/child ₽300/100; ⊗10am-6pm Wed & Fri-Mon, 11am-9pm Thu; ⓂPloshchad Revolyutsii) Part Russian Revival, part neo-Renaissance, this red-brick beauty was built in the 1890s as the Moscow City Hall and later served as the Central Lenin Museum. It was converted into the War of 1812 Museum in honor of the war's 200-year anniversary. Artwork, documents, weapons and uniforms are all on display, offering a detailed depiction of the events and effects of the war.

MANEGE EXHIBITION CENTRE   ART GALLERY
Map p255 (Выставочный центр Манеж; www.moscowmanege.ru; Manezhnaya pl; exhibits ₽200-300; ⊗11am-8pm Tue-Sun; ⓂBiblioteka Imeni Lenina) The long, low neoclassical building west of Alexander Garden is Moscow Manege, a vast space that is used for art exhibits and other events. The recent 'Golden Age of Russian Avant-Garde' exhibit attracted the attention of art connoisseurs, but it also hosts wide-ranging events such as poetry readings, film screenings and literary festivals.

Among others, Manege regularly hosts stimulating events organised by the **Moscow Design Museum** (www.moscowdesignmuseum.ru) and Media Art Lab.

ZAIKONOSPASSKY
MONASTERY   MONASTERY
Map p255 (Заиконоспасский монастырь; Nikolskaya ul 7-9; ⓂPloshchad Revolyutsii) This monastery was founded by Boris Godunov in 1600, although the church was built in 1660. The name means 'Behind the Icon Stall', a reference to the busy icon trade that once took place here. After being closed for more than 90 years, the monastery has recently reopened. The now-functioning, multitiered **Saviour Church** is tucked into the courtyard away from the street.

On the orders of Tsar Alexey, the Likhud brothers – scholars of Greek – opened the Slavonic Greek and Latin Academy on the monastery premises in 1687. (Mikhail Lomonosov was a student here.) The academy later became a divinity school and was transferred to the Trinity Monastery of St Sergius in 1814.

MONASTERY OF
THE EPIPHANY   MONASTERY
Map p255 (Богоявленский монастырь; Bogoyavlensky per 2; ⓂPloshchad Revolyutsii) This monastery is the second oldest in Moscow, founded in 1296 by Prince Daniil, son of

Alexander Nevsky. The current **Epiphany Cathedral** – with its tall, pink, gold-domed cupola – was constructed in the 1690s in the Moscow baroque style. If you're lucky, you may hear the bells ringing forth from the old wooden belfry nearby.

SYNOD PRINTING HOUSE
HISTORICAL BUILDING

Map p255 (Печатный двор Синод; Nikolskaya ul 15; MPloshchad Revolyutsii) Now housing the Russian State University for the Humanities, this elaborately decorated edifice is where Ivan Fyodorov reputedly produced Russia's first printed book, *The Apostle*, in 1563. (You can see the man himself near Tretyakovsky proezd.) Spiraling Solomonic columns and Gothic windows frame the lion and unicorn, who are facing off in the centre of the facade. Up until the early 19th century, Kitay Gorod was something of a printing centre, home to 26 of Moscow's 31 bookshops.

TRETYAKOVSKY PROEZD
HISTORIC SITE

Map p255 (Третьяковский проезд; MTeatralnaya) The gated walkway of Tretyakovsky proezd (originally built in the 1870s) leads from Teatralny proezd into Kitay Gorod. Nearby, you can see where archaeologists uncovered the 16th-century fortified wall that used to surround Kitay Gorod, as well as the foundations of the 1493 Trinity Church. There is also a statue of Ivan Fyodorov, the 16th-century printer responsible for Russia's first book. Back in the day, the archway was financed by the Tretyakov brothers (founders of the namesake art gallery). Apparently the construction of the medieval-style gate and the opening of the passageway were an attempt to relieve traffic on Nikolskaya ul. It was reopened in 2000 and is now lined with exclusive shops.

OLD ENGLISH COURT
MUSEUM

Map p255 (Палаты старого Английского двора; www.mosmuseum.ru; ul Varvarka 4a; MKitay-Gorod) This reconstructed 16th-century house, white with wooden roofs, was the residence of England's first emissaries to Russia (sent by Elizabeth I to Ivan the Terrible). It also served as the base for English merchants, who were allowed to trade duty free in exchange for providing military supplies to Ivan. Today, it houses a small exhibit dedicated to this early international exchange. It was closed for renovations at the time of research.

CHAMBERS OF THE ROMANOV BOYARS
MUSEUM

Map p255 (Палаты бояр Романовых; www.shm.ru; ul Varvarka 10; admission ₽200; ⊙10am-5pm Thu-Mon, 11am-6pm Wed; MKitay-Gorod) This small but interesting museum is devoted to the lives of the Romanov family, who were mere boyars (high-ranking nobles) before they became tsars. The house was built by Nikita Romanov, whose grandson Mikhail later became the first tsar of the 300-year Romanov dynasty.

Exhibits show the house as it might have been when the Romanovs lived here in the 16th century. Enter from the rear of the building.

CHURCH OF THE TRINITY IN NIKITNIKI
CHURCH

Map p255 (Церковь Троицы в Никитниках; Ipatyevsky per; MKitay-Gorod) This little gem of a church, built in the 1630s, is an exquisite example of Russian baroque. Its onion domes and tiers of red-and-white spade gables rise from a square tower. Its interior is covered with 1650s gospel frescoes by Simon Ushakov and others. A carved doorway leads into **St Nikita the Martyr's Chapel**, above the vault of the Nikitnikov merchant family, who were among the patrons who financed the construction of the church.

POLYTECHNICAL MUSEUM
MUSEUM

Map p270 (Политехнический музей; www.polymus.ru; Novaya pl 3/4; MLubyanka) Occupying the entire block of Novaya pl, this giant museum showcases the history of Russian science, technology and industry. Indeed, it has claimed to be the largest science museum in the world. The museum is closed for a long overdue renovation and update, promising a 'fundamentally new museum and education centre' by 2018. In the meantime, a temporary exhibit has been set up at the VDNKh (All Russia Exhibition Centre; p90).

While the museum's focus is scientific, the building is also architecturally interesting and visually appealing. Three different parts of the structure were built at different times and in different styles: the oldest, central section (1877) represents the Russian Byzantine era; the eastern section (1896) is inspired by 17th-century Russian styles; and the western section (1907) is art nouveau.

MAMONTOV'S METROPOL

The Hotel Metropol, among Moscow's finest examples of art nouveau architecture, is one of many contributions by famed philanthropist and patron of the arts, Savva Mamontov. The decorative panel on the hotel's central facade, facing Teatralny proezd, is based on a sketch by the artist Mikhail Vrubel. It depicts the legend of the Princess of Dreams, in which a troubadour falls in love with a kind and beautiful princess and travels across the seas to find her. He falls ill during the voyage and is near death when he finds his love. The princess embraces him, but he dies in her arms. Naturally, the princess reacts to his death by renouncing her worldly life. The ceramic panels were made at the pottery workshop at Mamontov's Abramtsevo estate.

The ceramic work on the side of the hotel facing Teatralnaya pl is by the artist Alexander Golovin. The script was originally a quote from Nietzsche: 'Again the same story: when you build a house you notice that you have learned something'. During the Soviet era, these wise words were replaced with something more appropriate for the time: 'Only the dictatorship of the proletariat can liberate mankind from the oppression of capitalism'. Lenin, of course.

MEMORIAL TO THE VICTIMS OF TOTALITARIANISM
MEMORIAL

Map p270 (Мемориал жертвам тоталитаризма) A humble Memorial to the Victims of Totalitarianism stands in the little garden southeast of the notorious Lubyanka Prison. This single stone slab comes from the territory of an infamous 1930s labour camp situated on the Solovetsky Islands in the White Sea.

EATING

STOLOVAYA 57
CAFETERIA €

Map p255 (Столовая 57; 3rd fl, GUM, Krasnaya pl 3; mains ₽200-300; ☺10am-10pm; 🖻; MOkhotny Ryad) Newly minted, this old-style cafeteria offers a nostalgic re-creation of dining in post-Stalinist Russia. The food is good – and cheap for such a fancy store. Meat cutlets and cold salads come highly recommended. This is a great place to try 'herring in a fur coat' (herring, beets, carrots and potatoes).

FRIENDS FOREVER CAFE
CAFE €

Map p255 (Кафе Друзья навсегда; www.friends-forever.ru; 5th fl, Nautilus Shopping Center, ul Nikolskaya 25; mains ₽200-400; ☺9am-11pm; 🛜🖉🖻📶; MLubyanka) A perfect place for breakfast or a light lunch, this comfy cafe has high ceilings, soothing colours and big windows overlooking Nikolskaya. Come in the afternoon for a pick-me-up coffee and choose from the irresistible selection of sweets.

COFFEE MANIA
CAFE €€

Map p255 (Кофе мания; www.coffeemania.ru; Mal Cherkassky per 2; breakfast ₽300-500, mains ₽500-1100; ☺8am-midnight Mon-Thu, 8am-2am Fri, 10am-2am Sat, 10am-midnight Sun; 🛜🖉🖻; MLubyanka) You'll find the same overpriced but appetising fare as other outlets of the ubiquitous chain, but the fabulous 'grand cafe' interior makes this a special experience. Marble floors, art-deco chandeliers and elaborate lattice work evoke another era. Efficient service too.

LOFT CAFÉ
FUSION €€

Map p255 (www.cafeloft.ru; 6th fl, Nautilus, Nikolskaya ul 25; lunch ₽450, mains ₽500-900; ☺9am-11pm; 🛜🖉🖻; MLubyanka) This tiny, trendy cafe, on the top floor of the Nautilus shopping centre, has a small terrace offering a fantastic view of Lubyanka pl. Innovative, modern dishes fuse the best of Russian cuisine with Western and Asian influences, such as grilled salmon with spinach and orange sauce, or beef stroganoff with morels.

BOSCO CAFE
ITALIAN €€€

Map p255 (☎495-620 3182; www.bosco.ru; GUM, Krasnaya pl 3; pasta ₽500-1000, mains ₽1200-2000; ☺10am-10pm; 🖻; MPloshchad Revolyutsii) Sip a coffee or take a meal while you view the Kremlin, watch the crowds line up at Lenin's Mausoleum or admire St Basil's domes – this cafe on the 1st floor of GUM is *the* place to marvel at the magnificence of Red Square The menu is wide-ranging, so you don't have to spend a fortune. Reservations are recommended for dinner.

🍷 DRINKING & NIGHTLIFE

CAFE TANTSY   BAR

Map p255 (Кафе Танцы; Nikolskaya ul 11; ⊙noon-midnight Sun-Thu, noon-6am Fri & Sat; 🛜; MPloshchad Revolyutsii) Truly, a hole in the wall. Moscow does not have enough of these cosy cafes, where the cramped quarters and rough-around-the-edges decor are a part of the attraction. High stools, exposed brick and hipster clientele create an atmosphere of convivial bohemia. It's a popular spot for a mid-afternoon tipple or a late-night top-off.

Incidentally, *tantsy* means 'dance', but there is no room for that. They must be speaking metaphorically.

DISSIDENT VINOTECA   WINE BAR

Map p255 (Диссидент Винотека; www.dissident.msk.ru; 5th fl, Nautilus, Nikolskaya 25; ⊙11am-midnight; MLubyanka) Comfortable and classy, this Moscow wine bar offers over 200 kinds of wine by the glass, along with appropriate accompaniments such as cheese, paté and other hors d'oeuvres. Certainly wine was considered a bourgeois beverage back in the day, but we're pretty sure that Soviet dissidents were not drinking wines like these. Panoramic views of Lubyanka prison are free.

MANDARIN COMBUSTIBLE   LOUNGE

Map p255 (☑495-745 0700; Mal Cherkassky per 2; ⊙24hr; 🛜; MLubyanka) Dining, drinking and dancing are all on offer in this sexy space. There is a long menu of Pan Asian cuisine – as well as sushi, pasta, tapas and more – served around the clock for Moscow's non-stop party people. Drinks are forgettable and service is slack, but everything (and everyone) looks fine – and sometimes that's what matters.

ROMANOV BAR   COCKTAIL BAR

Map p255 (Романов Бар; www.romanovbar.ru; Nikolskaya ul 19/21; ⊙noon-midnight Sun-Wed, noon-6am Thu-Sat; MLubyanka) The interior is over-the-top, with its velvet-covered furniture and crystal chandeliers. But the summer terrace is a delightful place for a drink or even a meal – the bartenders mix a mean cocktail.

If that doesn't keep you entertained, there are often dance parties, fashion events and karaoke.

🚶 Neighbourhood Walk
Ancient Moscow: Red Square & Kitay Gorod

START LUBYANSKAYA PL
END STARAYA PL
LENGTH 3KM; THREE HOURS

This walk shows off the oldest and most atmospheric part of Moscow, from the grandiosity of Red Square to the intimate, ancient streets of Kitay Gorod.

Start your tour at ❶**Lubyanskaya pl**, dominated by the forbidding facade of the (former) prison, a once notorious place. Nearby, the modest Memorial to the Victims of Totalitarianism remembers the people who suffered within these walls.

Leave behind heavy traffic when you enter Kitay Gorod, strolling down Nikolskaya ul. This was the main road to Vladimir and used to be the centre of a busy icon trade. Today it is a pleasant pedestrian street, lined with shops, churches and cafes. You'll pass the elaborate gated walkway at ❷**Tretyakovsky Proezd** (p80), now home to Moscow's fanciest designer boutiques. Look also for the decorated, Gothic facade of the ❸**Synod Printing House** (p80) – easily identified by the lion and the unicorn – and the gold-domed steeples of the ❹**Zaikonospassky Monastery** (p79), peeking out over the rooftops.

In Kitay Gorod it seems like there are churches and monasteries on every corner and in every courtyard. Duck down Bogoyavlensky per to get a look at another one – the ❺**Monastery of the Epiphany** (p79). This 13th-century monastery is the second oldest in Moscow, though the pink Baroque church that stands here now was built much later.

Cut through the courtyard and out to pl Revolyutsii. This busy square displays its own impressive array of architecture. The ❻**Hotel Metropol** (p177) is a stunning – if decaying – example of art nouveau architecture, featuring spectacular tile work by the painter Mikhail Vrubel.

Further west, the unusual ❼**Four Seasons Moscow** (p177) actually exhibits its two contrasting architectural styles,

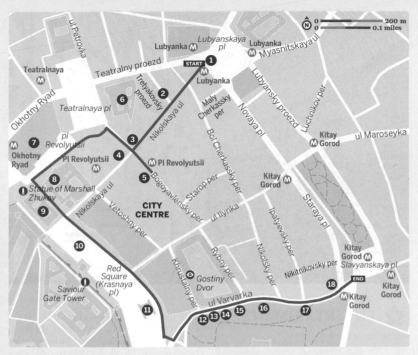

thanks to a fluke of history. The story goes that Stalin was shown two possible designs for the Hotel Moskva on Manezhnaya pl. Not realising they were alternatives, he approved both. The builders didn't dare point out his error, and so built half in constructivist style and half in Stalinist style.

On the south side of the square, you'll notice the impressive red-brick facade of the ❽ **War of 1812 Museum** (p79) and the ❾ **State History Museum** (p79), both exhibiting Russian Revival and neo-Renaissance grandeur. A statue of the WWII general (and hero) Marshal Zhukov stands stoically in front.

Turn south and walk between the two museums – through Resurrection Gate – and feast your eyes on the stunning expanse of ❿ **Red Square** (p75). On the south side, the mighty Kremlin wall is punctuated by tall towers, most notably the Saviour Gate Tower. Beneath the wall, Lenin's Mausoleum still receives visitors, paying their respects. On the north side, the pretty little Kazan Cathedral complements the ornate facade of GUM. And at the far end, with its electrifying assemblage of shapes, colours and textures, stands Russia's most famous landmark, ⓫ **St Basil's Cathedral** (p77). Walk across the expanse of cobblestones and get a good look at the amazing architecture.

At the southern end of Red Square, turn left on ul Varvarka, a small street with the neighbourhood's greatest concentration of ancient buildings. The area between ul Varvarka and the river is now slated to become the new Zaryadye Park. Walking from west to east, you'll pass the pink-and-white ⓬ **St Barbara's Church**, dating to 1804; the peak-roofed ⓭ **Old English Court** (p80), dating to the 16th century; the 17th-century ⓮ **Church of St Maxim the Blessed**; the monks' building and golden-domed cathedral of the ⓯ **Monastery of the Sign**; the ancient ⓰ **Chambers of the Romanov Boyars** (p80); and the 1658 ⓱ **St George's Church**. On the opposite side of the street is the trading arcades of Gostinny Dvor. Surrounded by this concentration of aged buildings, it's possible to imagine what 'Old Moscow' was like.

Continue east and emerge onto Staraya pl. In the underground passage at the corner, look out for the ⓲ **remains of the old city wall**. This *perekhod* (crosswalk) is also the entrance to the Kitay-Gorod metro stop.

GUM (p76)

☆ ENTERTAINMENT

KREMLIN BALLET   BALLET
Map p255 (Кремлевский балет; ☎495-628 5232; www.kremlinpalace.org; ul Vozdvizhenka 1; ☺box office noon-8pm; Ⓜ Aleksandrovsky Sad) The Bolshoi Theatre doesn't have a monopoly on ballet in Moscow – leading dancers also appear with the Kremlin Ballet, which performs in the Kremlin Palace. The Bolshoi is magical, but seeing a show inside the Kremlin is really something special as well.

The repertoire is unapologetically classical. The box office is near the entrance to the metro station.

🛍 SHOPPING

With hundreds of fancy stores and restaurants, GUM (p76) is a bright, bustling shopping mall that's worth a browse when you visit Red Square.

GUS-KHRUSTALNY
FACTORY STORE   SOUVENIRS
Map p255 (Гусь-Хрустальный заводской магазин; www.ghz.ru; Gostiny Dvor; ☺10am-8pm; Ⓜ Ploshchad Revolyutsii) Since the glass production factory was founded there in 1756, the town of Gus-Khrustalny (east of Moscow) has been known for its high-quality glassware. This little factory outlet carries a small but choice selection of beautiful and reasonably priced crystal and glassware, especially coloured glass.

ALENA AKHMADULLINA
BOUTIQUE   CLOTHING & ACCESSORIES
Map p255 (Бутик Алёны Ахмадулиной; www.alenaakhmadullina.ru; Nikolskaya ul 25; ☺11am-10pm; Ⓜ Lubyanka) Alena Akhmadullina's romantic, flowing fashions have been wowing trendsetters since 2005, when the St Petersburg designer first showed her stuff in Paris. She has received loads of international attention ever since (including an invitation to provide an outfit for Angelina Jolie in the film *Wanted*). The subtly seductive designs are known for offering a new perspective on Russian themes.

OKHOTNY RYAD   SHOPPING MALL
Map p255 (ТЦ Охотный ряд; www.ox-r.ru; Manezhnaya pl; ☺10am-10pm; Ⓜ Okhotny Ryad) The best part of this underground mall is the fanciful troika fountain that splashes shoppers as they enter and exit from Alexander Garden. Aside from the clothing and electronic stores, there is a big, crowded food court.

Tverskoy & Novoslobodsky

TVERSKOY | NOVOSLOBODSKY

Neighbourhood Top Five

1 Spending an evening at the **Bolshoi Theatre** (p87), where world-famous opera and ballet companies perform Russian classics.

2 Eating, drinking, dancing and otherwise frolicking at **Hermitage Gardens** (p88), one of the liveliest places in Moscow, where art, food or musical festivals take place almost weekly.

3 Learning how it felt to be Jewish in Russia, from the partition of Poland to the late USSR era, at the ultra-modern **Jewish Museum & Centre of Tolerance** (p89).

4 Sweating away your city stresses amid the luxury of **Sanduny Baths** (p99).

5 Admiring the fantastical **paintings of Viktor Vasnetsov** (p90) in the studio where he painted them.

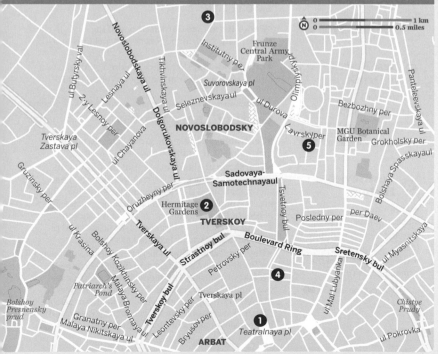

For more detail of this area see Map p258 ➡

Lonely Planet's Top Tip

While the Bolshoi is Russia's most famous theatre, it is not the only one. Several other opera and ballet theatres in Moscow offer the same level of professionalism and panache in their performances at a fraction of the price. If you have your heart set on going to the opera or ballet but can't get tickets to the Bolshoi, consider the **Novaya Opera** (p97) or the **Stanislavsky & Nemirovich-Danchenko Musical Theatre** (p97), both gorgeous theatres with highly skilled performers.

✗ Best Places to Eat

➡ Delicatessen (p94)

➡ Brasserie Most (p94)

➡ Lavka-Lavka (p94)

➡ Dzhondzholi (p94)

For reviews, see p91 ➡

🍷 Best Places to Drink

➡ Noor (p96)

➡ Enthusiast (p96)

➡ Cafe Mart (p96)

For reviews, see p95 ➡

◉ Best Soviet History

➡ Contemporary History Museum (p89)

➡ Gulag History Museum (p88)

➡ Central Museum of the Armed Forces (p91)

For reviews, see p88 ➡

Explore: Tverskoy & Novoslobodsky

Tverskoy is Moscow's busiest, swankiest and most commercialised district. Few people can afford to live here, but millions pour in daily to work, hunt for garments at shopping arcades or dine out.

Originating at the Kremlin, Moscow's main thoroughfare, Tverskaya ul, is a broad avenue of stately pre-Soviet and Stalin-era buildings. East of it, the majestic Teatralnaya pl (Theatre Sq), is home to the world-famous Bolshoi Theatre. This glittering jewel of a theatre is a sight to behold, often attracting tourists and shoppers to the benches and fountains that grace the square.

From here, several commercial streets radiate towards the Boulevard Ring, each filled with boutiques and cafes. Semi-pedestrianised ul Bolshaya Dmitrovka is linked with Tverskaya ul by the fully pedestrianised Kamergersky per. Further up, trendy Stoleshnikov per connects ul Bolshaya Dmitrovka with quaint ul Petrovka, which leads to charming Hermitage Gardens.

Beyond the Garden Ring, Tverskoy blends into the much more relaxed, uncrowded Novoslobodsky district, home of the Jewish Museum & Centre of Tolerance and a few nice bars and restaurants.

Local Life

➡**Parks** Hermitage Gardens is one of the city's liveliest places, with fresh air, greenery and cocktails at 3205 (p95).

➡**Crowd-drinking** Join a few hundred students for a pint of cheapish beer at mammoth Vokzal (p96).

Getting There & Away

➡**Teatralnaya pl** Take the green Zamoskvoretskaya metro line to Teatralnaya station.

➡**Tverskaya ul** Manezhnaya pl, at the bottom of Tverskaya ul, is accessible from the Okhotny Ryad metro station on the red Sokolnicheskaya line. The green Zamoskvoretskaya metro line provides easy access to Pushkinskaya pl (at Tverskaya station), Triumfalnaya pl (at Mayakovskaya station) and pl Tverskaya Zastava (at Belorusskaya station).

➡**Beyond Garden Ring** The green Zamoskvoretskaya metro line follows Tverskaya ul (which becomes Tverskaya-Yamskaya ul, then Leningradsky pr and eventually Leningradskoe sh) almost all the way to MKAD, terminating at Rechnoy Vokzal. Novoslobosky district is accessible via the connecting metro stations at Novoslobodskaya or Mendeleevskaya.

TOP SIGHT
BOLSHOI THEATRE

The Bolshoi Theatre (Большой театр) is still one of Moscow's most romantic and entertaining options for a night out. The glittering six-tier auditorium has an electric atmosphere, evoking over 235 years of premier music and dance. Both the ballet and opera companies perform a range of Russian and foreign works here.

The present pink-and-white beauty was built in 1824. This historic theatre saw the premier of Tchaikovsky's *Swan Lake* in 1877 and *The Nutcracker* in 1919. The facade of the Bolshoi is famed for the bronze troika that is flying off the front. Gracing Teatralnaya Sq, the fountain by Vitali, which features bronze sculptures of the three muses, is Moscow's oldest. A welcome supplement, Bolshoi's new stage was opened next door in 2002.

Opera and ballet directors come and go, leaving their imprint on the repertoire as well as generating heaps of controversy. But classic gems, such as the iconic *Swan Lake* and *Boris Godunov*, remain. There have been a few very successful experiments with 20th-century and modern music in recent years, but they don't tend to linger for long.

Juicy stories about the Bolshoi's singers and ballerinas regularly appear in tabloids. Following the collapse of the Soviet Union, the Bolshoi was marred by politics, scandal and even outright crime. Yet the show must go on – and it will.

Although it's not entirely impossible to get a ticket from the box office a few days in advance, don't bet on it – they sell like hot cakes. Your chances are higher in summer, while at the height of the season (October to December) they are minimal. Tickets can be purchased online on the theatre's website (go to bolshoi.ru/en/timetable for the English version). Reports suggest that from 2015 standing-room tickets will be available for ₽100.

It is also possible to buy tickets from a scalper. Scalpers are easy to find; the trick is negotiating a price – expect to pay upwards of ₽3000. Examine the ticket and the date of the show (even the year) before money changes hands.

DON'T MISS

➜ Fountain by Vitali
➜ Bronze troika
➜ Your performance!

PRACTICALITIES

➜ Map p258
➜ www.bolshoi.ru
➜ Teatralnaya pl 1
➜ tickets ₽200-4000
➜ ⓂTeatralnaya

 **SIGHTS**

⊙ Tverskoy

HERMITAGE GARDENS PARK
Map p258 (Сады Эрмитажа; mosgorsad.ru; ul Karetny Ryad 3; ⊘24hr; MPushkinskaya) FREE All the things that have improved Moscow parks no end in recent years fill this small, charming garden to the brim. Today it is possibly the most happening place in Moscow, where art, food and crafts festivals, and concerts occur almost weekly, especially in summer. Apart from welcoming lawns and benches, it boasts a large playground for children, a summer cinema and a cluster of curious food and crafts kiosks. Come here to unwind and mingle with the coolest Muscovites.

The garden was created in 1894 around a theatre that saw the screening of the Lumiere brothers' first film in 1896 and the 1898 Moscow premiere of Chekhov's *Seagull*, performed by the troupe that had just been scrambled together by Stanislavsky and Nemirovich-Danchenko.

GULAG HISTORY MUSEUM MUSEUM
Map p258 (Исторический музей ГУЛАГ; ☑495-621 7346; www.gmig.ru; ul Petrovka 16; adult/student ₽150/20; ⊘11am-6pm Tue, Wed & Fri-Sun, noon-8pm Thu; MTeatralnaya) Amid all the swanky shops on ul Petrovka, an archway leads to a courtyard that is strung with barbed wire and hung with portraits of political prisoners. This is the entrance to a unique museum dedicated to the Chief Administration of Corrective Labour Camps and Colonies, better known as the Gulag. Guides dressed like guards describe the vast network of labour camps that once existed in the former Soviet Union, and recount the horrors of camp life.

Millions of prisoners spent years in these labour camps, made famous by Alexander Solzhenitsyn's book *The Gulag Archipelago*. More than 18 million people passed through this system during its peak years, from 1929 to 1953, although many camps remained in operation until the end of the 1980s. The gulag became a chilling symbol of political repression, as many of the prisoners were serving time for 'antisocial' or 'counter-revolutionary' behaviour. The museum serves as a history lesson about the system, as well as a memorial to its victims.

MOSCOW MUSEUM OF MODERN ART MUSEUM
Map p258 (Московский музей современного искусства; MMOMA; www.mmoma.ru; ul Petrovka 25; adult/student ₽250/100; ⊘noon-8pm Tue-Wed & Fri-Sun, 1-9pm Thu; MChekhovskaya) A pet project of the ubiquitous Zurab Tsereteli, this museum is housed in a classical 18th-century merchant's home, originally designed by Matvei Kazakov (architect of the Kremlin Senate). It is the perfect light-filled setting for an impressive collection of 20th-century paintings, sculptures and graphics, which include both Russian and foreign artists. The highlight is the collection of avant-garde art, with works by Chagall, Kandinsky and Malevich.

Unique to this museum is its exhibit of 'nonconformist' artists from the 1950s and '60s – those whose work was not acceptable to the Soviet regime. The gallery also hosts temporary exhibits that often feature contemporary artists. Be sure not to bypass the whimsical sculpture garden in the courtyard. There are additional MMOMA outlets, used primarily for temporary exhibits, on **Tverskoy bul** (MMOMA; Map p264; www.mmoma.ru; Tverskoy bul 9; admission ₽150; ⊘noon-8pm; MPushkinskaya) and **Yermolayevsky per** (MMOMA; Map p264; www.mmoma.ru; Yermolayevsky per 17; adult/student ₽200/100; ⊘noon-8pm; MMayakovskaya).

UPPER ST PETER MONASTERY MONASTERY
Map p258 (Петровский монастырь; cnr ul Petrovka & Petrovsky bul; ⊘8am-8pm; MChekhovskaya) The Upper St Peter Monastery was founded in the 1380s as part of an early defensive ring around Moscow. The main, onion-domed **Virgin of Bogolyubovo Church** dates from the late 17th century. The loveliest structure is the brick Cathedral of Metropolitan Pyotr, restored with a shingle roof. (When Peter the Great ousted the Regent Sofia in 1690, his mother was so pleased she built him this church).

M'ARS CONTEMPORARY ART CENTRE ART GALLERY
Map p258 (Центр Современного Искусства М'АРС; www.marsgallery.ru; Pushkarev per 5; ⊘gallery noon-8pm Tue-Sun, cafe noon-11pm daily; MTsvetnoy Bulvar, Sukharevskaya) Founded by artists who were banned during the Soviet era, this gallery space includes 10 exhibit halls showing the work of top contemporary artists, as well as a cool club and cafe in the basement.

HOUSE OF UNIONS
& STATE DUMA

Мар p258 (Дом Союзов и Государственная Дума; Okhotny ryad 2/1; ⓂTeatralnaya) The glowering **State Duma** (Map p258) was erected in the 1930s for Gosplan (Soviet State Planning Department), source of the USSR's Five-Year Plans; it is now the seat of the Russian parliament. The green-columned House of Unions dates from the 1780s. Its ballroom, called the Hall of Columns, is famous as the location of one of Stalin's most grotesque show trials, that of Nikolai Bukharin, a leading Communist Party theorist who had been a close associate of Lenin.

Both buildings are closed to the public.

TVERSKAYA PLOSHCHAD

Map p258 (Тверская площадь) A statue of the founder of Moscow, **Yury Dolgoruky** (Map p258), presides over this prominent square near the bottom of Tverskaya ul. So does Mayor Sergei Sobyanin, as the buffed-up five-storey building opposite is the **Moscow mayor's office** (Map p258). Many ancient churches are hidden in the back streets, including the 17th-century **Church of Sts Kosma & Damian** (Map p258).

CHURCH OF THE NATIVITY
OF THE VIRGIN IN PUTINKI

Мар p258 (Церковь Рождества Богородицы в Путинках; ul Malaya Dmitrovka 4; ⓂPushkinskaya) When this church was completed in 1652, the Patriarch Nikon responded by banning tent roofs like the ones featured here. Apparently, he considered such architecture too Russian, too secular and too far removed from the Church's Byzantine roots. Fortunately, the Church of the Nativity has survived to grace this corner near Pushkinskaya pl.

CONTEMPORARY
HISTORY MUSEUM

Map p258 (Музей современной истории России; ☑495-699 6724; www.sovr.ru; Tverskaya ul 21; adult/student ₽250/100; ☺10am-6pm Tue-Sun; ⓂPushkinskaya) Formerly known as the Revolution Museum, this retro exhibit traces Soviet history from the 1905 and 1917 revolutions up to the 1980s. The highlight is the extensive collection of propaganda posters, in addition to all the Bolshevik paraphernalia. Look for the picture of the giant Palace of Soviets (Дворец Советов) that Stalin was going to build on

the site of the blown-up – and now rebuilt – Cathedral of Christ the Saviour. Complete with stone lions, the opulent mansion housing the museum was the home of the Moscow English Club – a venue favoured by Anglophile gentlemen and native Brits in tsarist times.

⊙ Novoslobodsky

JEWISH MUSEUM
& CENTRE OF TOLERANCE

(Еврейский музей и Центр терпимости; www.jewish-museum.ru; ul Obraztsova 11 str 1A; adult/student ₽400/200; ☺noon-10pm Sun-Thu; ⓂNovoslobodskaya) Occupying a heritage garage, purpose-built to house a fleet of Leyland double-deckers that plied Moscow streets in the 1920s, this vast museum, filled with cutting-edge multimedia technology, tackles the uneasy subject of relations between Jews and the Russian state over centuries. The exhibition tells the stories of pogroms, Jewish revolutionaries, the Holocaust and Soviet anti-Semitism in a calm and balanced manner. The somewhat limited collection of material exhibits is compensated for by the abundance of interactive video displays.

We especially like those that encourage visitors to search for answers to dilemmas faced by early 20th-century Jews – to stand up and fight, to emigrate or to assimilate and keep a low profile.

Russia's Jewish population was quite small until the 18th century, when the empire incorporated a vast chunk of Poland then inhabited by millions of Yiddish-speaking Jews. They were not allowed to move into Russia proper until the early 20th century – a policy that became known as the Pale of Settlement. This led to the perception of Jews as an ethnic rather than a religious group, which still lingers today.

GLINKA MUSEUM OF
MUSICAL CULTURE

Map p258 (Музей музыкальной культуры Глинки; ☑495-739 6226; www.glinka.museum; ul Fadeeva 4; admission ₽200; ☺noon-7pm Tue-Sun; ⓂMayakovskaya) This musicologist's paradise boasts over 3000 instruments – handcrafted works of art – from the Caucasus and the Far East. Russia is very well represented: a 13th-century *gusli* (traditional instrument similar to a dulcimer) from Novgorod, skin drums from Yakutia,

VDNKH & OSTANKINO

Palaces for workers! There is hardly a better place to see this slogan put into practice than at **VDNKh** (MVDNKh), which stands for Exhibition of Achievements of the National Economy. This Stalin-era name is being resurrected, replacing the post-Soviet VVTs (All-Russian Exhibition Centre).

VDNKh is like a Stalinesque theme park, with palatial pavilions, each designed in its own unique style to represent all Soviet republics and various industries, from geology to space exploration.

The highlights are two opulently decorated fountains. Positioned right behind the main gates, **People's Friendship Fountain** is surrounded by 16 gilded female figures dressed in ethnic costumes representing Soviet republics (the mysterious 16th figure stands for Karelo-Finnish republic disbanded in 1956).

It's currently undergoing reconstruction after years of post-Soviet neglect. The **Space Pavillion** has become a temporary shelter for the Polytechnical Museum (p80) and the venue for insightful natural science and technology exhibitions. Further on, the jaw-dropping **Stone Flower Fountain**, themed on Urals miners mythology, is covered in semi-precious stones from the Urals.

Approaching VDNKh from the metro, the soaring 100m titanium obelisk is a monument 'To the Conquerors of Space', built in 1964 to commemorate the launch of *Sputnik*. In its base is the **Cosmonautics Museum** (kosmo-museum.ru; admission ₽200; ⏰11am-7pm Tue-Sun, 11am-9pm Thu; MVDNKh), featuring cool space paraphernalia such as the first Soviet rocket engine and the moon-rover Lunokhod. An inspiring collection of space-themed propaganda posters evokes the era of the space race.

As (and if) you reach the far end of VDNKh you have the choice or either pressing on towards the extensive grounds of **Moscow Main Botanical Gardens**, or turning left towards the quaint **Ostankino Park**, surrounding a namesake palace.

You are unlikely to get lost if you simply head towards the looming **Ostankino TV Tower** (Останкинская башня; ☑8-800-100 5553; tvtower.ru; adult/child ₽980/490; ⏰10am-8pm Tue-Sun; MVDNKh), located right behind the park. Built in 1967, it was the tallest free-standing structure in the world (surpassing the Empire State Building). At 540m, it is now fourth on the list.

At 337m, the observation deck is open for visitors. A super-speedy lift whisks passengers up in less than 60 seconds. From the top, there are 360-degree views and (horror!) a bit of glass floor. Tours take place hourly and must be booked in advance; bring your passport. There's a 40% discount on 10am and 11am tours on weekdays.

a *balalaika* (triangular instrument) by the master Semyon Nalimov – but you can also see such classic pieces as a violin made by Antonio Stradivari. Recordings accompany many of the rarer instruments, allowing visitors to experience their sound.

This incredible collection started with a few instruments that were donated by the Moscow Tchaikovsky Conservatory at the end of the 19th century. The collection grew exponentially during the Soviet period. It was named after Mikhail Glinka in 1945, in honour of the nationalist composer's 150th birthday.

VASNETSOV HOUSE-MUSEUM   ART MUSEUM
Map p258 (Дом-музей Васнецова; ☑495-681 1329; www.tretyakovgallery.ru; per Vasnetsova 13; adult/student ₽250/100; ⏰10am-5pm Tue-Sat; MSukharevskaya) Viktor Vasnetsov was a Russian-revivalist painter, who drew inspiration from fairy tales and village mysticism. In 1894, he designed his own house in Moscow, which is now a museum. Fronted by a colourful gate, it is a charming home in neo-Russian style filled with the original wooden furniture, a tiled stove and many of the artist's paintings. The attic studio, where he once worked, is now adorned with paintings depicting Baba Yaga and other characters from Russian fairy tales.

Early on, Vasnetsov was scorned for his fantastical style, as it was such a startling contrast to the realism of the Peredvezhniki (Wanderers, 19th-century art movement). Even Pavel Tretyakov, the most prominent patron of the arts at the time, refused to buy his paintings. However, by the turn of the century, he found a source of support in Savva Mamontov, whose financing drove the Russian revivalist movement.

MUSEUM OF DECORATIVE & FOLK ART
ART MUSEUM

Map p258 (Всероссийский музей декоративно-прикладного и народного искусства; ☑495-609 0146; www.vmdpri.ru; Delegatskaya ul 3 & 5; adults/students ₽200/100; ◎10am-6pm Wed-Mon; Ⓜ Tsvetnoy Bulvar) Just beyond the Garden Ring, this museum showcases centuries-old arts-and-crafts traditions from around Russia and the former Soviet republics. Of the 40,000 pieces in the collection, you might see painted *khokhloma* woodwork from Nizhny Novgorod, including wooden toys and *matryoshka* dolls; baskets and other household items made from birch bark, a traditional Siberian technique; intricate embroidery and lacework from the north, as well as the ubiquitous Pavlov scarves; and playful Dymkovo pottery and Gzhel porcelain.

Look also for the so-called 'propaganda porcelain' – fine china decorated with revolutionary themes. The museum is known for its impressive collection of *palekh* – black lacquer boxes and trays painted with detailed scenes from Russian fairy tales. The collection fills two rooms. It features, among others, pieces by Ivan Golikov and Ivan Markichev, often considered the originators of the *palekh* style.

EXPERIMENTANIUM
MUSEUM

(Экспериментаниум; ☑495-789 3658; http://experimentanium.ru, in Russian; ul Butyrskaya 46/2; ◎9.30am-7pm Mon-Fri, 10am-8pm Sat, Sun & holidays; Ⓜ Savylovskaya) Travelling with children who ask too many questions about life, the universe and everything? Here is a place that provides answers for them to ponder for a while. Experimentanium is an exciting place where children learn physics, chemistry, mechanics, acoustics, anatomy and whatnot by playing, and indeed experimenting, with a vast number of interactive exhibits.

An English-language excursion costs a whooping ₽4500, so you might set up an experiment on yourself by measuring how much secondary-school material is still deposited in your head and allow it to serve as your child's own guide into the world of science.

CENTRAL MUSEUM OF THE ARMED FORCES
MUSEUM

Map p258 (Центральный музей Вооружённых Сил; ☑495-681 6303; www.cmaf.ru; ul Sovetskoy Armii 2; adult/student ₽120/60; ◎10am-4.30pm Wed-Sun; Ⓜ Novoslobodskaya) Covering the history of the Soviet and Russian military since 1917, this massive museum has 800,000 military items, including uniforms, medals and weapons, are displayed. Highlights include remnants of the American U2 spy plane (brought down in the Urals in 1960) and the victory flag raised over Berlin's Reichstag in 1945. Take trolleybus 69 (or walk) 1.3km east from Novoslobodskaya metro.

DOSTOEVSKY HOUSE-MUSEUM
MUSEUM

Map p258 (Дом-музей Достоевского; ☑495-681 1085; ul Dostoevskogo 2; adult/student ₽150/50; ◎11am-6pm Thu, Sat & Sun, 2-7pm Wed & Fri; Ⓜ Novoslobodskaya) Though this renowned Russian author is more closely associated with St Petersburg, Fyodor Dostoevsky was actually born in Moscow, where his family lived in a tiny apartment on the grounds of Marinsky Hospital. He lived here until the age of 16, when he went to St Petersburg to enter a military academy. The family's Moscow flat has been recreated according to descriptions written by Fyodor's brother.

Visitors can see the family's library, toys and other personal items, including Fyodor's quill pen and a wooden chest with vaulted cover he slept on during his childhood, which clearly contributed to his view of the world as a place full of pain. In addition, the house stood next to a morgue and asylum that received beggars and madmen from all over the city. From Novoslobodskaya metro station, walk east on Seleznevskaya ul and turn left on per Dostoevskogo.

✖️ EATING

✖️ Tverskoy

⭐ ZUPPERIA
INTERNATIONAL €

Map p258 (☑915-391 8309; www.facebook.com/Zupperia; ul Sadovaya-Samotechnaya 20; mains ₽250-300; ◎8am-11pm; 🛜💳; Ⓜ Tsvetnoy Bulvar) Designed to look like a transplant from some old-worldish European city, this

FLAKON

Like the Bolsheviks a hundred years ago, Moscow hipsters are capturing one factory after another and redeveloping them, according to their hipster tastes. **Flakon** (www.flacon.ru; ul Bolshaya Novodmitrovskaya 36; ⊙variable; MDmitrovskaya) is arguably the most visually attractive of all the redeveloped industrial areas around town, looking a bit like the far end of Portobello Rd, especially during the weekends. Once a glassware plant, it is now home to dozens of funky shops and other businesses. Shopping for designer clothes and unusual souvenirs is the main reason for coming here. The main shopping area covers two floors of the factory's central building. For clothes you won't find outside Moscow, go to the second floor and check out the **Charismas Show Room**, a Russian brand producing streetwear as well as fancy dresses. Weekends are the best time to visit as this is when you are most likely to encounter a festival or crafts fair. You'll also find cafes, a cinema and even a small Ayurvedic spa on the premises.

unpretentious eatery is run by local celebrity chef William Lamberti. The minimalist menu includes soups, bruschettas and salads. At first glance, the place seems to consist of one long table, but there is more seating downstairs. Takeaway is available.

SHAWARMA REPUBLIC
MIDDLE EASTERN €

Map p258 (Республика Шаурма; shawarma-republic.ru; Hermitage Gardens; mains ₽250; MPushkinskaya) If only the Middle East was like the menu of this funky shawarma shop, where 'Lebanese', 'Syrian' and 'Israeli' shawarma peacefully coexist. Authenticity is beyond the point – the owners have devised their own style, whereby shawarmas look like geometrically impeccable cylinders filled with falafel, meat, salad and pickles. It's located right at the entrance to Hermitage Garden. Ideal for lunch on a park bench.

FRESH
VEGETARIAN €

Map p258 (Свежий; ☑965-278 90 89; freshrestaurant.ru; ul Bolshaya Dmitrovka 11; mains ₽450; ⊙11am-11pm; 🛜🍴🍱; MTeatralnaya) Fresh out of Canada, this is the kind of vegetarian restaurant that people pour into – not for lifestyle reasons, but because the modern, post-ethnic food and the escapist ambience are actually great. Definitely go for the smoothies. Vegans and rawists will not feel neglected.

ANDERSON
DELI €

Map p258 (Андерсон; cafe-anderson.ru; Strastnoy bul 4; mains ₽360-460; ⊙9am-11pm; 🍱🍴; MPushkinskaya) This sweet, child-friendly deli serves salads, soups and cakes, as well as smoothies and lemonades. The honey

latte might be a little too experimental, but the tea with raspberry puree and sage is quite exceptional.

DARY PRIRODY
INTERNATIONAL €

Map p258 (Дары природы; ☑8-985-600 8035; mains ₽250-350; MPushkinskaya) This trailer permanently stationed in Hermitage Gardens contains a kitchen run by people on a mission to transform Moscow's culinary scene, churning out all kinds of international foods from burgers to Asian noodles (but only a few at a time – the menu changes weekly).

You can eat at a stand-up table by the trailer or find a suitable bench in the park.

SELENGE
MONGOLIAN €

Map p258 (Сэлэнгэ; selenge.ru; ul Malaya Dmitrovka 23/15; mains ₽250-490; ⊙noon-midnight; MMayakovskaya) If you want a foretaste of your future Trans-Eurasian adventure, come here to sample food hailing from all cultures affiliated with Mongolia – Buryat, Kalmyk, Tyvan and Tibetan. For a safe introduction, try *Buryat buuza* dumplings. Brave ones tuck into Kalmyk lamb giblet soups and main courses, watering them down with *kumys* – fermented horse milk.

BUTERBRO
SANDWICH SHOP €

Map p258 (БутерБро; www.facebook.com/ButerBro; ul Karetny Ryad 3; sandwiches ₽250; ⊙noon-8pm) This little place at the entrance to Hermitage Gardens makes gourmet sandwiches and yummy soups. Stand-up tables are helpfully equipped with telephone chargers. You can also savour your sandwich on a bench in the park.

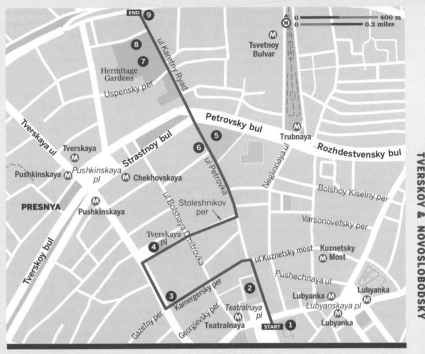

Neighbourhood Walk
Tverskoy

START TEATRALNAYA PL
END CHAIKHONA NO 1
LENGTH 2.5KM, THREE HOURS

Start your tour at the stately Teatralnaya pl (metro Teatralnaya), ringed with eye-popping architecture. The magnificent **1 Hotel Metropol** (p177) is an art-nouveau masterpiece. Across the street, the **2 Bolshoi Theatre** (p87) is the centrepiece of the square. The Maly Theatre and the National Youth Theatre frame it on either side.

Head up ul Petrovka and turn left onto Kamergersky per. Lined with restaurants and cafes with outdoor seating, this pleasant pedestrian strip is Moscow's prime people-watching spot. Look out for the **3 Moscow Art Theatre** (p97), founded by Konstantin Stanislavsky in 1898.

From here walk up Tverskaya ul to **4 Tverskaya pl** (p89), home to two of

Moscow's heroes: the centre statue is Yury Dolgoruky, founder of Moscow; across in city hall sits Sergei Sobyanin, mayor of Moscow. East of here, Stoleshnikov per is another quaint cobblestone strip, lined with fancy boutiques and trendy cafes.

From Stoleshnikov per turn left into ul Petrovka and walk north to pl Petrovskie Vorota, named for the gates that used to guard the city. Here, you can wander around the ancient **5 Upper St Peter Monastery** (p88) or the fresh **6 Moscow Museum of Modern Art** (p88).

Cross the Boulevard Ring and walk your way up ul Karenty Ryad to finish your tour amid the shady greenery of **7 Hermitage Gardens**.

Stop for a drink at **8 3205** (p95), then stroll west on the Garden Ring to reach Mayakovskaya metro station, or head for a meal and – quite possibly – much more drinking at **9 Delicatessen** (p94).

★**DELICATESSEN** INTERNATIONAL €€

Map p258 (Деликатесы; www.newdeli.ru; Savodvaya-Karetnaya ul 20; mains ₽450-700; ⊘noon-midnight Tue-Sat; 🛜◨; Ⓜ️Tsvetnoy Bulvar) The affable (and chatty) owners of this place travel the world and experiment with the menu a lot, turning burgers, pizzas and pasta into artfully constructed objects of modern culinary art. The other source of joy is a cabinet filled with bottles of ripening fruity liquors, which may destroy your budget if consumed uncontrollably (a pointless warning, we know).

The latter asset brought Delicatessen into World's Top 50 Bars list – admittedly at number 50. Go through the archway next to Shokoladnitsa cafe, turn left and look out for a green door on your right. The sign above it reads: 'Thank you for finding us'.

★**LAVKA-LAVKA** INTERNATIONAL €€

Map p258 (Лавка-Лавка; 🗹495-724 3532; http://lavkalavka.com; ul Petrovka 21 str 2; dishes ₽400-600; ⊘6pm-midnight Mon-Fri, 11am-midnight Sat & Sun; 👪; Ⓜ️Teatralnaya) 🥢 Welcome to the Russian Portlandia – all the food here is organic and hails from little farms where you may rest assured all the lambs and chickens lived a very happy life before being served to you on a plate. Irony aside, this a great place to sample local food cooked in a funky improvisational style.

Each item on the menu is attributed to an individual farmer. Geography spans from central Russia to Sakhalin. Of special note are the ales and different kinds of *kvas* (fermented rye-bread drink) produced on farms near Moscow. The restaurant comes with a great (if expensive) shop selling farm produce.

DZHONDZHOLI GEORGIAN €€

Map p258 (Джонджоли; 🗹495-650 5567; www. ginzaproject.ru; Tverskaya ul 20/1; mains ₽420-670; ⊘11am-midnight; 🛜◨; Ⓜ️Pushkinskaya) Exposed brick walls, wood and wicker furniture, and muted tones ensure that the focus of the Dzhondzholi dining room is in fact the open kitchen, where the chefs are busy preparing delicious *dolma* (stuffed vine leaves), *khachapuri* (cheese bread), *kharcho* (rice with beef or lamb soup) and other authentic favourites.

The food is fabulous, and happily it comes with none of the kitsch that we've come to expect from Moscow's Georgian restaurants.

Fun fact: food connoisseur and cookbook author Darra Goldstein explains in her book *A Georgian Feast* that *dzhondzholi* is 'a garlicky long-stemmed green, usually eaten pickled', that is common in Georgian cuisine. Try it for ₽190.

SISTERS GRIMM RUSSIAN €€

Map p258 (Сёстры Гримм; www.sgrimm.ru; Stoleshnikov per 11; meals ₽400-600; 🛜◨🍴; Ⓜ️Chekhovskaya) Sabrina and Daphne would be right at home in this cosy country cottage, well stocked with canned fruits and vegetables, books, photos and board games. The menu features 'home-cooking', Russian-style, with an enticing selection of mulled wine, lemonades and fruity cocktails to complete the fantasy.

COURVOISIER CAFE EUROPEAN €€

Map p258 (🗹495-632 9995; courvoisier-cafe. ru; Malaya Sukharevskaya pl 8; meals ₽380-550; ⊘24hr; 🍴◨; Ⓜ️Sukharevskaya) This informal, French-themed cafe is furnished with picnic tables and park benches, evoking an idyllic outdoor setting. (There is outdoor seating too, but fronting the Garden Ring, it is not so peaceful.) Serving breakfast, soups, pasta and grills, it's a popular spot for breakfast, happy hour (4pm to 7pm) or a late-night snack.

TRATTORIA VENEZIA ITALIAN €€

Map p258 (trattoria-venezia.ru; Strastnoy bul 4/3; meals ₽400-800; ⊘11am-midnight; Ⓜ️Chekhovskaya) Pretend that the Boulevard Ring is the Grand Canal. Imagine the cars ensconced in traffic are really gondolas, and the billboard-plastered facade of the Pushkinsky Cinema is actually the Ducal Palace. If you're still reading, then the Trattoria Venezia is for you. The long menu includes more than 25 pasta plates, as well as pizza, risotto, lasagne and Italian-style meat and fish dishes.

STARLITE DINER AMERICAN €€

Map p258 (Strastnoy bul 8a; mains ₽430-600; ⊘24hr; 🛜; Ⓜ️Chekhovskaya) Corporate Russia meets vintage America, and the result is a shiny version of an all-night diner. Sit at the polished chrome counter or sink into a vinyl booth to eat burgers, drink milkshakes and listen to that old-time rock 'n' roll.

★**BRASSERIE MOST** FRENCH €€€

Map p258 (🗹495-660 0706; brasseriemost. ru; ul Kuznetsky most 6/3; mains ₽620-2200;

⊗8am-midnight Mon-Fri, 9am-midnight Sat & Sun; MTeatralnaya) Moscow's most venerated and erudite restaurateur Aleksander Rappoport shares his love for regional French cuisine in this classy and expensive place on Kuznetsky most. The menu is a grand gastrotour taking in seemingly every major area of France from Bretagne to Alsace. Authenticity is religion. If they say bouillabaisse, be sure it will taste exactly like Marseille's best.

BARASHKA — AZERI €€€

Map p258 (Барашка; ☑495-625 2895; www.novikovgroup.ru; ul Petrovka 20/1; mains ₽750-1500; ⊗noon-midnight; MTeatralnaya) Yes, it's expensive – but it's also a sophisticated setting, done up as an understated Baku courtyard, adorned with jars of pickled lemons and blooming plants. Barashka offers a menu full of fresh tasty salads, grilled meats and slow-cooked stews, many of which feature the little lamb, for which the restaurant is named.

UZBEKISTAN — UZBEK €€€

Map p258 (Узбекистан; ☑495-623 0585; www.uzbek-rest.ru; Neglinnaya ul 29; mains ₽750-1900; ⊗noon-3am; 🖟; MTrubnaya) This place opened in 1951 by order of the Ministry of Trade of the Uzbek Soviet Republic. Six decades later, the place has expanded its menu to include Chinese, Arabic and Azeri food, in addition to the Uzbek standards. Make yourself comfortable on the plush cushions, order some spicy plov (pilaf-like meat and rice) or delicious fried kebabs. Now brace yourself for a belly-dancing show.

✘ Novoslobodsky

FARMER'S DINER — BISTRO €

Map p258 (Новослободский; ul Lesnaya 5; ₽300-450; ⊗11am-11pm; MBelorusskaya) This little bistro is run by people obsessed with Williamsburg gastroculture. The burger with caramelised onion is the trademark dish, but the place's main virtue is the two-course set lunch that costs ₽350 including a drink. It's a convenient pit stop before getting the Aeroexpress to Sheremetyevo airport.

IZYA GRILL — INTERNATIONAL €

Map p258 (Изя Гриль; izia-grill.ru; ul Sushchevskaya 27/1; mains ₽200-450; ⊗noon-midnight Sun-Thu, noon-6am Fri & Sat; 🕾; MNovoslobod-

skaya) The menu here reflects the three pillars of a modern Israelite's experience – a Jewish mother's cooking, an adventure in Southeast Asia and a stint in the US. Following this sequence, you can easily have forshmak herring paste for starters, spicy coconut milk soup as the first course and a burger for the main.

It's an easygoing place with an open-plan kitchen married with a bar that serves cheap (₽100) beer. Apart from many other virtues, it makes a logical stop en route to the Jewish Museum.

DRUZHBA — CHINESE €€

Map p258 (Дружба; ☑499-973 1212; www.drugba.ru; Novoslobodskaya ul 4; meals ₽600-800; ⊗11am-11pm; 🖟; MNovoslobodskaya) Druzhba earns high marks for authenticity, and as far as Sichuan cuisine goes that means spicy. Chinese restaurants in Moscow are notorious for turning down their seasoning to appeal to Russian taste buds, but Druzhba is the exception, which explains why this place is often packed with Chinese patrons. The chicken with peppers gets red-hot reviews.

MI PIACE — ITALIAN €€

Map p258 (☑495-970 1129; mipiace.ru; 1-ya Tverskaya-Yamskaya 7; mains ₽300-720; MMayakovskaya) This outlet of the cool, contemporary pizzeria chain near Triumfalnaya pl boasts big windows that allow loads of light into the dining room, and diamond-shaped wine racks filled with bottles and books. You can take a seat at a table if you like, but it's much more appealing to hunker down on one of the couches with your pizza pie.

🍷 DRINKING & NIGHTLIFE

★3205 — CAFE

Map p258 (☑905-703 3205; www.veranda3205.ru; ul Karetny Ryad 3; ⊗11am-3am; MPushkinskaya) The biggest drinking/eating establishment in Hermitage Gardens, this verandah positioned at the back of the main building looks a bit like a greenhouse. In summer, tables (and patrons) spill out into the park, making it one of the city's best places for outdoor drinking. With its long bar and joyful atmosphere, the place also heaves in winter.

★ENTHUSIAST BAR

Map p258 (Энтузиаст; per Stoleshnikov str 5; ⊗noon-11pm; MTeatralnaya) Scooter enthusiast, that is. But you don't have to be one in order to enjoy this superbly laidback bar hidden at the far end of a fancifully shaped courtyard and disguised as a spare-parts shop. On a warm day, grab a beer or cider, settle into a beach chair and let harmony descend on you.

NOOR BAR

Map p258 (☑499-130 6030; www.noorbar.com; ul Tverskaya 23; ⊗3pm-3am Mon-Wed, noon-6am Thu-Sun; MPushkinskaya) There is little to say about this misleadingly unassuming bar, apart from the fact that everything in it is close to perfection. It has it all – prime location, convivial atmosphere, eclectic DJ music, friendly bartenders and superb drinks. Though declared 'the best' by various magazines on several occasions, it doesn't feel like they care.

CAFE MART CAFE

Map p258 (Кафе Март; www.cafemart.ru; ul Petrovka 25; meals ₽800-1200; ⊗11am-midnight Sun-Wed, 11am-6am Thu-Sat, jazz concert 9pm Thu; 🖷; MChekhovskaya) It looks like another cellar bar, but if you walk all the way through the underground maze you'll find yourself in the huge overground 'orangerie' hall with mosaic-covered walls, warm lighting and possibly a jazz concert. When the weather is fine, Mart spills into the sculpture-filled courtyard of the adjacent Moscow Museum of Contemporary Art.

CAFE VOKZAL BAR

Map p258 (Кафе вокзал; cafe-vokzal.ru; ul Sushchevskaya 21; ⊗11am-midnight; MNovoslobodskaya) Packed with revellers, the railway-themed Vokzal looks and feels like a pub that has somehow grown to the size of a supermarket. The ₽100 price tag on the trademark beer and cheap food in the adjoining cafeteria ensure students from the nearby university have no doubts as to where to waste their young years.

KAMCHATKA BAR

Map p258 (Камчатка; novikovgroup.ru; ul Kuznetsky most 7; ⊗10am-1am Sun-Thu, noon-3am Fri & Sat; MTeatralnaya) Kamchatka is a generic term for all things fringe, and this cavernous pub seems to have been designed to prove that beer can go for ₽80 even in a prime location in front of the TsUM. But make sure you ask for their trademark Kamchatka beer, otherwise you'll get an expensive one. Kamchatka is best in summer, when you and your friend the pint can walk out into the street to enjoy the sunshine with fellow lumpen intellectuals.

GOGOL CLUB

Map p258 (Гоголь; www.gogolclubs.ru; Stoleshnikov per 11; ⊗noon-5am; MTeatralnaya) Fun, informal and affordable (so surprising on swanky Stoleshnikov), Gogol is great for food, drinks and music. The underground club takes the bunker theme seriously, notifying customers that their food is ready with an air-raid siren. In summer the action moves out to the courtyard, where the gigantic tent is styled like an old-fashioned street scene.

SIMACHYOV BAR

Map p258 (Симачёв; www.bar.denissimachev. com; Stoleshnikov per 12/2; ⊗11am-last guest; MChekhovskaya) By day it's a boutique and cafe, owned and operated by the famed fashion designer of the same name; by night, it becomes a hip-hop-happening nightclub that combines glamour and humour. The eclectic decor includes leopard-skin rugs tossed over tile floors, toilet stools pulled up to a wash-basin bar, Catholic confessionals for private dining, and more. You still have to look sharp to get in here, but at least you can be bohemian about it.

ARTEFAQ CLUB, CAFE

Map p258 (☑495-650 3971; www.artefaq.ru; ul Bolshaya Dmitrovka 32; ⊗24hr, concerts Fri-Sun; MChekhovskaya) It's a club! It's a restaurant! It's a gallery! Set on four levels, ArteFAQ makes use of every inch of space, with music in the basement, a bar and outdoor terrace at ground level and dining upstairs. If you choose to check out the underground, be ready to get your groove on, as the music is heavy on the disco.

KUKLY PISTOLETY BAR

Map p258 (Куклы Пистолеты; kuklypistolety. ru; Novoslobodskaya ul 16A; ⊗noon-midnight Sun-Thu, noon-5am Fri & Sat; MMendeleevskaya) It's a local that attracts a regular crowd of regular people who like to hang out there on a regular basis. Come to quaff a few cold ones, watch the big screen and enjoy the camaraderie. While you're here, you can ponder the dolls and guns that adorn the walls, thus earning the bar its strange name.

⭐ ENTERTAINMENT

BOLSHOI THEATRE BALLET, OPERA
See p87.

MASTERSKAYA LIVE MUSIC
Map p258 (Мастерская; www.mstrsk.ru; Teatralny proyezd 3 str 3; ⊙noon-6am; 🔊; ⓂLubyanka) All the best places in Moscow are tucked into far corners of courtyards, and they often have unmarked doors. Such is the case with this super-funky music venue. The eclectic, arty interior makes a cool place to chill out during the day. Evening hours give way to a diverse array of live-music acts or the occasional dance or theatre performance.

12 VOLTS CLUB
Map p258 (12 Вольт; www.12voltclub.ru; bldg 2, Tverskaya ul 12; ⊙6pm-6am; ⓂMayakovskaya) The founders of Moscow's lesbian movement opened this cafe-cum-social club, hidden away in a courtyard off Tverskaya ul. Buzz for admission. Once you're in, you'll find both gays and lesbians socialising together in a cosy environment, enjoying great drink specials and listening to pop music.

MOSCOW ART THEATRE (MKHT) THEATRE
Map p258 (Московский художественный театр (МХАТ); http://art.theatre.ru; Kamergersky per 3; ⊙box office noon-7pm; ⓂTeatralnaya) Often called the most influential theatre in Europe, this is where method acting was founded over 100 years ago, by Stanislavsky and Nemirovich-Danchenko. Besides the theatre itself and an acting studio, there's a small museum about the theatre's history.

NOVAYA OPERA OPERA
Map p258 (Новая опера; ☑495-694 0868; www.novayaopera.ru; ul Karetny Ryad 3; ⊙box office noon-7.30pm; ⓂTsvetnoy Bulvar) This theatre company was founded in 1991 by then-mayor Luzhkov and artistic director Evgeny Kolobov. Maestro Kolobov stated, 'we do not pretend to be innovators in this beautiful and complicated genre of opera'. As such, the 'New Opera' stages the old classics, and does it well. The gorgeous, modern opera house is set amid the Hermitage Gardens.

STANISLAVSKY & NEMIROVICH-DANCHENKO MUSICAL THEATRE OPERA
Map p258 (Музыкальный театр Станиславского и Немирович-Данченко; ☑495-629 2835; www.stanislavskymusic.ru; ul Bolshaya Dmitrovka 17; ⊙box office 11.30am-7pm; ⓂChekhovskaya) This historic company was founded when two legends of the Moscow theatre scene – Konstantin Stanislavsky and Vladimir Nemirovich-Danchenko – joined forces in 1941. Their newly created theatre became a workshop for applying the innovative dramatic methods of the Moscow Art Theatre to opera and ballet.

DOME CINEMA CINEMA
Map p258 (☑495-931 9873; www.domecinema.ru; Renaissance Moscow Hotel, Olympiysky pr 18/1; ⓂProspekt Mira) This is one of Moscow's first deluxe American-style theatres. These days films are shown in the original language – usually English – with dubs in Russian on the headphones.

RUSSIAN BALL AT YAR CABARET
(Яр; ☑495-960 2004; www.sovietsky.ru; Leningradsky pr 32/2, Sovietsky Hotel; tickets ₽1000, dinner ₽800-1200; ⓂDinamo) Everything about Yar is over the top, from the vast, gilded interior to the traditional Russian menu to the Moulin Rouge–style dancing girls. The thematic show is infamous for its elaborate costumes. The old-fashioned Russian food is pretty elaborate, too. Buy tickets in advance.

Walk 1km southeast from Dinamo metro station.

NIKULIN CIRCUS ON TSVETNOY BULVAR CIRCUS
Map p258 (Цирк Никулина на Цветном бульваре; ☑495-625 8970; www.circusnikulin.ru; Tsvetnoy bul 13; tickets ₽400-2500; ⊙box office 11am-2pm & 3-7pm; ⓂTsvetnoy Bulvar) Founded in 1880, this circus is now named after beloved actor and clown Yury Nikulin (1921–97), who performed at the studio here for many years. Nikulin's shows centre on a given theme, which serves to add some cohesion to the productions. There are lots of trapeze artists, tightrope walkers and performing animals.

OBRAZTSOV PUPPET THEATRE & MUSEUM CHILDREN'S THEATRE
Map p258 (Театр и музей кукол Образцова; ☑495-699 5373; www.puppet.ru; Sadovaya-Samotechnaya ul 3; ⊙box office 11am-2.30pm & 3.30-7pm; ⓂTsvetnoy Bulvar) The country's largest puppet theatre performs colourful Russian folk tales and adapted classical plays. Kids can get up close and personal with the incredible puppets at the museum, which holds a collection of over 3000.

DUROV ANIMAL THEATRE
CHILDREN'S THEATRE

Map p258 (Театр животных Дурова; ☑495-631 3047; www.ugolokdurova.ru; ul Durova 4; tickets ₽150-600; ☺show times vary, 11am-5pm Wed-Sun; Ⓜ Prospekt Mira) Dedushka Durov (Grandpa Durov) founded this zany theatre for kids as a humane alternative to the horrible treatment of animals he saw at the circus. His shows feature mostly domestic animals, including cats and dogs, farm animals and the occasional bear. His most popular show is Railway for Mice. Guided tours of the museum give kids a closer look at the railway. Take tram 7 from Prospekt Mira metro station, or walk 1.5km west on ul Durova.

BB KING
LIVE MUSIC

Map p258 (☑495-699 8206; www.bbkingclub.ru; Sadovaya-Samotechnaya ul 4/2; ☺noon-midnight, music from 8.30pm; Ⓜ Tsvetnoy Bulvar) This old-style blues club hosts an open jam session on Wednesday night, acoustic blues on Sunday and live shows other nights. The restaurant is open for lunch and dinner, when you can listen to jazz and blues on the jukebox. Enter from the courtyard.

LENKOM THEATRE
THEATRE

Map p258 (Ленком театр; ☑495-699 9668, box office 495-699 0708; www.lenkom.ru; ul Malaya Dmitrovka 6; tickets ₽200-2000; ☺box office noon-3pm & 4-7pm; Ⓜ Pushkinskaya) The Lenkom isn't the most glamorous theatre, but it's widely considered to have the strongest acting troupe in the country. The flashy productions and musicals performed here keep non-Russian speakers entertained.

MALY THEATRE
THEATRE

Map p258 (Малый театр; ☑495-624 4046; www.maly.ru; Teatralnaya pl 1/6; ☺box office 11am-8pm; Ⓜ Teatralnaya) Maly means 'small', meaning smaller than the Bolshoi across the street. Actually, these names date back to the time when there were only two theatres in town: the opera theatre was always called the 'Bolshoi', while the drama theatre was the 'Maly'. Founded in 1824, it mainly features performances of 19th-century works by Ostrovsky and fellow playwrights.

SATIRIKON THEATRE
THEATRE

(Театр Сатирикон; ☑495-602 6583; www.satirikon.ru; Sheremetyevskaya ul 8; ☺box office 11am-8pm; Ⓜ Marina Roshcha) Boasting one of Moscow's most talented theatre producers, Konstantin Raikin, as well as a host of big-name directors, the Satirikon earned a reputation in the early '90s with its outrageously expensive production of the *Threepenny Opera*. It has since broken its own record for expenditure with *Chantecler,* which featured dancing ducks and chickens.

CSKA ARENA
SPORTS

(Арена и Стадион ЦСКА; ☑495-225 2600; Leningradsky pr 39a; Ⓜ Aeroport) This 5500-person arena was built in the lead-up to 1980, when it hosted the Olympic basketball tournament. These days it is home to Moscow's most successful basketball and hockey teams. About 1.5km south of Aeroport metro station.

🛍 SHOPPING

DEPST
FASHION ACCESSORIES

Map p258 (www.depst.ru; Tsvetnoy bul 15 (inside Tsvetnoy shopping mall); ☺10am-10pm) This is the ultimate place to shop for Russian designer items, from jewellery to clothes, furniture and cutlery. The shop occupies pretty much the entire underground floor of Tsvetnoy shopping centre, which also has a nice food court on the top floor.

PODARKI VMESTE S VOROVSKI
SOUVENIRS

Map p258 (Подарки вМесте с Воровски; www.m-rosemarie.ru; Kuznetsky most 21/5; ☺10am-9pm; Ⓜ Lubyanka) This sweet little boutique houses a cooperative of four designers. The rather cramped space is filled with hundreds of useful and useless (but pretty) items, including Galereyka's felt slippers and hats (some shaped as Soviet tanks) and Ptitsa Sinitsa's stylish ceramics with East European folklore motifs.

★ TRANSYLVANIA
MUSIC

Map p258 (☑495-629 8786; www.transylvania.ru; Tverskaya ul 6/1, Bldg 5; ☺11am-10pm; Ⓜ Teatralnaya) From the courtyard, look for the black metal door that leads down into this dungeon of a shop, which houses room after room of CDs, in every genre imaginable. If you are curious about the *russky* rock scene, this is where you can sample some songs.

YELISEEV GROCERY
FOOD & DRINK

Map p258 (Елисеевский магазин; Tverskaya ul 14; ☺8am-9pm Mon-Sat, 10am-6pm Sun; Ⓜ Pushkinskaya) Peek in here for a glimpse of pre-revolutionary grandeur, as the store is set in the former mansion of the successful merchant Yeliseev. It now houses an upscale market selling caviar and other delicacies. It's a great place to shop for souvenirs for your foodie friends back home.

RESPUBLIKA
BOOKS

Map p258 (Республика; ☑495-251 6527; www.respublica.ru; 1-ya Tverskaya Yamskaya 10; ☻10am-9pm; ⓜMayakovskaya) It's a bookstore, but it's also a gift shop, a music shop and a cafe. This is the place to shop for a quirky gift for your friend who (you think) has everything. You will surely be proven wrong. For example, do they have a frog shower cap? Swarovski eye mask? A French toast imprint of the Eiffel Tower?

SIMACHYOV BOUTIQUE & BAR
CLOTHING, ACCESSORIES

Map p258 (☑495-629 5701; www.denissimachev. com; Stoleshnikov per 12/2; ⓜChekhovskaya) The wild child of Russian fashion, Denis Simachyov has become a household name in Moscow thanks to his popular nightclub and irreverent clothing. His collections have been inspired by themes as diverse as Russian sailors, Chechen war, Siberian peasants, hip-hop gangsters and gypsy nomads.

PODIUM CONCEPT STORE
CLOTHING, ACCESSORIES

Map p258 (Kuznetsky most 14; ☻noon-midnight; ⓜKuznetsky Most) This gorgeous 'concept store' offers six storeys of high fashion and fun design. Huge windows framed with heavy drapes, an embossed tin ceiling and plush furniture provide an exquisite setting for edgy and exotic (and expensive) clothing.

TSUM
DEPARTMENT STORE

Map p258 (ЦУМ; www.tsum.ru; ul Petrovka 2; ⓜTeatralnaya) TsUM stands for Tsentralny Universalny Magazin (Central Department Store). Built in 1909 as the Scottish-owned Muir & Merrilees, it was the first department store aimed at middle-class shoppers. These days it's filled with designer labels and luxury items.

DOM FARFORA
HOUSEWARES

Map p264 (Дом Фарфора; www.domfarfora. ru; 1-ya Tverskaya-Yamskaya 17; ☻10am-9pm; ⓜBelorusskaya) The 'house of china' sells the world's most famous brands of fine china, including Russia's own *Imperatorsky farforovy zavod* (Imperial china factory). Designs are tasteful, traditional, and whimsical and wonderful, and sometimes all of the above. A Moscow-themed tea set makes a perfect souvenir.

RUSSIAN BRONZE
SOUVENIRS

Map p258 (Русская бронза; www.russkaya-bronza.com; ul Kuznetsky most 20; ☻9am-9pm; ⓜKuznetsky Most) The factory outlet for the Vel metallurgical company is chock-full of bronze sculptures and figurines, as well as office accessories, tableware, teaspoons, candelabras, piggy banks and other potential souvenirs.

DOM INOSTRANNOY KNIGI
BOOKS

Map p258 (Дом иностранной книги; www. mdk-arbat.ru; Kuznetsky most 18/7; ⓜKuznetsky Most) The House of Foreign Books is a small place with a wide selection of literature in foreign languages. Most books are in English, though there are smaller selections of German, French and other European languages.

★YEKATERINA
CLOTHING, ACCESSORIES

Map p258 (Екатерина; www.mexa-ekaterina. ru; ul Bolshaya Dmitrovka 11; ⓜTeatralnaya) One of Russia's oldest furriers, this place has been manufacturing *shapky* (fur hats) and *shuby* (fur coats) since 1912. While Yekaterina has always maintained a reputation for high-quality furs and leather, its designs are constantly changing and updating to stay on top of fashion trends.

🏃 SPORTS & ACTIVITIES

★SANDUNY BATHS
BANYA

Map p258 (☑495-628 4633; www.sanduny.ru; Neglinnaya ul 14; male & female 1st class ₽1500, male 2nd class & female premium ₽1850, male premium class ₽2300; ☻8am-10pm; ⓜKuznetsky Most) Sanduny is the oldest and most luxurious *banya* in the city. The Gothic Room is a work of art with its rich wood carving, while the main shower room has an aristocratic Roman feel to it. There are several classes, as on trains, though regulars say that, here, second male class is actually better than the premium class.

No matter which class you choose, it will be a costly experience, especially if you rent the essential items – a sheet to wrap yourself into (₽170), a felt hat to avoid burning your hair (₽410) and a pair of slippers.

Presnya

INNER PRESNYA | OUTER PRESNYA

Neighbourhood Top Five

1 Admiring Presnya's unique collection of architecture, including the art nouveau **Ryabushinsky Mansion** (p102) and the constructivist **Narkomfin** (p103).

2 Following *The Master and Margarita* from its opening scene at **Patri-** **arch's Ponds** (p103) to its climax at the **Central House of Writers** (p103), following up with a visit to the author's **Bulgakov House** (p103).

3 Stargazing and braving flight simulation at the **Moscow Planetarium** (p105).

4 Indulging in an *haute russe* feast at **Café Pushkin** (p107).

5 Attending the **Tchaikovsky Concert Hall** (p110) or **Moscow Tchaikovsky Conservatory** (p110) to listen to a world-class concert (perhaps Tchaikovsky!).

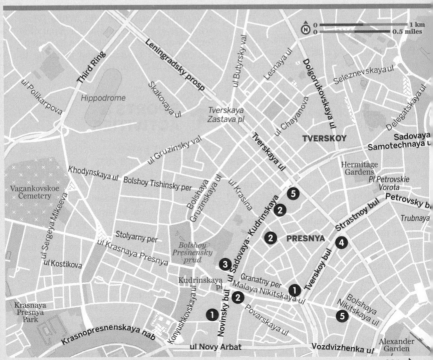

For more detail of this area see Map p264 ➡

Explore: Presnya

Presnya encompasses some of the capital's oldest neighbourhoods as well as its newest development. Start by exploring the lovely residential areas of Inner Presnya, chock-full of evocative architecture, historic parks and fantastic drinking and dining spots. The whole neighbourhood is a wonderful place for a wander, especially with a copy of Bulgakov's *The Master and Margarita* in hand. Come in the late afternoon, then stay for dinner: the area around Patriarch's Ponds has emerged as a dining hotspot, with restaurants lined up along Spiridonovsky per.

The more traditional sights – the newly reopened planetarium and the huge zoo – are set on the busy Garden Ring (the ring road 3km from the Kremlin). Either attraction could entertain you for a few hours.

Further out, the wide roads, heavy traffic and ongoing construction in Outer Presnya are not particularly user-friendly. Make the trip only if you have your heart set on a particular destination.

Local Life

➡**Parks** Packs of teens, grandmothers with wee ones and starry-eyed couples all congregate at Patriarch's Ponds to sit on the shady benches and feed the ducks.

➡**Bakery** The queue often runs out the door, as loyal patrons wait their turn for the city's best freshly baked breads, pastries and pies at Volkonsky (p104).

➡**Brunch** Weekends at Correa's (p108) are an expat institution.

Getting There & Away

➡**Metro** Inner Presnya is most easily accessed from Mayakovskaya station on the green line or Pushkinskaya station on the purple line.

➡**Metro** For the more western parts of the district, the most useful metro stations are at Kudrinskaya pl (Barrikadnaya and Krasnopresnenskaya stations) and ul 1905 goda (Ulitsa 1905 Goda station).

➡**Metro** The new development around the International Business Center (Moskva-City) has its own minimetro spur branching off from Kievskaya station, with a convenient stop at Vystavochnaya.

Lonely Planet's Top Tip

In the back streets around Bolshaya Nikitskaya ul, many old mansions have survived – some renovated, others dilapidated. Most of those on the streets closest to the Kremlin were built by the 18th-century aristocracy, while those further away were built by rising 19th-century industrialists. These days many of these buildings are occupied by embassies and cultural institutions. With little traffic, Bolshaya Nikitskaya ul is excellent for a quiet ramble.

PRESNYA

✖ Best Places to Eat

➡ Café Pushkin (p107)
➡ Volkonsky (p104)
➡ As Eat Is (p105)
➡ Khachapuri (p105)

For reviews, see p104 ➡

☐ Best Places to Drink

➡ Bar Klava (p109)
➡ Kvartira 44 (p109)
➡ Art Lebedev Cafe Studio (p109)

For reviews, see p109 ➡

◉ Best Kids' Outings

➡ Moscow Planetarium (p105)
➡ Moscow Zoo (p104)
➡ Patriarch's Ponds (p103)
➡ Tsereteli Studio-Museum (p104)

For reviews, see p102 ➡

⊙ SIGHTS

⊙ Inner Presnya

CHURCH OF THE RESURRECTION CHURCH
Map p264 (Церковь Воскресения; Bryusov per 2; ⓂPushkinskaya) Through the arch off of Tverskaya ul, the unexpected, gold-domed Church of the Resurrection was one of the few churches to remain open throughout the Soviet period. As such, it is full of fine icons and artwork rescued from churches torn down during the Soviet era.

CHURCHES OF THE GRAND & SMALL ASCENSION CHURCH
(Церковь Большого Вознесения и Церковь Малого Вознесения; Bolshaya Nikitskaya ul; ⓂArbatskaya) In 1831 poet Alexander Pushkin married Natalya Goncharova in the elegant **Church of the Grand Ascension** (Map p264), on the western side of pl Nikitskie Vorota. Six years later he died in St Petersburg, defending her honour in a duel. Such passion, such romance… The celebrated couple is featured in the Rotunda Fountain, erected in 1999 to commemorate the poet's 100th birthday.

Down the street, the festive **Church of the Small Ascension** (Map p264) sits on the corner of Voznesensky per. Built in the early 17th century, it features whitewashed walls and stone embellishments carved in a primitive style.

RYABUSHINSKY MANSION MUSEUM
Map p264 (Особняк Рябушинского; Malaya Nikitskaya ul 6/2; ⊙11am-5.30pm Wed-Sun; ⓂPushkinskaya) FREE Also known as the Gorky House-Museum, this fascinating 1906 art-nouveau mansion was designed by Fyodor Shekhtel and gifted to celebrated author Maxim Gorky in 1931. The house is a visual fantasy with sculpted doorways, ceiling murals, stained glass, a carved stone staircase and exterior tilework. Besides the fantastic decor it contains many of Gorky's personal items, including his extensive library.

MUSEUM OF ORIENTAL ART MUSEUM
Map p264 (Музей искусства народов востока; ☎495-691 0212; www.orientmuseum.ru; Nikitsky bul 12a; admission ₽300; ⊙11am-8pm Tue-Sun; ⓂArbatskaya) This impressive museum on the Boulevard Ring holds three floors of exhibits spanning the Asian continent. Of particular interest is the 1st floor, dedicated mostly to the Caucasus, Central Asia and North Asia (which means the Russian republics of Cukotka, Yakutiya and Priamurie).

But the entire continent is pretty well represented, including the countries that were not part of the Russian or Soviet empires. The collection covers an equally vast time period, from ancient times through to the 20th century, including painting, sculpture and folk art. One unexpected highlight is a special exhibit on Nikolai Rerikh, the Russian artist and explorer who spent several years travelling and painting in Asia.

ART4.RU ART GALLERY
Map p264 (☑499-136 5656; www.art4.ru; Khlinovsky tupik 4; admission ₽200; ⊙by appointment; ⓂOkhotny Ryad) Anyone can be a museum director, as demonstrated by Moscow businessman-turned-art-collector Igor Markin. His 700-plus–piece collection had outgrown his private properties, so he decided to start a museum where he could display his art and share it with the public. And so art4.ru ('Art for Russia') was born.

The small gallery space is used to exhibit not only pieces from Markin's own collection, but also up-and-coming artists that he has 'discovered'. It's a unique experience that is worth investigating if you're interested in Russia's hot contemporary art scene.

GOGOL HOUSE MUSEUM
Map p264 (Дом Гоголя; www.domgogolya.ru; Nikitsky bul 7; admission ₽100; ⊙noon-7pm Wed & Fri, 2-9pm Thu, noon-5pm Sat & Sun; ⓂArbatskaya) Nineteenth-century writer Nikolai Gogol spent his final tortured months here. The rooms – now a small but captivating museum – are arranged as they were when Gogol lived here. You can even see the fireplace where he famously threw his manuscript of *Dead Souls*.

An additional reading room contains a library of Gogol's work and other reference materials about the author. The quiet courtyard contains a statue of the emaciated, sad author surrounded by some of his better-known characters in bas-relief.

LYUBAVICHESKAYA SYNAGOGUE SYNAGOGUE
Map p264 (Любавическая синагога; Bolshaya Bronnaya ul 6; ⓂPushkinskaya) Converted to a theatre in the 1930s, this building was still

used for gatherings by the Jewish community throughout the Soviet period. Today the building serves as a working synagogue, as well as a social centre for the small but growing Jewish community in Moscow.

PATRIARCH'S PONDS PARK

Map p264 (Патриаршие пруды; Bolshoy Patriarshy per; Ⓜ Mayakovskaya) Patriarch's Ponds harks back to Soviet days, when the parks were populated with children and *babushky* (grandmothers) You'll see grandmothers pushing strollers and lovers kissing on park benches. In summer children romp on the swings, while winter sees them ice skating on the pond. The small park has a huge statue of 19th-century Russian writer Ivan Krylov, known to Russian children for his didactic tales.

Patriarch's Ponds were immortalised by writer Mikhail Bulgakov, who had the devil appear here in *The Master and Margarita*. The initial paragraph of the novel describes the area to the north of the pond, where the devil enters the scene and predicts the rapid death of Berlioz. Contrary to Bulgakov's tale, a tram line never ran along the pond. Bulgakov's flat, where he wrote the novel and lived up until his death, is around the corner on the Garden Ring.

BULGAKOV HOUSE-MUSEUM MUSEUM

Map p264 (Дом-музей Булгакова; www.dombulgakova.ru; Bolshaya Sadovaya ul 10; admission ₽70; ⊙1-11pm, to 1am Fri & Sat; Ⓜ Mayakovskaya) Author of *The Master and Margarita* and *Heart of a Dog,* Mikhail Bulgakov was a Soviet-era novelist who was labelled a counterrevolutionary and was censored throughout his life. His most celebrated novels were published posthumously, earning him a sort of cult following in the late Soviet period. Bulgakov lived with his wife Yelena Shilovskaya (the inspiration for Margarita) in a flat in this block, which now houses a small museum and theater.

Back in the 1990s the empty flat was a hang-out for dissidents and hooligans, who painted graffiti and wrote poetry on the walls. Nowadays, the walls have been whitewashed and the doors locked, but there is a small museum and cafe on the ground floor. The exhibit features some of his personal items, as well as posters and illustrations of his works. More interesting are the readings and concerts that are held here (check the website), as well as the off-beat tours on offer. A black cat hangs out in the courtyard.

CENTRAL HOUSE OF WRITERS (CDL) NOTABLE BUILDING

Map p264 (Центральный дом литераторов; ЦДЛ; www.moscowwriters.ru; Povarskaya ul 50; Ⓜ Barrikadnaya) The Central House of Writers is an elaborate art nouveau mansion dating to 1889. The historic mansion housed the administrative offices of the writers' union for most of the Soviet period. As such, it was featured in Bulgakov's novel *The Master and Margarita.*

CHEKHOV HOUSE-MUSEUM MUSEUM

Map p264 (Дом-музей Чехова; ul Sadovaya-Kudrinskaya 6; admission ₽150; ⊙11am-6pm Tue, Wed & Fri-Sun, 2-8pm Thu; Ⓜ Barrikadnaya) 'The colour of the house is liberal, ie red', Anton Chekhov wrote of his house on the Garden Ring, where he lived from 1886 to 1890. The red house now contains the Chekhov House-Museum, with bedrooms, drawing room and study all intact. Musical performances are held here several times a week in the late afternoon.

The overall impression is one of a peaceful and cultured family life. The walls are decorated with paintings that were given to Chekhov by Levitan (painter) and Shekhtel (art nouveau architect), who often visited him here. Photographs depict the playwright with literary greats Leo Tolstoy and Maxim Gorky. One room is dedicated to Chekhov's time in Melikhovo, showing photographs and manuscripts from his country estate.

☉ Outer Presnya

NARKOMFIN NOTABLE BUILDING

Map p264 (Наркомфин; Novinsky bul 25; Ⓜ Barrikadnaya) The model for Le Corbusier's Unitè d'Habitation design principle, this architectural landmark was an early experiment in semi-communal living (p104). Designed and built between 1928 and 1930 by Moisei Ginzburg and Ignatii Milinis, Narkomfin offered housing for members of the Commissariat of Finances. In line with constructivist ideals, communal space is maximised and individual space is minimised. Apartments have minute kitchens to encourage residents to eat in the communal dining room.

INSIDE NARKOMFIN

What is it like to live inside an innovative – even revolutionary – architectural landmark (p103)? Even more intriguing, what is it like to live inside such a landmark that has been left to rot? Those are the questions local filmmakers sought to explore, when making **Narkomfin: A Web Documentary** (www.narkomfin.net). Their goal was to give viewers a glimpse inside this celebrated building, which many have talked about but few have seen, as access is restricted. The film also introduces some of the residents – mostly artists – who discuss their daily interactions with their surroundings.

Having been in a semi-ruinous state for many years, a Russian property development group has been buying up apartments in the building with the long-term intention of preserving the constructivist landmark and converting it into condos. In the meantime, the dilapidated apartments are being leased to artists for very low rents. Unfortunately, the future remains in limbo, especially amid reports of 'cosmetic repairs' that threaten the integrity of the architecture.

MOSCOW ZOO   ZOO
Map p264 (Московский зоопарк; www.moscow zoo.ru; Yaroslavskoe shosse; adult weekday/weekend ₽300/500, children free; ⊙10am-8pm Tue-Sun Apr-Sep, to 5pm Oct-Mar; ♿; ⓜ Barrikadnaya) In 2014, the zoo underwent a huge renovation in honour of its 150th anniversary, so it should be in great shape in coming years. Huge flocks of feathered friends populate the central ponds, making for a pleasant stroll for bird-watchers. For a new perspective on Moscow's nightlife, check out the nocturnal animal exhibit. Other highlights include the big cats (featuring Siberian tigers), and the Dolphinarium. For more four-legged fun, follow the footbridge to see exhibits featuring animals from each continent.

TSERETELI STUDIO-MUSEUM   MUSEUM
Map p264 (Музей-мастерская Зураба Церетели; www.mmoma.ru; Bolshaya Gruzinskaya ul 15; admission ₽250; ⊙11am-6pm Fri-Wed, 1-8pm Thu; ♿; ⓜ Belorusskaya) Moscow's most prolific artist has opened up his 'studio' as a space to exhibit his many masterpieces. You

can't miss this place – whimsical characters adorn the front lawn. They give just a tiny hint of what's inside: a courtyard crammed with bigger-than-life bronze beauties and elaborate enamel work.

The highlight is undoubtedly Putin in his judo costume, although the huge tile Moscow cityscapes are impressive. You'll also recognise some smaller-scale models of monuments that appear around town. Indoors, there are three floors of the master's sketches, paintings and enamel arts.

WHITE HOUSE   NOTABLE BUILDING
Map p264 (Белый дом; Krasnopresnenskaya nab 2; ⓜ Krasnopresnenskaya) The White House – officially the House of Government of the Russian Federation – fronts a stately bend in the Moscow River, just north of the Novoarbatsky most.

It was here that Boris Yeltsin rallied the opposition that confounded the 1991 hardline coup, then two years later sent in tanks and troops to blast out conservative rivals, some of them the same people who backed him in 1991. The images of Yeltsin climbing on a tank in front of the White House in 1991, and of the same building ablaze after the 1993 assault, are among the most unforgettable from those tumultuous years.

✖ EATING

✖ Inner Presnya

★ VOLKONSKY   BAKERY €
Map p264 (Волконский; www.wolkonsky.com; Bolshaya Sadovaya ul 2/46; pastry items ₽100-200; ⊙7.30am-11pm Mon-Fri, 8am-1pm Sat & Sun; 🛜♿; ⓜ Mayakovskaya) The queue often runs out the door, as loyal patrons wait their turn for the city's best freshly baked breads, pastries and pies. It's worth the wait, especially if you decide on a fruit-filled croissant or to-die-for olive bread. Next door there are big wooden tables where you can get large bowls of coffee or tea.

CAFE RECEPTOR   FUSION €
Map p264 (Кафе Рецептор; www.cafereceptor. ru; Bolshaya Nikitskaya ul 22/2; mains ₽200-400; ⊙noon-midnight; 🛜🍴♿; ⓜ Okhotny Ryad) Colourful graffiti, amateur artwork and old photographs adorn the walls of this quirky basement cafe. It creates an arty setting f

TOP SIGHT
MOSCOW PLANETARIUM

Since reopening in 2011 after a 17-year closure, the Moscow Planetarium (Московский планетарий) has become the 'star' of educational attractions in Moscow. The planetarium shines bigger and brighter than before, having expanded in area by more than three times and incorporating high-tech gadgetry, interactive exhibits and educational programs.

The centrepiece is the **Large Star Hall** (Большой Звездный Зал; ₽550-600) (the biggest in Europe!), with its 25m silver dome roof. Your ticket includes access to the old-school exhibits in the Urania Museum (think meteorite collection). After the show (from May to October), you can explore the **Sky Park**, sprinkled with astronomical instruments from sun dials to solar panels.

The new facility also includes the innovative interactive **Lunarium** (Лунариум; ₽450), where visitors can perform experiments. Fun hands-on activities include generating electrical energy, riding a cosmic bicycle and determining your weight on another planet. Another favourite attraction is the **four-dimensional cinema** (4D Кинотеатр; ₽450), which features 3D images plus other special sensual effects such as sounds, smells and movement.

DON'T MISS...
➡ Large Star Hall
➡ Interactive 'Lunarium' museum
➡ Sky Park

PRACTICALITIES
➡ Map p264
➡ www.planetarium -moscow.ru
➡ ul Sadovaya-Kudrinskaya 5
➡ exhibits ₽300-600
➡ ⊙museum 10am-9pm, theatre 10am-midnight Wed-Mon
➡ MBarrikadnaya

---

healthy, veg-heavy meals, fresh juices, fancy teas and free-flowing wine, house cocktails and occasional live music. There's another outlet near **Patriarch's Ponds** (Map p264; Bolshoy Kozikhinsky per 10; MTverskaya).

COOL KULINARIYA   RUSSIAN €
Map p264 (Cool Кулинария; www.coolkulinariya. ru; Bolshaya Nikitskaya ul 24/1, bldg 6; mains ₽200-400; ⊙8am-11pm Mon-Fri, 10am-11pm Sat & Sun; 🛜🍴; MOkhotny Ryad) Tucked into a cosy basement crowded with comfy tables, this inviting little hovel makes it easy to sample fresh Russian soups and salads, as well as more exotic fare from the wok. Just take a peek inside the glass case and see what looks good. The only hard part is saving room for one of the tempting pastries.

PUSHKIN KONDITERSKAYA   CAFE €
Map p264 (www.cafe-pushkin.ru; Tverskoy bul 26; desserts ₽100-300; ⊙noon-midnight; 🚹; MPushkinskaya) If you want to impress your date, but you can't afford the Café Pushkin for dinner, head next door to the *konditerskaya* (confectioner) for dessert. It's every bit as opulent as the restaurant, from the crystal chandeliers down to the marble floors, with plenty of embellishments in between (including the glass case displaying the sweets).

★AS EAT IS   INTERNATIONAL €€
Map p264 (Как Есть; ☑495-699 5313; www.aseatis.ru; Tryokhprudny per 11/13; mains ₽500-900; ⊙noon-11pm; 🍴📶; MMayakovskaya) We love the understated, eclectic interior, with its mismatched textures, appealingly packed bookshelves and vintage detailing. Even more, we love the contemporary seasonal fare, which is delightful to look at and divine to eat. It's the kind of food that would normally cost big bucks, but prices are reasonable. Extra love for the pun of a name.

★KHACHAPURI   GEORGIAN €€
Map p264 (☑8-985-764 3118; hacha.ru; Bolshoy Gnezdnikovsky per 10; khachapuri ₽200-350, mains ₽400-600; 🛜📶; MPushkinskaya) Unassuming, affordable and appetising, this urban cafe exemplifies what people love about Georgian culture: the warm hospitality and the freshly baked *khachapuri* (cheese bread). Aside from seven types of delicious *khachapuri,* there's also an array of soups, shashlyki (kebabs), *khinkali* (dumplings) and other Georgian favourites.

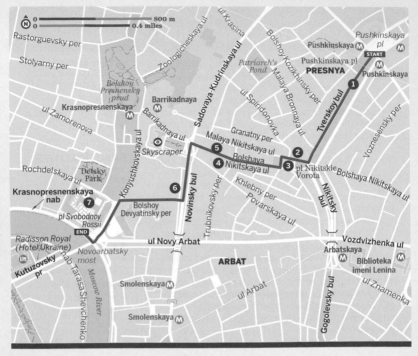

🏃 Neighbourhood Walk
Presnya Past & Present

START PUSHKINSKAYA PL
END KRASNOPRESNENSKAYA NAB
LENGTH 4KM; TWO HOURS

Walk from the previous century into the present (and beyond). From Pushkinskaya pl, stroll south along **①Tverskoy bul**. This is the loveliest stretch, lined with grand architecture and colourful blooms. At the end, sneak a peak at **②Ryabushinsky Mansion** (p102), an art nouveau beauty where Maxim Gorky lived.

The **③Church of the Grand Ascension** (p102) looming over the intersection hosted the wedding of Alexander Pushkin and Natalya Goncharova, and a sculpture of the lovebirds graces the fountain out front. Walk up Bolshaya Nikitskaya ul, which is studded with mansions. Some of the most striking include the elaborate facade at **④No 51** and the tiled edifice of **⑤Lopatina Building** at No 54.

At the end of Bolshaya Nikitskaya, use the underground crosswalk to reach Kudrin-skaya pl, dominated by a massive skyscraper (one of Stalin's Seven Sisters). Just south is one of Moscow's last and best examples of modernist architecture, **⑥Narkomfin** (p103). Amid talk of reconstruction, legal barriers and lack of financing mean the building continues to crumble.

Turn right into Bolshoy Devyatinsky per, then left into Konyushkovskaya ul, continuing south to Krasnopresnenskaya nab. On the banks of the Moscow River is the massive facade of the **⑦White House** (p104), home of the Russian parliament and site of several decisive events in recent history. The Radisson Royal, another of Stalin's Seven Sisters, stands on the opposite side of the river.

In the distance, the International Business Centre sprouts up along the Moscow River. Note the double-pronged City of Capitals building, representing Moscow and St Petersburg. Mercury City Tower, the tallest building in Europe, towers some 340m above the city.

★FAVORITE
AMERICAN €€

Map p264 (☑495-691 1850; www.favorite-pub.ru; ul Spiridonovka 24; mains ₽500-800; ☺8am-last guest; ⓓ; ⓂMayakovskaya) Moscow's Favorite Pub is this cool and casual Brooklyn-style hang-out, serving tasty gourmet burgers and grilled steaks. There's microbrewed beer on tap (Brickstone Beer, made in Moscow) and a football game on the TV.

UILLIAM'S
EUROPEAN €€

Map p264 (Вилльямʼс; ☑495-650 6462; www.ginzaproject.ru; Malaya Bronnaya ul 20a; mains ₽700-1200; ☺10.30am-11.30pm; ⓓ; ⓂMayakovskaya) This tiny little spot is always packed with patrons who come to watch the action in the open kitchen, which is basically the centrepiece of the restaurant. Chef Uilliam Lamberti prides himself on using only the highest quality ingredients and offering his heart and soul in the preparation. The results are perfection on a plate.

JEAN-JACQUES
FRENCH €€

Map p264 (Жан-Жак; www.jan-jak.com; Nikitsky bul 12; mains ₽300-600; ☺8am-6am; ⓢ; ⓂArbatskaya) In a prime location on the Boulevard Ring, this friendly wine bar welcomes everybody wanting a glass of wine, a bite to eat, some music and a few smiles. The basement setting is cosy but not dark, making it an ideal spot to share a bottle of Bordeaux (₽1200 to ₽2500) and nibble on brie.

MARI VANNA
RUSSIAN €€

Map p264 (Мари Ванна; ☑495-650 6500; www.marivanna.ru; Spiridonyevsky per 10; mains ₽600-800; ☺8am-midnight; ⓓⓓⓗ; ⓂPushkinskaya) Don't look for the sign (there is none), just ring the doorbell at No 10. You'll be ushered into homey environs, complete with overstuffed bookcases and black-and-white TV showing old Soviet shows. You will be served delicious Russian home cooking on little plates. Just when you begin to think it is 1962, you will be handed your bill with prices from modern-day Moscow. Ouch.

SCANDINAVIA
SWEDISH €€

Map p264 (☑495-937 5630; www.scandinavia.ru; Maly Palashevsky per 7; mains ₽600-1000; ⓢⓓⓗ; ⓂPushkinskaya) Much loved by Moscow expats, Scandi offers an enticing interpretation of what happens 'when Sweden meets Russia'. A delightful summer cafe features sandwiches, salads and treats from the grill (including the best burgers in Moscow, by some accounts).

PAVILION
RUSSIAN €€

Map p264 (Павильон; ☑495-697 5110; www.restsindikat.com; Bolshoy Patriarshy per 7; mains ₽500-900; ☺noon-midnight; ⓢⓓ; ⓂMayakovskaya) Occupying the old boathouse overlooking Patriarch's Ponds, this place is hard to beat for atmosphere. The pavilion dates from the 19th century, but the interior has a 'high Soviet' design and a menu to match. All the old favourites are here, exquisitely prepared, and sometimes with a surprising twist.

TWENTY-TWO
INTERNATIONAL €€

Map p264 (☑495-776 8622; www.twentytwo22.ru; ul Novy Arbat 22; mains ₽600-900; ☺noon-6am; ⓢⓓⓓ; ⓂSmolenskaya) Can one restaurant be all things to all people? We're not sure, but Twenty-Two is sure going to try. Downstairs, it's a cosy place for coffee and cupcakes. Upstairs, it's a slick wine bar with a vast menu spanning the globe. Despite the lack of specialisation, the food gets rave reviews, as do the views from the floor-to-ceiling windows.

★CAFÉ PUSHKIN
RUSSIAN €€€

Map p264 (Кафе Пушкинь; ☑495-739 0033; www.cafe-pushkin.ru; Tverskoy bul 26a; business lunch ₽750, mains ₽1000-2200; ☺24hr; ⓢⓓ; ⓂPushkinskaya) The tsarina of *haute-russe* dining, with an exquisite blend of Russian and French cuisines – service and food are done to perfection. The lovely 19th-century building has a different atmosphere on each floor, including a richly decorated library and a pleasant rooftop cafe.

★UGOLYOK
EUROPEAN €€€

Map p264 (Уголёк; ☑495-629 0504; Bolshaya Nikitskaya 12; ☺9am-midnight Sun-Wed, 9am-1.30am Thu-Sat; ⓂBiblioteka im Lenina) Everything at Ugolyok is perfectly pleasing to the eye, from the slick post-industrial interior, to the funky but fine tableware, to the tantalising food and drinks laid before you. Fortunately, it tastes good too, as deliciously fresh ingredients are mixed up in unusual ways. A+ for brunch.

NEDALNY VOSTOK
ASIAN FUSION €€€

Map p264 (Недальний Восток; ☑495-694 0641; www.novikovgroup.ru; Tverskoy bul 15; mains ₽900-1300; ⓓⓓ; ⓂPushkinskaya) Moscow is raving about the 'Near East'. Foodies love the superfresh seafood prepared in the wok, on the grill or in the oven – all in plain sight of the diners. It's one for a splurge.

✄ Outer Presnya

★STOLLE
CAFE €

Map p264 (Штолле; www.stolle.ru; Bolshaya Sadovaya ul 3; mains ₽200-300; ⊗8am-10pm; 🛜📶♿; ⓂMayakovskaya) The entire menu at Stolle is excellent, but the *pirogi* (pies) are irresistible. A *stolle* is a traditional Saxon Christmas cake: the selection of sweets and savouries sits on the counter, fresh from the oven. It may be difficult to decide (mushroom or meat, apricot or apple?), but you really can't go wrong.

BOTANIKA
FUSION €

Map p264 (Ботаника; 📞495-251 9760; www.cafebotanika.ru; Bolshaya Gruzinskaya ul 61; mains ₽300-500; ⊗11am-midnight; 🛜📶📱; ⓂBelorusskaya) Rare is the restaurant in Moscow that is both fashionable and affordable, but Botanika pulls it off. It offers light, modern fare, with plenty of soups, salads and grills. Wood furniture and subtle floral prints complement the garden-themed decor, all of which makes for an enjoyable, all-natural eating experience.

SOUP CAFE
RUSSIAN €

Map p264 (Суп кафе; www.soupcafe.ru; 1-ya Brestskaya ul 62; soup ₽200; ⊗24hr; 📶; ⓂBelorusskaya) This aptly named restaurant takes the most appetising element of Russian food to new heights, offering some 40 varieties of hot and cold on any given day. If you can't decide, go for the sampler. The atmosphere is loungey: dim lights, modern furniture and DJs spinning house music at night.

ANDERSON FOR POP
INTERNATIONAL €

Map p264 (Андерсон для Пап; 📞499-753 1601; www.cafe-anderson.ru; Mal Gruzinskaya ul 15/1; mains ₽390-620; ⊗9am-11pm Mon-Fri, 10am-11pm Sat-Sun; ♿; ⓂBarrikadnaya) The ultimate in family-friendly, this place is designed for dads and kids. It has a play area (complete with Foosball), a reading area and a creative area – plenty for the 'kids' to do while the mums enjoy some downtime. The food and drinks are reliably good for all family members, with the right mix of traditional and new cuisine.

BULKA
BAKERY €

Map p264 (Булка пекарня; www.bulkabakery.ru; Bolshaya Gruzinskaya ul 69; pastries ₽100-200; ⊗8am-11pm; 🛜♿; ⓂBelorusskaya) The coffee is good but the pastries are even better.

Whether you're hankering for something savoury or sweet, you're sure to find it in the big glass display case. Late in the day, everything goes on sale so they can start afresh the following morning.

UPSIDE DOWN CAKE CO
BAKERY €

Map p264 (www.upsidedowncake.ru; Bolshaya Gruzinskaya ul 76; desserts ₽150-300; ⊗9am-11pm Mon-Fri, 10am-11pm Sat & Sun; 🛜📶📱; ⓂBelorusskaya) We hope you saved room for dessert. This corner bakery features lots of cupcakes and pastries, delicious sorbet and a great selection of herbal teas by the pot.

★RAGOUT
FUSION €€

Map p264 (📞495-662 6458; www.caferagout.ru; Bolshaya Gruzinskaya ul 69; mains ₽600-900; ⊗8am-midnight; 🛜📶📱; ⓂBelorusskaya) Muscovites are raving about Ragout. The vibe is cool, but not cooler than thou. The food choices are creative, but not crazy. This gastropub is part of a culinary movement to provide fine dining at reasonable prices – a concept that's long overdue in Moscow.

CORREA'S
EUROPEAN €€

Map p264 (📞495-933 4684; www.correas.ru; Bolshaya Gruzinskaya ul 32; mains ₽400-600; ⊗8am-11pm Mon-Fri, 9am-11pm Sat & Sun; 🛜📶📱; ⓂBelorusskaya) The original Correa's occupies a tiny space and there are only a handful of tables. But the large windows and open kitchen guarantee it does not feel cramped, just cosy. The menu – sandwiches, pizza and grills – features nothing too fancy, but everything is prepared with the freshest ingredients. There's another outlet on **ul Grasheka** (Map p264; 📞495-789 9654; ul Grasheka 7; 🛜📶📱; ⓂMayakovskaya).

CORNER BURGER
BURGERS €€

Map p264 (CBBG76; www.cornerburger.ru; Bolshaya Gruzinskaya ul 76; burgers ₽500-650; 🛜📶📱; ⓂBelorusskaya) We know you didn't come to Moscow to eat burgers, but just in case you have a hankering, we know where you can get one. These babies feature high-quality ground beef, grilled the way you like it and served on an English muffin or on pretzel bread, with a variety of toppings.

SHINOK
UKRAINIAN €€

Map p264 (Шинок; 📞495-651 8101; www.shinok.ru; ul 1905 goda 2; mains ₽750-1100; ⊗noon-midnight; 📶📱♿; ⓂUlitsa 1905 Goda) In case you didn't think Moscow's themed dining was over the top, this restauran has re-created a Ukrainian peasant farm in central Moscow – though with an oddly pared-back, contemporary style. The house speciality is *vareniki* (boiled dumplings), which are superb.

DOLKABAR INTERNATIONAL €€

Map p264 (Долкабар; www.dolkabar.ru; ul Krasina 7; lunch ₽400, mains ₽400-900; ⏱noon-11pm; 🛜⬚; ⓂMayakovskaya) Dolkabar is the creation of traveller and blogger Sergei Kolya, who wanted to make a place where people could come to share their adventures and get inspired for their next trip. Maps on the tables and photos on the walls create the perfect setting for a menu of international favourites.

BARASHKA AZERI €€€

Map p264 (Барашка; ☎495-653 8303; ul 1905 goda 2; mains ₽500-1000; ⬚; ⓂUlitsa 1905 Goda) Step off a busy Moscow street and into a charming Azeri courtyard, where you can dine on delectable salads, grilled meats and hearty stews.

🍷 DRINKING & NIGHTLIFE

🍸 Inner Presnya

TIME-OUT BAR COCKTAIL BAR

Map p264 (www.timeoutbar.ru; 12th fl, Bolshaya Sadovaya ul 5; ⏱noon-2am Sun-Thu, noon-6am Fri & Sat; ⓂMayakovskaya) On the upper floors of the throwback Pekin Hotel, this trendy bar is nothing but 'now'. That includes the bartenders sporting plaid and their delicious concoctions, especially created for different times of day. The perfect place for sundowners (or sun-ups, if you last that long).

BAR KLAVA BAR

Map p264 (Бар Клава; www.bar-klava.com; Malaya Bronnaya ul 26; ⏱noon-6am; 🛜; ⓂMayakovskaya) The chic interior and intimate atmosphere make for a sophisticated little bar, which manages to be trendy but not pretentious. The menu features a full page of whiskeys and some enticing house cocktails. It's an expensive place to drink, if that's your activity for the evening, but a perfectly pleasant place to pop in for a sip before or after your night out.

ART LEBEDEV CAFE STUDIO CAFE

Map p264 (Кафе Студия Артемия Лебедева; lik.artlebedev.ru; Bolshaya Nikitskaya ul 35b; 🛜; ⓂArbatskaya) Owned by design guru Artemy Lebedev, this tiny space invites an attractive arty crowd to sip fancy tea and coffee. Regulars love the house-made *kasha* (porridge) for breakfast and the shady terrace in summer. Don't miss the shop downstairs.

KVARTIRA 44 BAR

Map p264 (Квартира 44; www.kv44.ru; Bolshaya Nikitskaya ul 22/2; mains ₽300-500; ⏱noon to late; 🛜; ⓂOkhotny Ryad) Somebody had the brilliant idea to convert an old Moscow apartment into a crowded, cosy bar, with tables and chairs tucked into every nook and cranny, and jazz and piano music on Friday and Saturday nights.

CONVERSATION CAFE

Map p264 (Разговор; www.conversationcafe.ru; Bolshaya Nikitskaya ul 23/14/9; 🛜🔌; ⓂArbatskaya) Considering its three specialties – coffee, pasta and ice cream – we can't imagine why anybody wouldn't want to stop in at this inviting, contemporary cafe. Soups and sandwiches are also on the menu, but it's the decadent desserts and wake-me-up coffee drinks that keep the seats filled.

RYUMOCHNAYA BAR

Map p264 (Рюмочная; Bolshaya Nikitskaya ul 22/2; meals ₽300-500; ⏱11am-11pm; ⓂOkhotny Ryad) This is a hold-over (or a comeback?) from the days when a drinking establishment needed no special name. The *ryumochnaya* was the generic place where comrades stopped on their way to or from work to toss back a shot or two before continuing on their way. This particular Ryumochnaya also offers some tasty food to accompany your *sto grammov* (100g).

CAFE MARGARITA CAFE

Map p264 (Кафе Маргарита; ☎495-699 6534; www.cafe-margarita.ru; Malaya Bronnaya ul 28; meals ₽400-600; ⏱noon-2am; ⓂMayakovskaya) With walls lined with bookshelves, and a site opposite Patriarch's Ponds, this offbeat cafe is popular with a well-read, young crowd. The place livens up in the evening, when it often hosts live acoustic, folk and jazz.

MAYAK BAR

Map p264 (Маяк; www.clubmayak.ru; Bolshaya Nikitskaya ul 19; business lunch ₽270, mains ₽300-350; ⏱noon-6am; 🛜; ⓂOkhotny Ryad)

Named for the Mayakovsky Theatre downstairs, this is a remake of a much beloved club that operated in this spot throughout the 1990s. The reincarnated version is more pub than club, exuding the air of a welcoming, old-fashioned inn. But it still attracts actors, artists and writers, who come to see friendly faces and eat filling European fare.

COFFEE MANIA — CAFE

Map p264 (Кофемания; www.coffeemania.ru; Moscow Conservatory, Bolshaya Nikitskaya ul 13; ⊙24hr; ☎; Ⓜ Okhotny Ryad) A popular place for the rich and beautiful to congregate, this friendly, informal cafe is beloved for its homemade soups, freshly squeezed juices and steaming (if overpriced) cappuccinos, not to mention its summer terrace overlooking the leafy courtyard of the conservatory.

🍴 Outer Presnya

JAGGER — NIGHTCLUB, BAR

Map p264 (www.ginza.ru; Rochdelskaya ul 15, Bldg 30; ⊙noon-midnight Mon-Wed, noon-6am Thu-Sat, 2pm-midnight Sun; Ⓜ Ulitsa 1905 Goda) Tucked into the courtyard in the Tryokhgornaya Manufacturing complex, Jagger is a superhot bar with a supercool vibe – excellent cocktails, sharp clientele and laidback atmosphere. Still, you have to know where to look for this place. And you have to look good. Enter from ul 1905 goda and head to the inner courtyard.

MANON CLUB — NIGHTCLUB

Map p264 (Клуб Манон; www.manon-club.ru; ul 1905 goda 2; ⊙noon-6am; Ⓜ Ulitsa 1905 goda) Come for amazing views and great music, and dance the night away. It's a popular, romantic spot for dinner, though the food gets mixed reviews. But folks who stay for drinking and dancing are not disappointed by the party that continues until sunrise. Dress up.

VINTAGE — WINE BAR

Map p264 (Винтаж; www.barvintage.ru; ul Krasina 7, str 3; ⊙noon-11pm; Ⓜ Mayakovskaya) Duck into the courtyard and look for the sign pointing the way into this understated dining room. Vintage is all about the vino. The wine list (mostly from Europe) reads like a novel, and it's nicely complemented by a menu of cheese and charcuterie. There is other food too, but you're really here to relax, enjoy good company and drink wine.

RED — CAFE

Map p264 (www.redespressobar.com; Sadovaya-Kudrinskaya ul 1; ⊙8am-midnight Sun-Wed, 24hr Thu-Sat; ☎; Ⓜ Barikadnaya) With minimalist decor and free wi-fi, Red is a popular spot to look cool while getting a caffeine fix. Delicious coffee is roasted in-house.

☆ ENTERTAINMENT

SIXTEEN TONS — LIVE MUSIC

Map p264 (Шестнадцать тонн; ☏495-253 1550; www.16tons.ru; ul Presnensky val 6; cover ₽600-1200; ⊙11am-6am, concerts 8pm Sun-Thu, 9pm Thu-Sat, midnight Fri & Sat; ☎; Ⓜ Ulitsa 1905 Goda) Downstairs, the brassy English pub-restaurant has an excellent house-brewed bitter. Upstairs, the club gets some of the best Russian bands that play in Moscow, hosting such names as Mara and Theodor Bastard, among others.

TCHAIKOVSKY CONCERT HALL — CLASSICAL MUSIC

Map p264 (Концертный зал имени Чайковского; ☏495-232 0400; www.melo man.ru; Triumfalnaya pl 4/31; tickets ₽300-3000; ⊙closed Jul-Aug; Ⓜ Mayakovskaya) Home to the famous Moscow State Philharmonic, the capital's oldest symphony orchestra, Tchaikovsky Concert Hall was established in 1921. It's a huge auditorium, with seating for 1600 people, and hosts Russian classics such as Stravinsky, Rachmaninov and Shostakovich, as well as other European favourites, plus special children's concerts.

MOSCOW TCHAIKOVSKY CONSERVATORY — CLASSICAL MUSIC

Map p264 (Московская консерватория имени Чайковского; ☑box office 495-629 9401; www.mosconsv.ru; Bolshaya Nikitskaya ul 13; Ⓜ Okhotny Ryad) The country's largest music school, named for Tchaikovsky of course, has two venues, both of which host concerts, recitals and competitions. It's best known for the prestigious International Tchaikovsky Competition (www.tchaikovsky-competition.net), which takes place every four years, awarding titles of top pianist, singer, cellist and violinist.

SPARTAK STADIUM — SPORTS

(Стадион Спартак; ☑495-411 5200; www.ot kritiearena.ru; Volokolamskoe shosse 67; Ⓜ Tushinskaya) Home to FC Spartak, this bizarre-

TREKHGORNAYA MANUFACTURING FACTORY

Trekhgornaya Manufaktura (Трёхгорная Мануфактура) is one of the oldest textile factories in Russia, founded in 1799 on the banks of the Moscow River. The factory played a key role in the development of the Presnya district. Over the years, it has employed hundreds of thousands of mill girls, weavers and designers. The company survived conflict (the War of 1812, the uprisings of 1905 and WWII), nationalisation and privatisation. Now, it is learning to survive capitalism.

Although the company continues to design and produce fabrics, the level of production has dropped dramatically since its peak in the early 1980s, and most of the company's production has moved to Yaroslavl. Many of its warehouses have been converted into studios and showrooms, especially for interior design. Like other re-purposed industrial zones, Trekhgornaya has become a hot spot for nightlife, as restaurants and clubs take advantage of the prime location and vast postindustrial spaces. Clubs such as Jagger remember their roots, displaying the looms and other paraphernalia that built this place.

Despite this nostalgia, Trekhgornaya is still going strong. If you need any proof, just check out their product line at the **Factory Outlet** (Трёхгорная Мануфактура фирменный магазин; Map p264; www.trekhgorka.ru; Rochdelskaya ul 15; ⊙9.30am-8.30pm Mon-Sat, 10am-6pm Sun; ⓂBarrikadnaya).

looking arena was new in 2014, built for the upcoming World Cup. In addition to the 42,000-capacity stadium, the complex includes an indoor arena and extensive other sports facilities.

SHOPPING

PROSTO TAK   SOUVENIRS
Map p258 (Просто Так; www.buro-nahodok. ru; Maly Gnezdnikovsky per 12/27; ⊙11am-9pm; ⓂPushkinskaya) For quirky, clever souvenirs, stop by this network of artists' cooperatives. Each outlet has a different name, but the goods are more or less the same: uniquely Russian gifts such as artist-designed *tapki* (slippers) and hand-woven linens, though artist Yury Movchan has a line of funky fixtures (lights, clocks etc) made from old appliances and other industrial discards.

BOLSHE   ART, SOUVENIRS
Map p264 (Больше; www.bolshe-chem.ru; Malaya Bronnaya ul 28/2; ⊙11am-9pm Mon-Fri, noon-9pm Sat & Sun; ⓂMayakovskaya) This outlet of the clever artists' cooperative that has shops scattered around Moscow, features handmade, original and totally impractical stuff – great gifts or fun souvenirs.

MOSTOK   ART, SOUVENIRS
Map p264 (Мосток; www.mostok.ru; Bolshaya Sadovaya ul 3; ⊙10am-7pm Mon-Fri, noon-7pm Sat; ⓂMayakovskaya) Shelves are stacked

with trade books and counters are piled high with postcards. The walls are crammed with posters, prints and original artwork, some portraying unusual panoramas and historic Moscow scenes. Part frame store, part graphic-design service, part print shop – you never know what treasures you might find.

CHOCOLATE SALON   FOOD & DRINK
Map p264 (Шоколадный салон; Povarskaya ul 29/36; ⊙10am-9pm; ⓂBarrikadnaya) This bustling store is the factory outlet for several local candy makers, including the most famous, Krasny Oktyabr (Red October). The display case is filled with tempting filled candies and chocolate sculptures in all forms. We can't resist the old-fashioned Alyonka candybar.

SPORTS & ACTIVITIES

KRASNOPRESNKIYE BANY   BANYA
Map p264 (Краснопресненские бани; ☑men's banya 495-255 5306, women's banya 495-253 8690; www.baninapresne.ru; Stolyarny per 7; general admission ₽1200-1700; ⊙8am-11pm; ⓂUlitsa 1905 Goda) Lacking an old-fashioned, decadent atmosphere, this modern, clean, efficient place nonetheless provides a first-rate *banya* (hot-bath) experience. The facility has Russian steam room, Finnish sauna, plunge pool and massage services.

Arbat & Khamovniki

ARBAT | KHAMOVNIKI

Neighbourhood Top Five

1 Perusing the collections at the **Pushkin Museum of Fine Arts** (p117), especially the incredible array of Impressionist and post-Impressionist art in its Gallery of European & American Art of the 19th & 20th Centuries.

2 Wandering around **Novodevichy Convent & Cemetery** (p114), soaking up five centuries of artistry and history.

3 Strolling, shopping, and doing the cafe scene on **ul Arbat** (p122).

4 Marvelling at the ostentation and sheer size of the **Cathedral of Christ the Saviour** (p121).

5 Recalling Russia's greatest tragedy and triumph of the 20th century at the Museum of the Great Patriotic War and the monuments at **Park Pobedy** (p119).

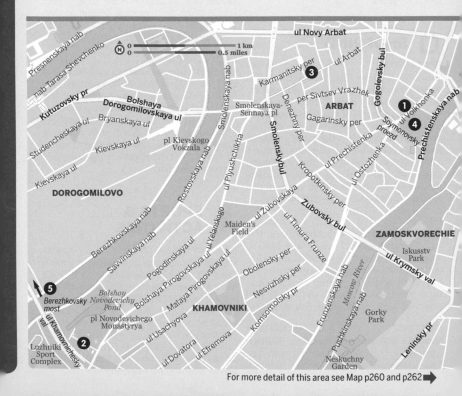

For more detail of this area see Map p260 and p262

Explore: Arbat & Khamovniki

These two adjacent districts are an art-lover's dream. The Arbat district is packed with world-class art museums and smaller artist-dedicated galleries, not to mention the elaborate Cathedral of Christ the Saviour. One might spend an entire day wandering the area, starting at the world-class Pushkin Museum of Fine Arts, then strolling up ul Prechistenka in the afternoon and dropping into sights along the way.

Evening is also a wonderful time to wander the storied cobblestoned streets around the old Arbat, the historic haunt of artists, musicians and street performers. Though Arbat today has been taken over by souvenir stands and is often packed with tourists, it still evokes the free-thinking artistic spirit of yesteryear.

In Khamovniki, the Unesco-recognised Novodevichy Convent & Cemetery is a worthwhile half-day destination – a welcome break from art-gallery row. Further away from the city centre, the roads become wider, the traffic faster and the distances greater. As such, Dorogomilovo and Sparrow Hills are not great for wandering. But it's worth making a special trip for a few choice destinations, such as Park Pobedy (Victory Park) and the forested hillsides of Vorobyovy Gory Nature Preserve.

Local Life

➡ **Al fresco** None of Moscow's many summer terraces can beat the pedestrian bridge behind the Cathedral of Christ the Saviour for fabulous Kremlin views. It's also an economical choice: bring your own bottle of Shampanskoe and pull up a bench.

Getting There & Away

➡ **Metro** The light-blue line and dark-blue lines run parallel across the Arbat district. They both have stations called Arbatskaya, with the entrance near Arbatskaya pl; and they both have stations called Smolenskaya, with the entrance near Smolenskaya pl. None of these same-named stations are connected to each other, however, so make sure you know which line you are getting on.

➡ **Metro** The red line traverses Khamovniki district, from Kropotkinskaya station at pl Prechistenskie Vorota (near the Cathedral of Christ the Saviour); to Park Kultury station along the Garden Ring; to Sportivnaya station in the southwestern corner (near Novodevichy).

Lonely Planet's Top Tip

Many of the neighbourhood museums stay open in the evening one day per week. On Thursday, for example, the Pushkin Museum of Fine Arts and its Gallery of European & American Art of the 19th & 20th Centuries stay open until 9pm, as does the Tsereteli Gallery. The Shilov Gallery does the same on Wednesday evenings.

✕ Best Places to Eat

➡ Elardzhi (p127)
➡ Black Market (p128)
➡ Varenichnaya No 1 (p126)
➡ Zhurfak Cafe (p127)

For reviews, see p126 ➡

♙ Best Places to Drink

➡ Gavroche Wine Bar (p128)
➡ Carabas (p129)
➡ Zhiguli Beer Hall (p128)
➡ Sky Lounge (p128)

For reviews, see p128 ➡

◉ Best Art Galleries

➡ Gallery of European & American Art of the 19th & 20th Centuries (p118)
➡ Rerikh Museum (p122)
➡ Pushkin Museum of Fine Arts (p117)
➡ Multimedia Art Museum (p125)
➡ Burganov House (p123)

For reviews, see p122 ➡

ARBAT & KHAMOVNIKI

 TOP SIGHT
NOVODEVICHY CONVENT & CEMETERY

In 1524 Grand Prince Vasily III founded the Novodevichy Convent and Cemetery (Новодевичий монастырь
и кладбище) to celebrate the taking of Smolensk from
Lithuania. From early on, the 'New Maidens' Convent'
was a place for women from noble families to retire –
some more willingly than others.

Walls & Towers

Enter the convent through the red-and-white Moscow-
baroque **Transfiguration Gate-Church** (Преображенская
надвратная церковь), built in the north wall between 1687
and 1689. All of these striking walls and towers, along with
many other buildings on the grounds, were rebuilt around
this time, under the direction of Sofia Alexeyevna. The
elaborate **bell tower** (Колокольня) against the east wall
towers 72m over the rest of the monastery. When it was
built in 1690 it was one of the tallest towers in Moscow.

Smolensk Cathedral

The centrepiece of the monastery is the white **Smolensk Cathedral** (Смоленский собор;
1524–25), built to house the precious *Our Lady of Smolensk* icon. The sumptuous interior
is covered in 16th-century **frescoes**, considered to be among the finest in the city. The
gilded **iconostasis** includes icons that date from the time of Boris Godunov. The icons on
the fifth tier are attributed to 17th-century artists Simeon Ushakov and Feodor Zubov. The
tombs of Sofia Alexeyevna and Eudoxia Lopukhina are in the south nave.

Chambers of Sofia Alexeyevna

Sofia Alexeyevna used the Novodevichy Convent as a residence when she ruled Russia
as regent in the 1680s. During her rule, she rebuilt the convent to her liking – which was

DON'T MISS...

➡ Smolensk Cathedral
frescoes and icons

➡ The 72m bell tower

➡ Graves of Nikita
Khrushchev and Boris
Yeltsin

PRACTICALITIES

➡ www.novodev.msk.ru

➡ adult/child ₽300/100

➡ ⏱8am-8pm, museums
9am-5pm

➡ Ⓜ Sportivnaya

fortunate, as she was later confined here when her half-brother, Peter the Great, came of age. After being implicated in the Streltsy rebellion, she was imprisoned here for life, primarily inhabiting the **Pond Tower** (Напрудная башня).

Chambers of Eudoxia Lopukhina

Eudoxia Lopukhina, the first wife of Peter the Great, stayed in the **Chambers of Tsarina Eudoxia Miloslavkaya** (Палаты царевны Евдокии Милославской). Although she bore him a son, Peter detested her conservative, demanding personality, and soon rejected her for the beautiful daughter of a Dutch wine merchant. Eudoxia retired to a monastery in Suzdal, where she further estranged herself by taking her own lover and founding an opposition movement within the church. The tsar responded by executing the bishops involved and banishing his former wife to a more remote location.

Upon Peter's death, he was succeeded by Peter II, who recalled his grandmother Eudoxia back to Moscow. She lived out her final years in high style at Novodevichy.

Other Buildings

Other churches include the red-and-white **Assumption Church** (Успенская церковь), dating from 1685 to 1687, and the 16th-century **St Ambrose's Church** (Амвросиевская церковь). Boris Godunov's sister, Irina, lived in the building adjoining the latter. Today, **Irina's Chambers** (Палаты Ирины Годуновой) hold exhibits of religious artwork.

Novodevichy Cemetery

The **Novodevichy Cemetery** (Новодевичье кладбище; Map p262; ☺9am-5pm; Ⓜ Sportivnaya) **FREE** is one of Moscow's most prestigious resting places – a veritable who's who of Russian politics and culture. Here you will find the tombs of Rostrovpovich, Bulgakov, Chekhov, Gogol, Mayakovsky, Prokofiev, Stanislavsky and Eisenstein, among many other Russian and Soviet cultural notables.

In Soviet times Novodevichy Cemetery was used for eminent people the authorities judged unsuitable for the Kremlin wall, most notably Khrushchev. The intertwined white-and-black blocks around his bust were intended by sculptor Ernst Neizvestny to represent Khrushchev's good and bad sides.

The tombstone of Nadezhda Alliluyeva, Stalin's second wife, is covered by unbreakable glass to prevent vandalism. The grave of former president Boris Yeltsin, who died in 2007, is marked by an enormous sculpture of a Russian flag, rippling in the wind.

DISCRETION ADVISED

Novodevichy is a functioning monastery. Women are advised to cover their heads and shoulders when entering the churches; men should wear long pants.

It is said that Novodevichy was a favourite wintertime destination for Leo Tolstoy, who lived in the neighbourhood and liked to go ice skating on the pond outside the monastery walls. One of the main characters of *Anna Karenina* – Konstantin Levin – meets his future wife, Kitty, when she is ice skating here.

GRAVE DIGGING

If you want to investigate Novodevichy Cemetery, buy the Russian map (on sale at the kiosk), which pinpoints nearly 200 graves of notable citizens.

The Soviets shut down Novodevichy in 1922 and – always ironic – converted it into a Museum of Women's Emancipation. The nuns were invited to return to the convent in 1994, with services recommencing the following year.

ARBAT & KHAMOVNIKI NOVODEVICHY CONVENT & CEMETERY

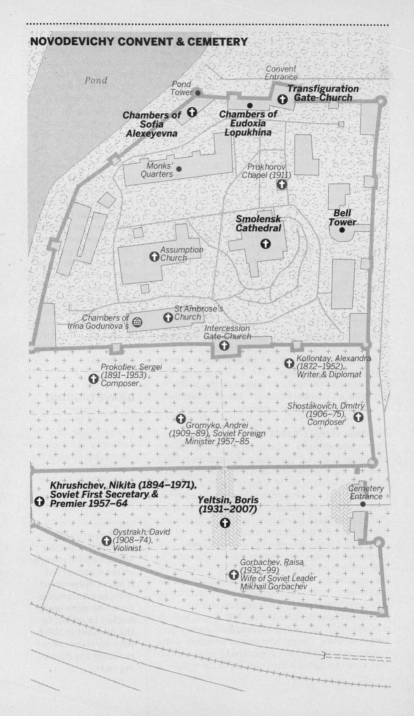

NOVODEVICHY CONVENT & CEMETERY

Pond

Convent Entrance

Pond Tower

Transfiguration Gate-Church

Chambers of Sofia Alexeyevna

Chambers of Eudoxia Lopukhina

Monks' Quarters

Prokhorov Chapel (1911)

Smolensk Cathedral

Bell Tower

Assumption Church

St Ambrose's Church

Chambers of Irina Godunova's

Intercession Gate-Church

Prokofiev, Sergei (1891–1953) Composer

Kollontay, Alexandra (1872–1952), Writer & Diplomat

Shostakovich, Dmitry (1906–75), Composer

Gromyko, Andrei (1909–89), Soviet Foreign Minister 1957–85

Khrushchev, Nikita (1894–1971), Soviet First Secretary & Premier 1957–64

Yeltsin, Boris (1931–2007)

Cemetery Entrance

Oystrakh, David (1908–74), Violinist

Gorbachev, Raisa (1932–99), Wife of Soviet Leader Mikhail Gorbachev

TOP SIGHT
PUSHKIN MUSEUM OF FINE ARTS

Pushkin Museum of Fine Arts (Музей изобразительных искусств им Пушкина), **Moscow's premier foreign-art museum, displays a broad range of European works. The collections are located not only in the main building, but also in the nearby Museum of Private Collections and the Gallery of European & American Art of the 19th & 20th Centuries. The museum is likely to close during an upcoming renovation and expansion, which is scheduled for completion in 2018.**

Main Building

The **main building** (Главное здание; ul Volkhonka 12; adult/student ₽300/150; Ⓜ Kropotkinskaya) opened in 1912 as the museum of Moscow University. It now exhibits the bulk of the holdings that date from antiquity through the 18th century.

The excellent **Ancient Civilisation exhibits** in rooms 1 and 2 contain ancient Egyptian weaponry, jewellery, ritual items and tombstones. Most of the items were excavated from burial sites, including two haunting mummies. Room 3 houses the impressive **Treasures of Troy** exhibit, with excavated items dating back to 2500 BC.

The highlight of the museum are the **Dutch masterpieces** from the 17th century, located in rooms 9 through 11. **Rembrandt** is the star of the show, with many paintings on display, including his moving *Portrait of an Old Woman*.

The **Greek and Italian Courts** (rooms 14 and 15) contain examples from the museum's original collection, which was made up of plaster-cast reproductions of the masterpieces from Ancient Greece and Rome, as well as from the Renaissance. You'll find more plaster casts upstairs, including a special room devoted to Michelangelo (room 29). The 17th and 18th centuries dominate the second floor. Room 17 contains a diverse collection of **Italian paintings**, including some formidable large-scale canvases. Rooms 21 through 23 are

DON'T MISS...

➡ Treasures of Troy
➡ Golden Age of Dutch Art
➡ Impressionist and post-Impressionist collections

PRACTICALITIES

➡ Map p260
➡ www.arts-museum.ru
➡ ul Volkhonka 12
➡ admission each branch ₽200-300
➡ ⊙10am-7pm Tue-Sun, to 9pm Thu
➡ Ⓜ Kropotkinskaya

Culture vultures flock to the Pushkin Museum of Fine Arts in December. Since 1981, the unique December Nights Festival pairs musical performances with accompanying art exhibits, highlighting works from a particular artist, composer, era or theme.

MUSEUM TOWN

Museum administration has announced plans for a massive overhaul of the museum buildings and the surrounding area. The original idea was to restore and adapt the current museum buildings, along with three historic mansions, creating a cultural quarter, with greatly expanded exhibit space and other facilities. The plan will allow the museum to display more art, to receive more visitors and – most importantly – to implement the security and conditions necessary to preserve this incredible collection.

Exhibits at the Museum of Private Collections are organised around the collections, each as a whole, to maintain the integrity of each private collection. Details of the collectors are displayed alongside the art.

devoted to France, with a separate gallery for the Rococo period, featuring some appropriately dreamy paintings by Boucher.

Gallery of European & American Art of the 19th & 20th Centuries

The separate **Gallery of European & American Art of the 19th & 20th Centuries** (Map p260; www.new-paintart.ru; ul Volkhonka 14; adult/child ₽300/150; ⓂKropotkinskaya) contains a famed assemblage of Impressionist and post-Impressionist works, based on the collection of two well-known Moscow art patrons, Sergei Shchukin and Ivan Morozov.

The **Impressionists** occupy rooms 8 through 10, with paintings by Degas, Manet, Renoir and Pisarro, and an entire room dedicated to Monet. Rodin's sculptures include pieces from *The Gates of Hell* and *The Monument to the Burghers of Calais*.

Room 11 is dedicated to **post-Impressionism**, most notably Van Gogh. The museum contains several of his lesser-known gems, including the scorching *Red Vineyards* and the tragic *Prison Courtyard*, painted in the last year of his life. Room 14 is almost exclusively Cézanne, featuring his sensuous *Bathers*. Room 15 is devoted to works by Gauguin, representing his prime period. Rooms 19 and 20 display many of the most famous paintings by Matisse, such as *Goldfish*. There are a few exquisite, primitive paintings by Rousseau in room 21, and some lesser-known pieces by Picasso in room 22. The final rooms complete the rich collection of 20th-century art, featuring Miro, Kandinsky, Chagall, Arp and others.

Museum of Private Collections

The **Museum of Private Collections** (Музей личных коллекций; Map p260; www.artprivatecollections.ru; ul Volkhonka 10; adult/child ₽200/100; ⓂKropotkinskaya) shows off art collections donated by private individuals. The centrepiece is the **collection of Ilya Silberstein** (rooms 16 to 19), the museum's founder and an accomplished historian of Russian literature and art. This collection is especially rich in pieces by early-20th-century 'Mir Iskusstva' artists such as Benois, Serebryakova, Serov and Kustodiev. Other highlights include the **Inna Koretskaya and Boris Mihailovsky Collection** (room 2) featuring works by Rerikh, Golovin and Kuznetsov; the **Lemkul room** (room 20) with graphic art by Fyodor Lemkul, as well as the artist's collection of glassworks from Russia and Europe; the **Sergei Solovyov Collection** (room 21), with paintings by Perov and Repin; and the impressive collection of **Old Believer icons** from the 16th to 20th centuries in rooms 14 and 15.

◉ TOP SIGHT
PARK POBEDY

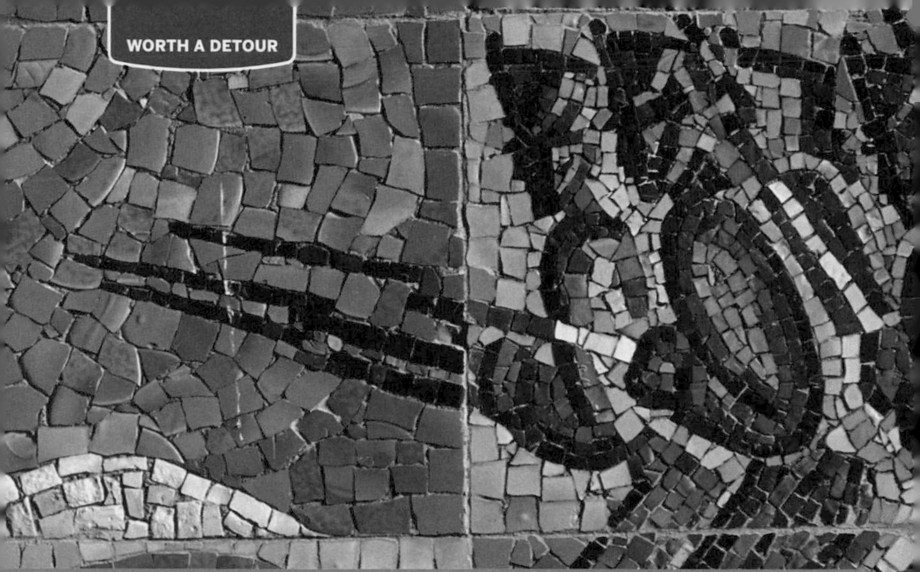

Magnificent Park Pobedy (Парк Победы; Victory Park) at Poklonnaya Hill is an enormous memorial complex commemorating the sacrifice and celebrating the triumph of the Great Patriotic War – as WWII is known in Russia. Unveiled on the 50th anniversary of the victory, the park includes endless fountains and monuments, as well as the memorial church, synagogue and mosque.

Obelisk

The dominant monument is an enormous obelisk, topped with a sculpture of St George slaying the dragon (the work of Zurab Tsereteli). Its height is exactly 141.8m, with every 10cm representing one day of the war. At the 60th Victory Day celebrations in 2005, Putin unveiled 15 mighty **bronze cannons**, symbolic of the war's 15 fronts. The ensemble is surrounded by fountains and benches, as well as the sweet **Church of St George**.

Museum of the Great Patriotic War

The **Museum of the Great Patriotic War** (Центральный музей Великой Отечественной Войны; www.poklonnayagora.ru; ul Bratiev Fonchenko 10; adult/child ₽250/100; ⊙10am-6pm Tue-Sun Nov-Mar, to 8pm Apr-Oct; Ⓜ Park Pobedy) is the centrepiece of the park and a destination for many children's groups.

The museum contains two impressive memorial rooms: the **Hall of Glory** honours the many heroes of the Soviet Union, while the moving **Hall of Remembrance and Sorrow** is hung with strings of glass-bead 'teardrops' in memory of the fallen.

There are hundreds of exhibits here, including dioramas of every major WWII battle the Russians fought in, as well as weapons, photographs, documentary films, letters and many other authentic wartime memorabilia.

DON'T MISS...

➡ Towering Obelisk

➡ Hall of Remembrance and Sorrow

➡ Memorial to the Victims of the Holocaust

PRACTICALITIES

➡ Kutuzovsky pr

➡ ⊙dawn-dusk

➡ Ⓜ Park Pobedy

Park Pobedy has been a war memorial since the 1960s, but it was dedicated to the War of 1812. It was only in the 1990s that the museum opened and the WWII memorials were built.

METRO ART

Check out the artwork in Park Pobedy metro station. Created by the tireless Zurab Tsereteli, the two mosaics depict events from the War of 1812 and the Great Patriotic War, respectively. This station rivals the more central stations for artistry – and it is also the deepest metro station in the city.

Just east of Park Pobedy, the Triumphal Arch celebrates the defeat of Napoleon in 1812. The original arch was demolished at its site in front of the Belorusskaya metro station during the 1930s and reconstructed here in a fit of post-WWII public spirit.

Exposition of Military Equipment

The unique **Exposition of Military Equipment** (Площадка боевой техники; www.poklonnayagora.ru; adult/child ₽250/100; ☉10am-7pm Tue-Sun; Ⓜ Pak Pobedy) displays more than 300 examples of weapons and military equipment from the World War II era. There are plenty of Red Army tanks, armoured cars and self-propelled artillery, not to mention the famous Katyusha rocket launcher. Every branch of the armed forces is represented, so you'll also see train cars, used by the civil engineering unit, fighter planes and naval destroyers.

The exhibit also includes equipment captured from Germany and Japan, and other equipment that was used by the Allies.

Memorial Synagogue

The **Memorial Synagogue at Poklonnaya Hill** (Мемориальная синагога на Поклонной горе; ☎499-148 1907; www.poklonnaya.ru; ☉by appointment; Ⓜ Park Pobedy) FREE opened in 1998 as a memorial to Holocaust victims, as well as a museum of the Russian Jewry. Admission is with a guide only, so you must make arrangements in advance, especially if you want a tour in English. Not far from the synagogue, a moving **sculpture** commemorates the victims of the Holocaust.

Borodino Museum-Panorama

Park Pobedy is a monument to the Great Patriotic War, but historians find many parallels with the War of 1812, not the least of which is the route taken by attacking and retreating armies. Following the vicious, inconclusive battle at Borodino in August 1812, Moscow's defenders retreated along what are now Kutuzovsky pr and ul Arbat, pursued by Napoleon's Grand Army. Less than 1km east of Park Pobedy is a museum commemorating this event.

The centrepiece is the **Borodino Panorama** (Музей-панорама "Бородинская битва"; www.1812panorama.ru; Kutuzovsky pr 38; adult ₽160; ☉10am-5pm Sat-Wed, 10am-8pm Thu), a pavilion with a giant 360-degree painting of the Borodino battle. Painted by Franz Roubaud, the canvas is 115m around and 15m high. Standing inside this tableau of bloodshed – complete with sound effects – is a powerful way to visualise the event. The museum also contains other artefacts and artwork related to the battle.

In honour of the 200th anniversary of the battle, the museum opened a two-room exhibit dedicated to 'Man & War'. It displays more than 400 items – paintings, weapons, uniforms and more. Multimedia displays bring the battle to life.

TOP SIGHT
CATHEDRAL OF CHRIST THE SAVIOUR

Dominating the skyline along the Prechistenskaya nab, the gargantuan Cathedral of Christ the Saviour (Храм Христа Спасителя) was completed in 1997 – just in time to celebrate Moscow's 850th birthday. It is amazingly opulent, garishly grandiose and truly historic.

The cathedral's sheer size and splendour guarantee its role as a love-it-or-hate-it landmark. Considering Stalin's plan for this site (a Palace of Soviets topped with a 100m statue of Lenin), Muscovites should at least be grateful they can admire the shiny domes of a church instead of the shiny dome of Ilyich's head.

The cathedral sits on the site of an earlier and similar church of the same name, built in the 19th century to commemorate Russia's victory over Napoleon. The original was destroyed in 1931, during Stalin's orgy of explosive secularism. His plan to replace the church with a 315m-high Palace of Soviets never got off the ground – literally. Instead, for 50 years the site served an important purpose: the world's largest swimming pool.

The Cathedral replicates its predecessor in many ways. The central altar is dedicated to the Nativity, while the two side altars are dedicated to Sts Nicholas and Alexander Nevsky. Frescoes around the main gallery depict scenes from the War of 1812, while marble plaques remember the participants.

The original cathedral was built on a hill (since levelled). The contemporary Cathedral has been constructed on a wide base, which contains the smaller (but no less stunning) **Church of the Transfiguration**. This ground-level chapel contains the venerated icon *Christ Not Painted by Hand,* by Sorokin, which was miraculously saved from the original cathedral.

DON'T MISS...

➡ Fresco-covered interior dome

➡ *Christ Not Painted by Hand* in the Church of the Transfiguration

➡ Views from the Patriarshy footbridge

PRACTICALITIES

➡ Map p260

➡ ul Volkhonka 15

➡ ☺1-5pm Mon, 10am-5pm Tue-Sun

➡ Ⓜ Kropotkinskaya

◉ SIGHTS

◉ Arbat

PUSHKIN MUSEUM OF FINE ARTS MUSEUM
See p117.

**MUSEUM OF PRIVATE
COLLECTIONS** MUSEUM
See p118.

**GALLERY OF EUROPEAN &
AMERICAN ART OF THE 19TH
& 20TH CENTURIES** MUSEUM
See p118.

**CATHEDRAL OF CHRIST
THE SAVIOUR** CHURCH
See p121.

SHILOV GALLERY MUSEUM
Map p260 (Галерея Шилова; www.shilov.su; ul Znamenka 5; adult/student ₽160/80; ◉11am-7pm Tue-Sun, noon-9pm Thu; ⓂBiblioteka imeni Lenina) 'What is a portrait? You have to attain not only an absolute physical likeness… but you need to express the inner world of the particular person you are painting.' So Alexander Shilov described his life work as contemporary Russia's most celebrated portrait painter in an interview posted on the gallery's website. Known for his startling realism, the artist provides great insight into his subjects, with some high-level political figures among them.

GLAZUNOV GALLERY MUSEUM
Map p260 (Галерея Глазунова; www.glazunov.ru; ul Volkhonka 13; adult/student ₽80/20; ◉11am-6pm Tue-Sun, to 9pm Thu; ⓂKropotkinskaya) This elaborate Russian Empire–style mansion, opposite the Pushkin Museum of Fine Arts, houses a gallery dedicated to the work of Soviet and post-Soviet artist Ilya Glazunov. Glazunov is famous for his controversial, colourful paintings that depict hundreds of people, places and events from Russian history in one monumental scene. His most famous work is *Eternal Russia (Bechnaya Rossiya)*, while more recent examples are *Mystery of the 20th Century* and *Market of Our Democracy*.

RERIKH MUSEUM MUSEUM
Map p260 (Центр-музей Рериха; www.icr.su; Maly Znamensky per 3/5; admission ₽650; ◉11am-6pm Tue-Sun; ⓂKropotkinskaya) Nikolai Rerikh (known internationally as Nicholas Roerich) was a Russian artist from the late 19th and early 20th centuries, whose fantastical artwork is characterised by rich colours, primitive style and mystical themes. This museum, founded by the artist's son Sergei, includes work by father

---

ARBAT, MY ARBAT

Arbat, my Arbat, you are my calling. You are my happiness and my misfortune.
Bulat Okudzhava

For Moscow's beloved bard Bulat Okudzhava, the Arbat was not only his home, it was his inspiration. Although he spent his university years in Georgia dabbling in harmless verse, it was only upon his return to Moscow – and to his cherished Arbat – that his poetry adopted the free-thinking character for which it is known.

He gradually made the transition from poet to songwriter, stating, 'Once I had the desire to accompany one of my satirical verses with music. I only knew three chords; now, 27 years later, I know seven chords, then I knew three'. While Bulat and his friends enjoyed his songs, composers, singers and guitarists did not, resenting the fact that somebody with no musical training was writing songs. The ill feeling subsided when a well-known poet announced that '…these are not songs. This is just another way of presenting poetry'. And so a new form of art was born. The 1960s were heady times, in Moscow as elsewhere, and Okudzhava inspired a whole movement of liberal-thinking poets to take their ideas to the streets. Vladimir Vysotsky and others – some political, others not – followed in Okudzhava's footsteps, their iconoclastic lyrics and simple melodies drawing enthusiastic crowds all around Moscow.

The Arbat today, crowded with tacky souvenir shops and pricey cafes, bears little resemblance to the haunt of Okudzhava's youth. But its memory lives on in the bards and buskers, painters and poets who perform for strolling crowds on summer nights.

and son, as well as family heirlooms and personal items. The artwork is intriguing: Rerikh spent a lot of time in Central Asia, India and the Altai Mountains of Siberia, so his paintings feature distinctive landscapes and mythological scenes. The building – the 17th-century Lopukhin manor – is a grand setting in which to admire the artwork.

BURGANOV HOUSE MUSEUM

Map p260 (Дом Бурганова; www.burganov.ru; Bolshoy Afanasyevsky per 15; ⊙11am-7pm; ⓂKropotkinskaya) FREE Part studio, part museum, the Burganov House is a unique venue in Moscow, where the craft goes on around you, as you peruse the sculptures and other artwork on display. Comprising several interconnected courtyards and houses, the works of sculptor Alexander Burganov are artfully displayed alongside pieces from the artist's private collection. The surrounding streets of the Arbat and Khamovniki also contain many examples of the artist's work.

HOUSE OF FRIENDSHIP WITH PEOPLES OF FOREIGN COUNTRIES NOTABLE BUILDING

Map p264 (Дом дружбы с народами зарубежных стран; Vozdvizhenka ul 16; ⓂArbatskaya) Studded with seashells, this 'Moorish Castle' was built in 1899 for an eccentric merchant, Arseny Morozov, who was inspired by a real Moorish castle in Spain. The inside (not open to the public) is sumptuous and equally over the top. Morozov's mother, who lived next door, apparently declared of her son's home, 'Until now, only I knew you were mad; now everyone will'.

MELNIKOV HOUSE NOTABLE BUILDING

Map p260 (Дом Мельникова; www.melnikovhouse.org; Krivoarbatsky per 10; ⓂArbatskaya) The only private house built during the Soviet period, the home of Konstantin Melnikov stands as testament to the innovation of the Russian avant-garde. The architect created his unusual home from two interlocking cylinders – an ingenious design that employs no internal load-bearing wall. It was also experimental in its designation of living space, as the whole family slept in one room, divided by narrow wall screens.

The future of Melnikov House is in jeopardy due to the corrosion caused by construction in the surrounding area. Family members are working with the Russian Avantgarde Heritage Preservation Foundation to turn the house into a state-run museum (and thus guarantee its preservation), but the process has been tied up in court for years due to ownership disputes.

PUSHKIN HOUSE-MUSEUM MUSEUM

Map p260 (Дом-музей Пушкина; www.pushkinmuseum.ru; ul Arbat 53; admission ₽120; ⊙10am-6pm Tue-Sun, noon-9pm Thu; ⓂSmolenskaya) After Alexander Pushkin married Natalya Goncharova at the nearby Church of the Grand Ascension, they moved to this charming blue house on the old Arbat. The museum provides some insight into the couple's home life, a source of much Russian romanticism. (The lovebirds are also featured in a statue across the street.)

This place should not be confused with the Pushkin Literary Museum, which focuses on the poet's literary influences.

TOLSTOY LITERARY MUSEUM MUSEUM

Map p260 (Литературный музей Толстого; www.tolstoymuseum.ru; ul Prechistenka 11; adult/student ₽200/100; ⊙11am-6pm Tue-Sun; ⓂKropotkinskaya) The Tolstoy Literary Museum is supposedly the oldest literary memorial museum in the world (founded in 1911). In addition to its impressive reference library, the museum contains exhibits of manuscripts, letters and artwork focusing on Leo Tolstoy's literary influences and output. Family photographs, personal correspondence and artwork from the author's era all provide insight into his work.

This museum undoubtedly contains the largest collection of portraits of the great Russian novelist. Entire exhibits are dedicated to his major novels such as *Anna Karenina* and *War and Peace*. The museum does not contain much memorabilia from Tolstoy's personal life, which is on display at the Tolstoy Estate-Museum (p125).

PUSHKIN LITERARY MUSEUM MUSEUM

Map p260 (Литературный музей Пушкина; www.pushkinmuseum.ru; ul Prechistenka 12/2; admission ₽120; ⊙10am-5pm Tue-Sun; ⓂKropotkinskaya) Housed in a beautiful empire-style mansion dating to 1816, this museum is devoted to the life and work of Russia's favourite poet. Personal effects, family portraits, reproductions of notes and handwritten poetry provide insight into the work of the beloved bard. Perhaps the most interesting exhibit is 'Pushkin & His Time', which puts the poet in a historical context, demonstrating the influence of the Napoleonic Wars, the Decembrists'

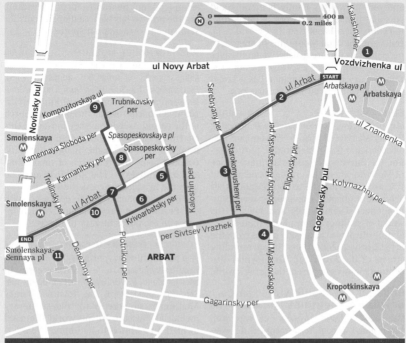

🏃 Neighbourhood Walk
A Stroll down the Stary Arbat

START ARBATSKAYA PL
END SMOLENSKAYA PL
LENGTH 3KM, TWO HOURS

Your stroll down *stary* Arbat ('old' Arbat) starts at traffic-filled Arbatskaya pl. Take note of the **❶ House of Friendship with Peoples of Foreign Countries** (p123), flaunting its incongruous Moorish style.

Strolling up **❷ ul Arbat**, sidewalk art and street performers stand beside souvenir stalls and costumed characters. Wander down some of the quiet lanes, such as **❸ Starokonyushenny per**, which has exemplary art nouveau architectural details.

Around the corner on Sivtsev Vrazhek per, look out for strange and beautiful sculptures dotting the yards and courtyards. They are the work of Alexander Burganov, whose nearby **❹ studio** (p123) is filled with whimsical treasures.

Get a glimpse of the counterculture of the old Arbat at the corner of Krivoarbatsky per and ul Arbat, where the **❺ Viktor**

Tsoy memorial wall is dedicated to the lead singer of the Soviet rock band Kino. Tsoy achieved cult-idol status in 1990 when he died in a car crash at a tragically young age. Further along Krivoarbatsky per, the cylindrical **❻ Melnikov House** (p123) is an important constructivist architectural site.

Back on the Arbat, you can't miss the statue of the bard **❼ Bulat Okudzhava**. Cross the street and continue north on Spasopeskovsky per. This little lane contains architectural gems such as the lovely 17th-century **❽ Church of the Saviour in Peski.** The handsome neoclassical mansion at No 10 is **❾ Spaso House**, famous as the scene of Satan's ball in Bulgakov's *The Master and Margarita.*

Return to the Arbat and the house where Alexander Pushkin and Natalya Goncharova lived after they wed, now holding the **❿ Pushkin House-Museum** (p123). Continue to Smolenskaya pl – the **⓫ Ministry of Foreign Affairs**, a towering Stalinist skyscraper, is one of Stalin's Seven Sisters.

revolt and other historic events. This literary museum provides more in-depth insights than the Pushkin House-Museum (p123) on the Arbat.

TSERETELI GALLERY
MUSEUM

Map p260 (Галерея Церетели; www.tsereteli.ru; ul Prechistenka 19; admission ₽300; ⊘noon-8pm Tue-Sun, to 9pm Thu; ⓂKropotkinskaya) Housed in the 18th-century Dolgoruky mansion, this is the endeavour of the tireless Zurab Tsereteli. The gallery shows how prolific this guy is. The rooms are filled with his often over-the-top sculptures and primitive paintings. If you don't want to spend the time or money exploring the gallery, just pop into the Galereya Khudozhnikov cafe (p127), which is an exhibit in itself.

RUSSIAN ACADEMY OF ARTS
ART GALLERY

Map p260 (Российская академия художеств; www.rah.ru; ul Prechistenka 21; admission varies; ⊘noon-8pm Tue-Sun; ⓂKropotkinskaya) The Russian Academy of Arts hosts rotating exhibits in the historic 19th-century mansion of the Morozov estate. Despite the institutional name, this is part of the Zurab Tsereteli empire; it puts on inspired and varied shows featuring mostly contemporary Russian and foreign artists.

MULTIMEDIA ART MUSEUM
ART GALLERY

Map p260 (Мультимедиа Арт Музей; www.mamm-mdf.ru; ul Ostozhenka 16; admission ₽300; ⓂKropotkinskaya) This slick, modern gallery is home to an impressive photographic library and archives of contemporary and historic photography. The facility usually hosts several simultaneous exhibits, often featuring works from prominent photographers from the Soviet period, as well as contemporary artists.

TOCHKA-G MUSEUM OF EROTIC ART
MUSEUM

Map p260 (Музей эротического искусства Точка-G; www.tochkag.net; ul Novy Arbat 17; admission ₽500; ⊘noon-midnight; ⓂArbatskaya) It means 'G-spot', in case you didn't already guess. Among this gigantic display of erotica, you're bound to find something that will titillate yours. Look for 'artistic' interpretations of sex through the ages, from ancient Kama Sutra–style carvings to contemporary (and perhaps controversial) sexual-political commentary. Also on site: sex shop and cafe! Look for the Om Cafe and enter from the back.

◉ Khamovniki

NOVODEVICHY CONVENT & CEMETERY
CONVENT

See p114.

MOSCOW MUSEUM
MUSEUM

Map p262 (Музей Москвы; www.mosmuseum.ru; Zubovsky bul 2; adult/child ₽300/120; ⊘10am-8pm Tue, Wed & Fri-Sun, 11am-9pm Thu; ♿; ⓂPark Kultury) Formerly the Museum of the History of Moscow, this excellent museum has a new name, a new location and a new mission. The permanent history exhibit demonstrates how the city has spread from its starting point at the Kremlin. It is heavy on artefacts from the 13th and 14th centuries, especially household items and weapons. More exciting, the museum has space to launch thought-provoking temporary exhibits, including artists' and other local perspectives on the city. It's in the former warehouses and garages of the Defense Ministry, with a central courtyard that displays outdoor art and interactive exhibits.

TOLSTOY ESTATE-MUSEUM
MUSEUM

Map p262 (Музей-усадьба Толстого 'Хамовники'; www.tolstoymuseum.ru; ul Lva Tolstogo 21; adult/student ₽200/100; ⊘10am-6pm Tue-Wed & Fri-Sun, noon-8pm Thu; ⓂPark Kultury) Leo Tolstoy's winter home during the 1880s and 1890s now houses an interesting museum dedicated to the writer's home life. While it's not particularly opulent or large, the building is fitting for junior nobility – which Tolstoy was. Exhibits here demonstrate how Tolstoy lived, as opposed to his literary influences, which are explored at the Tolstoy Literary Museum (p123). See the salon where Rachmaninov and Rimsky-Korsakov played piano, and the study where Tolstoy himself wove his epic tales.

CHURCH OF ST NICHOLAS IN KHAMOVNIKI
CHURCH

Map p262 (Церковь Святого Николая в Хамовниках; ul Lva Tolstogo 2; ⓂPark Kultury) This church, commissioned by the weavers' guild in 1676, is among the most colourful in Moscow. The ornate green-and-orange-tapestry exterior houses an equally exquisite interior, rich in frescoes and icons. Leo Tolstoy, who lived up the street, was a parishioner at St Nicholas, which is featured in his novel *Resurrection*. Look also for the old white stone house, built in 1689, which

WORTH A DETOUR

SPARROW HILLS

The green hills in the south of Moscow are known as Sparrow Hills, or Vorobyovy Gory. Running along the south side of the river bank, opposite the tip of the Khamovniki peninsula, there is a pleasant strip of greenery, known as **Vorobyovy Gory Nature Preserve** (Воробёвы горы; www.vorobyovy-gory.ru; Ⓜ Vorobyovy Gory) `FREE`. This wooded hillside is a less developed, less crowded extension of Gorky Park and Neskuchny Garden. The paved path that originates further north continues along the river for several kilometres, and bikes and skates are available to rent here.

Walking trails from the river bank wind up through the woods to **Moscow State University** (Московский Государственный Университет; MGU; Universitetskaya pl; Ⓜ Universitet). From the lookout point, the city spreads out before you. It is an excellent vantage point to see Luzhniki, the huge stadium complex built across the river for the 1980 Olympics, as well as Novodevichy Convent and the Cathedral of Christ the Saviour.

The Stalinist spire of MGU towers over the square. One of the 'Seven Sisters', the building is the result of four years of hard labour by convicts between 1949 and 1953. It boasts an amazing 36 storeys and 33km of corridors. The shining star that sits atop the spire is supposed to weigh 12 tonnes. Among other socialist realist frills on the facade, note the eager students looking forward to communism. The building is not open to the public, which is a shame, because the lobby is equally elaborate, featuring bronze statues of distinguished Soviet scientists.

housed the office of the **weavers' guild and textile shop** (Бывшая ткацкая гильдия; ul Lva Tolstogo 10).

AUTOVILLE MUSEUM
(Автовиль; www.autoville.ru; ul Usachyova 2; admission ₽300; ☺10am-10pm; Ⓜ Sportivnaya) This impressive facility brings together under one roof dozens of exquisite automobiles from around the world and across the decades. The cars, which are in pristine condition, come from some 50 different private collections. Some date back as far as 1907, while some are from the present day. It's a form of art exhibit, presenting the vehicles as objects of great beauty as well as functionality.

✖ EATING

✖ Arbat

⭐**VARENICHNAYA NO 1** RUSSIAN €
Map p260 (www.varenichnaya.ru; ul Arbat 29; mains ₽200-400; ☺10am-midnight; 🍴🐾👶; Ⓜ Arbatskaya) Retro Soviet is all the rage in Moscow, but this old-style Varenichnaya does it right, with books lining the walls, old movies on the B&W TV, and Cold War–era prices. The menu features tasty, filling

vareniki and *pelmeni* (different kinds of dumplings), with sweet and savoury fillings. Bonus: an excellent housemade pickled veggie plate to make you pucker.

RUKKOLA ITALIAN €
Map p260 (Руккола; rucola.com.ru; ul Arbat 19; mains ₽300-500; ☺10am-midnight; 🛜🐾👶; Ⓜ Arbatskaya) Rukkola offers perfectly crispy, artfully topped, thin-crust pizza, which you'd be happy to eat in Napoli, let alone Moscow. A stylish interior, friendly service and affordable prices make this a great find. Lounge on comfy couches and watch the pizza chef toss his pies high in the sky; or take advantage of outdoor seating to watch the action on the Arbat.

CAFE SINDBAD LEBANESE €
Map p264 (Кафе Синдбад; Nikitsky bul 14; mains ₽200-300; ☺noon-midnight; 🐾👶; Ⓜ Arbatskaya) The interior of this cosy restaurant resembles a traditional Lebanese village house, complete with Arabian music and the scent of fresh-brewed cardamom coffee. It's the perfect setting to enjoy Lebanese home cooking, including *kefta*, kebabs, *fettoush* and felafel. And hookahs, obviously.

MOO-MOO CAFETERIA €
Map p260 (My-My; ul Arbat 45/24; mains ₽200-300; ☺10am-11pm; 🛜; Ⓜ Smolenskaya) You will recognise this popular cafeteria by its

black-and-white Holstein-print decor. The cafeteria-style service offers an easy approach to all the Russian favourites. There are other outlets all over town.

⭐ELARDZHI
GEORGIAN €€

Map p260 (Эларджи; ☑495-627 7897; www.ginzaproject.ru; Gagarinsky per 15a; mains ₽600-800; ⬛❖; ⓂKropotkinskaya) Moscow's Georgian restaurants are all very tasty, but this one is also tasteful. You'll be charmed from the moment you enter the courtyard, where live rabbits and lambs greet all comers. Sink into a sofa in the romantic dining room or on the light-filled porch; then feast on delicacies, such as the namesake dish, *elarji* (cornmeal with Sulguni cheese).

⭐ZHURFAK CAFE
RUSSIAN €€

Map p260 (Кафе Журфак; ☑985-212 5050; www.jurfak-cafe.ru; Bolshoy Afanasyevsky per 3; mains ₽500-800; ❖9.30am-11pm; 🕾; ⓂKropotkinskaya) One of our favourite secret spots, this smart cafe is named for the MGU Journalism Faculty, which is located nearby. In summer, there's a shady outside eating area. Otherwise, descend into the comfy basement quarters for lively conversation, traditional food, jazz music (Wednesday and Friday) and a hint of Soviet nostalgia.

CAFE SCHISLIVA
RUSSIAN €€

Map p260 (Кафе Щислива; ul Volkhonka 9; mains ₽400-600; ❖8am-midnight Mon-Fri, 10am-midnight Sat & Sun; 🕾⬛❖; ⓂKropotkinskaya) With a prime location in the midst of the art museums along ul Volkhonka, this small cafe strikes the right balance between trendy and traditional, serving up classic Russian soups, salads and mains, and presenting them in artful and appetising ways. Highlights include hearty breakfast, fresh fruit drinks and an excellent 'business lunch'.

VOSTOCHNY KVARTAL
UZBEK €€

Map p260 (Восточный квартал; ul Arbat 45/24; mains ₽400-800; ✎⬛; ⓂSmolenskaya) Vostochny Kvartal lives up to its name, acting as the 'Eastern Quarter' of the Arbat. Uzbek cooks and plenty of Uzbek patrons are a sign that this is a real-deal place to get your *plov* (meat and rice).

Despite the Arbat address, it's actually on Plotnikov per, behind the Bulat Okudzhava statue.

TIFLIS
GEORGIAN €€

Map p260 (Тифлис; www.tiflis.ru; ul Ostozhenka 32; mains ₽500-900; ⬛; ⓂKropotinskaya) The name of this restaurant comes from the Russian word for the Georgian capital, Tbilisi, and when you enter this restaurant you might think you are there. Its airy balconies and interior courtyards recall a 19th-century Georgian mansion – an atmospheric setting for tasty Georgian fare.

AKADEMIYA
ITALIAN €€

Map p260 (Академия; www.academiya.ru; Volkhonka ul 15/17; lunch ₽400, mains ₽400-800; ❖8am-midnight Mon-Fri, 10am-midnight Sat & Sun; ⓂKropotkinskaya) Sip fancy coffee drinks or munch on crispy-crust pizza and watch the world go by. Steps from the Pushkin Museum of Fine Arts and the Cathedral of Christ the Saviour, this is the perfect place to recover from a day of art and architecture. There is another outlet on **Gogolevsky bul** (Map p260; Gogolevsky bul 33/1; ❖9am-midnight; ⓂArbatskaya), near the old Arbat.

BALKON
ASIAN, ITALIAN €€

Map p260 (Балкон; www.ginzaproject.ru; Novinsky bul 8; mains ₽500-1000; ❖noon-last customer; ✎⬛; ⓂSmolenskaya) On the 7th floor of the Lotte Plaza, this trendy spot has the requisite outdoor terrace (the largest in the city) and superb city views. But it also gives you something to look at right in the dining area: various islands of activity give a glimpse of the preparation of different kinds of food – a 'gastronomic show'.

GALEREYA KHUDOZHNIKOV
FUSION €€€

Map p260 (Галерея художников; ☑495-637 2866; www.gal-h.ru; ul Prechistenka 19; mains ₽800-1200; ❖noon-midnight; ✎⬛; ⓂKropotkinskaya) This fantastical restaurant next to the Tsereteli Gallery lives up to its name, which means 'Artist Gallery'. The huge, light-filled atrium is wallpapered with stained glass and primitive paintings. The menu is a fusion of European and Asian influences. Though it is secondary to the art, the food is well prepared and, appropriately enough, artistically presented.

✗ Khamovniki

GOLUBKA
RUSSIAN €

Map p262 (Голубка; www.golubka-moscow.com; Bolshaya Pirogovskaya ul 53/55; mains ₽300-500; ❖9am-11pm; 🕾✎⬛❖; ⓂSportivnaya)

SKY LOUNGE

High up on the top floor of the Russian Academy of Sciences building (fondly known as 'the Brains') the **Sky Lounge** (www.skylounge.ru; Leninsky prospekt 29, fl 22; ⊘1pm-midnight Sun-Wed, to 1am Thu-Sat; ⓜLeninsky Prospekt) is a sweet spot to go for a sundown drink. The party picks up after dark, when a DJ spins tunes and the Moscow lights twinkle in the distance.

Opposite the entrance to Novodevichy Convent is this sweet place where you can snuggle into big armchairs, enjoy the view out the picture windows, and feast on fresh bread, hot soup and other old-fashioned goodness. The menu is mostly Russian cuisine, but includes pasta, sandwiches and other international favourites.

STOLLE   CAFE €

Map p262 (Штолле; www.stolle.ru; Malaya Pirogovskaya ul 16; mains ₽200-400; ⊘9am-9pm; ⓘ; ⓜSportivnaya) After wandering the grounds and examining the graves at Novodevichy, an energy boost is usually in order. The perfect place for this is Stolle, specialising in tasty Saxon pies. Choose from the selection of savoury and sweet pastries sitting on the counter, or order something more substantial from the sit-down menu.

BLACK MARKET   AMERICAN €€

Map p262 (www.blackmarketcafe.ru; ul Usachyova 2/1; mains ₽500-1000, steaks ₽900-1500; ⊘10am-midnight; ⓐⓘ; ⓜFrunzenskaya) Whether you come for the 'burger bar' or the 'meat market', you'll get your protein at this upscale American bar and grill. Preparation of the meat is perfect, down to the fresh, homemade burger rolls. You'll also appreciate the well-stocked bar, super slick interior and good-looking patrons.

PANE & OLIO   ITALIAN €€€

Map p262 (www.paneolio.ru; ul Timura Frunze 22; pasta ₽600-1000, mains ₽1200-1600; ⊘noon-midnight; ⓐⓘ; ⓜPark Kultury) Forgoing the trends that characterise many Moscow restaurants, Pane & Olio is a classic Italian trattoria, offering homemade pasta, thin-crust pizza and fine grilled meats and fish. A chef named Giuseppe makes the rounds to ensure his guests are sated and happy.

CHEMODAN   SIBERIAN €€€

Map p260 (Чемодан; ☑495-695 3819; www.chemodan-msk.ru; Gogolevsky bul 25; mains ₽900-1500; ⓘ; ⓜKropotkinskaya) A unique opportunity to sample Siberian cuisine (rare, for those of us who don't frequent Siberia). The menu highlights game meat (elk, reindeer, bear and even yak) as well as regional seafood (salmon and crab). The dining room is decorated with old photos and antiques, creating a romantic atmosphere that any adventurer would be happy to return home to.

🍷 DRINKING & NIGHTLIFE

🍸 Arbat

ZHIGULI BEER HALL   BREWERY

Map p260 (Пивной зал Жигули; www.zhiguli.net; ul Novy Arbat 11; 500mL beers ₽210-350; ⊘10am-2am Sun-Thu, 10am-4am Fri & Sat; ⓐ; ⓜArbatskaya) It's hard to classify this old-style *stolovaya* (cafeteria) that happens to brew great beer. The place harks back to the Soviet years, when a popular bar by the same name was a Novy Arbat institution. The minimalist decor and cafeteria-style service recalls the heyday, although this place has been updated with big-screen TVs and a separate table-service dining room.

GOGOL-MOGOL   CAFE

Map p260 (Гоголь-Моголь; www.gogol-mogol.ru; Gagarinsky per 6; desserts ₽200-300; ⊘10am-11pm; ⓐ; ⓜKropotkinskaya) The front door is painted with a cake recipe in French, which should give you a pretty good idea of what you are getting into. There are a few lunch items on the menu, but this is really a place to come to indulge in rich French pastries and sweet drinks such as the namesake Gogol-Mogol (which is like egg-nog, but it rhymes).

🍸 Khamovniki

GAVROCHE WINE BAR   WINE BAR

Map p262 (Винный бар Гаврош; www.thewine-bar.ru; ul Timura Frunze 11; ⊘9am-midnight Sun-Wed, 9am-2am Thu-Sat; ⓐ; ⓜPark Kultury) First came the beer bars, and then the cocktail lounges. It only stands to reason that wine bars would be next. This one is stylish but not pretentious, with exposed brick walls and wines listed on a blackboard behind the bar. You'll find dozens of vintages from around the world, with a menu of Med-style small plates to complement them.

CARABAS
LOUNGE

Map p262 (www.carabasbar.ru; ul Lva Tolstogo 18; ⊙noon-6am; 🖥; Ⓜ Park Kultury) Spacious, elegant and eclectic, the interior of Carabas somehow blends leather armchairs and crystal chandelier balls with exposed brick and concrete walls, and neon signs. It's a pricey but popular spot to sip a cocktail in high style, groove to DJ-spun tunes, or grab a late-night bite to eat.

SOHO ROOMS
CLUB

Map p262 (☑495-988 7474; www.sohorooms. ru; Savvinskaya nab 12; ⊙club 11pm-last guest, restaurant 24hr; Ⓜ Sportivnaya) Still one of the hottest clubs in Moscow, this uberexclusive nightclub offers scantily clad women, cool music and expensive cocktails. Of course, many clubs in Moscow can boast such things, but only Soho Rooms has a swimming pool and a poolside terrace, too. Face control.

☆ ENTERTAINMENT

RHYTHM BLUES CAFE
LIVE MUSIC

Map p260 (Блюз Кафе Ритм; ☑499-697 6008; www.rhythm-blues-cafe.ru; Starovagankovsky per; ⊙shows 9pm; Ⓜ Aleksandrovsky Sad) If your dog got run over by a pick-up truck, you might find some comfort at the Rhythm Blues Cafe, with down-and-out live music every night, plus cold beer and a whole menu of salty cured meats. Great fun and a friendly vibe, with people actually listening to the music. Book a table if you want to sit down.

GELIKON OPERA
OPERA

Map p260 (Геликон опера; ☑495-695 6584; www.helikon.ru; ul Novy Arbat 11; tickets ₽300-3000; ⊙box office noon-2pm & 2.30-7pm; Ⓜ Arbatskaya) Named after famous Mt Helicon, home to the muses and inspiration for musicians, this opera company is unique in Moscow for its innovative, even experimental, opera performances. Director Dmitry Bertman is known for 'combining musical excellence with artistic risk', according to one local dramaturge. The Gelikon's 250-seat theatre provides an intimate setting that allows for some interaction between the performers and the audience.

ENTERTAINMENT FOR LITTLE PEOPLE

Russia's rich tradition of theatre and entertainment extends to all segments of the population, even the little people. If you are travelling with children, you are likely to find yourself in the southwest corner of the city, which is home to some of the best options for kids' entertainment.

Bolshoi Circus on Vernadskogo (☑495-930 0300; www.bolshoicircus.ru; pr Vernadskogo 7; tickets ₽600-3000; ⊙shows 7pm Wed-Fri, 1pm & 5pm Sat & Sun; 👶; Ⓜ Universitet) This huge circus holds 3400 spectators, but the steep pitch means that everyone has a view of the action. The company includes hundreds of performers – mostly acrobats, but some animals too (bears, sea lions, monkeys). It is a great spectacle that is certain to entertain and amaze.

Kuklachev Cat Theatre (Театр кошек Куклачёва; ☑495-243 4005; www.kuklachev.ru; Kutuzovsky pr 25; tickets ₽300-2000; ⊙shows noon, 2pm or 4pm Thu-Sun, daily in summer; 👶; Ⓜ Kutuzovskaya) At this unusual theatre, acrobatic cats do all kinds of stunts for the audience's delight. Director Yury Kuklachev says: 'We do not use the word "train" here because it implies forcing an animal to do something, and you cannot force cats to do anything they don't want to. We *play* with the cats.'

Moscow Children's Musical Theatre (Детский Музыкальный Театр им Н.И.Сац; ☑495-930 7021; www.teatr-sats.ru; pr Vernadskogo 5; tickets ₽200-1200; ⊙times vary Wed-Sun Sep-Jun; 👶; Ⓜ Universitet) Founded by theatre legend Natalya Sats in 1965, this was the country's first children's theatre. Apparently, Sats was the inspiration for Prokofiev's famous rendition of *Peter and the Wolf*, which is still among the most popular performances here. But all shows are entertaining and educational, with actors appearing in costume beforehand to talk with the children.

WORTH A DETOUR

YUDASHKIN

Russia's best-known fashion designer is Valentin Yudashkin, whose classy clothes are on display at the Louvre and the Met, as well as the State History Museum in Moscow (look but don't touch!). If you wish to try something on, head to this swanky **boutique** (www.yudashkin.com; Kutuzovsky pr 19; MKievskaya), which seems like a museum but has many things that you can buy.

LUZHNIKI STADIUM   SPORT

Map p262 (Олимпийский Комплекс Лужники; 495-780 0808; www.luzhniki.ru; Luzhnetskaya nab 24; MSportivnaya) This giant stadium (home to FC Torpedo) is the capital's largest, seating nearly 80,000. It was the chief venue for the 1980 Summer Olympics, and more recently has been selected to host the final game of the 2018 World Cup.

🛍 SHOPPING

ASSOCIATION OF ARTISTS OF THE DECORATIVE ARTS   SOUVENIRS

Map p260 (Ассоциация художников декоративно-прикладного искусства; AHDI; www.ahdi.ru; ul Arbat 21; 11am-8pm; MArbatskaya) Look for the ceramic plaque and the small sign indicating the entrance to this 'exposition hall', which is actually a cluster of small shops, each one showcasing arts and crafts by local artists. In addition to paintings and pottery, the most intriguing items are the gorgeous knit sweaters, woolly coats and embroidered dresses – all handmade and unique.

RUSSIAN EMBROIDERY & LACE   SOUVENIRS

Map p260 (Русская вышивка и кружево; www.yp.ru/vishivka; ul Arbat 31; 11am-8pm Mon-Sat, 11am-5pm Sun; MSmolenskaya) Considering the lack of flashy signs and kitsch, it would be easy to miss this plain shopfront on the Arbat. But inside there are treasures galore, from elegant napery to delicate handmade sweaters and embroidered shirts.

BURO NAHODOK   ART GALLERY

Map p260 (Бюро находок; www.buro-nahodok.ru; Smolensky bul 7/9; 10am-9pm Mon-Fri, 11am-8pm Sat & Sun; MPark Kultury) In 2003

three Moscow artists opened this shop to sell their fun and funky gifts and souvenirs. It was the first of what would become a network of artists' cooperatives around the city.

You'll find quirky knick-knacks, clothing and home decor, most exhibiting more than a hint of irony.

DOM KNIGI   BOOKS

Map p264 (Дом Книги; www.mdk-arbat.ru; Novy Arbat 8; 9am-11pm Mon-Fri, 10am-11pm Sat & Sun; MArbatskaya) Among the largest bookshops in Moscow, Dom Knigi has a selection of foreign-language books to rival any other shop in the city, not to mention travel guidebooks, maps, and reference and souvenir books. This huge, crowded place holds regularly scheduled readings, children's programs and other bibliophilic activities.

ARTEFACT GALLERY CENTRE   ART GALLERY

Map p260 (ul Prechistenka 30; 10am-6pm, individual gallery hours vary; MKropotkinskaya) Near the Russian Academy of Art, the Artefact Gallery Centre is a sort of art mall, housing a few dozen galleries under one roof. Look for paintings, sculptures, dolls, pottery and other kinds of art that people actually might like to buy, as opposed to the more avant-garde exhibits at other art centres.

RUSSKIE CHASOVYE TRADITSII   JEWELLERY

Map p260 (Русские часовые традиции; www.smirs.com; ul Arbat 11; 10am-9pm; MArbatskaya) If you are in the market for a fancy timepiece, pop into the Arbat outlet of 'Russian Watch Traditions'. On this touristy drag, these small shops cater primarily to tourists, so they carry exclusively Russian brands, including Aviator, Buran, Vostok, Poljot, Romanoff and Denissov.

CHAPURIN BOUTIQUE   CLOTHING & ACCESSORIES

Map p262 (www.chapurin.com; Savvinskaya nab 21; 10am-10pm; MSportivnaya) Fashion maven Igor Chapurin got his start designing theatre costumes, but his creativity knows no bounds: in addition to men's and women's clothing, he has lines of children's clothing and sportswear. His signature style? Rich fabrics, playful textures and solid colours.

Zamoskvorechie

Neighbourhood Top Five

1 Strolling, cycling, roll-erblading, dancing, drinking, sunbathing, playing petanque and otherwise being hyperactive (or hyper-lazy, if you wish) in the revived and gentrified **Gorky Park** (p133).

2 Spending a half-day at the **Tretyakov Gallery** (p135), admiring the

superb collection of Russian icons, the cutting social commentary of the Peredvizhniki (Wanderers), the whimsy of the symbolists, and other prerevolution-ary art.

3 Watching the day and short summer night go by from one of **Red October's** (p137) rooftop bars.

4 Walking through a forest of sculptures, including fallen Soviet idols at **Art Muzeon Sculpture Park** (p137).

5 Escaping to **Kolomenskoe** (p141) – a patch of idyllic countryside not far from the centre.

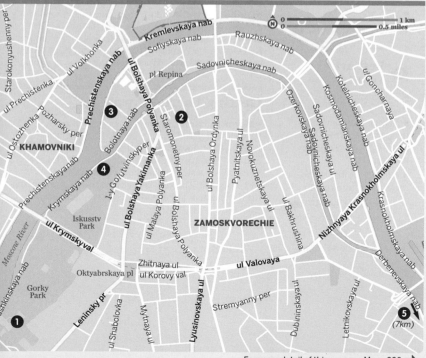

For more detail of this area see Map p266

Lonely Planet's Top Tip

The northern part of Zamoskvorechie – including the Red October complex on Bolotny Island – is easiest to access by walking over the Bolshoy Moskvoretsky most from the Kremlin or walking over the Patriarshy most from the Cathedral of Christ the Saviour.

✗ Best Places to Eat

➡ Mizandari (p140)

➡ Produkty (p140)

➡ Chugunny most (p140)

For reviews, see p140 ➡

🍷 Best Places to Drink

➡ Bar Strelka (p142)

➡ Le Boule (p142)

➡ WT4 (p142)

For reviews, see p142 ➡

◉ Best Art Venues

➡ Tretyakov Gallery (p135)

➡ Garage Museum of Contemporary Art (p137)

➡ Art Muzeon Sculpture Park (p137)

➡ Lumiere Brothers Photography Centre (p138)

For reviews, see p137 ➡

Explore: Zamoskvorechie

With its markedly low old buildings, quaint courtyards and a multitude of onion domes, Zamoskvorechie is a bit of a provincial Russian town that somehow ended up inside central Moscow. The people responsible for its outlook and for the lingering old-world ambience are *kuptsy* (merchants) who populated the area until the 19th century and had completely different lifestyles and habits to the nobility living across the river. Their most outstanding legacy is Tretyakov Gallery, containing the largest collection of Russian art.

But it is in this district that the face of the new, cool, liveable, sophisticated Moscow is being born. The fledgling gentrification belt is now spreading along the river from the red-brick buildings of the Red October chocolate factory (Moscow's inner hipster galaxy) to the revived Gorky Park, via the freshly-renovated Krymskaya Naberezhnaya embankment. Dump your cliches into the river – welcome to post-historical Moscow!

Local Life

➡**Markets** The Danilovsky Market is a trek from the centre but it's worth it, especially in the summer and early autumn, when stalls are filled with fruit and berries you can't hope to find in a supermarket.

➡**Outdoor activities** Closed for vehicles, but welcoming cyclists, rollerbladers and pedestrians, Moscow's answer to London's South Bank stretches for 8km from Red October to Vorobyovy Gory via Gorky Park, which offers a few zillion activities, from petanque to dancing.

Getting There & Away

➡**Metro** Three different metro lines cut through Zamoskvorechie in a north–south direction. The green Zamoskvoretskaya line has stops at Novokuznetskaya and Paveletskaya. The orange Kaluzhsko-Rizhskaya line also has a stop at Novokuznetskaya, as well as at Oktyabrskaya. The grey Serpukhovsko-Timiryazevskaya line has stations at Polyanka and Serpukhovskaya.

TOP SIGHT
GORKY PARK

Moscow's main escape from the city within the city is not your conventional expanse of nature preserved deep inside an urban jungle. It is not a fun fair either, though it used to be one. Its official name says it all – Maxim Gorky's Central Park of Culture & Leisure (Парк Горького). That's exactly what it provides: culture and leisure in all shapes and forms. Designed by avant-garde architect Konstantin Melnikov as a piece of Communist utopia in the 1920s, these days it showcases the enlightened transformation Moscow has undergone in the recent past.

DON'T MISS
➡ Olive Beach
➡ Le Boule

PRACTICALITIES
➡ Map p266
➡ ⊘24hr
➡ 🛜 🚹
➡ ⓂOktyabrskaya

Activities

The list of activities on offer could easily cover a Rosetta Stone, although on sunny days thousands opt for complete inactivity either atop one of the giant cushions scattered around the park or on the sundecks at the **Olive Beach** (Map p266; sunbed per day ₽1000; ⊘10am-11pm) located on the embankment by the pedestrian bridge.

Cyclists and rollerbladers create a bit of a traffic jam inside the park during weekends, but they can enjoy a vehicle-free, 16km riverside ride to Vorobyovy Gory and back. There are several bicycle- and skate-rental places around the park, with one conveniently located under the pedestrian bridge.

Sport fans will find dedicated areas for beach volleyball, urban and extreme sports, table tennis and even petanque – played by local Francophones and hipsters at Le Boule (p142) bar.

In summer, the park is totally engulfed in the dance craze – young people gather in their hundreds to learn every conceivable type of dance, from acrobatic rock 'n' roll to salsa and polka. The epicentre of this madness is located on the boardwalk under **Novoandreyevsky most**, but there are a few more dancing venues inside the park.

When the temperatures drop, Gorky Park becomes a winter wonderland. The ponds are flooded, turning the park into the city's biggest **ice-skating rink** (Парк Горького; Map

NESKUCHNY GARDEN

As you head west along the river, past Andreyevsky most, you'll find yourself in what looks more like a conventional park. Neskuchny is much less crowded than Gorky Park, full of shade, and criss-crossed by walking and cycling paths that go up and down through deep ravines.

Neskuchny Garden contains several sports facilities, including tennis courts, as well as open-air table tennis and chess clubs. There is also an open-air gym.

LOST IN TRANSLATION

Neskuchny literally means 'not dull', which sounds as weird in Russian as it does in English. 'Sad' simply means 'gardens' – it's not sad at all!

p266; ☑495-237 1266; ul Krymsky val; morning/evening Tue-Thu ₽200/300, Fri-Sun 300/500; ☺10am-3pm & 5-11pm Tue-Sun; Ⓜ Park Kultury). Tracks are created for cross-country skiers to circumnavigate the park. Ice skates and cross-country skis are available to rent. Bring your passport.

Culture

After decades spent as a tacky and neglected fun fair, Gorky Park is once again a real Park Kultury (or park of culture) as Muscovites normally call it. It is the venue for almost weekly musical, theatre, art and culinary festivals.

Art objects pop up throughout the park as part of various exhibitions and festivals, but Darya Zhukova's Garage Museum of Contemporary Art (p137) plays the flagship role. Unfortunately little is preserved of the pre-war Soviet sculptures that adorned the park's alleys, but you will find a bronze female swimmer about to jump into the Moscow River, if you walk further into Neskuchny Garden.

In Neskuchny Garden the open-air **Stas Namin Theatre** (Театр Стаса Намина; Green Theatre; Map p266; stasnamintheatre.ru; ul Krymsky Val 9, str 33) hosts concerts as well as its own performances, mostly from the rock-opera genre. The new open-air **Pioner cinema** shows films after dark, but almost all are entirely in Russian.

Bar Hopping

Gorky Park's new management is on a mission to change the city's food and drink culture, so all the coolest culinary projects are welcome here. There are a multitude of eateries around the park from small kiosks, such as AC/DC in Tbilisi (p140), to large restaurants and open-air bars, the most popular ones being Lebedinoe Ozero (p142) and Le Boule (p142).

TOP SIGHT
TRETYAKOV GALLERY

Designed by Russian-revivalist artist Viktor Vasnetsov to resemble an exotic boyar castle, the Tretyakov Gallery (Главный отдел Государственной Третьяковской галереи) houses the world's biggest collection of Russian icons and prerevolutionary Russian art.

The Collection

The tour of the gallery begins on the 2nd floor, where 18th- to 20th-century artists are exhibited. On the 1st floor, visitors are treated to more *fin de siècle* art before finding themselves surrounded by medieval icons.

Second Floor

Rooms 1 through 7 display paintings and sculpture from the 18th century, while rooms 8 through 15 have landscapes, character paintings and portraits from the 19th century. The real gems of the collection, however, start with room 16. In the 1870s daring artists started to address social issues, founding the **Peredvizhniki** (Wanderers) movement.

Room 17 is dedicated to **Vasily Perov**, one of the founders of the movement. Look for his portrait of Dostoevsky and the moving painting *Troika*, with its stark depiction of child labour. Others associated with the movement were **Ivan Kramskoi** (room 20) and **Ivan Shishkin** (room 25).

Viktor Vasnetsov (room 26) paints fantastical depictions of fairy tales and historical figures. His painting *Bogatyry* (Heroes) is perhaps the best example from the revivalist movement, although *A Knight at the Crossroads* is more dramatic. By contrast, **Vasily Vereshchagin** (room 27) is known for his harsh realism, especially in battle scenes. **Vasily Surikov** (room 28) excels at large-scale historical scenes. *Boyarina*

DON'T MISS...

➡ *Vladimir Icon of the Mother of God*

➡ *The Princess of the Dream*

➡ *A Knight at the Crossroads*

➡ *Ivan the Terrible and his Son Ivan*

PRACTICALITIES

➡ Map p266

➡ www.tretyakovgallery.ru/en/

➡ Lavrushinsky per 10

➡ adult/student ₽400/250

➡ ⏰10am-6pm Tue, Wed, Sat & Sun, to 9pm Thu & Fri, ticket office closes 1hr before closing

➡ Ⓜ Tretyakovskaya

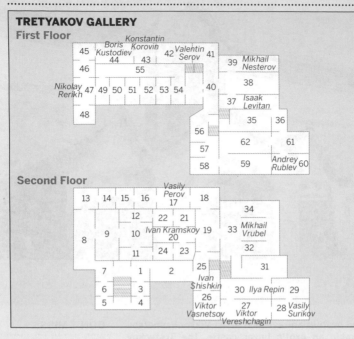

TRETYAKOV GALLERY

First Floor

Second Floor

Morozova captures the history of the schism in the Orthodox Church and how it tragically played out for one family.

Ilya Repin (rooms 29 and 30) is perhaps the most beloved Russian realist painter. *Ivan the Terrible and his Son Ivan* is downright chilling. Room 31 has a few masterpieces by **Nicholas Ge**, another founder of the Peredvizhniki movement. **Mikhail Vrubel** (rooms 32 to 34) was a symbolist-era artist who defies classification. One entire wall is covered with his fantastic art nouveau mural *The Princess of the Dream*.

First Floor

A selection of **Isaac Levitan**'s landscapes is in room 37. **Mikhail Nesterov** (room 39) combines symbolism with religious themes. *The Vision of the Youth Bartholomew* depicts an episode from the life of St Sergei of Radonezh (patron saint of Russia). In rooms 41 and 42, **Valentin Serov** was the most celebrated portraitist of his time.

Moving into the 20th century, artists began to reject the rules of realism. Room 43 displays **Konstantin Korovin's** foray into Impressionism. **Alexander Golovin** and **Boris Kustodiev** represent the 'World of Art' art nouveau movement in room 44. In room 46, **Pavel Kuznetsov** was the founder of the Blue Rose, the Moscow group of symbolist artists. **Nikolai Rerikh** (Nicholas Roerich) shows off his fantastical storytelling style in room 47. Rooms 49 to 54 contain drawings, watercolours, pastels and prints, with rotating exhibits of works from the museum's permanent collection. Room 55 houses the **Treasury**, with its collection of metals, jewellery, embroidery and precious knick-knacks.

Icons are found on the 1st floor in rooms 56 to 62. Andrei Rublyov's *Holy Trinity* (1420s) from Sergiev Posad, regarded as Russia's greatest icon, is in room 60. Within the museum grounds is the **Church of St Nicholas in Tolmachi** (Map p266; ☉noon-4pm Tue-Sun), which was transferred to this site and restored in 1997. The centrepiece is the revered 12th-century *Vladimir Icon of the Mother of God,* protector of all Russia, which was transferred here from the Assumption Cathedral in the Kremlin.

👁 SIGHTS

GORKY PARK   PARK
See p133.

STATE TRETYAKOV GALLERY   GALLERY
See p135.

RED OCTOBER   ARTS CENTRE
Map p266 (Завод Красный Октябрь; Bersenevskaya nab; M Kropotkinskaya) **FREE** This defiant island of Russian modernity and European-ness is a vibrant arts centre filled with cool bars, restaurants and galleries. With an aptly revolutionary name, the former Red October chocolate factory looks straight into Kremlin's eyes – a vivid reminder that Russia is not all about totalitarian control and persecution.

Made of red brick, like its imperial vis-à-vis across the river, the factory was built by German national Theodor Ferdinand von Einem and proudly bore his name until the Bolshevik takeover. Production was suspended in the noughties when its conversion into Moscow's hottest restaurant and entertainment area began. These days it is a key part of the hipster belt stretching along the river into Gorky Park and beyond. Come here to rub shoulders with Moscow's smart, cool and beautiful in one of the rooftop bars or check out an exhibition at the flagship Strelka Institute (p145) or Lumiere Brothers Photography Centre (p138).

Sadly, Red October might be losing a part of its pull as the embattled independent Dozhd TV channel (that is, half of the trendy crowd in local bars) is moving out and the pro-Putin LifeNews channel is taking over the premises.

**ART MUZEON & KRYMSKAYA
NABEREZHNAYA**   SCULPTURE PARK
Map p266 (ul Krymsky val 10; M Park Kultury) **FREE** Now fully revamped and merged with the wonderfully reconstructed Krymskaya Naberezhnaya embankment, **Art Muzeon** is a motley collection of (mostly kitschy) sculpture and monuments to Soviet idols (Stalin, Sverdlov, a selection of Lenins and Brezhnevs) that were ripped from their pedestals in the post-1991 wave of anti-Soviet feeling. All of these stand in a lovely garden with boardwalks and many inviting benches.

Moscow's answer to London's South Bank, **Krymskaya Naberezhnaya** features wave-shaped street architecture with many Scandinavian-style wooden elements, beautiful flower beds and a moody fountain that ejects water randomly from many holes in the ground – a sure way to make children (and some adults) run and laugh unstoppably for hours on a hot sunny day.

Moored here, the cruise ship **Valery Bryusov** is being converted into an art and educational venue, complete with a cinema, a musical venue, cafes, a co-working space and even a barber shop!

The **Vernisage**, an artists' market, is about the only place left here from the old days. The embankment begins near the tip of Bolotny Island, where the gargantuan **statue of Peter the Great** (Bersenevskaya nab; M Polyanka) created by the controversial sculptor Zurab Tsereteli surveys the area from a giant column. We'd call it fully pedestrianised, if not for the cyclists and in-line skaters who often create what resembles a very normal Moscow traffic jam. There is a shop renting bicycles and in-line skating equipment. This is the starting point of the vehicle-free 8km route that runs through Gorky Park, Neskuchny Garden and Vorobyovy Gory.

**GARAGE MUSEUM OF
CONTEMPORARY ART**   GALLERY
Map p266 (www.garageccc.com; ul Krymsky val 9; adult/student ₽300/150; ⏱11am-9pm Mon-Thu; M Oktyabrskaya) The brainchild of Moscow art fairy Darya Zhukova, incidentally the girlfriend of oligarch Roman Abramovich, has seen better times, but it remains one of the hottest modern art venues in the capital. Retaining its original name, Garage is now housed in a temporary, though not-able, Gorky Park structure – architect Sigeru Ban used recycled paper as the construction material.

It vacated the spectacular premises of Bakhmetyev Garage in northern Moscow, which is now used by the Jewish Museum, but the name stuck. The construction of a large permanent building nearby its current location in the park was announced some years ago, but appears to have stalled.

BOLOTNAYA PLOSHCHAD   SQUARE
Map p266 (Болотная площадь) Named after the swamp it used to be, Bolotnaya has a lot to tell about those who rebelled against the Kremlin, which views it warily from the other side of the river. Comprising gardens and a bulging section of the city's main avenue, flanked by the grim constructivist Dom na Naberezhnoy, it was the scene of

DARK TIMES ENLIGHTENED

In September 2011 Vladimir Putin decided to run for a third presidential term; meanwhile, many Muscovites decided they had had enough of Putin. Later that year, suspicions of a rigged parliamentary election prompted a series of demonstrations and marches, mostly held on Bolotnaya ploshchad. The protests were peaceful and good-natured, with participants bearing funny posters, such as the one reading 'We are 146%' (both a nod to the Occupy NY slogan, and a reference to the fact that at one point during the election coverage, state TV showed a digram indicating Putin's party had 146% of the vote).

Young, middle-class urbanites (often referred to as *khipstery* – hipsters), were in the lead, full of bright ideas. A desire to turn Moscow into a more liveable and modern city was high on their agenda, although their main concern was for fair elections.

On 6 May 2012 – the eve of Putin's inauguration – a protest march on Bolotnaya was brutally dispersed in what marked the start of a wave of repression. Dozens of rank and file activists ended up in prison on seemingly dubious charges.

But with the whip, came the carrot. Seizing the opposition activists' agenda, Moscow mayor Sergei Sobyanin embarked on an ambitious program to turn the city into a modern European capital. Vice-mayor Sergei Kapkov led the drive. The former right-hand man of oligarch Roman Abramovich, was responsible for the incredible transformation of Gorky Park into a modern and attractive space. His enlightened approach eventually spread to all of Moscow's parks, while the city authorities continued to help industrial redevelopment projects, such as Winzavod (p148) and Flakon (p92).

As gentrification engulfed the city, the anti-Putin protests subsided. Moscow hipsters did sympathise with Ukrainian protesters who toppled president Viktor Yanukovych. But the standoff in Kiev was too long, too nervous and too violent for their tastes. As the political regime became more oppressive, they retreated back into the golden cage of art lectures at Strelka, Winzavod exhibitions and petanque games at Gorky Park. The feeling that this situation cannot last for long is widespread; many young, cultured Muscovites fear they will eventually be chased out of their hipster Eden.

---

the public executions of the leaders of two of Russia's main peasant uprisings – Stepan Razin and Emelyan Pugachev.

Centuries later, prominent Bolsheviks, who proudly moved into the newly built **Dom na Naberezhnoy** in the 1920s, were disappearing from their flats almost every night in Stalin's purges. A small **museum** (Map p266; ☑495-959 0317; www.museumdom. narod.ru; ul Serafimovicha 2; ⊙5-8pm Wed, 2-6pm Sat; MKropotkinskaya) **FREE** tells the story of the house's most prominent inhabitants. The gardens draw punks, hippies and *Lord of the Rings* re-enactment fans on summer nights. It contains an intriguing sculpture by Mikhail Shemyakin, *Children are Victims of Adults' Vices* (with the vices depicted in delightful detail). In 2012, it became the site of anti-Putin protests commonly known as the Bolotnaya movement.

NEW TRETYAKOV GALLERY   GALLERY
Map p266 (Новая Третьяковская галерея; www.tretyakovgallery.ru/en/; ul Krymsky val 10; adult/student ₽400/250; ⊙10am-6pm Tue-Wed

& Sat & Sun, 10am-9pm Thu & Fri, ticket office closes 1hr before; MPark Kultury) The premier venue for 20th-century Russian art is this branch of the State Tretyakov Gallery, better known as the New Tretyakov. This place has much more than the typical socialist realist images of muscle-bound men wielding scythes, and busty women milking cows (although there's that too). The exhibits showcase avant-garde artists such as Malevich, Kandinsky, Chagall, Goncharova and Popova.

In the same building as the Tretyakov, **TsDKh**, or Central House of Artists, is a huge exhibit space used for contemporary-art shows. A number of galleries are also housed here on a permanent basis.

LUMIERE BROTHERS
PHOTOGRAPHY CENTRE   GALLERY
Map p266 (www.lumiere.ru; Bolotnaya nab 3, Bldg 1; ⊙noon-9pm Tue-Sun) One of the main pilgrimage destinations for photography fanatics, is this modern and competently curated space that hosts frequently changing exhibi-

tions of Russian and Western photo artists. There is a nice shop selling photo albums and postcards in the premises.

CHURCH OF ST JOHN
THE WARRIOR   CHURCH

Map p266 (Церковь Иоанна Воина; ul Bolshaya Yakimanka 48; MOktyabrskaya) The finest of all Zamoskvorechie's churches mixes Moscow and European baroque styles, resulting in a melange of shapes and colours. It was commissioned by Peter the Great in thanks for his 1709 victory over Sweden at Poltava. The gilt, wood-carved iconostasis was originally installed in the nearby **Church of the Resurrection at Kadashi** (Церковь Воскрессения на Кадашах; Map p266; 2-y Kadashevsky per 7).

BAKHRUSHIN THEATRE MUSEUM   MUSEUM

Map p266 (Театральный музей Бахрушина; www.gctm.ru; ul Bakhrushina 31/12; adult/student ₽200/100; ☉noon-7pm Tue-Wed & Fri-Sun, 1-9pm Thu; MPaveletskaya) Russia's foremost stage museum, founded in 1894, is in the neo-Gothic mansion on the north side of Paveletskaya pl. The museum exhibits all things theatrical – stage sets, costumes, scripts and personal items belonging to some of Russia's stage greats. The exhibits are not limited only to drama, also tracing the development of opera, ballet and puppetry. Highlights include the costumes and stage set from *Boris Godunov* (starring the famous bass, Fyodor Shalyapin) and the ballet shoes worn by Vaslav Nijinsky.

DANILOV MONASTERY   MONASTERY

(Даниловский монастырь; msdm.ru; ul Danilovsky val; ☉7am-7pm; MTulskaya) **FREE** The headquarters of the Russian Orthodox Church stands behind white fortress walls. On holy days this place seethes with worshippers murmuring prayers, lighting candles and ladling holy water into jugs at the tiny chapel inside the gates. The Danilovsky Monastery was built in the late 13th century by Daniil, the first Prince of Moscow, as an outer city defence.

The monastery was repeatedly altered over the next several hundred years, and served as a factory and a detention centre during the Soviet period. It was restored in time to replace Sergiev Posad as the Church's spiritual and administrative centre, and became the official residence of the Patriarch during the Russian Orthodoxy's millennium celebrations in 1988.

Enter beneath the pink **St Simeon Stylite Gate-Church** on the north wall. The oldest and busiest church is the **Church of the Holy Fathers of the Seven Ecumenical Councils**, where worship is held continuously from 10am to 5pm daily. Founded in the 17th century and rebuilt repeatedly, the church contains several chapels on two floors: the main one upstairs is flanked by side chapels to St Daniil (on the northern side) and Sts Boris and Gleb (south). On the ground level, the small main chapel is dedicated to the Protecting Veil, and the northern one to the prophet Daniil.

Built in the 1830s, the yellow neoclassical **Trinity Cathedral** is an austere counterpart to the other buildings. West of the cathedral are the patriarchate's External Affairs Department and, at the far end of the grounds, the Patriarch's Official Residence. Against the north wall, to the east of the residence, there's a 13th-century **Armenian carved-stone cross**, or *khachkar*, a gift from the Armenian Church. The church guesthouse, in the southern part of the monastery grounds, has been turned into the elegant Danilovskaya Hotel (p181).

DONSKOY MONASTERY   MONASTERY

(Донской монастырь; ☏495-952 1646; www.donskoi.org; Donskaya ul; MShabolovskaya) Moscow's youngest, Donskoy Monastery was founded in 1591 as the home of the *Virgin of the Don* icon (now in the Tretyakov Gallery). This icon is credited with the victory in the 1380 battle of Kulikovo; it's also said that, in 1591, the Tatar Khan Giri retreated without a fight after the icon showered him with burning arrows in a dream.

Most of the monastery, surrounded by a brick wall with 12 towers, was built between 1684 and 1733 under Regent Sofia and Peter the Great. The **Virgin of Tikhvin Church** over the north gate, built in 1713 and 1714, is one of the last examples of Moscow baroque. In the centre of the grounds is the large brick **New Cathedral**, built between 1684 and 1693. Just to its south is the smaller **Old Cathedral**, dating from 1591 to 1593.

When burials in central Moscow were banned after the 1771 plague, the Donskoy Monastery became a graveyard for the nobility, and it is littered with elaborate tombs and chapels. Donskoy Monastery is a five-minute walk from Shabolovskaya metro. Go south along ul Shabolovka, then take the first street west, 1-y Donskoy proezd.

EATING

★MIZANDARI
GEORGIAN €

Map p266 (☑8-903-263 9990; nab Bolotnaya 5, str 1; mains ₽300-400; ⊗11am-11pm; ⋈Kropotkinskaya) Georgian restaurants in Moscow tend to be either expensive or tacky. This small family-run place is neither. Come with friends and order a selection of appetisers, such as *pkhali* and *lobio* (both made of walnut paste), *khachapuri* (cheese pastry) and *kharcho* (spicy lamb soup). Bless you if you can still accomodate a main course after all that! A bottle of Kindzmarauli red wine might help to increase your capacity.

MARUKAME
JAPANESE €

Map p266 (Марукамэ; marukame.ru; ul Pyatnitskaya 29; mains ₽150-200; ⊗11am-11pm; ⋈Novokuznetskaya) This superpopular and conveniently located self-service noodle shop draws crowds of office workers during lunchtime break – hence a long, but fast-moving queue. Apart from udon noodles, the menu also features *domburi* rice dishes, tempura skewers and rolls.

OCHEN DOMASHNEYE KAFE
RUSSIAN €

Map p266 (Очень домашнее кафе; ☑495-951 1734; www.dom-cafe.ru; ul Pyatnitskaya 9/28, str 1; ₽380-550; ⊗8am-11pm Mon-Fri, 11am-11pm Sat & Sun; ⋈Novokuznetskaya) The name, which translates as 'a very homey cafe', is also its motto. This is as close as it gets to the kind of food Russians eat at home, which inevitably means borsch (beetroot soup) or mushroom soup for starters, and all kinds of *kotlety* meatballs (meat, chicken or fish) as the main course. Portions are fairly small, and appetisers go for about the same price as mains.

AC/DC IN TBILISI
GEORGIAN €

Map p266 (facebook.com/acdcintbilisi; Gorky Park; mains ₽250-350; ⊗10am-10pm; ⋈Oktyabrskaya) Burgers and Georgia (the one in the Caucasus, that is) seem to inhabit parallel universes, but they get together in this summer-only Gorky Park kiosk. An otherwise very ordinary burger turns Georgian with the help of hot *adjika* sauce and *suluguni* cheese. The meatballs in walnut *satsivi* sauce are another thing to try here.

SOK
VEGETARIAN €

Map p266 (Сок; Lavrushinsky per 15; mains ₽340-400; ⊗11am-11pm; ⋈Tretyakov-skaya) Citrus-coloured walls and delicious fresh-squeezed juices are guaranteed to brighten your day. All the soups, salads, pasta and fabulous desserts are vegetarian, with many vegan options too. The menu even features a few Russian classics such as beef stroganoff, made with seitan (a wheat-based meat substitute).

NASHA CHEBURECHNAYA
TATAR €

Map p266 (Наша чебуречная; Bolshoy Tolmachevsky per 3; chebureks ₽80-100; ⊗11am-11pm; ⋈Tretyakovskaya) If you can bear with some post-Soviet shabbiness, this is the place to try competently cooked *chebureks* – the Tatar meat-filled (well, mostly) pastry cooked in sizzling oil. Lamb *cheburek* is the golden standard, but there are about a dozen kinds on offer, including meat-free options.

GRABLY
CAFETERIA €

Map p266 (Грабли; www.grably.ru; Pyatnitskaya ul 27; mains ₽200-300; ⊗10am-11pm; ⋈Novokuznetskaya) The big buffet features an amazing array of fish, poultry and meat, salads, soups and desserts. After you run the gauntlet and pay the bill, take a seat in the elaborate winter-garden seating area. This Zamoskvorechie outlet is particularly impressive, with two levels of tiled floors, vines draped over wrought-iron rails, and chandeliers suspended from the high ceilings. Beer and wine are available at the bar upstairs.

★PRODUKTY
ITALIAN €€

Map p266 (Продукты; ☑8-903-789 3474; facebook.com/productscafe; Bersenevsky per 5, Bldg 1; meals ₽600-1000; ⊗noon-midnight Sun-Thu, to 6am Fri & Sat; ⋈Kropotkinskaya) The success of this Red October highlight is determined by the cool, postindustrial decor, simple Italian food and the proximity to the premises of several editorial offices, including the embattled Dozhd TV. It's not really visible from the street – enter the courtyard on the left of the Burger Brothers window.

CHUGUNNY MOST
BISTRO €€

Map p266 (Чугунный мост; ☑495-959 4418; facebook.com/chugunniimost; ul Pyatnitskaya 6; mains ₽360-550; ⊗9am-midnight12am; ⋈Tretyakovskaya) This place illustrates the direction in which the entire Moscow restaurant scene seems to be heading – a bistro-cum-bar that would not be out of

KOLOMENSKOE MUSEUM-RESERVE

It only takes a couple of metro stops to get to Moscow's internal countryside. Set amid 4 sq km of picturesque parkland, on a bluff above a bend in the Moscow River, **Kolomenskoe** (Музей-заповедник 'Коломенское'; www.mgomz.com; ⊗grounds 8am-9pm; ⋈Kolomenskaya or Kashirskaya) **FREE** is an ancient royal country seat and a Unesco World Heritage Site. Shortly after its founding in the 14th century, the village became a favourite destination for the princes of Moscow. The royal estate is now an eclectic mix of churches and gates, as well as other buildings that were added to the complex over the years.

Churches & Gates

From Bolshaya ul, enter the grounds of the museum-reserve through the 17th-century **Saviour Gate** to the star-spangled **Our Lady of Kazan Church**. Ahead, the white-washed, tent-roofed 17th-century **Front Gate** – guarded by two stone lions – was the main entrance to the royal palace.

Ascension Church

Outside the front gate, overlooking the river, rises Kolomenskoe's loveliest structure, the **Ascension Church** (pr Andropova 39; ⊗10am-6pm Tue-Sun; ⋈Kolomenskoye) **FREE**, sometimes called the 'white column'. Built between 1530 and 1532 for Grand Prince Vasily III, it probably celebrated the birth of his heir, Ivan the Terrible. It was a revolutionary structure at the time, which experts attribute to Italian masters.

Wooden Buildings

Among the old wooden buildings on the grounds is the **cabin** where Peter the Great lived while supervising ship- and fort-building at Arkhangelsk. The cabin is surrounded by a re-creation of the tsar's orchards and gardens. There are also a few handsome structures that were brought here from other regions, specifically the **Bratsk fortress tower** and the **gate-tower of St Nicholas Monastery** from Karelia.

Great Wooden Palace

In the mid-17th century, Tsar Alexey built a palace so fabulous it was dubbed 'the eighth wonder of the world'. This whimsical building was famous for its mishmash of tent-roofed towers and onion-shaped eaves, all crafted from wood and structured without a single nail. Unfortunately, this legendary building had fallen into disrepair and was demolished in 1768 by Catherine the Great. Some 230 years later, a kitschy gingerbread replica of **Tsar Alexey's palace** (Дворец царя Алексея Михайловича; pr Andropova 39; admission ₽400; ⊗10am-6pm Tue-Sun; ⋈Kashirskaya) was constructed on the grounds of Kolomenskoe Park. Come here for the opulent interiors, which allegedly replicate the originals, based on historical records.

place somewhere like Prenzlauerberg, Berlin. The subdued, wood-dominated decor is almost therapeutic and the inventive post-ethnic food makes you want to live or work in the vicinity, just so it can be your local. The ₽390 set lunch deal is about the best value for money in town. It's a good breakfast choice, too.

CORREA'S
EUROPEAN €€

Map p266 (✆495-725 6035; ul Bolshaya Ordynka 40/2; mains ₽400-600; ⊗8am-11pm; 🖙🍴📶; ⋈Polyanka) Correa's has outlets all over the city, and though none are quite as cosy and quaint as the original in Presnya (p108),

a restaurant with a bit more space has its advantages. This one is oddly located in a cement courtyard, but it does have outdoor seating, and the spacious, light-filled interior is inviting too. Fresh ingredients and simple preparations guarentee the food is impeccable.

DANILOVSKY MARKET
MARKET €€

(www.danrinok.ru; Mytnaya ul 74; ⊗8am-8pm; ⋈Tulskaya) One of many Soviet-era giant farmer's markets, Danilovsky has been engulfed by the same wave of gentrification as Moscow's parks and old factories. With uniformed vendors and thoughtfully designed premises, it looks very orderly, if a tiny bit artificial. But it retains the flavour of a good old Russian *rynok* – a busy, bustling place, full of activity and colour.

Even if you're not shopping, it's entertaining to peruse the tables piled high with multicoloured produce: homemade cheese and jam; golden honey straight from the hive; vibrantly coloured spices pouring out of plastic bags; slippery silver fish posing on beds of ice; and huge slabs of meat hanging from the ceiling.

STARLITE DINER
AMERICAN €€

Map p266 (www.starlite.ru; Bolotnaya pl 16/5; mains₽350-700; ⊘24hr; ⊕⊅⊠⊛; ⋒Tretyakovskaya) You're never far from a burger and a beer. Or breakfast any time of day or night. Bring on the nostalgia with classic diner decor and no-frills, filling food.

🍷 DRINKING & 🍸 NIGHTLIFE

★GIPSY
NIGHTCLUB, CAFE

(www.bargipsy.ru; Bolotnaya nab 3/4; ⊘6pm-1am Sun-Thu, 2pm-6am Fri & Sat) Euphoria reins in this postmodern, nomad camp of a bar that has a strategic rooftop position on Red October. The decor is bright-coloured kitsch, which among other oddities means fake palm trees and toilet doors covered with artificial fur. The DJ and live-music repertoire are aptly eclectic. You don't have to be rich to pass the face control, but some natural coolness does help.

BAR STRELKA
CAFE, NIGHTCLUB

Map p266 (barstrelka.com; Bldg 5a, Bersenevskaya nab 14/5; ⊘9am-midnight Mon-Thu, to 3am Fri & Sat, from noon Sat & Sun; ⊕; ⋒Kropotkinskaya) Located just below the Patriarshy most, the bar-restaurant at the Strelka Institute is the ideal starting point for an evening in the Red October complex. The rooftop terrace has unbeatable Moscow River views, but the interior is equally cool in a shabby-chic sort of way. The bar menu is excellent and there is usually somebody tinkling the ivories.

LEBEDINOE OZERO
BAR

Map p266 (Лебединое озеро; ⊅495-782 5813; http://s-11.ru/lebedinoe-ozero; Gorky Park; ⊘noon-5am Apr-Oct; ⋒Frunzenskaya) The name means 'Swan Lake' and, yes, it over-

looks a little pond where resident swans float contentedly. Aside from the idyllic setting at the southern end of Gorky Park, this place is a happening summertime haunt thanks to lounge chairs in the sun, (expensive) fruity cocktails and a small swimming pool for cooling dips or late-night aquatic dancing. There is face control, which gets stricter in the bar-hopping rush hour around midnight.

KVARTIRA 44
BAR

Map p266 (⊅499-238 8234; kv44.ru; ul Malaya Yakimanka 24/8; ⊘noon-midnight Sun-Thu, noon-4am Fri & Sat; ⊕; ⋒Polyanka) Back in the olden days, the best place to go for a drink was your neighbour's flat, which would be crowded with mismatched furniture and personal memorabilia. This is the atmosphere evoked at 'Apartment 44', where the drinks flow, the music plays and life is merry.

HUB
BAR

Map p266 (https://www.facebook.com/hub yousomuch; ul Pyatnitskaya 82/34; ⊘8am-3am; ⋒Serpukhovskaya) Somewhat unexpectedly placed in the ever-so-hectic pl Serpukhovskaya, this garage-style bar exudes the air of a permanent vacation on Aloha Beach. The menu focuses on quality rather than quantity – there are three types of draft beer (including Fuel ale brewed in Moscow), a limited number of cocktails, great freshly-roasted coffee and milkshakes.

Three delicious gourmet sandwiches on offer ensure that you don't have to survive on drinks alone.

LE BOULE
BAR

Map p266 (⊅8-926-376 9366; Gorky Park; ⊘noon-midnight; ⊕; ⋒Oktyabrskaya) The goatee and mustache factor is high in this hipster-ridden verandah bar that comes with a dozen petanque lanes. Grab a pitcher of sangria or a pint of cider and have a go at what is arguably the most alcohol-compatible sport. Live bands often play on the verandah in the early evening.

WT4
BAR

Map p266 (⊅495-771 7446; Bersenevskaya nabm 6/3; ⊘noon-midnight Sun-Thu, to 6am Fri & Sat; ⋒Kropotkinskaya) Finally, a Russian bar matching the size of the country, not the standard cramped affair. Kick back on caramel leather sofas or perch at the very long central bar, eying a giant crocodile

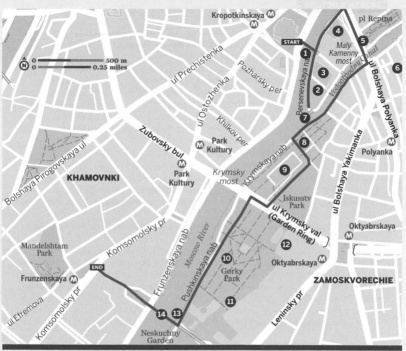

🏃 Neighbourhood Walk
Zamoskvorechie

START CATHEDRAL OF CHRIST
THE SAVIOUR
END NOVOANDREYEVSKY MOST
LENGTH 3KM; TWO HOURS

From the Cathedral of Christ the Saviour a pedestrian bridge leads across the Moscow River to Bolotny Island, a slice of land south of the Kremlin.

The **1 Patriarshy most** offers a fantastic panorama of the Kremlin towers and of the cathedral itself.

South of the bridge on Bolotny Island is the old **2 Red October chocolate factory** (p137), now housing a heaving art and entertainment cluster, as well as the centrepiece **3 Strelka Institute** (p145).

Detour north along Sofiyskaya nab to **4 Dom na Naberezhnoy** (p138), which was a prestigious residential building during Soviet times. It faces **5 Bolotnaya ploshchad** (p137), the scene of anti-Putin protests in 2012.

Walk across the Maly Kamenny most. The **6 Tretyakov Gallery** (p135) is a few blocks to the east, but if you don't want to be sidetracked for the rest of the day, head south along the embankment passing Zurab Tsereteli's monstrous sculpture of **7 Peter the Great** (p137).

From the embankment, along the beautifully revamped Krymskaya Naberezhnaya, enter the **8 Art Muzeon Sculpture Park** (p137), an art museum and history lesson all in one. From here, you can enter the **9 New Tretyakov** (p138), dedicated to 20th-century art.

Head to **10 Gorky Park** (p133) via the passage under Krymsky most and face numerous detour choices – from a game of petanque at **11 Le Boule** to browsing modern art objects at the **12 Garage Museum of Contemporary Art** (p137) to sunbathing at **13 Olive Beach** (p133). **14 Novoandreyevsky most** (pedestrian bridge; p133) will take you to Frunzenskaya metro station.

WORTH A DETOUR

TSARITSYNO

On a wooded hill in far southeast Moscow, **Tsaritsyno Palace** (Музей-заповедник Царицыно; ☑495-355 4844; www.tsaritsyno-museum.ru; ⊗grounds 6am-midnight, exhibits 11am-6pm Tue-Fri, 11am-8pm Sat & Sun; ⓂTsaritsino) **FREE** is a modern-day manifestation of the exotic summer home that Catherine the Great began in 1775 but never finished. Architect Vasily Bazhenov worked on the project for 10 years before he was sacked. She hired another architect, Matvey Kazakov, but the project was eventually abandoned after she ran out of money. For hundreds of years, the palace was little more than a shell, until the Russian government finally decided to finish and refurbish it in 2007.

Nowadays, the **Great Palace** (Большой дворец; admission ₽150) is a fantastical building that combines old Russian, Gothic, classical and Arabic styles. Inside, exhibits are dedicated to the history of Tsaritsyno (Царицыно), as well as the life of Catherine the Great. The nearby kitchen building, or **khlebny dom** (Хлебный дом; admission ₽300), also hosts rotating exhibits, sometimes culinary and sometimes less tantalising topics such as icons and art.

The *khlebny dom* is a pleasant place to hear classical **concerts** (☑499-725 7291; tickets ₽150-300; ⊗5pm Sat & Sun) in summer.

The extensive grounds include some other lovely buildings, such as the **Small Palace**, the working **Church of Our Lady Lifegiving Spring**, the cavalier buildings and some interesting bridges. A pond is bedecked by a fantastic fountain set to music. The English-style wooded park stretches all the way south to the **Upper Tsaritsynsky Pond**, which has rowing boats available for hire in summer, and west to the Tsaritsyno Palace complex.

Tsaritsyno is easy to find: just follow the signs from the eponymous metro station.

swallowing a train on the inner wall mural. On the menu, there are 24 cocktails to quench your thirst (and inhibition) and Asian food to eliminate hunger.

Besides food and drinks, the place holds all kinds of art events and film screenings. DJs spin tunes until the wee hours.

PROGRESSIVE DADDY & DADDY'S TERRACE
BAR

Map p266 (www.progressivedaddy.ru; Bersenevskaya nab 6/2; ⓂKropotkinskaya) Daddy managed to snag the prime location in the Red October complex: at the tip of the island, on the top floor of the factory, the restaurant-bar-club has the best views in the joint (if not the city). Sit on the terrace and sip a bellini while you admire the Cathedral of Christ the Saviour in the distance. It's very modern Moscow.

ROLLING STONE
NIGHTCLUB

Map p266 (Bolotnaya nab 3; ⊗10pm-7am Thu-Sat; ⓂKropotkinskaya) Plastered with covers of the namesake magazine and lit by naked bulbs, this place has the feel of an upscale dive bar. What makes it upscale is its location in the ultratrendy Red October complex, and the clientele – they might be dressed in casual gear but they still have to look impeccable to get past the face control. The music spans all genres and there is a small dance floor if you are so inclined.

COFFEE BEAN
CAFE

Map p266 (www.coffeebean.ru; Pyatnitskaya ul 5; ⊗8am-11pm; ⓂTretyakovskaya) One could claim that Coffee Bean started the coffee thing in Moscow. While the original location on Tverskaya is no longer open, there are a few of these excellent, affordable cafes around town.

KARLSON
BAR

Map p266 (Карлсон; ☑8-964-571 6370; www.ginza.ru/msk; nab Ovchinnikovskaya 20/1; ⊗noon-midnight Sun-Thu, to 3am Fri & Sat; ⓂNovokuznetskaya) It's posh (though not at all tasteless) and it boasts a spectacular view of Moscow from its rooftop position, which is the main reason to throw a few thousand rubles on wine and cocktails, or even super-expensive food, here. Rest assured that quality will match the price. The bar is located inside a business centre.

Just say you are going to Karlson at the entrance.

⭐ ENTERTAINMENT

STRELKA INSTITUTE FOR ARCHITECTURE, MEDIA & DESIGN
ART CENTRE

Map p266 (www.strelkainstitute.ru; Bersenevskaya nab 14/5; ⓂKropotkinskaya) This institute is the focal point of the development at the Red October chocolate factory. Aside from the course offerings and the popular bar, Strelka brings a healthy dose of contemporary culture to Moscow, hosting lectures, workshops, film screenings and concerts.

MOSCOW INTERNATIONAL HOUSE OF MUSIC
CLASSICAL MUSIC

Map p266 (☑495-730 1011; www.mmdm.ru; Kosmodamianskaya nab 52/8; tickets ₽200-2000; ⓂPaveletskaya) This graceful, modern, glass building has three halls, including Svetlanov Hall, which holds the largest organ in Russia. Needless to say, organ concerts held here are impressive. This is the usual venue for performances by the **National Philharmonic of Russia** (☑495-730 3778; www.nfor.ru), a privately financed, highly lauded, classical music organisation. Founded in 1991, the symphony is directed and conducted by the esteemed Vladimir Spivakov.

🛍 SHOPPING

CENTRAL HOUSE OF ARTISTS (TSDKH)
ART, SOUVENIRS

Map p266 (Центральный дом художника; www.cha.ru; admission ₽200; ⓢ11am-7pm Tue-Sun; ⓂPark Kultury) Sometimes called by its initials (ЦДХ), this huge building attached to the New Tretyakov contains studios and galleries, as well as exhibition space for rotating collections. This is a great place to browse if you're in the market to acquire a painting or print from Moscow's red-hot contemporary art scene.

ROTFRONT
FOOD & DRINK

Map p266 (per 2nd Novokuznetsky 13/15; ⓢ9am-8pm Mon-Sat, 9am-5pm Sun; ⓂNovokuznetskaya) You know you are in an ex-Soviet country when a candy factory is named after a phrase German socialist workers

greeted each other with in the 1920s. The factory is actually much older than its Soviet name, having catered to Moscow's sweet teeth since 1826. The shop sells largely the same toffees, caramel and chocolate candies as it did in the 1970s.

BOOKHUNTER
BOOKSTORE

Map p266 (www.bookhunter.ru; ul Tatarskaya Bolshaya 7; ⓢ9am-7pm; ⓂNovokuznetskaya) Inside a business centre, this small shop is stuffed with fiction and nonfiction books in English (not to mention German, French and Spanish). You'll find all sorts of art, academic and other reference books (including a good selection of travel guides), as well as Russian and foreign literature.

🏃 SPORTS & ACTIVITIES

BERSENEVSKIYE BANY
BANYA

Map p266 (Берсеневские бани; ☑495-281 5086; Bersenevskaya nab 16, str 5; 2hr ₽1200, each subsequent hour ₽600; ⓢ8am-11pm, women only Mon-Wed, men only Thu-Sun) Proof that Red October hipsters have no aversion to century-old traditions, this new bathhouse is both elegant and competently run. The vaulted cellars of the former Smirnov distillery (yes, this is the birthplace of Smirnoff vodka) create just the right circulation in the steam room. Unless you are an old Russian *banya* hand, splash some extra money and let them pamper you.

If being beaten with twigs qualifies as pampering, that is.

OLIVER BIKES
CYCLING

Map p266 (Оливер Байкс; ☑499-340 2609; www.bikerentalmoscow.com; Pyatnitskaya ul 2; per hour/day from ₽100/500, tours ₽900; ⓢ2-10pm Tue-Fri, 11am-10pm Sat & Sun; ⓂNovokuznetskaya) Oliver rents all kinds of two-wheeled vehicles, including cruisers, mountain bikes, folding bikes and tandem bikes, all of which are in excellent condition. Its location is convenient for bike rides along the Moscow River. Oliver also offers weekend bike tours, but only occasionally in English.

Meshchansky & Basmanny

MESHCHANSKY | BASMANNY

Neighbourhood Top Five

❶ Contemplating Moscow's hot contemporary art scene at any one of the city's post-industrial art complexes, such as **Winzavod Center for Contemporary Art** (p148), **ArtPlay** (p148) and **Proekt_Fabrika** (p157).

❷ Descending 60m underground to explore the Cold War communications centre at **Bunker-42** (p149).

❸ Stocking up on junk souvenirs and Soviet paraphernalia at **Izmaylovsky market** (p150).

❹ Putting on a Soviet child's hat at the **Soviet Arcade Games Museum** (p149).

❺ Whiling away some hours with food, music and art at **Art Garbage** (p156).

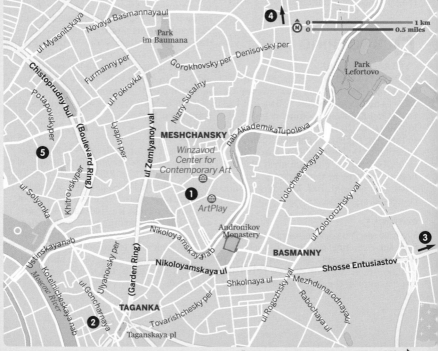

For more detail of this area see Map p270 ➡

Explore: Meshchansky & Basmanny

Markedly laidback compared with other central districts, Meshchansky covers a large swath of central Moscow dominated by pre-revolutionary residential buildings – many of them painted in the uniform yellow.

Its busiest artery is ul Maroseyka, which originates in Kitay Gorod and becomes ul Pokrovka just before reaching Boulevard Ring. It is absolutely packed with good places to eat and drink.

Gracious boulevards create a leafy pedestrian belt running all the way down to the Moscow River. With a beautiful pond that becomes a skating rink in winter, Chistoprudny Boulevard is about the cutest area in Moscow and is great for leisurely walks.

Beyond the Garden Ring and Kursky train station, a belt of centenarian factories is becoming one of Moscow's hottest art, shopping and start-up scenes. The flagship Winzavod Center for Contemporary Art, a former winery, is packed with galleries, while the nearby ArtPlay area specialises in modern design.

Local Life

➡ **New Moscow** Watch the city's game-changers plot new projects and start-ups at Winzavod Center for Contemporary Art and ArtPlay.

➡ **Budget Joint** What are young Russians up to? Find out at Tsiferblat (p154), where 20-somethings spend time engaging in a few dozen different activities.

➡ **Outdoors** Whatever the weather, locals stroll and socialise around Chistye Prudy.

Getting There & Away

➡ **Meshchansky** Several metro lines pass through Meshchansky. Both the purple Tagansko-Krasnopresnenskaya line and the orange Kaluzhsko-Rizhskaya line have stops at Kitay-Gorod. Along the Boulevard Ring, Chistye Prudy is on the red Sokolnicheskaya line; Turgenevskaya is on the orange Kaluzhsko-Rizhskaya line; and Sretensky Bulvar is on the light green Lyublinskaya line.

➡ **Basmanny** Converted factories are best accessed from Kurskaya metro station where the ring links with the dark blue Arbatsko-Pokrovskaya line and the light green Lyublinskaya line.

Lonely Planet's Top Tip

Trams departing from Chistye Prudy metro station are a nice way of touring this section of the Boulevard Ring. All of them go down to the river and across the bridge to Novokuznetskaya metro in Zamoskoverchie.

✕ Best Places to Eat

➡ Darbazi (p152)

➡ Kitayskaya Gramota (p152)

➡ Odessa-Mama (p153)

For reviews, see p152 ➡

⚑ Best Places to Drink

➡ Art Garbage (p156)

➡ Solyanka (p155)

➡ Chaynaya Vysota (p154)

➡ Tsurtsum Cafe (p154)

For reviews, see p154 ➡

⊙ Best Art Centres

➡ Winzavod Center for Contemporary Art (p148)

➡ Proekt_Fabrika (p157)

➡ ArtPlay (p148)

For reviews, see p148 ➡

TOP SIGHT
WINZAVOD & ARTPLAY

A hundred years ago, industrialisation was a buzz word in Moscow. Nowadays it is gentrification, bringing the old-world, centenarian red-brick factories back into the spotlight. The huge former industrial area behind Kursky train station is being redeveloped as a hotspot for modern culture and start-ups.

It all began with **Winzavod Center for Contemporary Art** (pictured), once a wine-bottling factory. Its buildings still bear names like 'Fermentation Workshop', but now are packed with art galleries, funky shops and fashion boutiques.

M&J Guelman Gallery (entrance 23) is the flagship gallery; its self-declared mission is to display modern art from outside Moscow. At **Aidan Studio** (entrance 20), you can see venerable owner Aidan Salakhova and her students at work on weekends. The **pop/off/art gallery** (entrance 22) is dedicated to 'sots-art' – the Soviet non-conformist's answer to Andy Warhol. **Fotoloft** (entrance 4) is all about photography. **Red & White Wine Workshop** houses temporary art exhibitions.

The nearby Manometer factory has also been touched by the magic wand of gentrification and is known as **ArtPlay** (Map p270; ☎495-620 0882; www.artplay.ru; Nizhny Syromyatnichesky per 10; ☉noon-8pm Tue-Sun; ⓂChkalovskaya) **FREE**. ArtPlay focuses on design, housing many furniture showrooms and antique stores. It's a bit of a maze, at the far end of which you'll find the building housing permanent art exhibitions. Halfway between it and the entrance, Edward's (p155) is a convenient pit stop, if your engine has run out of beer.

ArtPlay and Winzavod are being joined by the much bigger **Arma factory**, which is undergoing a major reconstruction.

To find Winzavod and ArtPlay, walk down Verkhnyaya Syromyatnicheskaya ul from Garden Ring, looking for passages under the railway line on your left. The first one leads to Winzavod (100m along on your left). Take the second one for ArtPlay.

DON'T MISS

➡ M&J Guelman Gallery
➡ Fotoloft
➡ Tsurtsum Cafe (p154)
➡ Edward's (p155)

PRACTICALITIES

➡ Винзавод
➡ Map p270
➡ www.winzavod.ru
➡ 4 Syromyatnichesky per 1
➡ ⓂChkalovskaya

👁 SIGHTS

👁 Meshchansky

CHISTYE PRUDY
PARK

Map p270 (Чистые пруды; Chistoprudny bul; ⓂChistye Prudy) Chistye Prudy (Clean Ponds) is the lovely little pond that graces the Boulevard Ring at the ul Pokrovka intersection. The Boulevard Ring is always a prime location for strolling, but the quaint pond makes this a desirable address indeed. Paddle boats in summer and ice skating in winter are essential parts of the ambience. Pick a cafe and sip a beer or a coffee while watching strollers and skaters go by.

CHORAL SYNAGOGUE
NOTABLE BUILDING

Map p270 (Московская Хоральная Синагога; Bolshoy Spasoglinishchevsky per 10; ⊙9am-6pm; ⓂKitay-Gorod) Construction of a synagogue was banned inside Kitay Gorod, so Moscow's oldest and most prominent synagogue was built just outside the city walls, not far from the Jewish settlement of Zaryadye. Construction started in 1881 but dragged on due to roadblocks by the anti-Semitic tsarist government. It was completed in 1906 and was the only synagogue that continued to operate throughout the Soviet period, despite attempts to convert it into a workers' club.

BUNKER-42 COLD WAR MUSEUM
MUSEUM

Map p270 (☑495-500 0554; www.bunker42.com; 5-ya Kotelnichesky per 11; admission ₽1300; ⊙by appointment; ⓂTaganskaya) On a quiet side street near Taganskaya pl, a nondescript neoclassical building is the gateway to the secret Cold War–era communications centre. The facility was meant to serve as the communications headquarters in the event of a nuclear attack. As such, the building was just a shell, serving as an entryway to the 7000-sq-metre space 60m underground. Now in private hands, the facility has been converted into a sort of a museum dedicated to the Cold War.

Unfortunately, not much remains from the Cold War days. The vast place is nearly empty, except for a few exhibits set up for the benefit of visitors, such as a scale model of the facility. Visitors watch a 20-minute film about the history of the Cold War, followed by a guided tour of the four underground 'blocks'.

VYSOTSKY CULTURAL CENTRE
MUSEUM

Map p270 (Культурный центр Высоцкого; www.vysotsky.ru; Nizhny Tagansky tupik 3; admission ₽80; ⊙11am-6pm Thu-Sat; ⓂTaganskaya) Part museum, part performance space, part art exhibit, this cultural centre pays tribute to local legend Vladimir Vysotsky. Singer and songwriter, poet and actor, Vysotsky was one of the Soviet Union's most influential pop-culture figures, thanks to the witty lyrics and social commentary in his songs. The permanent exhibit features a slew of photos and documents, as well as personal items such as the bard's guitar. Theatre, dance and musical performances take place every night in the performance hall.

MUSEUM OF THE RUSSIAN ICON
ART MUSEUM

Map p270 (Частный музей русской иконы; www.russikona.ru; ul Goncharnaya 3; ⊙11am-7pm Thu-Tue; ⓂTaganskaya) 🆓 This museum houses the private collection of Russian businessman and art patron Mikhail Abramov. He has personally amassed a collection of more than 4000 pieces of Russian and Eastern Christian art, including some 600 icons. The collection is unique in that it represents nearly all schools of Russian iconography. Highlights include Simon Ushakov's 17th-century depiction of the Virgin Odigitria and an icon of St Nikolai Mirlikiisky.

LUBYANKA PRISON
HISTORICAL BUILDING

Map p270 (Лубянка; Lubyanskaya pl; ⓂLubyanka) In the 1930s Lubyanka Prison was the feared destination of thousands of innocent victims of Stalin's purges. Today the grey building looming on the northeastern side of Lubyanskaya pl is no longer a prison, but is the headquarters of the Federal Security Service (Federalnaya Sluzhba Bezopasnosti). The FSB keeps a pretty good eye on domestic goings on. The building is not open to the public.

👁 Basmanny

SOVIET ARCADE GAMES MUSEUM
MUSEUM

(Музей советских игровых автоматов; www.15kop.ru; ul Baumanskaya 11; ⊙1-8pm; ⓂBaumanskaya) Growing up in 1980s USSR was a peculiar, but not necessarily entirely bleak experience. Here is an example – a collection of about 40 mostly functional

WORTH A DETOUR

IZMAILOVO

Izmaylovsky Market

Never mind the kitschy faux 'tsar's palace' it surrounds, **Izmaylovsky flea market** (www.kremlin-izmailovo.com; Izmaylovskoye shosse 73; ⊙10am-8pm; MPartizanskaya) is the ultimate place to shop for *matryoshka* dolls, military uniforms, icons, Soviet badges and some real antiques. Serious antiquarians occupy the 2nd floor of the wooden trade row surrounding the palace, but for really good stuff you need to come here at an ungodly hour on Saturday morning and compete with pros from Moscow galleries. Keep in mind that Russia bans the export of items older than 100 years.

Izmaylovsky Park & Royal Estate

Across a lake from the Izmaylovsky Market, Izmaylovsky Park is a former royal estate developed by Peter the Great's father, Tsar Alexey Mikhaylovich. Its 15 sq km contain a **recreation park** and a much larger expanse of **woodland** (Izmaylovsky Lesopark) east of Glavnaya alleya (the road that cuts north–south across the park). Trails wind throughout, making it a good place to escape the city for hiking or biking.

Past an extensive 18th-century barracks is the beautiful five-domed 1679 **Intercession Cathedral**, an early example of Moscow baroque. The nearby triple-arched, tent-roofed **Ceremonial Gates** (1682) and the squat brick **bridge tower** (1671) are the only other original buildings remaining.

Stalin's Bunker

A branch of the Central Museum of Armed Forces, **Stalin's Bunker** (Бункер Сталин; www.cmaf.ru; Sovietskaya ul 80; MPartizanskaya) was built under a sports stadium in the late 1930s in anticipation of the conflict with Germany. It would later be designated the 'command centre of the Supreme commander-in-chief of Red Army'. You must book in advance for a group tour of this facility, which includes the command room, dining room, an elegant marble meeting hall, and Stalin's office and living area. Tours are in Russian, but tour companies occasionally bring groups here for English tours.

Soviet arcade machines. At the entrance, visitors get a paper bag full of 15-*kopeck* Soviet coins, which fire up these recreational dinosaurs. Most of the games test your shooting or driving skills. Times and attitudes were different, so don't be surprised by having to target fluffy squirrels and rabbits in Winter Hunt. You can also measure your force by pulling out a rather defiant turnip or playing table ice hockey. If the effort makes you sweat, get some fruit-flavoured fizzy water from an authentic machine – it's only three *kopecks*!

APTEKARSKY OGOROD
GARDEN

(Аптекарский огород; www.hortus.ru; pr Mira 26; admission day/evening ₽100/150; ⊙10am-10pm May-Sep, 10am-5pm Oct-Apr; MProspekt Mira) This lovely, thoroughly revamped gardens is simply full of flowers interspersed by dozens of inviting benches. Established in 1706, the garden was originally owned by the Moscow general hospital to grow herbs

and other medicinal plants – hence the name, which translates as Pharmacy Garden. Visitors can wander along the trails, enjoy an exhibition of ornamental plants and explore three greenhouses containing plants from various climate zones. There is a choice of restaurants with verandahs facing the garden. During weekends, Aptekarsky Ogorod becomes a venue for concerts, fashion shows and craft fairs.

SOKOLNIKI
PARK

(Сокольники; MSokolniki) FREE Sokolniki park has changed beyond recognition in recent years. Criss-crossed by cycling paths, it blends into a proper forest bordering on **Losiny Ostrov National Park** (Национальный парк Лосиный остров). The area by the entrance, centred around a fountain, is full of cool eateries and welcoming benches. Further away, to the left of the entrance, is a funfair with rides and carousels. Another attraction is the **Rosarium** (Розариум), a manicured rose garden. At least three outlets in the central part of the park hire out bicycles and other sporting equipment. In summer, beach bums head to the **Basseyn** (Бассейн) open-air swimming pool, which turns into a party zone in the evening.

Come winter, the park opens a skating rink and Moscow's longest (200m) sledding hill. All kinds of urban culture and sporting festivals, including the popular **Equestrian Fest** (Конный Фестиваль; August 29 to September 1), take place year round.

SAKHAROV CENTRE MUSEUM

Map p270 (☑495-623 4401; www.sakharov -center.ru; ul Zemlyanoy val 57; ☺11am-7pm Tue-Sun; Ⓜ Chkalovskaya) **FREE** South of Kursky vokzal, by the Yauza River, is a small park with a two-storey house containing a human-rights centre named after Russia's most famous dissident. Inside, there is a museum recounting the life of Andrei Sakharov, the nuclear physicist-turned-human rights advocate, detailing the years of repression in Russia and providing a history of the courage shown by the dissident movement. The centre holds numerous presentations and debates on contemporary political and human-rights issues. It is under constant pressure from the authorities.

The park is dotted with unusual sculptures, most built from weapons and other military-industrial waste. Look out for a piece of the Berlin Wall that has been repurposed in to a poignant display. Temporary exhibitions cover current human-rights issues and contemporary art.

YELOKHOVSKY CATHEDRAL CHURCH

Map p270 (www.mospat.ru; Spartakovskaya ul 15; Ⓜ Baumanskaya) **FREE** Built between 1837 and 1845, the Church of the Epiphany in Yelokhovo has been Moscow's senior Orthodox cathedral since 1943. With five domes in a Russian eclectic style, the cathedral is full of gilt and icons, not to mention old women kneeling, polishing, lighting candles, crossing themselves and kissing the floor. In the northern part is the **tomb of St Nicholas the Miracle Worker**. A shrine in front of the right side of the iconostasis contains the remains of St Alexey.

RUBLYOV MUSEUM OF EARLY RUSSIAN CULTURE & ART ART MUSEUM

Мар p270 (Музей древнерусской культуры и искусства им Андрея Рублёва; www. rublev-museum.ru; Andronevskaya pl 10; adult/ student ₽350/200; ☺11am-6pm Mon-Tue & Fri & Sat, 2-9pm Thu; Ⓜ Ploshchad Ilycha) On the grounds of the former Andronikov Monastery, the Rublyov Museum exhibits icons from days of yore and the present. Unfortunately, it does not include any work by its acclaimed namesake artist. It is still worth visiting, not least for its romantic location. Andrei Rublyov, the master of icon painting, was a monk here in the 15th century. He is buried in the grounds, but no one knows quite where.

In the centre of the monastery grounds is the compact **Saviour's Cathedral**, built in 1427, the oldest stone building in Moscow. The cluster of *kokoshniki* (gables of colourful tiles and brick patterns) is typical of Russian architecture from the era. To the left is the combined rectory and 17th-century Moscow-baroque **Church of the Archangel Michael**; to the right, the old monks' quarters house the museum.

NOVOSPASSKY MONASTERY MONASTERY

Map p270 (Новоспасский монастырь; ☑495-676 9570; www.spasnanovom.ru; Verkhny Novospassky proezd; ☺7am-7pm; Ⓜ Proletarskaya) **FREE** Novospassky Monastery, a 15th-century fort-monastery, is about 1km south of Taganskaya pl. The centrepiece of the monastery, the **Transfiguration Cathedral**, was built by the imperial Romanov family in the 1640s in imitation of the Kremlin's Assumption Cathedral. Frescoes depict the history of Christianity in Russia, while the Romanov family tree, which goes as far back as the Viking Prince Rurik, climbs one wall. The other church is the 1675 **Intercession Church**. Under the river bank, beneath one of the towers of the monastery, is the site of a mass grave for thousands of Stalin's victims. At the northern end of the monastery's grounds are the brick **Assumption Cathedral** and an extraordinary **Moscow-baroque gate tower**.

ECCLESIASTIC RESIDENCE HISTORICAL BUILDING

(Крутицкое подворье; www.krutitsy.ru; 1-y Krutitsky per; ☺10am-6pm Wed-Mon; Ⓜ Proletarskaya) **FREE** Across the road running south of Novospassky Monastery is the sumptuous Ecclesiastic Residence. It was the home of the Moscow metropolitans after the founding of the Russian patriarchate in the 16th century, when they lost their place in the Kremlin.

OLD BELIEVERS' COMMUNITY

One of Russia's most atmospheric religious centres is the **Old Believers' Community** (Старообрядческая Община; ul Rogozhsky posyolok 29; ☺9am-6pm Tue-Sun; MPloshchad Ilycha), at Rogozhskoe, 3km east of Taganskaya pl. The Old Believers split from the main Russian Orthodox Church in 1653, when they refused to accept certain reforms. They have maintained the old forms of worship and customs ever since. In the late 18th century, during a brief period free from persecution, rich Old Believer merchants founded this community, which is among the most important in the country.

The yellow, classical-style **Intercession Church** contains one of Moscow's finest collections of icons, all dating from before 1653, with the oldest being the 14th-century *Saviour with the Angry Eye (Spas yaroe oko)*, protected under glass near the south door. The icons in the Deesis row (the biggest row) of the iconostasis are supposedly by the Rublyov school, while the seventh, *The Saviour*, is attributed to Rublyov himself. North of the church is the **Rogozhskoe Cemetery**.

Visitors are welcome at the church, but women should wear long skirts (no trousers) and headscarves. The community is a 30-minute walk from pl Ilycha, or take trolleybus 16 or 26, or bus 51, east from Taganskaya pl and get off after crossing a railway.

✕ EATING

✕ Meshchansky

LIUDI KAK LIUDI
FAST FOOD €

Map p270 (Люди как люди; www.ludikakludi.ru; Solyansky tupik 1/4; meals ₽300; ☺11am-10pm Mon-Sat, 11am-8pm Sun; MKitay-Gorod) This cute cafe has a few things going for it: its location makes it the perfect lunch stop for anyone strolling around Kitay Gorod; its warm welcome and tasty food make it a perfect lunch stop for anyone who is tired or hungry; and its prices make it the perfect lunch stop for anyone who is not made of money.

FILIAL
INTERNATIONAL €

Map p270 (Филиал; ☏495-621 2143; www.filial moscow.ru; per Krivokolenny 3 str 1; mains ₽270-450; ☺noon-midnight Sun-Thu, noon-6am Fri & Sat; MChistye Prudy) The woodwork interior makes it look like a pub or even a Gothic chapel, but the menu is a bit of a culinary ping-pong – Italian pasta sits next to Asian noodles, while risotto meets Thai curry in the same section. DJs play all night on Fridays and Saturdays.

KARAVAYEV BROTHERS CULINARY SHOP
DELI €

Map p270 (Кулинарная лавка братьев Караваевых; www.karavaevi.ru; ul Pokrovka 14, str 2; mains ₽200-300; ☺8am-11pm; MChistye Prudy, Kitay-Gorod) It's a deli and it's easy to use. Take a ticket at the entrance, then – while waiting for your turn – browse the ready-made meals on display and take your pick. Russian classics, such as *vinegret* beetroot salad, mingle on the menu with Western European and Asian favourites.

AVOCADO
VEGETARIAN €

Map p270 (www.avocadocafe.ru; Chistoprudny bul 12/2; mains ₽290-420; ☺10am-11pm; 🕾✎♿; MChistye Prudy) With a slightly austere interior, Avocado has a diverse menu drawing on cuisines from around the world. Meatless versions of soups and salads, pasta and *pelmeni* (dumplings) are all featured. Vegans and rawists will find specially dedicated sections on the menu.

★DARBAZI
GEORGIAN €€

Map p270 (☏495-915 3632; www.darbazirest. ru/; ul Nikoloyamskaya 16; mains ₽390-860; ☺noon-midnight; 🕾🅿; MTaganskaya) The vast majority of Georgian restaurants focus on the most popular, tried-and-true fare, such as shashlyk and *khinkali* (dumplings). This classy place goes far beyond these, listing less well-known delicacies with almost encyclopedic meticulousness. Our favourite is *chakapuli* (lamb cooked in white wine with estragon) and *Megreli kharcho* (duck in walnut sauce).

★KITAYSKAYA GRAMOTA
CHINESE €€

Map p270 (Китайская грамота; ☏495-625 4757; ul Sretenka 1; mains ₽300-900; ☺noon-midnight) Never mind the dubious humour in dressing waitresses as Mao's soldiers, this is the place to try outstanding Cantonese fare in an atmosphere echoing that of the Opium Wars decadence. A true culinary magician, the Chinese chef turns any ingredient – from hog paw to octopus to simple milk – into mouth-watering delicacies.

★ODESSA-MAMA
UKRAINIAN €€

Map p270 (✆8-964-647 1110; www.cafeodessa. ru; per Krivokolenny 10 str 5; mains ₽380-540; ☺noon-midnight; Ⓜ Chistye Prudy) Come here to celebrate Odessa, affectionately called 'mama' by the residents of this port city. What mama cooks is a wild fusion of Jewish, Ukrainian and Balkan foods, with a strong emphasis on Black Sea fish. It's like island hopping – from *forshmak* (Jewish herring pate) to Ukrainian borsch and eventually to fried Odessa gobies. If seafood is not your thing, try Ukrainian *varenyky* dumplings or Greek meatballs. Also, worth checking out – for cultural as much as gastronomical reasons – are *makarony po-flotski* (navy-style pasta), a classic Soviet staple, filling locals with nostalgia for the good old times.

MOSCOW-DELHI
INDIAN €€

Map p270 (✆8-925-193 1916; per Khokhlovsky 7; set meal ₽1000; ☺5-11.30pm; ✍; Ⓜ Kitay-Gorod) Finding yourself in an Indian village shack complete with a tandoori oven after searching for this poorly marked place in a decrepit mews is part of the fun, especially when it's -25°C outside. The thali meal, cooked by an Indian chef who stocks up on spices in Delhi, is of course the other part. To find Moscow-Delhi, enter the courtyard and look for a tiny passage between two single-storey buildings. The place is right behind it. Bookings are essential.

SHCHERBET
UZBEK €€

Map p270 (www.scherbet.ru; ul Sretenka 32; mains ₽350-400; ☺24hr; Ⓜ Sukharevskaya) Sitting amid plush pillows and woven tapestries, you'll feel like a sheik in this extravagantly decorated eatery. Feast on *plov* (rice mixed with lamb and vegetables), shashlyk and other Uzbek specialities. And of course, it wouldn't be Moscow if they didn't also offer hookahs and an evening belly-dance show.

EXPEDITION
RUSSIAN €€€

Map p270 (Экспедиция; ✆495-775 6075; www. expedicia.ru; Pevchesky per 6; meals ₽940-2000; 🅾🆖; Ⓜ Kitay-Gorod) This outrageously themed restaurant takes diners beyond the Polar circle, capturing the adventure and excitement of Siberia. You can imagine you arrived by chopper, as the vehicle is the centrepiece of the dining room. Feast on typical 'northern cuisine' – famous Baikal fish soup *(ukha); pelmeni* stuffed with wild boar or Kamchatka crab; and venison stroganoff. There is also an expensive but authentic Siberian *banya* (hot bath) on the premises.

✗ Basmanny

★DUKHAN CHITO-RA
GEORGIAN €

Map p270 (ul Kazakhova 10, str 2; mains ₽200-300; ☺noon-11pm; Ⓜ Kurskaya) It's a blessing when one of the most revered Georgian eateries in town is also one of the cheapest. The object of worship here is *khinkali* (large, meat-filled dumplings), but the traditional veggie starters are also great. The rather inevitable downside is that the place is constantly busy and there is often a queue to get in. Beware – there is a lot of delicious broth inside the dumplings, so bite a little and suck it out before proceeding with the rest.

ART CLUMBA
INTERNATIONAL €

Map p270 (✆499-678 0225; www.art-clumba.ru; Nizhnyaya Syromyatnicheskaya ul 5/7, Bldg 10; mains ₽310-480; ☺11am-11pm; 🅾✍🅿; Ⓜ Chkalovskaya) On the grounds of ArtPlay, this is an appropriately artistic venue, where creative types come to socialise or poke away on their MacBooks. The excellent menu is accurately described as 'eclectic with a strong accent of Russian home-cooking'. You'll find the traditional Russian favourites, done up with delightfully unexpected accompaniments. Even the basics (soups, *pelmeni* dumplings) are expertly prepared with subtle seasoning and impeccable ingredients.

LAVKA-LAVKA
INTERNATIONAL €€

Map p270 (www.lavkalavka.com; per Nizhny Susalny 5, str 10; mains ₽400-600; ☺11am-10pm; Ⓜ Kurskaya) Located inside the former Arma factory, this is the original outlet of a chain whose mission is to promote local farmers' products, and culinary experiments involving them. The garage-style place is part shop, part cafe with a long common table and no permanent menu, since they cook what they get and how they fancy at the time. Nizhny Susalny per is accessed via a long underground passage connected to Kurskaya metro (ring line) and Kursky vokzal (follow ul Kazakova signs). Once you get out, look out for the gates leading into Arma about 100m further on you right.

MADAM GALIFE
GEORGIAN €€

(www.madamgalife.ru; Prospect Mira 26/1; mains ₽370-800; ⊘noon-5am; 🛜; Ⓜ Prospekt Mira) A brainchild of famous Georgian film director Rezo Gabriadze, this is much more than just another Caucasian restaurant. It faces the charming Aptekarsky Ogorod gardens for starters, and the interior design – mixing naive art with antiques brought from Georgia – is superb. Food is a mixture of Georgian and European (to avoid disapointment, stick to the former). Also adding to the awesome atmosphere is the nightly live music: mostly piano and other jazzy ensembles.

🍷 DRINKING & NIGHTLIFE

🍷 Meshchansky

★ SISTERS CAFE
CAFE

Map p270 (📞 495-623 0932; www.facebook.com/sistacafe; ul Pokrovka 6; ⊘noon-11pm; 🛜; Ⓜ Kitay-Gorod) This cosy and quiet cafe-cum-bar has a distinct feminine touch about it – as if Chekhov's sisters have finally made their way to Moscow and started a new life here. Cheapish smoothies, lemonades and teas are on offer, but the wine and cocktail lists are equally impressive. If you're hungry, they serve lovingly prepared Italian standards. Retro furniture creates a cosy, homely feeling, but a striking mural with a girl facing a blue abyss suggests that this place is about dreams and new horizons.

CHAYNAYA VYSOTA
TEAHOUSE

Map p270 (Чайная высота; http://cha108.ru/; ul Pokrovka 27, str 1; 🛜; Ⓜ Chistye Prudy) Tearoom? Gelateria? This place looks more like an academic library of tea and ice cream, an impression enhanced by the fact that it shares premises with a bookshop. The tea menu is an endless list of pu'ers and oolongs, while ice-cream flavours range from gooseberry or fir-needle juice to chestnuts and Crimean rose petals. The emphasis is on the most unusual and hard-to-find ingredients, which unfortunately makes the place quite pricey.

BEAVERS & DUCKS
BAR

Map p270 (Бобры и утки; bobryiutki.ru; Chistoprudny bul 1A; ⊘24hr; Ⓜ Chistye Prudy) This convivial bar is run by two joyful women who mingle with the punters and invent risque names for cocktails, that we will not cite here for decency reasons. The place is open round the clock and starts serving breakfasts at 4am, which lures in herds of hungry party animals.

TSIFERBLAT
ANTICAFE

Map p270 (Циферблат; www.domnadereve.ziferblat.net; ul Pokrovka 12, str 1; for 1st hour ₽120, subsequent hours ₽80; 🛜; Ⓜ Kitay-Gorod) How often do you head to a cafe just because you need somewhere nice to spend some time in, not because you are desperate to get a coffee? Tsiferblat was the first establishment in Moscow that put the idea of a coffeeshop upside down. Here you pay for time, while coffee, as well as lemonade and cookies, are free. Enter at the back of the building, then walk to the 2nd floor.

🍷 Basmanny

TSURTSUM CAFE
CAFE

Map p270 (Цурцум кафе; 4th Syromyatnichesky per 1, str 6; ⊘10am-11pm) Synonymous with Winzavod, where it is located, Tsurtsum is a watering hole where all the beasts of the post-industrial savannah at the back of Kursky vokzal gather to sit on the verandah and plot new start-ups, performances and revolutions. Great for people-watching and non-malicious, self-educating eavesdropping – if you speak Russian.

OMG! COFFEE
CAFE

Map p270 (📞 495-722 6954; www.omgcoffee.net/; ul Staray Basmannaya 6, str 3; ⊘8.30am-11pm Mon-Fri, 11am-11pm Sat & Sun; Ⓜ Krasnye Vorota) The more Russia falls out with the US, the more Brooklyn-esque the Moscow cafe scene becomes. This smallish local is very scientific (or in their own words – psychotic) about coffee, which they buy from trusted roasting specialists and brew using seven different methods. They also serve delightful gourmet burgers and sandwiches.

KHITRYE LYUDI
CAFE

Map p270 (Хитрые люди; 4th Syromyatnichesky per, str 10; ⊘noon-midnight Sun-Thu, noon-5am Fri & Sat) Occupying what looks like an abandoned classroom in its Winzavod premises, is this easygoing cafe with hip, likeable waiters, an intriguing list of lemonades as well as alcoholic drinks, and a Hemingway portrait hanging above the bar and contributing to the slightly devil-may-care atmosphere.

EDWARD'S
PUB

Map p270 (ul Nizhnyaya Syromyatnicheskaya 10, str 9; ◯8am-midnight; Ⓜ Kurskaya) Ambushing unexpecting visitors from its hidden location inside a strategic passage at the ArtPlay converted factory area, Edward's is a tiny but noisy place with a few ales and lagers on tap and the kind of mediocre food that makes it an almost authentic 1980s English pub. Great for watching artsy types rushing through the passage.

PROPAGANDA
CAFE, NIGHTCLUB

Map p270 (www.propagandamoscow.com; Bolshoy Zlatoustinsky per 7; ◯noon-6am; 🛜; Ⓜ Kitay-Gorod) This long-time favourite looks to be straight from the warehouse district, with exposed brick walls and pipe ceilings. It's a cafe by day, but at night they clear the dance floor and let the DJ do his stuff. This is a gay-friendly place, especially on Sunday nights.

TEMA BAR
BAR

Map p270 (📞495-624 2720; www.temabar.ru; Potapovsky per 5; ◯24hr; Ⓜ Chistye Prudy) There are too many cocktails to count...but we know that Tema serves more than 20 different martinis, so that should give you an idea of the extent of the drinks menu. The talented bar staff are sure to serve up something that you like. Popular among both expats and locals, Tema has a fun, friendly and sometimes raucous vibe.

UKULELESHNAYA
CAFE

Map p270 (www.uku-uku.ru; ul Pokrovka 3/7; ◯noon-11pm; Ⓜ Kitay-Gorod) It doesn't make much sense to buy an ukulele in Moscow, but this music shop has the miniature 'uku-bar', which serves a few dozen types of coffee drinks and teas. In the evening, your bar stool becomes a vantage point from which to observe people learning to play ukulele and its Russian equivalent – *balalayka*.

SOLYANKA
CAFE, NIGHTCLUB

Map p270 (http://s-11.ru; ul Solyanka 11; cover Fri & Sat ₽500; ◯11am-6am; 🛜) Solyanka No 11 is a historic 18th-century merchant's mansion that has been revamped into an edgy, arty club. Wide plank–wood floors, exposed

brick walls, leather furniture and funky light fixtures transform the space. By day it's an excellent restaurant, serving contemporary, creative Russian and European food. On Thursday, Friday and Saturday nights, the big bar room gets cleared of tables and the DJ spins hip-hop, techno and rave. The music usually starts at 11pm (and so does the face control).

LIGA PAP
SPORTS BAR

Map p270 (📞495-624 3636; www.ligapap.ru; ul Bolshaya Lubyanka 24; ◯24hr; Ⓜ Lubyanka) It's a sports bar, but it sure is a snazzy one. The gorgeous interior features big windows, tiled floors and Gothic arched ceilings, in addition to the 20-plus flat-screen TVs. The centrepiece of the main hall is the huge screen, complete with projector as well as dramatic auditorium-style seating.

CAFE DIDU
BAR

Map p270 (📞495-624 1320; www.cafe-didu.ru; Myasnitskaya ul 24; lunch ₽190-320, meals ₽1000; 🛜👶; Ⓜ Chistye Prudy) This playful club-cafe invites relaxation and fun with lounge furniture, tantalising cocktails and colourful modelling clay. Containers of pliable playdough are found on each table (right next to the condiments) and the sculpted results are on display all around the restaurant.

ART LEBEDEV CAFE
CAFE

Map p270 (http://store.artlebedev.com/offline/lik; Myasnitskaya ul, 22/1; ◯9am-11pm; Ⓜ Chistye Prudy) Artemy Lebedev is a minor celebrity in Moscow, famed for his crafty creations and innovative designs. Check out the shop, then join his beautiful bohemian entourage for coffee and sweets at the cosy cafe upstairs. When the weather is fine, the courtyard is a delightful place to see and be seen.

SECRET
NIGHTCLUB

Map p270 (www.secret-club.ru; Nizhny Susalny per 7, Bldg 8; Ⓜ Kurskaya) The 'sliding scale' cover charge and cheap drinks attract a young, student crowd to this gay nightclub. The earlier you arrive, the cheaper the admission, but if you're a male aged 18 to 22, it's free any time. Two dance floors, plus live music or drag shows on weekends.

COFFEE BEAN
CAFE

Map p270 (www.coffeebean.ru; ul Pokrovka 21; ◯8am-11pm; Ⓜ Chistye Prudy) Winds of change brought US national Jerry Ruditser to Moscow in the early 1990s on a mission to create the nation's first coffee chain, which he succeeded in long before Starbucks found Russia on the map. Some argue it's still the best coffee served in the capital. That might be disputed, but on the friendliness front Coffee Bean is unbeatable.

⭐ ENTERTAINMENT

KRIZIS ZHANRA
LIVE MUSIC

Map p270 (www.kriziszhanra.ru; ul Pokrovka 16/16; ⊗11am-5am; MChistye Prudy) Everybody has something good to say about Krizis: expats and locals, old-timers and newcomers, young and old. What's not to love? Good cheap food, copious drinks and rockin' music every night, all of which inspires those gathered to get their groove on.

ART GARBAGE
LIVE MUSIC

Map p270 (www.art-garbage.ru; Starosadsky per 5; ⊗noon-6am; ⊛; MKitay-Gorod) Enter this funky club-cafe through the courtyard littered with sculpture. Inside, the walls are crammed with paintings of all genres, and there are DJs spinning or live music playing every night. The restaurant is relatively minimalist in terms of decor, but the menu is creative. Is it art or is it garbage? You decide.

PLATFORMA PROJECT
THEATRE

Map p270 (www.platformaproject.ru; per 4-y Syromyatnichesky 1, str 6) When drama, dance and visual art all come together, what do you call it? They call it 'platform' and they let visiting artists shape it as they please. Appropriately located in Winzavod, the venue hosts diverse events united by a mission of exploring distant artistic frontiers.

GOGOL CENTRE
THEATRE

Map p270 (Гоголь-центр; ☎499-262 9214; www.gogolcenter.com/; ul Kazakhova 8; MKurskaya) One of the most talked about theatres in Moscow is under constant political pressure due to its nonconformist position. Gogol Centre is a modern venue that hosts many musical and dance performances as well as cutting-edge drama. The latter is obviously difficult to appreciate without knowing Russian.

35MM
CINEMA

Map p270 (☎495-917 1748; www.kino35mm.ru/en; ul Pokrovka 47/24; MKrasnye Vorota) Unique in Moscow, this cinema has a policy of showing all films in their original language with Russian subtitles. The emphasis is on art-house and European films, but Hollywood sneaks in anyway.

PIROGI ON MAROSEYKA
LIVE MUSIC, CINEMA

Map p270 (www.ogipirogi.ru; ul Maroseyka 9/2; ⊗24hr; ⊛; MKitay-Gorod) If you have ever visited PirOGI's earlier incarnations, you might be surprised by the club's slick storefront. Inside, it's not dark and it's not grungy. Do not fear, however, as the crucial elements have not changed: decent food, affordable beer and movies and music every night, all of which draw the young, broke and beautiful.

NEW BALLET
DANCE

Map p270 (☎495-265 7510; www.newballet.ru; Novaya Basmannaya ul 25/2; ⊗box office 11am-7pm; MKrasnye Vorota) If you can't stand to see another *Swan Lake,* you will be pleased to know that the New Ballet performs innovative contemporary dance. This performance art, called 'plastic ballet', incorporates elements of classical and modern dance, as well as pantomime and drama. The theatre is tiny, providing an up-close look at original, cutting-edge choreography.

🛍 SHOPPING

TRICOTAGE CLUB
CLOTHING, ACCESSORIES

Map p270 (Трикотаж-клуб; www.sviterok.ru; ul Pokrovka 4; ⊗10am-10pm Mon-Fri, 11am-10pm Sat & Sun; MKitay-Gorod) There are not only hand-knitted sweaters, socks and mittens, but also a fun selection of toys and homemade souvenirs, and sleek and sexy styles of men's and women's clothing. This is not your grandmother's knitwear.

ODENSYA DLYA SCHASTYA
CLOTHING

Map p270 (Оденься для счастья; ul Pokrovka 31; ⊗11am-9pm; MKurskaya) This sweet boutique – encouraging shoppers to 'dress for happiness' – carries unique clothing by a few distinctive designers, including Moscow native Oleg Biryukov. The designer's eponymous label features refined styles with long, flowing lines and subdued, solid colours. The tastefulness and elegance exemplify the new direction of Russian fashion.

KHOKHLOVKA ORIGINAL
CLOTHING

Map p270 (http://xoxloveka.ru/; per Khokhlovsky 7; ⊗noon-10pm; MKitay-Gorod) This is about the world's most clandestine fashion shop. Enter a graffiti-covered courtyard, then look for a small gap between two single-storey buildings on your left – the door is inside the tiny passage. The showroom displays clothes and accessories produced by dozens of young (but often stellar) Russian designers. Designs can be controversial, but you won't see anyone wearing the same item back home.

BIBLIO-GLOBUS
BOOKSTORE

Map p270 (✆495-781 1900; www.biblio-globus. ru; Myasnitskaya ul 6; ◔9am-10pm Mon-Fri, 10am-9pm Sat & Sun; ⒨Lubyanka) Moscow's favourite bookshop is huge, with lots of reference and souvenir books devoted to language, art and history, and a good selection of maps and travel guides. A user-friendly computerised catalogue will help you find what you're looking for. Just to prove that Russia's consumer culture can keep up with the best of them, this old-school bookshop now has a coffee shop on the ground floor.

RAZU MIKHINA WORKSHOP
CLOTHING

Map p270 (www.razumikhina.com; 4-y Syromyatnichesky per 1, str 9, entrance 21; ◔11am-7pm; ⒨Kurskaya) London-trained designer Darya Razumikhina described her genre as 'ethnofuturism'. One may detect Russian and South Asian influences in her bright, multichrome clothes. The shop also sells jewellery.

OCHEVIDNOYENEVEROYATNOYE
SOUVENIRS

Map p270 (Очевидноеневероятное; www.orz-design.ru/; 4-y Syromyatnichesky per 1, str 6, entrance 13; ◔11am-9pm) True to its name, which translates as 'Evidentlyimprobable', this is the place to shop for surreal gifts and souvenirs – from a lamp shaped as an oil rig to a toilet-paper roll that allows the owner to learn a new Russian word before using each sheet. The Soviet theme is well represented in notebooks and passport covers.

COSMOTHEKA
PERFUMES

Map p270 (www.cosmotheca.com; 4-y Syromyatnichesky per 1/8, str 6; ◔10am-10pm; ⒨Kurskaya) Here you'll find perfume brands that you won't come by in a duty-free shop. All fringe international and Russian perfume producers are welcome, while Dior and the likes are not. The shop is located by the entrance to Winzavod art space.

BEL POSTEL
HOMEWARES

Map p270 (www.belpostel.com; ul Sretenka 27/29; ⒨Sukharevskaya) This lovely linens store carries a sumptuous selection of bathrobes,

WORTH A DETOUR

PROEKT_FABRIKA

Since 2004 the functioning October glass factory has shared its space with this innovative **arts venue** (www.proekt fabrika.ru; Perevedenovsky per 18; ◔10am-8pm Tue-Sun; ⒨Baumanskaya) 𝐅𝐑𝐄𝐄. Fabrika was the first independent, non-profit contemporary art organisation in Moscow and hosts dance, theatre and other interactive exhibits, plus visual art displays. The most active space is (appropriately enough) the **Aktovy Zal** (✆499-265 4935; www.aktzal.ru; tickets ₽250-300), a black box theatre that was formerly used by factory workers for amateur theatre and worker meetings. Contemporary dance, theatre and music are performed nightly.

blankets, sheets and towels. Take home a set of richly coloured tablecloths and napkins made from Russian linen. You will find some international designers, but most of the product line is soft Russian fabrics and Eastern prints.

MAGAZIN CHAI-KOFE
FOOD & DRINK

Map p270 (Магазин Чай-Кофе; ✆495-625 4656; Myasnitskaya ul 19; ◔9am-9pm Mon-Fri, 10am-7pm Sat & Sun; ⒨Turgenevskaya) In 1894 the old Perlov Tea House was redecorated in the style of a Chinese pagoda. Today this fantastical facade contains the Tea-Coffee Store, which is filled with coffee from Italy, Brazil, Costa Rica and Kenya, and tea from China, India and South Africa.

SRETENIE
SOUVENIRS

Map p270 (Сретение; ✆495-623 8046; ul Bolshaya Lubyanka 17; ⒨Lubyanka) Little remains of the 14th-century Sretensky Monastery: just the main church, Vladimirsky Cathedral, and, as it turns out, the gift shop. Get your icons – hanging icons, tabletop icons, triptych icons – and other souvenirs to soothe the spirit.

FACTORY-EXPEDITION
OUTDOOR GEAR

Map p270 (Фактория-Экспедиция; www.expe dicia.ru; Pevchesky per 6; ⒨Kitay-Gorod) For all your hunting expedition needs, find this tiny shop below the restaurant of the same name. As well as guns, knives and camping gear, you'll also find some strange and scary items from the great Russian countryside.

Day Trips from Moscow

Sergiev Posad p159

Home to the Trinity Monastery of St Sergius, Sergiev Posad's easy distance from Moscow and historic atmosphere ensure it's the most visited destination in the Golden Ring.

Abramtsevo p164

An artists colony and country estate, Abramtsevo was a font of artistic inspiration during the 19th-century renaissance of traditional Russian painting, sculpture, architecture and arts.

Vladimir p165

The 12th-century capital of medieval Rus was formative in establishing a distinctively Russian architectural style. Ancient Vladimir still shows off several remarkable structures that date back to its heyday.

Suzdal p168

Dating to the 11th century, Suzdal was a medieval capital and a spiritual centre. The village is still ringed with monasteries and peppered with merchant churches, making for an idyllic fairy-tale setting.

Borodino p172

The site of turning-point battles in the Napoleonic War of 1812 as well as the Great Patriotic War (WWII), Borodino Battlefield is also an idyllic destination far from the crowds, traffic and smog.

TRINITY MONASTERY OF ST SERGIUS

In Russia, it doesn't get any holier than Sergiev Posad (Сергиев Посад), founded in 1340 by the country's most revered saint, St Sergei of Radonezh. Since the 14th century, seekers have been journeying here to pay homage to him.

Sergiev Posad continues to be one of the most important spiritual sites in Russia and is usually crowded with pilgrims. It's an easy day trip from Moscow and that's how most people visit it. There are a handful of museums and other attractions, but the monastery is the main drawcard and it's more than enough to merit the trip here.

Note that visitors to the monastery should refrain from photographing the monks. Female visitors should wear headscarves, and men are required to remove their hats before entering the churches.

DON'T MISS

➜ Trinity Cathedral
➜ Vestry
➜ Chapel-at-the-Well

PRACTICALITIES

➜ **Area code** ☑496
➜ **Location** Sergiev Posad is 80km north of Moscow.

History

In 1340 St Sergei of Radonezh founded the **Trinity Monastery of St Sergius** (Troitse-Sergieva Lavra; ☑496 544 5356; www.stsl.ru; ⌚5am-9pm) **FREE**, which soon became the spiritual centre of Russian Orthodoxy. St Sergei is credited with providing mystic support to Prince Dmitry Donskoy during his improbable victory over the Tatars in the battle of Kulikovo Pole in 1380. Soon after his death at the age of 78, Sergei was named Russia's patron saint.

Spruced up on the occasion of St Sergius' 700-year anniversary in 2014, the monastery is an active religious centre with a visible population of monks in residence. This mystical place is a window into the age-old belief system that has provided Russia with centuries of spiritual sustenance.

Trinity Cathedral

Built in the 1420s, the squat, dark **Trinity Cathedral** (Троицкий собор) is the heart of the Trinity Monastery. The tomb of St Sergei stands in the southeastern corner, where a

IVAN VDOVIN / GETTY IMAGES ©

Nativity of the Virgin Cathedral, Suzdal (p169)
The town's 13th-century cathedral features iconic gold-spangled onion domes and sumptuous frescoes.

Rural house, Vladimir (p165)
The fusion of Western and Kyivian traditions first developed in 12th-century Vladimir influenced Russian architecture for centuries.

Saviour Monastery of St Euthymius, Suzdal (p169)
The 17th-century walls of this mighty monastery protect churches, bell towers and other notable buildings that today host art and history displays.

Restaurant sign, Suzdal (p168)
The wooden cottages that intermingle with Suzdal's many churches bring charm to this historical town.

JANE SWEENEY / GETTY IMAGES ©

WHILE YOU'RE HERE

The **Toy Museum** (Музей игрушек; www. museumot.ru; pr Krasnoy Armii 123; adults/students ₽150/70; ☺11am-5pm Wed-Sun) has a particularly good collection of nesting dolls, as Sergiev Posad was the centre of *matryoshka* production before the revolution.

EATING IN SERGIEV POSAD

Right by the monastery walls, **Gostevaya Izba** (Гостевая Изба; Aptekarsky per; ₽300-500; ☺11am-11pm) re-creates the kind of food metropolitans of the past would gorge on outside fasting periods, although – to the delight of vegetarians – the menu has a considerable fasting section, too. For salads, pastas and a couple of vegetarian options, try little **Art Café San Marino** (pr Krasnoy Armii 138/2; r ₽250-400; ☺11am-midnight). Looking utterly unorthodox in such close proximity to the holy site, this little cellar is filled with art and books.

memorial service for St Sergei goes on all day, every day. The icon-festooned interior, lit by oil lamps, is largely the work of the great medieval painter Andrei Rublyov and his students.

Cathedral of the Assumption

The star-spangled **Cathedral of the Assumption** (Успенский собор) was modelled on the cathedral of the same name in the Moscow Kremlin. It was finished in 1585 with money left by Ivan the Terrible in a fit of remorse over killing his son. Outside the west door is the **grave of Boris Godunov**, the only tsar not buried in either the Moscow Kremlin or St Petersburg's Sts Peter & Paul Cathedral. Another notable grave is that of **St Innokenty**, known as the apostle of America. He founded the Russian Orthodox community in Alaska.

Close by, the resplendent **Chapel-at-the-Well** (Накладезная часовня) was built over a spring that is said to have appeared during the Polish siege. The five-tier baroque **bell tower** took 30 years to build during the 18th century, and once had 42 bells, the largest of which weighed 65 tonnes.

Vestry

The **Vestry** (☺10am-5.30pm Wed-Sun), behind the Trinity Cathedral, displays the monastery's extraordinarily rich treasury, bulging with 600 years of donations from the rich and powerful – tapestries, jewel-encrusted vestments, solid-gold chalices and more. Recently closed for reconstruction, it was unclear when the museum would reopen.

Refectory Church of St Sergei

The huge block with the 'wallpaper' paint job is the **Refectory Church of St Sergei** (Трапезная церковь преподобного Сергия), so called because it was once a dining hall for pilgrims. Now it's the Cathedral of the Assumption's winter counterpart, holding morning services in cold weather. It is closed outside of service times, except for guided tours. The green building next door is the **metropolitan's residence**.

Getting There & Away

The fastest transport option to Sergiev Posad from Moscow is the express commuter train that departs from Moscow's Yaroslavsky vokzal (₽160, one hour, six daily). A couple of long-distance trains call at Sergiev Posad daily on the way to Yaroslavl (₽1200, three hours). There are no direct trains to Rostov-Veliky.

Bus 388 to Sergiev Posad (₽145; hourly from 7am to 10pm) departs from Moscow's VDNKh metro station. Transit buses for Kostroma (₽700), Yaroslavl

TRINITY MONASTERY OF ST SERGIUS

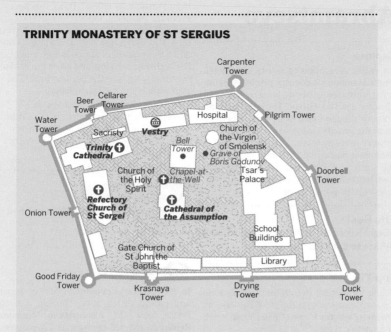

Carpenter Tower

Beer Tower — Cellarer Tower

Water Tower

Sacristy — **Vestry**

Hospital

Pilgrim Tower

Trinity Cathedral

Bell Tower

Church of the Virgin of Smolensk

● Grave of Boris Godunov

Tsar's Palace

Doorbell Tower

Church of the Holy Spirit

Chapel-at-the-Well

Onion Tower

Refectory Church of St Sergei

Cathedral of the Assumption

School Buildings

Gate Church of St John the Baptist

Library

Good Friday Tower

Krasnaya Tower

Drying Tower

Duck Tower

(₽500) or Rybinsk pass through Sergiev Posad almost hourly; each of these will take you to Pereslavl-Zalessky (₽150) and Rostov-Veliky (₽320) if you can get a ticket.

From the train and bus stations, walk 500m down ul Voznesenskaya until you reach an observation point with a splendid view of the Lavra. From there, it's another 300m along pr Krasnoy Armii.

To get here by car, it's a straightforward 80km trip from Moscow along the M8 (Yaroslavl road), but traffic at the exit from Moscow is horrendous. Definitely avoid heading out on afternoons and Saturday mornings.

Abramtsevo

Explore

An entire generation of artists considered Savva Mamontov's country estate, Abramtsevo (Абрамцево), to be an ideal retreat from Moscow, and you will too. The buildings and grounds remain much as they did when the great Russian revivalist artists worked here, so you can easily spend a half-day exploring the manor house and outbuildings, walking the trails and admiring the artwork that they left behind. Some buildings house interesting temporary exhibits.

The Best...

➡ **Sight** Saviour Church 'Not Made by Hand'
➡ **Place to Eat** Cafe Abramtsevo

Top Tip

While wandering the grounds, don't miss Viktor Vasnetsov's rendition of the *Hut on Chicken Legs,* the house of Baba Yaga, witch of fairy-tale fame.

Getting There & Away

➡ **Train** Suburban trains (headed to Sergiev Posad or Alexandrov) run every half-hour from Yaroslavsky vokzal (₽245, two hours). From the platform, follow the foot trail through the woods, straight across the fire road, through a residential community and down a rough set of stairs. Before reaching the highway, turn left and cross the bridge, continuing up into the parking area. The 1km walk is not well signposted.
➡ **Car** Turn west off the M8 Moscow–Yaroslavl highway just north of the 61km post (signs to Khotkovo and Abramtsevo mark the turn-off) and continue over the railroad tracks.

Need to Know

➡ **Area Code** ☑495
➡ **Location** Abramtsevo is 60km north of Moscow.

⊙ SIGHTS

In 1870 Savva Mamontov – railway tycoon and patron of the arts – bought a lovely estate, now the **Abramtsevo Museum-Reserve** (Музей-заповедник Абрамцево; www.abramtsevo.net; Museynaya ul 1, Abramtsevo; grounds ₽55, all exhibits ₽295; ◷10am-6pm Wed-Sun Apr-Sep, 10am-4pm Wed-Sun Oct-Mar), 60km north of Moscow. Here he hosted a whole slew of painters, who sought inspi-

---

RIDING THAT TRAIN

When taking trains from Moscow, note the difference between long-distance and 'suburban' trains. Long-distance trains run to places at least three or four hours out of Moscow (such as Vladimir), with limited stops and a range of classes. Suburban trains, known as *prigorodny poezdy* or *elektrichki,* run to places within 100km or 200km of Moscow (such as Abramtsevo, Sergiev Posad and Borodino).

Long-distance Trains

The regular long-distance service is a fast train *(skory poezd)* – a relative term. Foreigners booking rail tickets through agencies are usually put on a *skory* train. The best *(firmenny)* have cleaner cars and more convenient arrival and departure hours. Your ticket will normally give the numbers of your carriage *(vagon)* and seat *(mesto).*

Suburban Trains

Most Moscow train stations have a separate ticket hall for suburban trains, usually called the *prigorodny zal* (Пригородный Зал), which is often tucked away at the side or back of the building. Suburban trains are usually listed on separate timetables and depart from a separate group of platforms. These slow trains stop frequently, and have a single class of hard bench seats. You buy your ticket before the train leaves, and there's no capacity limit. *Prigorodny* trains often utilise an electronic ticket reader to enter the platform: be sure to save your ticket as it may be checked on the train or (more likely) as you exit the platform at your destination.

ration in the gardens and forests: painter Ilya Repin; landscape artist Isaak Levitan; portraitist Valentin Serov; and the quite un-Slavonic painter and ceramicist Mikhail Vrubel. Other artists came to dabble in the woodworking and ceramics workshop, and musicians (including Fyodor Shalyapin, who made his debut here) performed in the private opera.

MANOR HOUSE
MUSEUM

(Усадебный дом; adult/children ₽250/150) Several rooms of the manor house have been preserved intact, complete with artwork by various resident artists. The main attraction is Mamontov's dining room, featuring Repin's portraits of the patron and his wife, as well as Serov's luminous *Girl with Peaches*. A striking maiolica bench by Vrubel is in the garden.

SAVIOUR CHURCH 'NOT MADE BY HAND'
CHURCH

(Храм Спаса Нерукотворного) The prettiest building in the grounds is Saviour Church 'Not Made by Hand' (Tserkov Spasa Nerukotvorny). The structure epitomises Mamontov's intentions: it's a carefully researched homage by half-a-dozen artists to 14th-century Novgorod architecture. The iconostasis is by Repin and Vasily Polenov. The tiled stove in the corner, still working, is exquisite. It recently closed for renovations; check whether it is open at the time of your visit.

STUDIO & KITCHEN
MUSEUM

(Мастерская и Кухня; adult/child ₽100/60) Built in 1873 by Victor Gartman, the ornate Russian-style wooden studio is notable for the carved art nouveau detailing on the exterior. It contains an exhibit of Mikhail Vrubel's ceramic works, including an exquisite tile stove. Nearby, the former kitchen now contains a collection of folk art that was amassed by the Mamontovs.

BATHHOUSE
MUSEUM

(Баня-Теремок; adult/child ₽40/25) Completed in 1878, the bathhouse is another example of old Russian architecture, with a wood-carved exterior and painted roof. When the Mamontov family lived here, the building was used primarily as a guesthouse. It now houses an exhibit of carpentry and woodwork, including work by Yelena Polenova, who organised a woodcarving studio here back in the day.

EATING

CAFE ABRAMTSEVO
RUSSIAN €

(Кафе Абрамцево; www.cafe-abramtsevo.ru/; mains ₽250-400; ☺10am-6pm) Across the street and down the lane from the main entrance to the museum-reserve, you'll find this friendly cafe with outdoor seating and a full menu of Russian and international favourites. Portions are generous and preparations are tasty. There's also ice cream and *pirozhki* (pastries) for sale in the car park.

Vladimir

Explore

Vladimir (Владимир) looks like just another Soviet Gotham City, until you pass the medieval Golden Gate and spy the cluster of exquisite churches and cathedrals, some of the oldest in Russia. These are your first (and perhaps your only) destination in Vladimir. Prince Andrei Bogolyubsky chose Vladimir to be his capital in 1157, inviting the best European architects to design the town's landmarks. Fusing Western and Kyivan traditions, the style found here would influence Russian architecture for years to come.

It's possible to visit Vladimir as a day trip from Moscow, but it's better to combine it with a trip to nearby Suzdal and make a weekend of it. If you do stay, you'll have time to visit one of the interesting museums in the vicinity of the churches.

The Best...
➡**Sight** Cathedral of St Dmitry (p166)
➡**Place to Eat** Salmon & Coffee (p167)
➡**Place to Drink** Piteyny Dom Kuptsa Andreyeva (p167)

Top Tip

If you intend to visit Vladimir and Suzdal in one trip, spend the night in Suzdal, which offers more (and better) accommodation.

Getting There & Away

➡**Train** There are frequent services from Moscow, with the old-school Lastochka (₽300, three daily) and the modern Sapsan (₽900, two daily) being the fastest – they cover the distance in 1¾ hours. Both

Vladimir

Vladimir

of these continue to Nizhny Novgorod (Lastochka ₽300, Sapsan ₽1050; two hours). All long-distance trains heading towards Tatarstan and Siberia also call at Vladimir.

➡**Car** Vladimir is a 178km drive along the M7 from Moscow. Consider leaving in the morning (except Saturday) to lose less time at the exit from Moscow.

Need to Know
➡**Area Code** ☑4922
➡**Location** Vladimir is 178km east of Moscow.

◉ SIGHTS

ASSUMPTION CATHEDRAL   CHURCH
(Успенский собор; ☑4922-325 201; pl Sobornaya; adult/child ₽80/30; ⊙services 7am-8pm Tue-Sun, visitors 1pm-4.45pm) Set dramatically

on a high bluff above the Oka River, this fine piece of pre-Mongol architecture is the legacy of Prince Andrei Bogolyubsky, who started the shift of power from Kyiv to Northeastern Rus, which eventually evolved into Muscovy. Construction of this white-stone version of Kyiv's brick Byzantine churches began in 1158 – its simple but majestic form adorned with fine carving, innovative for the time.

Inside the church, a few restored 12th-century murals of peacocks and prophets can be deciphered about halfway up the inner wall of the outer north aisle. The real treasures, though, are the *Last Judgment* frescoes by Andrei Rublyov and Daniil Chyorny, painted in 1408, in the central nave and inner south aisle, under the choir gallery.

CATHEDRAL OF ST DMITRY   CHURCH
(Дмитриевский собор; Bolshaya Moskovskaya ul 60; adult/child ₽50/30; ⊙10am-5pm Wed-Mon summer, to 4pm winter) Never before or since this beauty was built have Russian stone

carvers achieved such artistic heights. Completed in 1197, the main attraction is the cathedral's exterior walls, covered in an amazing profusion of images. The top centre of the north, south and west walls all show King David bewitching the birds and beasts with music. Vladimir prince Vsevolod the Big Nest, who had this church built as part of his palace, appears at the top left of the north wall, with a baby son on his knee. Above the right-hand window of the south wall, Alexander the Great ascends into heaven, a symbol of princely might; on the west wall are the labours of Hercules.

CHAMBERS MUSEUM
(Палаты; ☑4922-323 320; Bolshaya Moskovskaya ul 58; adult/under 15yr ₽150/70; ◷10am-4pm Tue & Wed, 10am-5pm Thu-Sun) This grand 18th-century court building between two cathedrals is known as Palaty – the Chambers. It contains a children's museum, art gallery and historical exhibition. The former is a welcome diversion for little ones, who may well be suffering from old-church fatigue. The art gallery features art from the 18th century onwards, with wonderful depictions of the Golden Ring towns.

HISTORY MUSEUM MUSEUM
(Исторический музей; ☑4922-322 284; Bolshaya Moskovskaya ul 64; adult/child ₽50/30; ◷10am-5pm Wed-Mon) Across the small street from the Palaty, this museum has an extensive exhibition covering the history of Vladimir, from Kyivan princes to 1917 revolution displays, including many remains and reproductions of the ornamentation from Vladimir's two cathedrals. Reminiscent of Moscow's History Museum, the red-brick edifice was purpose-built in 1902.

GOLDEN GATE HISTORICAL BUILDING
(Золотые ворота; www.vladmuseum.ru; Zolotye Vorota; adult/child ₽50/30; ◷10am-6pm Fri-Wed) Vladimir's Golden Gate – part defensive tower, part triumphal arch – was modelled on a very similar structure in Kyiv. Originally built by Andrei Bogolyubsky to guard the western entrance to his city, it was later restored under Catherine the Great. You can climb the narrow stone staircase to check out the **Military Museum** (☑4922-322 559; adult/child ₽40/20; ◷10am-6pm Fri-Wed) inside. It's a small exhibit, the centrepiece of which is a diorama of old Vladimir being ravaged by nomadic raiders in 1238 and 1293.

CRYSTAL, LACQUER MINIATURES AND EMBROIDERY MUSEUM MUSEUM
(Выставка хрусталя, лаковой миниатюры и вышивки; vladmuseum.ru; Bolshaya Moskovskaya ul 2; adult/under 15yr ₽50/30; ◷11am-7pm Wed-Mon) Housed in the former Old Believers' Trinity Church this museum features the crafts produced in Gus-Khrustalny and other nearby towns. The shop in the basement sells a decent selection of crystal.

✗ EATING & DRINKING

SALMON & COFFEE INTERNATIONAL €€
(Лосось и кофе; www.losos-coffee.ru; Bolshaya Moskovskaya ul 19a; mains ₽300-600; ☎) Salmon is yet to be found in the Oka, while coffee is not exactly what medieval princes had for breakfast. But instead of hinting at the city's past, this DJ cafe serving Asian as well as European dishes is here to bring a cosmopolitan touch to the ancient town.

PITEYNY DOM KUPTSA ANDREYEVA RUSSIAN €€
(☑4922-232 6545; www.andreevbeer.com/dom; Bolshaya Moskovskaya ul 16; mains ₽250-400; ◷11am-midnight; ☎) Merchant Andreyev's Liquor House, as the name translates, makes a half-hearted attempt to pass off as an old-world Russian *kabak* (pub), but its main virtue is a dozen home-brewed beers on tap and hearty Russian meals, including all the classics – from *shchi* (cabbage soup) to bliny.

🛏 SLEEPING

Hotel prices include breakfast.

SAMOVAR HOSTEL €
(Самовар; ☑8-900-586 0151; www.samovarhostel.ru; ul Kozlov tupik 3; dm from ₽400, d ₽1400; ☎☀) For starters, they do have a real samovar – perfect for a tea party! More importantly, this is a brand new, purpose-built hostel with English-speaking staff, many amenities and a great atmosphere. The surroundings are slightly dingy, but the stairs leading to the garden by Assumption Cathedral are right in front of the entrance.

RUS HOTEL €€
(Русь; ☑4922-322 736; www.rushotel33.ru; ul Gagarina 14; s/d with breakfast from ₽2900/3400; ✳☎) As with everywhere along the Golden

BOGOLYUBOVO

Tourists and pilgrims alike flock to Bogolyubovo, just 12km northeast of Vladimir, to visit the 12th-century **Church of the Intercession on the Nerl** (Церковь Покрова на Нерли; ⊕10am-6pm Tue-Sun), the gold standard of Russian architecture.

Apart from ideal proportions, its beauty lies in a brilliantly chosen waterside location (floods aside) and the sparing use of delicate carving. Legend has it that Prince Andrei Bogolyubsky had the church built in memory of his favourite son, Izyaslav, who was killed in battle against the Bulgars. King David sits at the top of three facades, the birds and beasts entranced by his music. The interior has more carvings, including 20 pairs of lions. If the church is closed (from October to April the opening hours are more sporadic), try asking at the house behind.

To reach this famous church, take bus 152 from the Golden Gate or Sobornaya pl in Vladimir and get off by the hard-to-miss Bogolyubsky Monastery, which contains remnants of Prince Andrei's palace in the premises. Walk down Vokzalnaya ul, immediately east of the monastery. At the end of the street, cross the railroad tracks and follow the cobblestone path across the field.

Ring, the hotel scene in Vladimir is rapidly changing, with newer places offering better standards than old ones. Occupying an old mansion-house in a quieter street not far from the main drag, this new hotel offers nice, comfortable, if slightly faceless rooms.

★**VOZNESENSKAYA SLOBODA** HOTEL €€€
(Вознесенская слобода; ☎4922-325 494; www.vsloboda.ru; ul Voznesenskaya 14b; d with breakfast ₽4800; ℗❋☎) Perched on a bluff with tremendous views of the valley, this hotel might have the most scenic location in the whole of the Golden Ring area. It is very quiet in this neighbourhood, where old wooden cottages and new villas are dominated by the elegant Ascension church. The interior of this new building is tastefully designed to resemble art nouveau c 1900. The popular restaurant **Krucha** is on the premises.

Suzdal

Explore

The Golden Ring comes with a diamond, and that diamond is Suzdal (Суздаль). If you have time to visit only one place near Moscow, come here – even though everyone else will do the same. The place remains largely as it did as ages ago – its cute wooden cottages mingle with golden cupolas that reflect in the river, which meanders through gentle hills and flower-filled meadows.

Spend a morning exploring the Kremlin, shopping in Market Sq and admiring the rural views over the Klyazma River. In the afternoon, investigate the Saviour Monastery of St Euthymius. Along the way, you'll pass dozens of exquisite churches, colourful log cabins and other photogenic scenes. If you have the time or inclination, the surrounding countryside is a spectacular place for cycling or horse riding.

The Best...

➡**Sight** Kremlin
➡**Place to Eat** Chaynaya (p171)
➡**Place to Drink** Kvasnaya Izba (p171)

Top Tip

Most long-distance buses from Vladimir or Moscow pass the central square on their way to the Suzdal bus station. Ask the driver to let you out at the square to avoid the 2km trek back into town.

Getting There & Away

➡**Bus** The bus station is 2km east of Suzdal's centre on Vasilievskaya ul. A train/bus combination via Vladimir is by far the best way to get here from Moscow. Buses run every 45 minutes to/from Vladimir (₽115, one hour).

➡**Car** From Moscow, take the M7 to Vladimir, then follow the signs to Suzdal along the road that skirts Vladimir, before turning north towards Suzdal (220km in total).

Need to Know

➡ **Area Code** ☑49231
➡ **Location** Suzdal is 35km north of Vladimir.

⊙ SIGHTS

KREMLIN   FORTRESS

(Кремль; exhibits each ₽30-70, joint ticket adult/child ₽250/100; ⊙10am-6pm Wed-Mon) This kremlin is the grandfather of the one in Moscow. In the 12th century it was the base of prince Yury Dolgoruky, who ruled the vast northeastern part of Kyivan Rus and, among many other things, founded an outpost, which is now the Russian capital. The 1.4km-long earth rampart of Suzdal's kremlin encloses a few streets of houses and a handful of churches, as well as the main cathedral group on Kremlyovskaya ul.

NATIVITY OF THE
VIRGIN CATHEDRAL   CHURCH

(Церковь Казанской иконы Божьей Матери; Kremlyovskaya ul) The Nativity of the Virgin Cathedral, with its blue domes spangled with gold, was founded in the 1220s. Only its richly carved lower section is original white stone, though; the rest is 16th-century brick. The inside is sumptuous, with 13th- and 17th-century frescoes and 13th-century damascene (gold on copper) west and south doors.

ARCHBISHOP'S CHAMBERS   MUSEUM

(Архиерейские палаты; Kremlyovskaya ul; admission ₽70; ⊙10am-5pm Wed-Mon) Within the Kremlin, the Archbishop's Chambers houses the **Suzdal History Exhibition** (☑49231-21 624; admission ₽70; ⊙10am-5pm Wed-Mon), which includes the original 13th-century door from the Nativity of the Virgin Cathedral, photos of its interior and a visit to the 18th-century **Cross Hall** (Крестовая палата), which was used for receptions. The tent-roofed 1635 **kremlin bell tower** (звоница), on the east side of the yard, contains additional exhibits.

MARKET SQUARE   SQUARE

(Торговая площадь) Suzdal's Market Sq is dominated by the pillared **Trading Arcades** (1806–11) along its western side. There are four churches in the immediate vicinity, including the **Resurrection Church** (Воскресенская церковь; Torgovaya pl; admis-

sion ₽50). Make the precarious climb to the top of the bell tower and be rewarded with wonderful views of Suzdal's gold-domed skyline. The five-domed 1707 **Emperor Constantine Church** in the square's northeastern corner is a working church with an ornate interior. Next to it is the smaller 1787 **Virgin of All Sorrows Church**.

SAVIOUR MONASTERY
OF ST EUTHYMIUS   MONASTERY

(Спасо-Евфимиев мужской монастырь; ☑49231-20 746; grounds & individual exhibitions each adult/student ₽70/30, all-inclusive ticket adult/student ₽350/150; ⊙10am-6pm Tue-Sun) Founded in the 14th century to protect the town's northern entrance, Suzdal's biggest monastery grew mighty in the 16th and 17th centuries after Vasily III, Ivan the Terrible and the noble Pozharsky family funded impressive new stone buildings, and big land and property acquisitions. It was girded with its great brick walls and towers during the 17th century.

Right at the entrance, the **Annunciation Gate-Church** (Благовещенская надвратная церковь) houses an interesting exhibit on Dmitry Pozharsky (1578–1642), leader of the Russian army that drove the Polish invaders from Moscow in 1612.

A tall 16th- to 17th-century **cathedral bell tower** (Звонница) stands before the seven-domed **Cathedral of the Transfiguration of the Saviour** (Спасо-Преображенский собор). Every hour on the hour from 11am to 5pm a short concert of chimes is given on the bell tower's bells. The cathedral was built in the 1590s in 12th- to 13th-century Vladimir-Suzdal style. Inside, restoration has uncovered some bright 1689 frescoes by the school of Gury Nikitin from Kostroma. The tomb of Prince Dmitry Pozharsky is by the cathedral's east wall.

The 1525 **Assumption Refectory Church** (Успенская церковь), facing the bell tower, adjoins the old **Father Superior's chambers** (Палаты отца-игумена), which house a display of Russian icons and the excellent naive art exhibition showcasing works by local Soviet-era amateur painters.

The old **Monastery Dungeon** (Монастырская тюрьма), set up in 1764 for religious dissidents, is at the north end of the complex. It now houses a fascinating exhibit on the monastery's prison history, including displays of some of the better-known prisoners who stayed here. The Bolsheviks used the monastery as a concentration camp

Suzdal

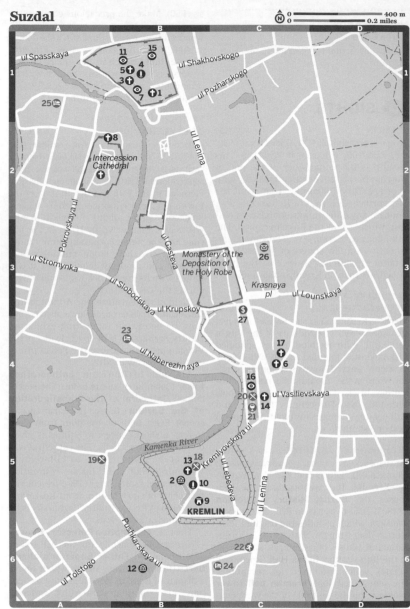

0 — 400 m
0 — 0.2 miles

after the 1917 revolution. During WWII, German and Italian officers captured in the battle of Stalingrad were kept here.

The combined **Hospital Chambers and St Nicholas Church** (Больничные кельи и Никольская церковь; 1669) features a rich museum of gold treasures.

INTERCESSION CONVENT   CONVENT
(Покровский монастырь; Pokrovskaya ul)
FREE It's one of the classic Suzdal pictures: whitewashed beauty surrounded by green meadows on the banks of a meandering river. Inside it's all flowers. The nuns, who live in wooden cottages left over from a for-

Suzdal

mer rustic hotel, seem to be quite obsessed with floriculture. This convent was founded in 1364, originally as a place of exile for the unwanted wives of tsars.

MUSEUM OF WOODEN
ARCHITECTURE & PEASANT LIFE   MUSEUM
(Музей деревянного зодчества и крестьянского быта; www.vladmuseum.ru; ul Pushkarskaya; adult/student ₽200/80; ◷9am-7pm Thu-Tue May-Oct, to 4pm Nov-Apr) This open-air museum illustrating old peasant life in this region of Russia is a short walk across the river, south of the Kremlin. Besides log houses, windmills, a barn and lots of tools and handicrafts, its highlights are the 1756 **Transfiguration Church** (Преображенская церковь) and the simpler 1776 **Resurrection Church** (Воскресенская церковь).

✖ EATING & DRINKING

Most hotels also have restaurants.

★CHAYNAYA   RUSSIAN €
(Чайная; www.restoran-suzdal.ru/chaynaya; ul Kremlyovskaya 10g; ₽120-350; ◷10am-9pm) It is hidden inside a kitschy crafts market, but this place is a gem. Russian standards – bliny, *shchi* (cabbage soup), mushroom dish-

es and pickles – are prominentd, but it is the unusual (and rather experimental) items on the menu that make the place so special. Red buckwheat pancakes anyone? Pickled apple stuffed with herring? Or the ultimate treat – fried salted cucumber with pickled ashberry on toast with sour cream and horseradish?

KVASNAYA IZBA   RUSSIAN €
(☑8-915-779 0577; www.kvasnaya-izba.ru; ul Pushkarskaya 51; ₽200-400; ◷10am-9pm; ☏) It is slightly out of the way, but it's worth the walk if you'd like to sample all kinds of *kvas* – Russia's traditional drink made of fermented rye bread. You may have it as a refreshment, but it goes equally well with the hearty Russian meals they cook here. *Kvas* is so synonymous with traditional lifestyle in Russia that it's even an ironic term – '*kvas* patriot'.

SALMON & COFFEE   INTERNATIONAL €€
(Лосось и кофе; www.losos-coffee.ru; Trading Arcades, ul Lenina 63a; mains ₽340-590; ◷10am-11pm) Suzdal's S&C is about the best place to go for an unhurried lunch or a cup of coffee. Quaint, it has a whitewashed wood interior aged to evoke the 'Cherry Orchard' dacha ambience. Despite the name, salmon is not really prominent on the menu, which includes European-fusion dishes and sushi.

GRAF SUVOROV & MEAD-TASTING HALL RUSSIAN

(Граф Суворов и зал дегустаций; Trading Arcades, ul Lenina 63a; tasting menu ₽130-350) With vaulted ceilings and kitschy wall paintings depicting Russian military hero Count Suvorov's exploits in the Alps, this place serves standard Russian food (mains ₽200 to ₽300) and a few dozen varieties of locally produced *medovukha,* a mildly alcoholic honey ale that was drunk by princes of old. Go for tasting sets, which include 10 samples each.

🏃 ACTIVITIES

BOAT CRUISE BOAT TRIPS

(₽250) Four times a day, a small tented boat takes tourists on a 40-minute cruise up and down the Kamenka River, leaving from the bridge by the Kremlin. It's a good chance to view Suzdal's many monasteries and churches from a different perspective.

HELIO SPA BANYA

(Горячие ключи; ☑49231-24000; www.parilka. com; ul Korovniki 14; ☺11am-1am) Rural Suzdal is a great place to cleanse the body and soul in a Russian *banya* (hot bath). Beautiful, lakeside *bani* are available for hire at Helio Park Hotel (former Goryachie Klyuchi) starting at ₽1200 per hour for up to four people. Each *bani* is an individually designed wooden cottage with different levels of steam and comfort zones.

🛌 SLEEPING

Suzdal is experiencing a tourist boom, which means there's plenty of choice in the midrange and high-end bracket – from quaint two- to three-room guesthouses to vast holiday resorts. You may save up to ₽1000 per night if you avoid staying during weekends or holidays. Breakfast is usually included.

GODZILLAS SUZDAL HOSTEL €

(☑in Moscow 495-699 4223; www.godzillashos tel.com; Naberezhnaya ul 32; dm with breakfast from ₽700; ☜) An affiliate of the namesake hostel in Moscow, this big log-cabin facility overlooking the river opened just a few years ago, but has already undergone a thorough renovation. Each dorm room has its own bathroom and balcony. Guests can also enjoy the blooming garden and Russian *banya,* as well as the chill-out lounge and the bar in the basement.

★ SURIKOV GUEST HOUSE GUESTHOUSE €€

(Гостевой дом Суриковых; ☑49231-21 568; www.surikovs.ru; ul Krasnoarmeyskaya 53; with breakfast, weekdays d/tr/q ₽2000/2500/3000, weekends d/tr/q ₽2500/3000/3500; ☜) Drifting into the boutique hotel category, this guesthouse positioned on a picturesque bend of the Kamenka River under the walls of St Euphimius Monastery, has modestly-sized, comfortable rooms furnished with antique-style pieces made by the owner. There's also a Russian restaurant. Visitors rave about this place.

PUSHKARSKAYA SLOBODA RESORT €€

(Пушкарская слобода; ☑49231-23 303; www. sloboda-gk.ru; ul Lenina 45; with breakfast, hotel d ₽2900, village d from ₽4300; ✳ ☒) This holiday village has everything you might want from your Disney vacation: there's accommodation in the log-cabin 'Russian inn', or the reproduction 19th-century 'Gunner's Village'; three restaurants, ranging from the rustic country tavern to a formal dining room; and every service you could dream up. It's an attractive, family-friendly, good-value option, though it might be too well-manicured for some tastes.

Borodino

Explore

Borodino (Бородино) battlefield is the site of turning-point battles in the Napoleonic War of 1812. Over two hundred years later, the rural site presents an amazing, vivid history lesson. Start at the Borodino Museum, which provides a useful overview, then spend the rest of the day exploring the 100-sq-km preserve. If you have your own car, you can see monuments marking the sites of the most ferocious fighting, as well as the headquarters of both the French and Russian armies. If you come by train, you'll probably be limited to the monuments along the road between the train station and the museum (which are many). The rolling hills around Borodino and Semyonovskoe are largely undeveloped, due to their historic status. Facilities are extremely limited; you may want to bring a picnic lunch.

The Best...

→**Sight** Borodino Field (p173)

Top Tip

The first Sunday in September, the museum complex hosts a re-enactment of the historic battle, complete with Russian and French participants, uniforms and weapons.

Getting There & Away

→**Train** Suburban trains leave from Moscow's Belorussky vokzal for Borodino (₽228, two hours) at 7.56am and 8.43am (with additional trains on weekends). Trains return to Moscow at 2.20pm and 4.02pm.

→**Car** Since the monuments are spread out, visiting by car is more convenient and probably more rewarding. If driving from Moscow, stay on the M1 highway (Minskoe sh) until the Mozhaysk turn-off, 95km beyond the Moscow outer ring road. It's 5km north to Mozhaysk, then 13km west to Borodino village.

Need to Know

→**Area Code** ✍49638
→**Location** Borodino is 130km west of Moscow.

◉ SIGHTS

BORODINO FIELD HISTORIC SITE
(Бородинское поле; www.borodino.ru) The entire battlefield – more than 100 sq km – is now the **Borodino Field Museum-Preserve**, basically vast fields dotted with dozens of memorials to specific divisions and generals (most erected at the centenary of the battle in 1912). The hilltop monument about 400m in front of the museum is **Bagration's tomb** (Могила Багратиона), the grave of Prince Bagration, a heroic Georgian infantry general who was mortally wounded in battle.

The **front line** was roughly along the 4km road from Borodino village to the train station: you'll see many monuments close to the road. Further south, a concentration of monuments around **Semyonovskoe**

marks the battle's most frenzied fighting. Here, Bagration's heroic Second Army, opposing far more numerous French forces, was virtually obliterated. Apparently, Russian commander Mikhail Kutuzov deliberately sacrificed Bagration's army to save his larger First Army, opposing lighter French forces in the northern part of the battlefield. **Kutuzov's headquarters** are marked by an obelisk in the village of Gorky. Another obelisk near Shevardino to the southwest, paid for in 1912 with French donations, marks **Napoleon's camp**. This battle scene was recreated during WWII, when the Red Army confronted the Nazis on this very site. Memorials to this battle also dot the fields, and **WWII trenches** surround the monument to Bagration. Near the train station are two WWII mass graves.

BORODINO MUSEUM MUSEUM
(Бородинский музей; www.borodino.ru; admission ₽50; ◷10am-5pm Tue-Sun Apr-Oct, 9am-3.30pm Tue-Sun Nov-Mar) The museum is an excellent starting place, as you can study an interactive diorama of the battle before setting out to see the site in person. Otherwise, the main exhibits feature original objects from the battle, including uniforms, weapons, documents and personal items. The displays, created by soldiers and their contemporaries, demonstrate the perception of the war and the battle at the time.

SAVIOUR BORODINO MONASTERY MUSEUM
(Спасо-Бородинскиймонастырь;www.borodino .ru; per exhibit ₽30; ◷10am-5pm Wed-Sun) Built by widows of the Afghan War, several exhibits on the grounds relate to the events at Borodino. Nowadays, the former hotel where Leo Tolstoy stayed when he was writing about the events that transpired nearby for his novel *War and Peace* contains an exhibit dedicated to the historical and fictional characters that populate his pages.

 EATING

ART CAFE BORODINO CAFE €€
(Арт-Кафе Бородино; mains ₽400-600) Do not be alarmed if you forgot to pack your picnic. On the grounds of the museum, there is now a small cafe serving bliny (crepes), *pelmeni* (dumplings) and other popular Russian standards.

Sleeping

With average hotel rates among the most expensive in the world, Moscow is not a cheap place to sleep. The city is flush with international luxury hotels, but more affordable hotels are harder to find. Fortunately, a slew of hostels have opened, and more midrange accommodations are now also appearing, usually in the form of 'minihotels'.

Hotels

The most visible type of accommodation in Moscow is the palatial four- or five-star hotel that has proliferated in the last decade. Priced for the business market, they may be prohibitively expensive for some travellers.

At the other end of the spectrum is the Soviet *gostinitsa* (hotel). These old-style institutions have gradually adapted to the needs of the modern traveller, and most have undertaken some degree of renovation. As a result, the quality of rooms can vary widely, and prices usually do too (even within the same hotel).

In recent years, some smaller private hotels have opened in Moscow. Many are housed in historic buildings, and their smaller size means they offer more intimacy than the larger chain hotels. However, the level of comfort and service at these smaller hotels can vary widely.

Minihotels

Privately owned 'minihotels' usually occupy a few floors in an apartment building. The rooms have been renovated to comfortably accommodate guests, but the hotel itself (which might have a dozen rooms or less) does not usually offer other facilities. Considering the shortage of midrange options, minihotels are among the best-value accommodation in the city.

Hostels

In recent years, dozens of hostels have opened in Moscow, much to the delight of budget travellers. Many have been converted from flats or *kommunalky* (communal apartments), so they are often located in innocuous, unmarked buildings on residential streets.

All hostels offer English-speaking staff, internet access, linen, kitchens and laundry facilities. Hostel prices do not usually include breakfast.

Room Rates

Moscow doesn't provide much value for money when it comes to the hospitality industry. Luxury hotels are indeed top notch, but they have prices to match. Expect to pay upwards of ₽10,000 for a night at one of Moscow's top-end hotels. If you can forgo a degree of luxury, you can stay in a classy, comfortable and centrally located hotel for ₽8000 to ₽10,000 for a double.

Midrange travellers can choose from a range of hotels, which offer decent rooms and amenities for ₽3000 to ₽8000 for a double. This wide-ranging category includes a variety of Soviet-era properties that have not come completely into the 21st century, though many are very atmospheric (as reflected in the price).

Budget accommodation is usually dorm-style, although there are a few private rooms available for less than ₽3000.

Accommodation is harder to find during the week than on weekends, and prices are usually lower on Friday and Saturday nights. Seasonal fluctuations are not significant. Prices include breakfast, unless otherwise indicated.

Lonely Planet's Top Choices

Hotel Metropol (p177) The ultimate in turn-of-the-century art nouveau luxury, sitting pretty a few steps from Red Square.

Hotel de Paris (p180) Chic rooms, super service and a vibrant neighbourhood – all at an affordable price.

Kitay-Gorod Hotel (p183) A simple, stylish place on the edge of ancient Kitay Gorod.

Blues Hotel (p180) This off-the-beaten-track boutique hotel offers excellent value for the price.

Godzillas Hostel (p178) A wide range of rooms and services for anyone watching their roubles.

Best by Budget

€

Godzillas Hostel (p178) The long-standing favourite that's more of a travellers' social club than hostel.

Anti-Hostel Cosmic (p178) How to marry dorm accommodation with privacy? Provide guests with a personal capsule.

€€

Blues Hotel (p180) Excellent-value, friendly hotel in a location that's off the beaten track.

Sleepbox Hotel (p178) It's neither rooms nor capsules, but immaculately clean and comfortable individual compartments such as you'll find on a train.

Danilovskaya Hotel (p182) Comfortable accommodation on the grounds of a monastery that serves as Russian Patriarch's HQ.

€€€

Hotel Metropol (p177) Artistic and historic, the Metropol offers a uniquely Moscow experience.

Hotel Baltschug Kempinski (p183) Ultimate luxury in the historic hotel facing the Kremlin across the river.

Nikitskaya Hotel (p180) This elegant boutique hotel is on one of Moscow's best dining streets.

Best Historic Hotels

Hotel Metropol (p177) An architectural marvel operating since 1907 that is steps from Moscow's most historic sites.

Hotel Baltschug Kempinski (p183) The recent renovation adds a modern touch to this 1898 beaut.

Radisson Royal (p181) Housed in a Stalinist skyscraper, this luxury hotel evokes the grandeur of an earlier era.

Best Hideaways

iVAN Hostel (p178) Stylish private rooms that would be more apt in a boutique hotel than a hostel.

Bulgakov Mini-Hotel (p181) Enter through the back door to find this homey place on the Arbat.

People Hotel (p181) Tucked into the courtyard of a palace dating to 1913.

NEED TO KNOW

Price Guide
The following codes represent the cost of a double room in high season.

€	under ₽3000
€€	₽3000-8000
€€€	over ₽8000

Book Your Stay Online
➡ www.hotels.lonely planet.com
➡ www.booking.com
➡ www.moscow-hotels. com

Price Units
Most hotels accept credit cards, but many hostels do not. Many hotels set their prices in dollars or euros. So-called *uslovie yedenitsiy* (often abbreviated as 'y.e.'), or standard units, are usually equivalent to euros. You will always be required to pay in roubles.

Taxes
Prices include the 18% value-added tax (VAT), but not the 5% sales tax, which is charged mainly at luxury hotels.

Reservations
Reservations are highly recommended. Unfortunately, some old-style hotels still charge a reservation fee, usually 20% but sometimes as much as 50% of the first night's tariff.

SLEEPING

Where to Stay

Neighbourhood	For	Against
Kremlin & Kitay Gorod	Close to the city's most prominent historic sites, including the Kremlin and Red Square; beautiful and atmospheric location; good transport connections	Touristy; few inexpensive options; heavy traffic in city centre
Tverskoy & Novoslobodsky	Excellent dining and entertainment options; easy access to Sheremetyevo Airport from Belorussky vokzal	Can be noisy; heavy traffic
Presnya	Excellent dining and entertainment options; lots of green space	
Arbat & Khamovniki	Close to the Pushkin Museum of Fine Arts and other art venues; excellent dining and entertainment options; lots of green space	
Zamoskvorechie	Close to Tretyakov Gallery; excellent dining and entertainment options; easy access to Domodedovo from Paveletskaya vokzal; lots of green space	
Meshchansky & Basmanny	Plenty of dining and entertainment options in Basmanny; easy access to Yaroslavsky vokzal; good transport connections	Can be noisy due to heavy traffic and multiple metro lines

🛏 Kremlin & Kitay Gorod

CAPITAL HOUSE
HOTEL €€

Map p255 (📞8-968-931 6646; www.capital house.su; Bol Cherkassky per 4, Bldg 1; r from ₽4500; 😊❄️🛜; 🇲Lubyanka) It feels a little sketchy when you enter through the courtyard, off a side street in the heart of Kitay Gorod. The surrounding buildings are rather decrepit, but the interior of this minihotel is fresh, with 20 simple rooms on the first two floors. It's nothing fancy, but you'll find acceptable, Ikea-style furnishings, high ceilings and plenty of natural light.

Breakfast is served in the rooms.

★HOTEL METROPOL
HISTORIC HOTEL €€€

Map p255 (📞499-5017800; www.metropol-moscow .ru; Teatralny proezd 1/4; d ₽9930-11,400, break-fast ₽2000; 😊❄️@😊; 🇲Teatralnaya) Nothing short of an art nouveau masterpiece, the 1907 Metropol brings an artistic, historic touch to every nook and cranny, from the spectacular exterior to the grand lobby, to the individually decorated (but small) rooms. The breakfast buffet is ridiculously priced, but it's served under the restaurant's gorgeous stained-glass ceiling (see also p81). The lower end of the price range is available on weekends and during other discounted periods.

FOUR SEASONS MOSCOW
HISTORIC HOTEL €€€

Map p255 (www.fourseasons.com; Okhotny ryad 2; d from ₽18,000; 😊❄️🛜😊🚶; 🇲Okhotny Ryad) Long a fixture on the Moscow skyline, the infamous Hotel Moskva was demolished in 2003, but Four Seasons has reconstructed the old exterior, complete with architectural quirks. The updated interior, of course, is contemporary and classy, with over 200 luxurious rooms and suites, as well as a fancy spa and a glass-roofed swimming pool.

The story goes that Stalin was shown two possible designs for the Hotel Moskva on Manezhnaya pl. Not realising they were alternatives, he approved both. The builders did not dare point out his error, so built half the hotel in constructivist style and half in Stalinist style. The incongruous result became a familiar and beloved feature of the Moscow landscape, even gracing the label of Stolichnaya vodka bottles.

SLEEPING KREMLIN & KITAY GOROD

SERVICED APARTMENTS

Entrepreneurial Muscovites have begun renting out apartments on a short-term basis. Flats are equipped with kitchens and laundry facilities and they almost always offer wi-fi access. The rental agency usually makes arrangements for the flat to be cleaned every day or every few days. Often, a good-sized flat is available for the price of a hotel room – or even less. It is an ideal solution for families or travellers in a small group.

Apartments are around ₽4300 to ₽8600 per night. Expect to pay more for fully renovated, Western-style apartments. Although there are usually discounts for longer stays, they are not significant, so these services are not ideal for long-term renters.

Moscow Suites (www.moscowsuites.ru; studio per night from US$199; 🛜) Slick apartments in central locations on Tverskaya or Novy Arbat. Airport pick-up and visa support are included in the price.

Intermark Serviced Apartments (www.intermarksa.ru; per night from ₽6800; 🛜) Four-star accommodation catering mostly to business travellers.

Enjoy Moscow (www.enjoymoscow.com; per night from US$155; 🛜) Has a range of apartments in the Tverskoy district. Apartments vary in size and decor, but the company provides responsive, reliable service.

Evans Property Services (www.evans.ru; 🛜) Caters mainly to long-term renters, but also offers some apartments for US$120 to US$200 per night.

HOFA (www.hofa.ru; apt from per night €44; 🛜) Authentic (and affordable) stays in a Russian family's apartment (with or without the family).

Moscow4rent.com (www.moscow4rent.com; per night from US$150) Centrally located flats, with internet, satellite TV and unlimited international phone calls.

3

⛭ Tverskoy & Novoslobodsky

GODZILLAS HOSTEL   HOSTEL €

Map p258 (☑495-699 4223; www.godzillashos
tel.com; Bolshoy Karetny per 6; dm from ₽760,
s/d ₽2400/2600; ❋@🛜; ⓂTsvetnoy Bulvar)
Tried and true, Godzillas is Moscow's best-
known hostel, with dozens of beds spread
out over four floors. The rooms come in
various sizes, but they are all spacious
and light-filled and painted in different
colours. To cater to the many guests, there
are bathroom facilities on each floor, three
kitchens and a big living room with satel-
lite TV.

CHOCOLATE HOSTEL   HOSTEL €

Map p258 (☑8-910-446 1778; www.chocohos
tel.com; Apt 4, Degtyarny per 15; dm ₽700-800,
tw/tr ₽2600/3300; @🛜; ⓂPushkinskaya)
Chocolate lovers rejoice – this charming,
friendly hostel will sooth your craving.
Bring your favourite brand from home
for their collection. In return you'll get
simple friendly accommodations – colour-
fully painted rooms with metal furniture
and old-style parquet floors. Bonus: bikes
available for rent!

ANTI-HOSTEL COSMIC   HOSTEL €

Map p258 (☑499-390 8132; http://anti-hostel.
ru/; ul Bolshaya Dmitrovka 7/5, str 3; capsules
from ₽1350; 🛜; ⓂTeatralnaya) Occupying a
converted apartment, this place marries
the idea of hostel with that of capsule hotel.
The location is hard to beat – Red Square is
just a five-minute walk away. Capsules create a tiny, though comfortable universe for
guests to enjoy on their own. There is also
a nice common area to mingle with fellow
capsule-dwellers.

IVAN HOSTEL   HOSTEL €

Map p258 (☑8-916-407 1178; www.ivanhostel.
com; per Petrovsky 1/30, apt 23; dm from ₽750,
d with shared bathroom from ₽2500; 🛜; ⓂChek-
hovskaya) iVAN consists of two clean and
quiet apartments located in the same tsarist-era residential building, a short walk
from Pushkin Sq. Being a hostel, it naturally has dorms – and very nice ones at
that – however its main virtue are several
simply-furnished, but tastefully designed
private rooms with whitewashed walls
and large windows. Bathrooms are shared
and there is no breakfast, but you can cook
it yourself in the fully-equipped communal
kitchen. Washing machine is available at
extra charge.

★SLEEPBOX HOTEL   HOTEL €€

Map p258 (☑495-989 4104; www.sleepbox
-hotel.ru; ul 1st Tverskaya-Yamskaya 27; s without bathroom from ₽3200, d from ₽4700, q from
₽5500; ❋🛜; ⓂBelorusskaya) It might draw
comparisons with capsule hotels, but it is
actually better. Think a comfortable train
compartment – it's close to what you get in
this immaculately clean and unusual hotel,
conveniently located for those arriving by
train from Sheremetyevo Airport. Common
showers and toilets are very modern and
clean; queues are unusual.

It also has more conventional doubles
with bathrooms, and larger family rooms.
Bicycles are available for rent.

GOLDEN APPLE   BOUTIQUE HOTEL €€

Map p258 (☑495-980 7000; www.goldenapple.
ru; ul Malaya Dmitrovka 11; d from ₽4900; ⊖❋🛜;
ⓂPushkinskaya) A classical edifice fronts the
street, but the interior is sleek and sophisticated. The rooms are decorated in a minimalist, modern style – subdued whites and
greys punctuated by contrasting coloured
drapes and funky light fixtures. Comfort is
paramount, with no skimping on luxuries
such as heated bathroom floors and down-
filled duvets.

Up to 30% discounts for those who book
in advance on the website.

PUSHKIN HOTEL   HOTEL €€

Map p258 (Отель Пушкин; ☑495-201 0222;
http://otel-pushkin.ru; per Nastasyinsky 5, str 1;
s/d from ₽7000/8000; ❋🛜; ⓂPushkinskaya)
Just off the eponymous square, this hotel
strives to fuse 19th-century style with the
modern perception of comfort. We'd call it
plush, if not for the tiny, B&B-style reception area. There is a restaurant in the premises, but no need to use it since the area is
packed with great places to eat and drink.

The entrance was poorly marked when
we visited, but it's the only one in the building, so hard to miss. Note huge discounts
are available during weekends.

GUEST HOUSE AMELIE   GUESTHOUSE €€

Map p258 (☑495-650 1789; www.hotel-amelie.ru;
Strastnoy bul 4, str 3, apt 17; s/d without breakfast
from ₽3000/3500; 🛜; ⓂChekhovskaya) Ame-
lie benefits from its superb location right
by Pushkin Sq – it's unlikely you will fin

a room cheaper than this in the vicinity, and it's a very nicely furnished room, too! On the downside, the hotel is a converted apartment, which means shared bathrooms and an unmarked entrance located on Kozitsky per.

Once you find this lane, look out for the entrance number in the building marked as per Kozitsky 3. Dial 17 and they will let you in.

HOTEL SAVOY
BOUTIQUE HOTEL €€€

Map p258 (Отель Савой; ☑495-620 8500; www.savoy.ru; ul Rozhdestvenka 3; s/d from ₽9500/12,600; ⊜✳🛜🏊; ⓂLubyanka) Built in 1912, the Savoy maintains an atmosphere of tsarist-era privilege for its guests, and is more intimate and affordable than other luxury hotels. All rooms are equipped with marble bathrooms and Italian fittings and furnishings. The state-of-the-art health club includes a glass-domed 20m swimming pool, complete with geysers and cascades to refresh tired bodies.

ARARAT PARK HYATT
HOTEL €€€

Map p258 (☑495-783 1234; www.moscow.park.hyatt.com; Neglinnaya ul 4; r from ₽23,000; ⊜✳🛜🏊; ⓂTeatralnaya) This deluxe hotel is an archetype of contemporary design: its glass-and-marble facade is sleek and stunning, yet blends effortlessly with the classical and baroque buildings in the surrounding area. The graceful, modern appearance extends inside to the atrium-style lobby and the luxurious rooms. Guests enjoy every imaginable amenity, and the service is top-notch (twice-daily housekeeping!).

Of the hotel's many restaurants, don't miss the **Conservatory Lounge**, which offers panoramic views of Teatralnaya pl.

🛌 Presnya

BEAR HOSTEL ON MAYAKOVSKAYA
HOSTEL €

Map p264 (☑495-649 6736; www.bear-hostels.com; ul Sadovaya-Kudrinskaya 32; dm ₽550-1000; ⊜✳@🛜; ⓂMayakovskaya) A less institutional atmosphere gives this place a leg up. Bold colours and words of wisdom stencilled on the walls lend some lightness and brightness to the otherwise standard place, which offers dorms ranging from four to 14 beds (including one women's dorm). We're fans of the location, just around the corner from Patriarch's Ponds.

BEAR HOSTEL ON ARBATSKAYA
HOSTEL €

Map p264 (☑495-649 6736; www.bear-hostels.com; ul Bolshaya Molchanovka 23; dm ₽500-1250, tw ₽3000, breakfast ₽130; ⊜✳@🛜; ⓂArbatskaya) Remove your shoes before entering this spotless, efficiently run hostel. Don't worry if you forgot your *tapochki* (slippers); you can always buy some from the vending machine. You can also buy items such as a toothbrush, underwear and breakfast-in-a-box.

Prices vary according to room size (two to 16 beds), and women can opt for an all-female dorm. The place is rather soulless but there are no surprises.

FRESH HOSTEL ARBAT
HOSTEL €

Map p264 (☑8-916-224 1212; www.freshhostel.ru; Merzlyakovsky per 16; dm ₽600-650; ⓂArbatskaya) This quiet, well-hidden gem near the Arbat is clean and cozy with a great air-conditioned kitchen/hangout area. It offers eight- and 10-bed dorms, with 50 beds in total. Look for the distinctive 'F' in the courtyard and get the door code before showing up.

MARCO POLO PRESNJA
HOTEL €€

Map p264 (Марко Поло Пресня; ☑495-660 0606; www.presnja.ru; Spiridonevsky per 9; d from ₽5400; ⊜✳🛜; ⓂMayakovskaya) If you could choose your best location – any location in the whole city – it might just be a quiet, leafy side street in the midst of Moscow's best restaurants. If that's what you chose, look no further. The place has a bit of that old-style institutional feel, but it's comfortable enough. And it's great value for your hard-earned cash.

There are some excellent deals available here – if you book far in advance, if you stay for five nights, or if you're lucky with the timing. Check it out.

ELEMENT HOTEL
HOTEL €€

Map p264 (Отель Элемент; ☑495-988 0064; www.hotel-element.ru; Bolshaya Nikitskaya ul 24/1, Bldg 5; d ₽3800-4500; ⊜✳🛜; ⓂArbatskaya) This location on trendy Bol Nikitskaya is prime, and prices are unbeatable; so you'll easily forgive the side-street entrance and the fact that rooms can be rented by the hour. It's actually a perfectly respectable place, with spotless rooms, pleasant decor and helpful staff.

The cheapest rooms are tiny, so unless you're travelling solo, you'll probably want to upgrade.

★**NIKITSKAYA HOTEL** BOUTIQUE HOTEL €€€
Map p264 (Гостиница Никитская ; ☑495-933 5001; www.assambleya-hotels.ru; Bolshaya Nikitskaya ul 12; s/d ₽9300/11,300, breakfast ₽500; ⊜✳︎☏; ⓂOkhotny Ryad) If you like small hotels in quaint neighbourhoods you will love the Nikitskaya Hotel. While the building and rooms are perfectly maintained, the hotel preserves an old-fashioned atmosphere of cosiness and comfort. And you can't beat the location, in the midst of the excellent restaurants and grand architecture of Bolshaya Nikitskaya. Breakfast is served in the popular attached restaurant, Ugolyok (p107).

Despite its superb location and Russian charm, we can't help feeling that this place is overpriced, unless you can take advantage of the special offers that are available at weekends and other low-occupancy times.

★**HOTEL DE PARIS** BOUTIQUE HOTEL €€€
Map p264 (☑495-777 0052; www.hotel-de paris.ru; Bol Bronnaya ul 23, Bldg 3; s/d from ₽9000/9450; ⊜✳︎☏; ⓂPushkinskaya) Steps from the madness of Tverskaya, this is a delightfully stylish hotel tucked into a quiet courtyard off the Boulevard Ring. Situated on the lower floors, the rooms do not get much natural light, but they feature king-size beds, Jacuzzi tubs and elegant design. Service is consistently friendly. Prices drop by 40% on weekends, offering terrific value.

ARBAT HOUSE HOTEL HOTEL €€€
Map p264 (Отель Арбат Хаус; ☑495-643 1910, reservations 495-695 5136; www.arbat-house.ru; Skatertny per 13; s/d from ₽7800/8300; ⊜✳︎☏; ⓂArbatskaya) With new management, a new name and new renovations, the Arbat House is still essentially a three-star hotel with four-star prices (but not bad value by Moscow standards). The rooms are small but comfortable places to crash. Service is friendly. The quaint location is not all that close to the Arbat, but tucked into a quiet residential street surrounded by embassies.

Discounted rates are often available on weekends and during slow periods: be sure to enquire about the 'best price of the day' when you book.

PEKING HOTEL HOTEL €€€
Map p264 (Гостиница Пекин; ☑495-650 0900; www.hotelpeking.ru; Bolshaya Sadovaya ul 5/1; s/d ₽7000/8600; ⊜✳︎☏; ⓂMayakovskaya) Towering over Triumfalnaya pl, this Stalin-ist building is blessed with high ceilings, parquet floors and a marble staircase. The rooms vary, but they have all been renovated in attractive jewel tones with relatively modern furniture. But the place can't shake its Soviet mood: sour staff and surly security really put a damper on things.

The up side is the excellent Time-Out Bar on the 13th floor, with amazing views and fun vibe. Welcome to the 21st century. PS Discounted 'nonrefundable' rates are available when you book online.

🛏 Arbat & Khamovniki

DA! HOSTEL HOSTEL €
Map p260 (Да! Хостел; ☑495-212 9383; www. da-hostel.ru; ul Arbat 11; dm ₽650-1025, tw ₽2900; ⊜@☏; ⓂArbatskaya) Da, this hostel is worthy of your roubles, with a wide-open, spacious common area and kitchen, a game room with PlayStation, and a nice mix of clean dorm rooms with sturdy wood beds. It has about 100 beds spread over two floors, including four-bed, women-only rooms. Most of the guests are Russian – some of whom are longer-term residents – which offers a unique vibe.

BEAR HOSTEL ON SMOLENSKAYA HOSTEL €
Map p260 (☑495-649 6736; www.bear-hostels. com; Smolensky bul 15; dm ₽600-950, breakfast ₽130; ⊜✳︎@☏; ⓂSmolenskaya) A smart, no-nonsense hostel with air-conditioned dorms (all co-ed) on the Garden Ring just west of the Arbat. The 50 wide bunk beds have guardrails to protect the young or inebriated. This is the nicest of the reliable Bear hostel chain, which also includes the run-of-the-mill Bear on Mayakovskaya and the larger flagship Bear on Arbatskaya.

★**BLUES HOTEL** BOUTIQUE HOTEL €€
Map p262 (☑495-961 1161; www.blues-hotel.ru; ul Dovatora 8; s/d from ₽5800/6300; ⊜✳︎☏; ⓂSportivnaya) The location is not exactly central, but is not a disadvantage. It is steps from the red-line metro (five stops to Red Square) and a few blocks from Novodevichy, with several worthwhile restaurants in the vicinity. Considering that, this friendly, affordable boutique hotel is a gem, offering stylish, spotless rooms with king-size beds and flat-screen TVs.

Even better – steeper discounts are available on weekends.

★ MERCURE
ARBAT HOTEL
BOUTIQUE HOTEL €€

Map p260 (Гостиница Меркурий Арбат; ☑495-225 0025; www.mercure.com; Smolenskaya pl 6; d from ₽7000; ❸❇☎; Ⓜ Smolenskaya) We're charmed by this sweet boutique hotel. It's not much to look at on the outside, but the rooms are attractive and rather plush to boot. The most affordable ones have queen-size beds, work space, flat-screen TVs and chic bathrooms with basin sinks. It's surprisingly quiet for its location right on the Garden Ring. Excellent value, especially on weekends.

You'll have to pay extra for the big buffet breakfast.

BULGAKOV MINI-HOTEL
HOTEL €€

Map p260 (☑495-229 8018; www.bulgakovhotel.com; ul Arbat 49; d ₽4000; ❸@☎; Ⓜ Smolenskaya) The classy rooms, graced by high ceilings and *Master and Margarita*–inspired art, are as good as it gets in Moscow for this price, especially considering the primo location. The bathrooms are tiny but they are private.

Enter the courtyard from Plotnikov per and use entrance No 2.

PEOPLE HOTEL
HOTEL €€

Map p260 (☑495-363 4581; www.hotelpeople.ru; Novinsky bul 11; s/d ₽3890/4290, without bathroom ₽2690/3290; ❸@☎; Ⓜ Smolenskaya) This delightful option occupies three wings in a stately neoclassical palace, just outside the Garden Ring. Rooms are small and sparse, walls are thin, and house cleaning comes every third day. But the sunlit, modern rooms represent rare good value in Moscow, and there is a nice kitchen and lounge for common use.

Note that summer nights can be hot with no air-con.

KEBUR PALACE
HOTEL €€€

Map p260 (Кебур Палас; ☑495-733 9070; www.keburpalace.ru; ul Ostozhenka 32; s/d ₽10,950/13,000; ❸❇☎❄; Ⓜ Kropotkinskaya) Georgians know hospitality. The proof is in the fine restaurants, such as the landmark Tiflis (p127), and in this refined four-star hotel under the same management. With 80 rooms, the hotel offers an intimate atmosphere and personalised service.

There are also a few small single rooms (costing ₽6600 to ₽9950) – ask for one with a balcony overlooking the fountain-filled patio.

ARBAT HOTEL
HOTEL €€€

Map p260 (Гостиница Арбат; ☑499-271 2801; www.president-hotel.net/arbat; Plotnikov per 12; s/d from ₽10,000/11,500; ❸❇☎; Ⓜ Smolenskaya) One of the few hotels that manages to preserve some appealing Soviet camp – from the greenery-filled lobby to the mirrors behind the bar. The guestrooms are decorated tastefully and comfortably, but the whole place has an anachronistic charm. Its location is excellent – a quiet residential street, just steps from the Arbat. Prices decrease by 40% on weekends.

RADISSON ROYAL
HISTORIC HOTEL €€€

(Радиссон; ☑495-221 5555; www.radissonblu.com; Kutuzovsky pr 2/1; r from ₽11,000; ❸❇☎❄; Ⓜ Kievskaya) Housed in one of Stalin's Seven Sisters, this bombastic beauty sits majestically on the banks of the Moscow River facing the White House. The place has retained its old-fashioned ostentation, with crystal chandeliers, polished marble and a thematic ceiling fresco in the lobby. Heavy drapes, textured wallpaper and reproduction antiques give the guestrooms a similar atmosphere of old aristocracy, but all the modern amenities are here.

Significant discounts are available if you book well in advance or if you're willing to prepay a nonrefundable room.

🛌 Zamoskvorechie

THREE PENGUINS
HOSTEL €

Map p266 (Три Пингвина; ☑8-910-446 1778; www.3penguins.ru; ul Pyatnitskaya 20, str 2; dm/d ₽750/₽2600; ☎; Ⓜ Novokuznetskaya) It's a very small hostel located in a converted flat with a comfy (we'd even say intimate) common area in the building best identified by cafe Illarion, just off ul Pyatnitskaya. Apart from the dorms, it features four doubles – two regular and two with bunk beds.

The Penguins scores high on friendliness and has a prime location in Zamoskovrechie's busiest area (also convenient for the Kremlin). Numerous cafes and Tretyakov Gallery are in close proximity.

DANILOVSKAYA HOTEL
HOTEL €€

(Даниловская гостиница; ☑495-954 0503; www.danilovsky.ru; Bul Starodanilovsky per; s/d ₽6000/6500; ❸❇@☎; Ⓜ Tulskaya) Moscow's holiest hotel is on the grounds of the 12th-century monastery of the same name – the exquisite setting comes complete with

18th-century churches and well-maintained gardens. The modern five-storey hotel was built so that nearly all the rooms have a view of the grounds. The recently renovated rooms are simple but clean, and breakfast is modest: no greed, gluttony or sloth to be found here.

MERCURE MOSCOW PAVELETSKAYA
HOTEL €€

Map p266 (☑495-720 5301; www.mercure.com; ul Bakhrushina 11; r from ₽5900; ☎; ⓂPaveletskaya) This Mercure branch seems to consist entirely of virtues. Convenient for Domodedovo Airport trains and close to Paveletskaya metro station, it is a quality hotel with plush rooms (purple colour prevailing), located in a quiet street of portly 19th-century houses, offering four-star comforts for a price that's hard to come by in Moscow.

The complimentary spa facilities are something you might be thankful for after a sweaty day in Moscow.

IBIS BAKHRUSHINA
HOTEL €€

Map p266 (☑495-720 5301; www.ibis.com; ul Bakhrushina 11; r from ₽3990; ✻☎; ⓂPaveletskaya) The Ibis' latest incursion into the city centre has improved the hotel scene here in a big way. Yes, it's just another Ibis; but in Moscow knowing exactly what you're getting is a big deal: affordable, comfortable rooms and professional, reliable service. Spa facilities in the adjacent Mercure hotel are available at extra charge.

OZERKOVSKAYA HOTEL
BOUTIQUE HOTEL €€

Map p266 (Озерковская гостиница; ☑495-783 5553; www.ozerkhotel.ru/eng; Ozerkovskaya nab 50; s/d from ₽5940/6900; ☻☎; ⓂPaveletskaya) This comfy, cosy hotel has only 27 rooms, including three that are tucked up under the mansard roof. The rooms are simply decorated, but parquet floors and comfortable queen-sized beds rank it above the standard post-Soviet fare. Add in attentive service and a central location (convenient for the express train to Domodedovo Airport), and you've got an excellent-value accommodation option.

WEEKEND INN APARTMENTS
GUESTHOUSE €€

Map p266 (☑495-648 4047; www.weekend-inn.ru; ul Pyatnitskaya 10, str 1; d/tr from ₽3900/4500; ⓂNovokuznetskaya) A short walk from the Kremlin across the river, this modest establishment occupies two upper floors in a 19th-century building. Rooms are spacious, with whitewashed walls and minimalist design. Shared bathrooms are immaculately clean and there is a common kitchen area, but there's honestly no reason to bother cooking – the area is packed with cafes.

ALROSA ON KAZACHY
BOUTIQUE HOTEL €€

Map p266 (Алроса на Казачьем; ☑495-745 2190; www.alrosa-hotels.ru; 1-y Kazachy per 4; s/d from ₽6400/6700; ☻✻☎♨; ⓂPolyanka) Set in the heart of Zamoskvorechie, one of the oldest and most evocative parts of Moscow, the Alrosa re-creates the atmosphere of an 18th-century estate. The light-filled atrium, bedecked with a crystal chandelier, and 15 classically decorated rooms provide a perfect setting for old-fashioned Russian hospitality. Reduced rates apply on weekends.

WARSAW HOTEL
HOTEL €€

Map p266 (Гостиница Варшава; ☑495-238 7701; www.hotelwarsaw.ru; Leninsky pr 2/1; s/d from ₽4600/5600; ☻✻☎; ⓂOktyabrskaya) In a traffic-ridden square dominated by a giant Lenin statue, but convenient for Gorky Park, this Soviet-era oldie has been fully renovated, as evidenced by the sparkling, space-age lobby adorned with lots of chrome, blue leather furniture and spider-like light fixtures. The new rooms are decent value for the location.

PARK INN SADU
HOTEL €€

Map p266 (☑495-644 4844; www.parkinn.ru; ul Bolshaya Polyanka 17; s/d from ₽3900/4500; ✻☎; ⓂPolyanka) It's a very regular branch of the Park Inn – think slightly impersonal, predictable comforts – which boasts a prime location within walking distance of the Kremlin and the Red October cluster of bars and galleries. Prices fall to a jaw-dropping low in the middle of summer.

SWISSÔTEL KRASNYE HOLMY
HOTEL €€€

Map p266 (☑495-787 9800; www.moscow.swissotel.com; Kosmodamianskaya nab 52; r from ₽17,000/19,800; ☻✻☎♨; ⓂPaveletskaya) The metallic skyscraper towering over the Moscow River is the swish Swissôtel Krasnye Holmy, named for this little-known neighbourhood of Moscow. Rooms are sumptuous, subtle and spacious. The decor is minimalist: rich, dark hardwood floors and a few modernist paintings, but nothing to detract from the striking city skyline.

If you don't want to dish out the cash to spend the night, you can still enjoy the views by heading up to the City Space Bar on the 32nd floor.

HOTEL BALTSCHUG KEMPINSKI
HISTORIC HOTEL €€€

Map p266 (Балчуг Кемпински; ☎495-287 2000; www.kempinski-moscow.com; ul Balchug 1; r without/with view from ₽13,000/16,000; ◉✴ 🛜🛏; ⓜKitay-Gorod, Ploshchad Revolyutsii) If you want to wake up to views of the sun glinting off the Kremlin's golden domes, this luxurious property on the Moscow River is the place for you. It is a historic hotel, built in 1898, with 230 high-ceilinged rooms that are sophisticated and sumptuous in design. The on-site restaurant is famous for its Sunday brunch, or 'linner' if you prefer, as it's served from 12.30pm to 4.30pm. Russian champagne and live jazz accompany an extravagant buffet.

Discounts on Friday and Saturday nights make this a great place for a weekend splurge.

🛏 Meshchansky & Basmanny

PRIVET HOSTEL
HOSTEL €

Map p270 (Хостел Привет; ☎495-374 5949; www.privethostels.ru; per Podsosensky 3, str 2; dm from ₽800; 🛜; ⓜKurskaya) Declaring itself the largest hostel in the ex-USSR, Privet occupies a mansion in the sweet and central Chistye Prudy neighbourhood. All painted in deep purple, four- and six-bed dorms have solid wooden bunk beds with orthopaedic mattresses, and some are equipped with smallish working tables. Showers and toilets look almost luxurious by Russian hostel standards. Also on the premises is a cafe serving breakfasts (at extra charge), a small communal kitchen, a gym and a small cinema showing films in Russian and English. The entrance is on per Barashevsky.

COMRADE HOSTEL
HOSTEL €

Map p270 (☎499-709 8760; www.comradehostel.com; ul Maroseyka 11; dm/s/d ₽650/1800/2200; ◉@🛜; ⓜKitay-Gorod) It's hard to find this tiny place – go into the courtyard and look for entrance No 3, where you might spot a computer-printed sign in the 3rd-floor window. Inside, is a great welcoming atmosphere, although the place is packed. Ten to 12 beds are squeezed into the dorm rooms,

plus there are mattresses on the floor if need be.

There is not really any common space, except the small foyer and kitchen, but everybody seems to get along like comrades. Breakfast is not included.

KITAY-GOROD HOTEL
HOTEL €€

Map p270 (Отель Китай-Город; ☎495-991 9971; www.otel-kg.ru; Lubyansky proezd 25; s ₽3800-5500, d ₽5200-7500; ◉✴🛜; ⓜKitay-Gorod) A rare chance for budget-conscious travellers to stay this close to Red Square, not to mention easy access to the metro and many restaurants in the vicinity. Forty-six small but comfortable rooms are situated on two floors of this residential building.

The location can be noisy: it's worth requesting air-con as you'll want to keep your windows closed. Prices are lower on weekends.

ELOKHOVSKY HOTEL
HOTEL €€

Map p270 (Отель Елоховский; ☎495-632 2300; http://elohotel.ru/; ul Spartakovskaya 24; s/d ₽3900/4600; ✴🛜; ⓜBaumanskaya) Admittedly not very central and occupying the top floor of a shopping arcade, this hotel is nevertheless about the best value for money you can find in Moscow. Room themes are based on the world's major cities, and are painted in soothing, homey colours. The coffee machine in the lobby is available 24 hours. Baumanskaya metro and Elokhovsky cathedral are a stone's throw away.

Watching shoppers move four floors below without being able to see you is actually quite meditative.

HOTEL SVERCHKOV 8
HOTEL €€

Map p270 (Сверчков 8; ☎495-625 4978; www.sverchkov-8.ru; Sverchkov per 8; s/d ₽6000/7000; ◉✴🛜; ⓜChistye Prudy) Situated on a quiet residential lane, this is a tiny 11-room hotel in a graceful 19th-century building. The hallways are lined with green-leafed plants, and paintings by local artists adorn the walls. Though rooms have old-style bathrooms and faded furniture, this place is a rarity for its intimacy and homey feel.

HILTON MOSCOW LENINGRADSKAYA
HISTORIC HOTEL €€

Map p270 (☎495-627 5550; www.hilton.com; Kalanchevskaya ul 21/40; d from ₽7000; ◉✴🛜; ⓜKomsomolskaya) Occupying one of the iconic Stalinist skyscrapers, the old Leningradskaya Hotel has a new life thanks to the Hilton and its upgrade. Hilton has maintained the Soviet grandiosity in the lobby, but has updated the rooms with contemporary design and state-of-the-art amenities.

This is the most convenient option if you are arriving or departing by train, due to its proximity to three stations. This beauty overlooks Komsomolskaya pl, in all its chaotic, commotion-filled glory.

BENTLEY HOTEL
HOTEL €€

Map p270 (☑495-917-4436; www.bentleyhotel.ru; ul Pokrovka 28; s/d from ₽4300/5500; ❷ ❋ ☎ ❋; Ⓜ Kitay-Gorod) Upstairs from a popular American-style diner, Bentley goes all out to make its guests feel right at home. Cheeseburgers and fries aside, the mini-hotel is a warm and inviting place, with a dozen spacious and richly decorated rooms. Bonus: guests receive a discount on massages and other services at a nearby spa – the perfect way to recover after a day of sightseeing.

GODZILLAS URBAN JUNGLE LODGE
GUESTHOUSE €€

Map p270 (☑8-925-347 4677; www.godzillashostel.com/ujl/; ul Pokrovka 21, 3rd fl; s/d with shared bathroom ₽2450/₽3150; ☎; Ⓜ Chistye Prudy) A branch of Moscow's most popular hostel, this place has about a dozen funky-looking singles and doubles above the popular Coffee Bean cafe in one of the city's loveliest neighbourhoods.

Bathrooms are shared, and it's a bit of a walk up a steep and slightly off-putting staircase. But it is about as good as it gets for this price.

SRETENSKAYA HOTEL
HOTEL €€€

Map p258 (Сретенская гостиница; ☑495-933 5544; www.hotel-sretenskaya.ru; ul Sretenka 15; s/d ₽7900/11,300; ❷ ❋ @ ☎; Ⓜ Sukharevskaya) Special for its small size and friendly staff, the Sretenskaya boasts a romantic Russian atmosphere. Rooms have high ceilings and tasteful, traditional decor. This place is welcoming in winter, when you can warm your bones in the sauna, or soak up some sun in the tropical 'winter garden'.

Understand Moscow

Moscow Today

More than two decades into its reign as the capital of the Russian Federation, Moscow has proven itself. In this time the city has weathered economic crises and political transitions, building sprees and demolition derbies, terrorist attacks and festive celebrations. Now – with a newly prosperous middle class and a new look to boot – the city has settled into an upbeat but sustainable rhythm. What Stalin said is finally true: 'Life has become better, comrades. Life has become more joyous.'

Best on Film

Elena (2011) Winner of a Jury Prize at Cannes, this drama examines the meaning of love, family and class in modern Moscow.

Moscow Doesn't Believe in Tears (1980) Great chick flick that bagged an Oscar for best foreign-language film.

My Perestroika (2010) An insightful documentary about coming of age during the *perestroika* (restructuring) era and navigating life in contemporary Moscow.

Best in Print

The Master and Margarita (Mikhail Bulgakov) The most telling fiction to come out of the Soviet Union.

On the Golden Porch (Tatyana Tolstaya) Short stories focusing on big souls in little flats in the 1990s.

Anna Karenina (Leo Tolstoy) A legitimate alternative for readers who don't have time for *War and Peace*.

Children of the Arbat (Anatoly Rybakov) A tragic but vivid portrait of 1930s Russia.

Good Manners

It was not long ago that Moscow topped the list of the most unfriendly cities in the world. By 2013 the Russian capital had dropped to number 16 on the list, compiled by CNN. Muscovites may not stop to chat with strangers on the street, but it's undeniable that this city is developing better manners.

➡ The police force has cleaned up its act, with new uniforms, new standards for behaviour and a new name (*politsiya*, replacing the ominous-sounding *militsiya*).

➡ Driving rules and parking restrictions are being enforced, resulting in more conscientious driving. Notably, automobiles often stop at crosswalks to allow pedestrians to cross the street.

➡ In 2014 a countrywide ban on smoking in public places went into effect. This includes restaurants, bars, train platforms, and even apartment stairwells. Breathe freely, comrades.

➡ Smoking was restricted to promote good health, but what about cursing? Profanity was banned from films and theatre productions, while warning labels are required for offending literature and music. The reaction from Muscovites to this legislation is mixed: many support the effort to make people more *kulturny*, while others scoff '#$%& that!'

Could it be that Moscow's notoriously gruff population is getting good manners? Can civility be legislated?

Liveability

When Sergei Sobyanin became mayor of Moscow in 2010, he promised a shift in focus for Moscow – away from big business and huge construction projects – towards improving the city for regular residents.

Four years down the line, the results are visible and the city is much more liveable. Millions of residents are rejoicing.

Not only is Moscow becoming more polite, she is gradually but noticeably becoming an easier, cleaner, more pleasant place to live.

One of Mayor Sobyanin's first orders of business, back in 2011, was to clear out the thousands of kiosks that littered the city sidewalks. It was a controversial move – not exactly supportive of small business – but nobody really misses those makeshift shops selling cigarettes, beer and candy.

While streets are still congested, driving is more closely regulated, meaning people are driving more sanely and more safely. Sobyanin introduced paid parking in the city centre, so there are fewer cars on the narrow old streets. Urban development in the centre has focussed on parks and pedestrian ways, making it easier to navigate on foot – or even on bike.

Hipsters

Hipsters are taking over Moscow. You'll see these educated, good-looking, well-travelled people, mostly in their 20s and 30s, browsing the art galleries at Winzavod Center for Contemporary Art, populating the pubs and clubs in Red October, and playing ping-pong in Gorky Park. They are not particularly politicised, but they want to lead rich, rewarding, 'normal' lives – like their counterparts in Europe and America. Most importantly, they know what this looks like.

So when Putin made moves to appoint himself to a third presidential term in 2012, they took to the streets. Analysts agree that the protests 'for fair elections' were a political flop, in that they failed to effect change in the elections or fix flaws in the system. Strict laws were subsequently enacted to make sure public manifestations of discontent did not continue.

But the protesters did succeed in getting the administration to pay attention to them. Suddenly, the city's parks were revamped; flowers were blooming; fountains were flowing; and the calendar was packed with art markets, yoga classes and beach volleyball. Sergei Kapkov, who directed the transformation of Gorky Park, was appointed to head up the city's cultural department. He's now overseeing the design and development of the new, high-profile park in Zaryadie (on the former site of the Hotel Rossiya) and a revamp of the municipal library system. Some analysts believe that Kapkov's main mission is to keep the hipsters busy and happy. And he's doing his job...

Putin (and by extension, Sobyanin) recognises the importance of popular appeal. The president enjoys high approval ratings, and he understands that this lends him a degree of legitimacy (perceived election fraud aside). His tenure has seen life improve dramatically for most people in Moscow – especially the hipsters. And it keeps getting better. Who wants to organise a protest when you can go out for a bike ride instead?

population per sq km

MOSCOW   RUSSIA

≈ 8 people

if Moscow were 100 people

91 would be Russian
2 would be Ukrainian
2 would be Tatar
1 would be Armenian

4 would be other

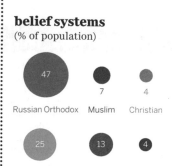

belief systems
(% of population)

47 Russian Orthodox
7 Muslim
4 Christian
25 Non-religious
13 Non-believers
4 Other

History

'Come to me, brother, please come to Moscow.' With these words, Yury Dolgoruky invited his allies to a celebratory banquet at the fortification he had erected on Borovitsky Hill, at the confluence of two rivers. The year was 1147. The settlement would prosper, eventually gaining power in the region and establishing itself as the capital of Ancient Rus. Nine centuries later – even as Russia has gone through multiple transformations – it is still ruled from the fortress that crowns Borovitsky Hill.

Medieval Moscow

Early Settlement

Moscow began as a trading post, set up by eastern Slav tribes who had migrated eastward from Kyivan Rus. Back in Kyiv, Grand Prince Vladimir I was anxious to secure his claim of sovereignty over all the eastern Slavs. He made his son Yaroslav the regional vicelord, overseeing the collection of tribute and the conversion of pagans.

After Vladimir's death, the descendants of Yaroslav inherited the northeastern territories of the realm, where they established a series of towns, fortresses and monasteries that is today known as the Golden Ring.

Political power gradually shifted eastward to these new settlements. During his reign, Grand Prince Vladimir Monomakh appointed his youngest son, Yury Dolgoruky, to look after the region. Legend has it that on his way back to Vladimir from Kyiv, Prince Yury stopped at Moscow. Believing that Moscow's Prince Kuchka had not paid him sufficient homage, Yury put the impudent boyar (high-ranking noble) to death and placed the trading post under his direct rule.

Moscow's strategic importance prompted Yury to construct a moat-ringed wooden palisade on the hilltop and install his personal vassal on site.

With its convenient access to rivers and roads, Moscow soon blossomed into a regional economic centre, attracting traders and artisans to the merchant rows just outside the Kremlin's walls. In the

History Books

....

Alexander Rodchenko: The New Moscow (Margarita Tupitsyn)

....

The Greatest Battle (Andrew Nagorski)

....

Lenin's Tomb (David Remnick)

....

Midnight Diaries (Boris Yeltsin)

TIMELINE	10th Century	1015	1113–25
	Eastern Slav tribes migrate from the Kyivan Rus principality further west, eventually assimilating or displacing the Ugro-Finnic tribes that had previously populated the region.	Vladimir I's realm is divided among his sons, leading to a violent period of family feuds. His son Yaroslav's descendants gain control over the eastern territories.	The Vladimir-Suzdal principality becomes a formidable rival in the medieval Russian realm. Grand Prince Vladimir appoints his son, Yury Dolgoruky, to look after the region.

early 13th century, Moscow became the capital of a small, independent principality, though it remained a prize contested by successive generations of boyar princes.

The Rise of Muscovy

In the 13th century, Eastern Europe was overwhelmed by the marauding Golden Horde, a Mongol-led army of nomadic tribespeople who appeared out of the eastern Eurasian steppes and were led by Chinggis (Genghis) Khaan's grandson, Batu. The ferocity of the Golden Horde raids was unprecedented, and quickly Russia's ruling princes acknowledged the region's new overlord. The Golden Horde's khan would constrain Russian sovereignty for the next two centuries, demanding tribute and allegiance from the Slavs.

The years of Mongol domination coincided with the rise of medieval Muscovy in a marriage of power and money. The Golden Horde was mainly interested in tribute, and Moscow was conveniently situated to monitor the river trade and road traffic. With Mongol backing, Muscovite officials soon emerged as the chief tax collectors in the region.

As Moscow prospered economically, its political fortunes rose as well. Grand Prince Ivan Danilovich earned the moniker of 'Moneybags' *(Kalita)* because of his remarkable revenue-raising abilities. Ivan Kalita used his good relations with the khan to manoeuvre Moscow into a position of dominance in relation to his rival princes. By the middle of the 14th century, Moscow had absorbed its erstwhile patrons, Vladimir and Suzdal.

Soon Moscow became a nemesis rather than a supplicant to the Mongols. In the 1380 Battle of Kulikovo, Moscow's Grand Prince Dmitry, Kalita's grandson, led a coalition of Slav princes to a rare victory over the Golden Horde on the banks of the Don River. He was thereafter immortalised as Dmitry Donskoy. This feat did not break the Mongols, who retaliated by setting Moscow ablaze only two years later. From this time, however, Moscow acted as champion of the Russian cause.

Towards the end of the 15th century, Moscow's ambitions were realised as the once-diminutive duchy evolved into an expanding autocratic state. Under the long reign of Grand Prince Ivan III, the eastern Slav independent principalities were forcibly consolidated into a single territorial entity.

After a seven-year assault, Ivan's army finally subdued the prosperous merchant principality of Novgorod and evicted the Hansa trading league. After Novgorod's fall, the 'gathering of the lands' picked up pace as the young Muscovite state annexed Tver, Vyatka, Ryazan, Smolensk and Pskov.

ST DANIIL

Prince Daniil became the first Grand Prince of Moscow at the end of the 13th century. Revered for his humbleness and diplomacy, he was canonised by the Russian Orthodox Church in 1652.

1147	1156	1237–38	1260s
Moscow is first mentioned in the historic chronicles when Yury Dolgoruky invites his allies to a banquet there: 'Come to me, brother, please come to Moscow.'	Moscow is fortified with a wooden fence and surrounded by a moat as protection against rival principalities and other attackers from the east.	The Mongols raze the city and kill its governor. Their menacing new presence levels the political playing field in the region, creating an opportunity for a small Muscovite principality.	Alexander Nevsky's youngest son, Daniil, inherits the territory of Moscow. The settlement is governed by his uncle until the child is old enough to rule.

In 1480 Ivan's army faced down the Mongols at the Ugra River without a fight. Ivan now refused outright to pay tribute or deference to the Golden Horde, and the 200-year Mongol yoke was lifted. A triumphant Ivan had himself crowned 'Ruler of all Russia' in a solemn Byzantine-style ceremony, earning him the moniker Ivan the Great.

Ivan the Terrible

At the time of Ivan the Great's death, the borders of Muscovy stretched from the Baltic region in the west to the Ural Mountains in the east and the Barents Sea in the north. The south was still the domain of hostile steppe tribes of the Golden Horde.

In the 16th century, the Golden Horde fragmented into four Khanates, which continued to raid Russian settlements. At this time, the grandson of Ivan the Great, Ivan IV (the Terrible), led the further expansion and consolidation of the upstart Muscovy state, defeating three out of four Khanates, securing control over the Volga River and opening up a vast wilderness east of the Urals. Ivan was less successful against the Crimean Tatars, who dominated the southern access routes to the Black Sea.

On the home front, the reign of Ivan IV spelt trouble for Moscow. Ivan came to the throne at age three with his mother as regent. Upon reaching adulthood, 13 years later, he was crowned 'Tsar of all the Russias'. (The Russian word 'tsar' is derived from the Latin term 'caesar'.) Ivan's marriage to Anastasia, a member of the Romanov boyar family, was a happy one, unlike the five that followed her early death.

When his beloved Anastasia died, it marked a turning point for Ivan. Believing her to have been poisoned, he started a reign of terror against the ever-intriguing and jealous boyars, earning himself the sobriquet 'the terrible'. Later, in a fit of rage, he even killed his eldest son and heir to the throne.

Ivan suffered from a fused spine and took mercury treatments to ease the intense pain. The cure, however, was worse than the ailment; it gradually made him insane.

The last years of Ivan's reign proved ruinous for Moscow. In 1571 Crimean Tatars torched the city, burning most of it to the ground. Ivan's volatile temperament made matters worse by creating political instability. At one point he vacated the throne and concealed himself in a monastery.

Upon his death, power passed to his 'feeble-minded' son, Fyodor. For a short time, Fyodor's brother-in-law and able prime minister, Boris Godunov, succeeded in restoring order to the realm. By the beginning of the 17th century, however, Boris was dead, Polish invaders occupied the

---

Medieval Moscow Sights

....

Kremlin

....

Kitay Gorod

....

St Basil's Cathedral

The Arbat is one of Moscow's oldest streets, dating back to the 15th century. Linguists believe the word Arbat comes from the Arabic word *arbad,* which means 'outskirts'. The Arabic word might have entered the Russian language by way of the Crimean Khanate, which was frequently attacking Moscow at this time.

1282	1303	1326	1328
On the southern outskirts of Moscow, Daniil founds the town's first monastery as a defensive outpost – now the Danilovsky Monastery.	Having become a monk before his death, Prince Daniil is buried in the cemetery at Danilovsky Monastery.	Moscow emerges as a political stronghold and religious centre. The head of the Russian episcopate departs Vladimir and moves into the Kremlin.	Grand Prince Ivan I (Kalita) gains the right to collect taxes from other Russian principalities, effectively winning control of the Vladimir-Suzdal principality.

Kremlin, and Russia slipped into a 'Time of Troubles'. Finally, Cossack soldiers relieved Moscow of its uninvited Polish guests and political stability was achieved with the coronation of Mikhail as tsar, inaugurating the Romanov dynasty.

Imperial Moscow

The Spurned Capital

Peter I, known as 'Peter the Great' for his commanding frame (reaching over 2m) and equally commanding victory over the Swedes, dragged Russia kicking and screaming into modern Europe. Peter spent much of his youth in royal residences in the Moscow countryside, organising his playmates in war games. Energetic and inquisitive, he was eager to learn about the outside world. As a boy, he spent hours in Moscow's European district; as a young man, he spent months travelling in the West. In fact, he was Russia's first ruler to venture abroad. Peter briefly shared the throne with his half-brother, before taking sole possession of it in 1696.

Peter wilfully imposed modernisation on Moscow. He ordered the boyars to shave their beards, imported European advisers and craftspeople, and rationalised state administration. He built Moscow's tallest structure, the 90m-high Sukharev Tower, and next to it founded the College of Mathematics and Navigation.

In Russian, Ivan IV is called Ivan Grozny, which usually gets translated as 'terrible'. It actually means something like 'dreadfully serious', in reference to the tsar's severity and strictness.

CHECK YOUR CALENDAR

For hundreds of years Russia was out of sync with the West. Until 1700 Russia dated its years from 'creation', which was determined to be approximately 5508 years before the birth of Christ. So at that time, the year 1700 was considered the year 7208 in Russia. Peter the Great – westward-looking as he was – instituted a reform to date the years from the birth of Christ, as they did in the rest of Europe.

Things got complicated again in the 18th century, when most of Europe abandoned the Julian calendar in favour of the Gregorian calendar, and Russia did not follow suit. By 1917, Russian dates were 13 days out of sync with European dates. Which explains how the October Revolution could have taken place on 7 November.

Finally, the all-powerful Soviet regime made the necessary leap. The last day of January 1918 was followed by 14 February 1918. All dates since 1918 have been identical to dates in the West.

We try to use dates corresponding to the current Gregorian calendar that is used worldwide. However, even history is not always straightforward, as other accounts may employ the calendars that were the convention at that time. Tell *that* to your history professor.

1327–33	1360	1380	1450s
The first stone structures are built within the Kremlin walls, including three elaborate limestone churches and a bell tower, each topped with a single dome.	The Kremlin is refortified and expanded. As the small village grows into an urban centre, Grand Prince Dmitry replaces the wooden walls with a limestone edifice.	Grand Prince Dmitry mounts the first successful Russian challenge to Tatar authority, earning his moniker Donskoy after defeating the Tatars in the Battle of Kulikovo on the Don River.	A Russian Orthodox Church is organised. When Constantinople falls to heathen Turks, Moscow is said to be the 'Third Rome', the rightful heir of Christendom.

Yet Peter always despised Moscow for its scheming boyars and archaic traditions. In 1712 he startled the country by announcing the relocation of the capital to a swampland, recently acquired from Sweden in the Great Northern War. St Petersburg would be Russia's 'Window on the West' and everything that Moscow was not – modern, scientific and cultured. Alexander Pushkin later wrote that 'Peter I had no love for Moscow, where, with every step he took, he ran into remembrances of mutinies and executions, inveterate antiquity and the obstinate resistance of superstition and prejudice'.

The spurned former capital quickly fell into decline. With the aristocratic elite and administrative staff departing for marshier digs, the population fell by more than a quarter in the first 25 years. The city suffered further from severe fires, a situation exacerbated by Peter's mandate to direct all construction materials to St Petersburg.

In the 1770s, Moscow was devastated by an outbreak of bubonic plague, which claimed more than 50,000 lives. It was decreed that the dead had to be buried outside the city limits. Vast cemeteries, including Danilovskoye and Vagankovskoye, were the result. The situation was so desperate that residents went on a riotous looting spree that was violently put down by the army. Empress Catherine II (the Great) responded to the crisis by ordering a new sanitary code to clean up the urban environment and silencing the Kremlin alarm bell that had set off the riots.

By the turn of the 19th century, Moscow had recovered from its gloom; Peter's exit had not caused a complete rupture. The city retained the title of 'First-Throned Capital' because coronations were held there. When Peter's grandson, Peter III, relieved the nobles of obligatory state service, many returned to Moscow. Moreover, many of the merchants had never left. After the initial shock of losing the capital, their patronage and wealth became visible again throughout the city.

The late 18th century also saw the construction of the first embankments along the Moscow River, which were followed by bridges. Russia's first university and first newspaper were started in Moscow. This new intellectual and literary scene would soon give rise to a nationalist-inspired cultural movement, which would embrace those features of Russia that were distinctly different from the West.

Moscow Boom Town

Moscow was feverishly rebuilt in just a few years following the Napoleonic War. Monuments were erected to commemorate Russia's hard-fought victory and Alexander's 'proudest moment'. A Triumphal Arch, inspired by their former French hosts, was placed at the top of Tvers-

In 1682 Peter I was installed as tsar. His half-sister, Sofia Alekseyevna, acted as regent, advising from her hiding place behind the throne. This two-seated throne – complete with hidden compartment – is on display at the Kremlin Armoury.

The Kremlin sat abandoned and empty from 1712 until 1773, when Catherine the Great commissioned a residence there. Construction of the palace did not move forward due to lack of funding. But several years later, architect Matvey Kazakov did build the handsome neoclassical Senate building, which stands today.

1475–1495	1478–80	1505–08	1508–16
Ivan III launches a rebuilding effort, importing Italian artisans and masons to construct the Kremlin's thick brick walls and imposing watchtowers.	Moscow subdues its rival principalities, and the Russian army defeats the Mongols at the Ugra River. Ivan III is crowned Ruler of all Russia, earning him the moniker 'Ivan the Great'.	Construction within the Kremlin continues, with the erection of the Ivan the Great Bell Tower, which would remain the highest structure in Moscow until the 20th century.	Alevizov moat is built outside the eastern wall of the Kremlin. The area outside the moat – present-day Red Square – is the town's marketplace.

kaya ul on the road to St Petersburg, and the immensely grandiose Cathedral of Christ the Saviour, which took almost 50 years to complete, went up along the river embankment outside the Kremlin.

The building frenzy did not stop with national memorials. In the city centre, engineers diverted the Neglinnaya River into an underground canal and created two new urban spaces: the Alexander Garden, running alongside the Kremlin's western wall; and Teatralnaya pl, featuring the glittering Bolshoi Theatre and later the opulent Hotel Metropol. The rebuilt Manezh, the 180m-long imperial stables, provided a touch of neoclassical grandeur to the scene.

A postwar economic boom changed the city forever. The robust recovery was at first led by the big merchants, long the mainstay of the city's economy. In the 1830s, they organised the Moscow Commodity Exchange. By midcentury, industry began to overtake commerce as the city's economic driving force. Moscow became the hub of a network of railroad construction, connecting the raw materials of the east to the manufacturers of the west. With a steady supply of cotton from Central

Imperial Moscow Sights
....
Kremlin Armoury
....
Cathedral of Christ the Saviour
....
Bolshoi Theatre
....
Triumphal Arch

THE BATTLE OF MOSCOW – 1812

In 1807 Tsar Alexander I negotiated the Treaty of Tilsit. It left Napoleon emperor of the west of Europe and Alexander emperor of the east, united (in theory) against England. The alliance lasted until 1810, when Russia resumed trade with England. A furious Napoleon decided to crush the tsar with his Grand Army of 700,000 – the largest force the world had ever seen for a single military operation.

The vastly outnumbered Russian forces retreated across their own countryside throughout the summer of 1812, scorching the earth in an attempt to deny the French sustenance, and fighting some successful rearguard actions.

Napoleon set his sights on Moscow. In September, with the lack of provisions beginning to bite the French, Russian general Mikhail Kutuzov finally decided to turn and fight at Borodino, 130km from Moscow. The battle was extremely bloody, but inconclusive, with the Russians withdrawing in good order. More than 100,000 soldiers lay dead at the end of a one-day battle.

Before the month was out, Napoleon entered a deserted Moscow. Defiant Muscovites burned down two-thirds of the city rather than see it occupied by the French invaders. Alexander, meanwhile, ignored Napoleon's overtures to negotiate.

With winter coming and supply lines overextended, Napoleon declared victory and retreated. His badly weakened troops stumbled westward out of the city, falling to starvation, disease, bitter cold and Russian snipers. Only one in 20 made it back to the relative safety of Poland. The tsar's army pursued Napoleon all the way to Paris, which Russian forces briefly occupied in 1814.

1524	1560	1571	1592
Novodevichy Convent is founded in honour of the conquest of Smolensk 10 years before. The fortress is an important link in the city's southern defence.	Provoked by the death of his wife, the ever-suspicious Ivan IV commences a reign of terror over the boyars (high-ranking nobles), thus earning him the moniker 'Ivan the Terrible'.	Moscow is burned to the ground by Crimean Tatars. As the city rebuilds, a stone wall is erected around the commercial quarters outside the Kremlin.	An earthen rampart is constructed around the city, punctuated by some 50 towers, marking the city limits at the location of the present-day Garden Ring.

Asia, Moscow became a leader in the textile industry. By 1890, more than 300 of the city's 660 factories were engaged in cloth production and the city was known as 'Calico Moscow'. While St Petersburg's industrial development was financed largely by foreign capital, Moscow drew upon its own resources. The Moscow Merchant Bank, founded in 1866, was the country's second-largest bank by century's end.

The affluent and self-assured business elite extended its influence over the city. The eclectic tastes of the nouveau riche were reflected in the multiform architectural styles of the mansions, salons and hotels. The business elite eventually secured direct control over the city government, removing the remnants of the old boyar aristocracy. In 1876, Sergei Tretyakov, artful entrepreneur and art patron, started a political trend when he became the first mayor who could not claim noble lineage.

The increase in economic opportunity in the city occurred simultaneously with a decline in agriculture and the emancipation of the serfs. As a result, the city's population surged, mostly driven by an influx of rural job seekers. In 1890, Moscow claimed over one million inhabitants. The population was growing so rapidly that the number increased by another 50% in less than 20 years. Moscow still ranked second to St Petersburg in population, but unlike the capital, Moscow was a thoroughly Russian city – its population was 95% ethnic Russian.

By 1900, over half of the city's inhabitants were first-generation peasant migrants. They settled in the factory tenements outside the Garden Ring and south of the river in the Zamoskvorechie district. The influx of indigents overwhelmed the city's meagre social services and affordable accommodation. At the beginning of the 20th century, Moscow's teeming slums were a breeding ground for disease and discontent. The disparity of wealth among the population grew to extremes. Lacking a voice, the city's less fortunate turned an ear to the outlawed radicals.

Red Moscow

Revolutionary Moscow

The tsarist autocracy staggered into the new century. In 1904 the impressionable and irresolute Tsar Nicholas II was talked into declaring war on Japan over some forested land in the Far East. His imperial forces suffered a decisive and embarrassing defeat, touching off a nationwide wave of unrest.

Taking their cue from St Petersburg, Moscow's workers and students staged a series of demonstrations, culminating in the October 1905 general strike, forcing political concessions from a reluctant Nicholas. In

---

Shortly after the Napoleonic War, the city's two outer defensive rings were replaced with the tree-lined Boulevard Ring and Garden Ring roads. The Garden Ring became an informal social boundary line: on the inside were the merchants, intellectuals, civil servants and foreigners; on the outside were the factories and dosshouses.

Tolstoy's most famous novel *War and Peace* tells the story of five aristocratic families in the lead-up to the Napoleonic invasion. The author used letters, journals, interviews and other first-hand materials to create the realist masterpiece, which includes some 160 real-life historical characters.

1591–1613	1601–03	1610–12	1613
Ivan IV dies with no capable heir, leaving the country in chaos. His death ushers in the so-called 'Time of Troubles', when Russia is ruled by a string of pretenders to the throne.	Russia suffers from widespread famine, which kills as much as two-thirds of the population. Over 100,000 people are buried in mass graves around Moscow.	The army of the Polish-Lithuanian Commonwealth occupies Moscow, until the arrival of a Cossack army, led by Dmitry Pozharsky and Kuzma Minin, which expels the Poles.	The Zemsky Sobor, a sort of parliament, elects Mikhail Romanov tsar. He is rescued from his exile in Kostroma and crowned, inaugurating the Romanov dynasty.

December the attempt by city authorities to arrest leading radicals provoked a new round of confrontation, which ended in a night of bloodshed on hastily erected barricades in the city's Presnya district.

Vladimir Ilych Ulyanov (Lenin) later called the failed 1905 Revolution the 'dress rehearsal for 1917'. He had vowed that next time Russia's rulers would not escape the revolutionary scourge. Exhausted by three years of fighting in WWI, the tsarist autocracy meekly succumbed to a mob of St Petersburg workers in February 1917. Unwilling to end the war and unable to restore order, the provisional government was itself overthrown in a bloodless palace coup, orchestrated by Lenin's Bolshevik Party. In Moscow, regime change was not so easy – a week of street fighting left more than 1000 dead. Radical socialism had come to power in Russia.

Fearing a German assault, Lenin ordered that the capital return to Moscow. In March 1918, he set up shop in the Kremlin and the new Soviet government expropriated the nicer city hotels and townhouses to conduct affairs. The move unleashed a steady stream of favour-seeking sycophants on the city. The new communist-run city government authorised the redistribution of housing space, as scores of thousands of workers upgraded to the dispossessed digs of the bourgeoisie.

The revolution and ensuing civil war, however, took its toll on Moscow. Political turmoil fostered an economic crisis. In 1921 the city's factories were operating at only 10% of their prewar levels of production. Food and fuel were in short supply. Hunger and disease stalked the darkened city. The population dropped precipitously from two million in 1917 to just one million in 1920. Wearied workers returned to their villages in search of respite, while the old elite packed up its belongings and moved beyond the reach of a vengeful new regime.

Red Moscow Sights

....

Lenin's Mausoleum

....

Moscow metro

....

VDNKh

....

Bunker-42

Stalin's Moscow

In May 1922 Lenin suffered the first of a series of paralysing strokes that removed him from effective control of the Party and government. He died, aged 53, in January 1924. His embalmed remains were put on display in Moscow, St Petersburg was renamed Leningrad in his honour, and a personality cult was built around him – all orchestrated by Josef Stalin.

The most unlikely of successors, Stalin outwitted his rivals and manoeuvred himself into the top post of the Communist Party. Ever-paranoid, Stalin later launched a reign of terror against his former party rivals, which eventually consumed nearly the entire first generation of Soviet officialdom. Hundreds of thousands of Muscovites were executed and secretly interred on the ancient grounds of the old monasteries.

1600s	1654–62	1682	1712
In the first half of the 17th century, the capital's population doubles to approximately 200,000 as settlements grow up outside the ramparts.	Wars with Poland and Sweden spur financial crisis. The production of copper coinage causes further economic hardship, sparking a massive uprising of 10,000 people on the streets.	A power struggle between two clans stirs up unrest among the Kremlin guard, which spreads to the Moscow mobs. Sofia Alekseyevna is installed as regent for her two brothers.	Peter I (the Great) surprises the country by moving the Russian capital from Moscow to St Petersburg.

In the early 1930s, Stalin launched Soviet Russia on a hell-bent industrialisation campaign. The campaign cost millions of lives, but by 1939 only the USA and Germany had higher levels of industrial output. Moscow set the pace for this rapid development. Political prisoners became slave labourers. The building of the Moscow–Volga Canal was overseen by the secret police, who forced several hundred thousand 'class enemies' to dig the 125km-long ditch.

The brutal tactics employed by the state to collectivise the countryside created a new wave of peasant immigrants who flooded into Moscow. Around the city, work camps and bare barracks were erected to shelter the huddling hordes who shouldered Stalin's industrial revolution. At the other end, Moscow also became a centre of a heavily subsidised military industry, whose engineers and technicians enjoyed a larger slice of the proletarian pie. The party elite, meanwhile, moved into new spacious accommodation such as the Dom na Naberezhnoy, on the embankment opposite the Kremlin.

Under Stalin, a comprehensive urban plan was devised for Moscow. On paper, it appeared as a neatly organised garden city; unfortunately, it was implemented with a sledgehammer. Historic cathedrals and bell towers were demolished in the middle of the night.

New monuments marking the epochal transition to socialism went up in place of the old. The first line of the marble-bedecked metro was completed in 1935. The enormous Cathedral of Christ the Saviour was razed with the expectation of erecting the world's tallest building, upon which would stand an exalted 90m statute of Lenin. This scheme was

In the 1940s the medieval Zaryadie district in Kitay Gorod was razed to make room for Stalin's 'Eighth Sister'. The massive skyscraper was never built, and the foundation eventually became the base of the gargantuan Hotel Rossiya (now demolished). The area is now slated for parkland.

THE BATTLE OF MOSCOW – 1941

In the 1930s Stalin's overtures to enter into an anti-Nazi collective security agreement were rebuffed by England and France. Vowing that the Soviet Union would not be pulling their 'chestnuts out of the fire', Stalin signed a nonaggression pact with Hitler instead.

Thus, when Hitler launched Operation Barbarossa in June 1941, Stalin was caught by surprise and did not emerge from his room for three days.

The ill-prepared Red Army was no match for the Nazi war machine, which advanced on three fronts. History repeated itself with the two armies facing off at Borodino. By December, the Germans were just outside Moscow, within 30km of the Kremlin. Only an early, severe winter halted the advance. A monument now marks the spot, near the entrance road to Sheremetyevo Airport, where the Nazis were stopped in their tracks. Staging a brilliant counter-offensive, Soviet war hero General Georgy Zhukov staved off the attack and pushed the invaders back.

1700s	1746	1755	1756
Moscow falls into decline in the first half of the century, when bureaucrats and aristocrats relocate to the north. By mid-century the population has dropped to 130,000.	The road to Tver becomes the road to St Petersburg, or Peterburskoye shosse, connecting the two capitals.	Compelled by Mikhail Lomonosov and Minister of Education Ivan Shuvalov, Empress Elizabeth establishes Moscow State University, the first university in Russia.	The country's first newspaper – the *Moscow News* (*Moskovskiye Vedemosti*) – is published at the new university, coming out on a weekly basis.

later abandoned and the foundation hole instead became the world's biggest municipal swimming pool. Broad thoroughfares were created and neo-Gothic skyscrapers girded the city's outer ring.

Post-Stalinist Moscow

When Stalin died, his funeral procession brought out so many gawkers that a riot ensued and scores of mourners were trampled to death. The system he built, however, lived on, with a few changes.

Nikita Khrushchev, a former mayor of Moscow, curbed the powers of the secret police, released political prisoners, introduced wide-ranging reforms and promised to improve living conditions. Huge housing estates grew up around the outskirts of Moscow; many of the hastily constructed low-rise projects were nicknamed *khrushchoby,* after *trushchoby* (slums). Khrushchev's populism and unpredictability made the ruling elite a bit too nervous and he was ousted in 1964.

Next came the long, stagnant reign of ageing Leonid Brezhnev. Overlooking Lenin's mausoleum, he presided over the rise of a military superpower and provided long-sought-after political stability and material security.

During these years, the Cold War shaped Moscow's development as the Soviet Union enthusiastically competed with the USA in the arms and space races. The aerospace, radio-electronics and nuclear weapons ministries operated factories, research laboratories and design institutes in and around the capital. By 1980 as much as one-third of the city's industrial production and one-quarter of its labour force was connected to the defence industry. Moscow city officials were not privy to what went on in these secretly managed facilities. As a matter of national security, the KGB discreetly constructed a second subway system, Metro-2, under the city.

Still, the centrally planned economy could not keep pace with rising consumer demands. While the elite lived in privilege, ordinary Muscovites stood in line for goods. For the Communist Party, things became a bit too comfortable. Under Brezhnev the political elite grew elderly and corrupt, while the economic system slid into a slow, irreversible decline. And the goal of turning Moscow into a showcase socialist city was quietly abandoned.

Nonetheless, Moscow enjoyed a postwar economic boom. Brezhnev showed a penchant for brawny displays of modern architecture. Cavernous concrete-and-glass slabs, such as the now defunct Hotel Rossiya, were constructed to show the world the modern face of the Soviet Union. The city underwent further expansion, accommodating more and more buildings and residents. The cement pouring reached a frenzy in

Many of Moscow's 'historic' sights are new buildings modelled after structures that were destroyed in the past. Kazan Cathedral and the Cathedral of Christ the Saviour were built in the 1990s, while the Great Wooden Palace at Kolomenskoe and the Great Palace at Tsaritsyno are both 21st-century constructions.

1770–80	1810–12	1824	1839–60
The bubonic plague breaks out in Moscow, killing as many as 50,000 people. By the end of the decade, the population of St Petersburg surpasses that of Moscow.	Russia defies its treaty with France, provoking Napoleon and his Grand Army to invade Russia. According to some, Muscovites burn down their own city in anticipation of the invasion.	The Bolshoi Theatre and the Maly Theatre are built on the aptly named Theatre Square, with the inauguration of the historic venues taking place the following year.	To celebrate the heroic victory over France in the Napoleonic Wars, the Cathedral of Christ the Saviour is built on the banks of the Moscow River.

ALCOHOLISM

the build-up to the 1980 Summer Olympics. However, Russia's invasion of Afghanistan caused many nations to boycott the Games and the facilities mostly stood empty.

Appreciation for Moscow's past began to creep back into city planning. Most notably, Alexander's Triumphal Arch was reconstructed, though plans to re-erect Peter's tall Sukharev Tower were not realised. Residential life continued to move further away from the city centre, which was increasingly occupied by the governing elite. Shoddy high-rise apartments went up on the periphery and metro lines were extended outward.

The attraction for Russians to relocate to Moscow in these years was, and continues to be, very strong. City officials tried desperately to enforce the residency permit system, but to no avail. In 1960 the population topped six million, and by 1980 it surpassed eight million. The spillover led to the rapid growth of Moscow's suburbs. While industry, especially the military industry, provided the city's economic foundation, many new jobs were created in science, education and public administration. The city became a little more ethnically diverse, particularly with the arrival of petty-market traders from Central Asia and the Caucasus.

Transitional Moscow

The Communist Collapse

The Soviet leadership showed it was not immune to change when Mikhail Gorbachev came to power in March 1985 with a mandate to revitalise the ailing socialist system. Gorbachev soon launched a multifaceted program of reform under the catchphrase 'perestroika' (restructuring). Gorbachev recognised that it would take more than bureaucratic reorganisations and stern warnings to reverse economic decline. He believed that the root of the economic crisis was society's alienation from the socialist system. Thus, he sought to break down the barrier between 'us' and 'them'.

His reforms were meant to engage the population and stimulate initiative. Glasnost (openness) gave new voice to both a moribund popular culture and a stifled media sector. Democratisation introduced multicandidate elections and new deliberative legislative bodies. Cooperatives brought the first experiments in market economics in over 50 years. Gorbachev's plan was to lead a gradual transition to reform socialism, but in practice, events ran ahead of him. Moscow set the pace.

In 1985 Gorbachev promoted Boris Yeltsin from his Urals bailiwick into the central leadership as the new head of Moscow. Yeltsin was giv-

In the 1970s, Moscow's most devastating social problem was alcoholism, cited as the major factor behind the high rate of absenteeism, abuse and truancy. Alcoholism was so rampant that Gorbachev tried to limit consumption to two bottles of vodka per week per family, which was not a popular policy initiative.

1861	1862	1905	1905
The 'liberator tsar' Alexander II enacts the Emancipation Reform, which liberates the serfs. Moscow's population surges as thousands of peasants descend on the big city.	Ivan Turgenev's novel Fathers and Sons kicks off the nihilist movement, an early forerunner of populism, anarchism and eventually Bolshevism.	Upon institution of the new position of 'city governor', the tsar appoints Alexander Adrianov as the first Mayor of Moscow.	The unpopular Russo-Japanese War provokes general strikes in Moscow and St Petersburg. In Moscow street barricades are set up, and fighting takes place in Presnya.

en the assignment of cleaning up the corrupt Moscow party machine and responded by sacking hundreds of officials. His populist touch made him an instant success with Muscovites, who were often startled to encounter him riding public transport or berating a shopkeeper for not displaying his sausage. During Gorbachev's ill-advised anti-alcohol campaign, Yeltsin saved Moscow's largest brewery from having to close its doors.

More importantly, Yeltsin embraced the more open political atmosphere. He allowed 'informal' groups, unsanctioned by the Communist Party, to organise and express themselves in public. Soon Moscow streets, such as those in the Arbat district, were hosting demonstrations by democrats, nationalists, reds and greens. Yeltsin's renegade

History Museums

Jewish Museum

State History Museum

Contemporary History Museum

Gulag History Museum

HISTORY TRANSITIONAL MOSCOW

LENIN UNDER GLASS

Red Square is home to the world's most famous mummy, that of Vladimir Ilych Lenin. When he died of a massive stroke on 22 January 1924, aged 53, a long line of mourners patiently gathered in the depths of winter for weeks to glimpse the body as it lay in state. Inspired by the spectacle, Stalin proposed that the father of Soviet communism should continue to serve the cause as a holy relic. So the decision was made to preserve Lenin's corpse for perpetuity, against the vehement protests of his widow, as well as Lenin's own expressed desire to be buried next to his mother in St Petersburg.

Boris Zbarsky, a biochemist, and Vladimir Voribov, an anatomist, were issued a political order to put a stop to the natural decomposition of the body. The pair worked frantically in a secret laboratory in search of a long-term chemical solution. In the meantime the body's dark spots were bleached, and the lips and eyes sewn tight. The brain was removed and taken to another secret laboratory, to be sliced and diced by scientists for the next 40 years in the hope of uncovering its hidden genius.

In July 1924 the scientists hit upon a formula to successfully arrest the decaying process, a closely guarded state secret. This necrotic craft was passed on to Zbarsky's son, who ran the Kremlin's covert embalming lab for decades. After the fall of communism, Zbarsky came clean: the body is wiped down every few days and then, every 18 months, thoroughly examined and submerged in a tub of chemicals, including paraffin wax. The institute has now gone commercial, offering its services and secrets to wannabe immortals for a mere million dollars.

In the early 1990s Boris Yeltsin expressed his intention to heed Lenin's request and bury him in St Petersburg, setting off a furore from the political left as well as more muted objections from Moscow tour operators. It seems that the mausoleum, the most sacred shrine of Soviet communism, and the mummy, the literal embodiment of the Russian Revolution, will remain in place for at least several more years.

1914–17	1917	1918	1922–24
Russia suffers immeasurably from losses in WWI. By 1916, Russia has sustained as many as 1.6 million casualties. High prices and food shortages affect the population.	Tsar Nicholas II succumbs to a mob of workers in St Petersburg and abdicates the throne. A provisional government is set up in an attempt to restore order.	The Bolshevik Party seizes power from the ineffective provisional government. In fear of a German attack, Vladimir Ilych Ulyanov (Lenin) moves the capital back to Moscow.	Lenin dies after a series of strokes and is succeeded by Josef Stalin. Nearly one million mourners arrive to pay their respects while Lenin lies in state.

GORBACHEV

style alienated the entire party leadership, one by one. He was summarily dismissed by Gorbachev in 1987, though he would be heard from again.

Gorbachev's political reforms included elections to reformed local assemblies in the spring of 1990. By this time, communism had already fallen in Eastern Europe and events in the Soviet Union were becoming increasingly radical. In their first free election in 88 years, Muscovites turned out in large numbers at the polls and voted a bloc of democratic reformers into office.

The new mayor was economist Gavril Popov, and the vice-mayor was Yury Luzhkov. Popov immediately embarked on the 'decommunisation' of the city, selling off housing and state businesses and restoring pre-revolutionary street names. He clashed repeatedly with the Soviet leadership over the management of city affairs. Popov soon acquired a key ally when Yeltsin made a political comeback as the elected head of the new Russian Supreme Soviet.

On 18 August 1991, the city awoke to find a column of tanks in the street and a 'Committee for the State of Emergency' claiming to be in charge. This committee was composed of leaders from the Communist Party, the KGB and the military. They had already detained Gorbachev at his Crimean dacha and issued directives to arrest Yeltsin and the Moscow city leadership.

But the ill-conceived coup quickly went awry and confusion ensued. Yeltsin, Popov and Luzhkov made it to the Russian parliament building, the so-called White House, to rally opposition. Crowds gathered at the White House, persuaded some of the tank crews to switch sides and started to build barricades. Yeltsin climbed on a tank to declare the coup illegal and call for a general strike. He dared the snipers to shoot him, and when they didn't, the coup was over.

The following day, huge crowds opposed to the coup gathered in Moscow. Coup leaders lost their nerve, one committed suicide, some fell ill and the others simply got drunk. On 21 August, the tanks withdrew; the coup was foiled. Gorbachev flew back to Moscow to resume command, but his time was up as well. On 23 August, Yeltsin banned the Communist Party in Russia.

Gorbachev embarked on a last-ditch bid to save the Soviet Union with proposals for a looser union of independent states. Yeltsin, however, was steadily transferring control over everything that mattered from Soviet hands into Russian ones. On 8 December, Yeltsin and the leaders of Ukraine and Belarus, after several rounds of vodka toasts, announced that the USSR no longer existed. They proclaimed a new Commonwealth of Independent States (CIS), a vague alliance of fully

It is well known that Mikhail Gorbachev won the Nobel Peace Prize, in 1990, for his efforts to end the Cold War. It is less known that he also won a Grammy Award in 2004, for his spoken word album for children *Peter and the Wolf, Wolf Tracks*.

1930s	1931	1935	1941–44
Stalin launches a campaign of modernisation and a reign of terror. Moscow becomes an industrial city, complete with poor workers and billowing factories.	The massive Cathedral of Christ the Saviour is destroyed by dynamite to make way for the Palace of Soviets, a Lenin-topped monument to socialism.	Members of the Komsomol (Communist youth) pitch in to construct the Komsomolskaya metro station. The first line of the metro, the Sokolniki line, starts operation.	Hitler defies a German-Soviet nonaggression pact and attacks Russia. The Nazi advance is halted by a severe winter, allowing the embattled Red Army to fight back.

independent states with no central authority. Gorbachev, a president without a country or authority, formally resigned on 25 December, the day the white, blue and red Russian flag replaced the Soviet red flag over the Kremlin.

Rebirth of Russian Politics

Buoyed by his success over Gorbachev and the coup plotters, Yeltsin (now Russia's president) was granted extraordinary powers by the parliament to find a way out of the Soviet wreckage. Yeltsin used these powers to launch radical economic reforms and rapprochement with the West. In so doing, he polarised the political elite. As Yeltsin's team of economic reformers began to dismantle the protected and subsidised command economy, the parliament finally acted in early 1992 to seize power back from the president. A stalemate ensued that lasted for a year and a half.

Historic Estates
....
Kolomenskoe
....
Tsaritsyno
....
Izmaylovsky Park
....
Ostankino Palace

The executive-legislative conflict at the national level was played out in Moscow politics as well. After the Soviet fall, the democratic bloc that had brought Popov to power came apart. In Moscow a property boom began, as buildings and land with no real owners changed hands at a dizzying rate with dubious legality. Increasingly, the mayor's office was at odds with the city council, as well as the new federal government. Popov began feuding with Yeltsin, just as he had previously with Gorbachev.

In June 1992 the impulsive Popov resigned his office in a huff. Without pausing to ask him to reconsider, Vice-Mayor Yury Luzhkov readily assumed the mayor's seat. The city council passed a vote of no confidence in Luzhkov and called for new elections, but the new mayor opted simply to ignore the resolution.

Throughout 1993, the conflict between President Yeltsin and the Russian parliament intensified. Eight different constitutional drafts were put forward and rejected. In September 1993 parliament convened with plans to remove many of the president's powers. Before it could act, Yeltsin issued a decree that shut down the parliament and called for new elections.

Events turned violent. Yeltsin sent troops to blockade the White House, ordering the members to leave it by 4 October. Many did, but on 2 and 3 October, a National Salvation Front appeared, in an attempt to stir popular insurrection against the president. They clashed with the troops around the White House and tried to seize Moscow's Ostankino TV Tower.

The army, which until this time had sought to remain neutral, intervened on the president's side and blasted the parliament into submission.

1953	1956	1961	1958
Stalin dies and is entombed on Red Square. Nikita Khrushchev becomes first secretary. His main rival, Lavrenty Beria, is arrested, tried for treason and executed.	Khrushchev makes a 'secret speech' at the Party Congress, denouncing Stalin's repressive regime and justifying his execution of Beria three years earlier.	Stalin is removed from the mausoleum on Red Square and buried in the Kremlin wall.	Nearly three decades after the destruction of the Cathedral of Christ the Saviour, the massive hole in the ground becomes the world's largest swimming pool.

In all, 145 people were killed and another 700 wounded – the worst such incident of bloodshed in the city since the Bolshevik takeover in 1917. Yeltsin, in conjunction with the newly subjugated parliament, put together the 1993 constitution that created a new political system organised around strong central executive power.

Throughout the 1990s Yeltsin suffered increasingly from heart disease. But come 1996, he was not prepared to step down from his 'throne'. It has been widely reported that in the time surrounding the 1996 presidential election, Russia's newly rich financiers, who backed Yeltsin's campaign, were rewarded with policy-making positions in the government and with state-owned assets in privatisation auctions. In a scene reminiscent of the medieval boyars, the power grabs of these 'oligarchs' became more brazen during Yeltsin's prolonged illness.

Economic Prosperity

In the new Russia, wealth was concentrated in Moscow. While the rest of Russia struggled to survive the collapse of the command economy, Moscow emerged quickly as an enclave of affluence and dynamism. By the mid-1990s Moscow was replete with all the things Russians had expected capitalism to bring, but had yet to trickle down to the provinces: banks, shops, restaurants, casinos, BMWs, bright lights and nightlife.

The city provided nearly 25% of all tax revenues collected by the federal government. Commercial banks, commodity exchanges, big businesses and high-end retailers all set up headquarters in the capital. By the late 1990s, Moscow had become one of the most expensive cities in the world.

When the government defaulted on its debts and devalued the currency in 1998, it appeared that the boom had gone bust. But as the panic subsided, it became clear that it was less a crisis and more a correction for a badly overvalued rouble. Russian firms became more competitive and productive with the new exchange rate. Wages started to be paid again and consumption increased.

Millennium Moscow

Cops in the Kremlin

In December 1999 Boris Yeltsin delivered his customary televised New Year's greeting to the nation. On this occasion the burly president shocked his fellow countryfolk yet again by announcing his resignation from office and retirement from politics. The once-combative Yeltsin had grown weary from a decade full of political adversity and physical infirmity.

After years of deteriorating health, Boris Yeltsin died of congestive heart failure in 2007. He is buried in Novodevichy Cemetery, where his grave is marked by an enormous Russian flag, which is sculpted out of stone but gives the appearance that it is rippling in the wind.

In 2005, Yelena Baturina, property magnate and wife of Mayor Luzhkov, became Russia's first female billionaire. The wife of the current mayor, Irina Sobyana, is also in the construction industry, although she has yet to register on any lists of richest people.

1964	1979–80	1982–85	1985
A coup against Khrushchev brings Leonid Brezhnev to power, ushering in the so-called 'years of stagnation'.	Russia invades Afghanistan to support its communist regime against US-backed Islamic militants. Relations between the superpowers deteriorate.	Brezhnev's death ushers in former KGB supremo Yury Andropov as general secretary for 15 months until his death. His successor, Konstantin Chernenko, dies 13 months later.	Mikhail Gorbachev is elected general secretary of the Communist Party. Intent on reform he institutes policies of *perestroika* (restructuring) and *glasnost* (openness).

Yeltsin turned over the office to his recently appointed prime minister, Vladimir Putin. As an aide to the president, Putin had impressed Yeltsin with his selfless dedication, shrewd mind and principled resolve. It was Yeltsin's plan to spring this holiday surprise on the unprepared political opposition to bolster Putin's chances in the upcoming presidential election. The plan worked. In March 2000 Putin became the second president of the Russian Federation.

Mystery surrounded the cop in the Kremlin: he was a former KGB chief, but an ally of St Petersburg's democratic mayor; well versed in European culture, but nostalgic for Soviet patriotism; diminutive in stature, but a black belt in karate.

In his first term, Putin's popular-approval ratings shot through the onion domes. He brought calm and stability to Russian politics after more than a decade of crisis and upheaval. The economy finally began to show positive growth. The improved economic situation led to budget surpluses for the first time since the 1980s and wages and pensions were paid in full and on time.

Putin vowed to restore the authority of the Moscow-based central state, engineering a constitutional reform to reduce the power of regional governors and launching a second war against radical Chechen separatists. His main opponent in the 2000 election, Moscow Mayor Yury Luzhkov, took note and hastily allied his political machine with Putin's new 'Unity' party.

Putin was reelected in 2004. His second term accelerated the trend toward a more authoritarian approach to politics. Former police officials were named prime minister and speaker of the parliament. Restraints on mass media, civil society and nongovernmental agencies were further tightened.

Terror in the Capital

Though the origins of the Russian–Chechen conflict date to the 18th century, it is only in recent times that Moscow has felt its consequences so close to home. In September 1999 mysterious explosions in the capital left more than 200 people dead. Chechen terrorists were blamed for the bombings, although the evidence was scant. Conspiracy theorists had a field day.

In 2002 Chechen rebels wired with explosives seized a popular Moscow theatre, demanding independence for Chechnya. Nearly 800 theatre employees and patrons were held hostage for three days. Russian troops responded by flooding the theatre with immobilising toxic gas, disabling hostage-takers and hostages alike and preventing the worst-case scenario.

Post-Soviet Moscow Sights

....

Art Muzeon

White House

....

Hotel Moskva

HISTORY MILLENNIUM MOSCOW

Moscow is estimated to be the world's seventh-largest city by population. In 2011 Moscow negotiated a land deal, whereby the city acquired a huge tract of sparsely populated land, more than doubling its size and making it the world's seventh-largest city by geographic area, too.

1991	1992	1993	1997
A failed coup in August seals the end of the USSR. Gorbachev resigns and Boris Yeltsin becomes the first popularly elected president of the Russian Federation.	The former Chairman of the Moscow City Council, Yury Luzhkov is appointed Mayor of Moscow, replacing his patron Gavril Papov.	Yeltsin sends in troops to deal with dissenters at Moscow's White House and Ostankino TV Tower. It is Russia's most violent political conflict since 1917.	To celebrate the 850th anniversary of the founding of Moscow, the Cathedral of Christ the Saviour is rebuilt in its original location.

The victims' unexpectedly severe reaction to the gas and a lack of available medical facilities resulted in 130 deaths and hundreds of illnesses. The incident refuelled Russia's campaign to force the Chechens into capitulation.

Chechen terrorists responded in kind, with smaller-scale insurgencies taking place regularly over the next several years. Between 2002 and 2005, suicide bombers in Moscow made strikes near Red Square, on the metro, on airplanes and at rock concerts, leaving hundreds of people dead and injured.

Things settled down for a few years, but the terror was not over. Towards the end of the decade, attacks resumed in full force, occurring on an annual basis in and around the capital. Again, the metro, the airport and other means of transportation were key targets.

The capital has been relatively quiet since 2011, but nothing has been resolved and nobody believes that this is over. Newspapers regularly report on Federal Security Service (FSB) successes at foiling terrorist plots. Federal officials promise retribution, city officials increase security, and the violence continues.

> Since the beginning of the Second Chechen War in 1999, nearly 900 people have been killed by terrorist attacks in and around Moscow.

The Party after the Party

Starting from 1999, Russia recorded positive economic growth. After the devaluation of the rouble, domestic producers became more competitive and more profitable. A worldwide shortage of energy resources heaped benefits on the economy. The Russian oil boom, going strong since 2000, enabled the government to run budget surpluses, pay off its foreign debt and lower tax rates.

Moscow, in particular, prospered. The city continued to undergo a massive physical transformation, with industry emptying out of the historic centre and skyscrapers shooting up along the Moscow River. The city's congested roadways were replete with luxury vehicles. The new economy spawned a small group of 'New Russians', who were alternately derided and envied for their garish displays of wealth. Following decades of an austere and prudish Soviet regime, Muscovites revelled in their new-found freedom. Liberation, libation, defiance and indulgence were all on open display.

By the start of the 2010s, the economic rhythms of the city steadied. More than a decade of economic growth meant that wealth was trickling down beyond the 'New Russians'. In Moscow, the burgeoning middle class endured a high cost of living, but enjoyed unprecedented employment opportunities and a dizzying array of culinary, cultural and consumer choices.

> Moscow Mayor, Sergei Sobyanin's early initiatives included a crack-down on corruption and a halt to construction. One of his first acts in office was, controversially, to do away with some 2000 kiosks that were scattered over Moscow's streets and squares.

1998	1999	2002–04	2008–09
An artificially high exchange rate and fiscal deficit bring on a financial crisis, resulting in the devaluation of the rouble and the government's default on international loans.	On New Year's Eve, Yeltsin announces his immediate resignation, entrusting the caretaker duties of president to Prime Minister Vladimir Putin.	Chechen rebels take 800 hostages in a Moscow theatre. Suicide bombers strike the metro, aeroplanes and rock concerts, leaving hundreds dead and injured.	A worldwide financial crisis hits Russia hard. The economic recession is exacerbated by the falling price of oil and military entanglements with Georgia.

SNOW REVOLUTION, NO REVOLUTION

In 2008 Putin's second term as president came to an end and the constitution did not allow him to run for a third consecutive term. Putin's hand-picked presidential successor was law professor and Deep Purple fan Dmitry Medvedev, who made haste to install his predecessor as prime minister.

The change in power registered barely a blip on Russia's political lifeline. Four years later, Medvedev declined to run for re-election. Putin stepped up, and suggested his main man Medvedev would make an excellent PM. They switched places in 2012.

For about six months between the election and the inauguration, Moscow's streets and squares saw regular protests 'for fair elections'. The demonstrations morphed into broader antigovernment unrest, sometimes called the 'Snow Revolution'. The largest of these events attracted 100,000 participants and more, according to organisers.

But this energy fizzled. Once in office, Putin enacted legislation that severely restricted such actions, making it more difficult to get permission to assemble, and levying harsh fines on anyone who participated in unsanctioned demonstrations. The opposition movement suffered from a lack of unity and organisation. Muscovites had jobs to do and families to support and sporting events and art exhibitions to attend. And in the end...the capital returned to business as usual. And the Kremlin breathed a sigh of relief.

A New Era

Since the time when the mayor of Moscow became a full-time bureaucratic job, rather than an honorary aristocratic title, no one has held the position longer than Yury Luzhkov. And certainly no one was more influential in shaping postcommunist Moscow than the 'mayor in the cap'. During Luzhkov's 18-year run, Moscow realised its claim of being a global centre of power and wealth. The skyline was transformed, the economy boomed and international culture thrived. In the tradition of urban political bosses, Luzhkov provided plenty of bread and circuses, bluster and cronyism.

In 2010 long-simmering tension between the Kremlin and the mayor's office finally boiled over. After a semipublic spat, then-President Medvedev simply fired the unrepentant chieftain. Just to make sure that everyone knew it was personal, Medvedev's decree explained that the mayor had 'lost the trust of the president'.

Luzhkov's replacement, Sergei Sobyanin, was previously the head of the presidential administration under Putin. Like other prized possessions in Putin's Russia, Moscow now belongs to the Kremlin.

In 2013 American whistleblower Edward Snowden became Moscow's most mysterious resident, when he spent 39 days in the transit area at Sheremetyevo Airport while seeking asylum from the US Department of Justice. He was finally granted a one-year temporary asylum in Russia, with hopes of staying longer.

2008–12	2009–11	2010	2011
Putin's chosen successor, Dmitry Medvedev, is elected President and serves one term. Putin acts as Prime Minister, until he is eligible to return to the presidency.	Chechen terrorists continue their deadly campaign. Attacks claim hundreds of victims, as bombs are detonated on trains, in metro stations and at the airport.	The long-serving, popular mayor Yury Luzhkov is removed from office. He is replaced by Sergei Sobyanin.	Moscow negotiates a land deal, whereby the city acquires a huge tract of sparsely populated land, more than doubling its geographic area.

Performing Arts

Moscow has always been known for the richness of its culture, ranging from the traditional to the progressive. Whether a Tchaikovsky opera or an Ostrovsky drama, the classical performing arts in Moscow are among the best (and cheapest) in the world. But New Russia comes with new forms of art and entertainment. This bohemian side of Moscow – be it a beatnik band or experimental theatre – provides a glimpse of Russia's future.

Music

The classics never go out of style. This is certainly true for music in Moscow, where Mussorgsky, Stravinsky and especially Tchaikovsky still feature in concert halls on an almost daily basis. The atmosphere in these places is a little stuffy, but the musicianship is first rate and the compositions are timeless. However, music in Moscow takes many forms, and these days rock, blues and jazz are ubiquitous in the capital; you can also hear alternative contemporary styles like funk, ska, house, hip hop, trip-hop and more.

Classical & Opera

The defining period of Russian classical music was from the 1860s to 1900. As Russian composers (and painters and writers) struggled to find a national identity, several influential schools formed, from which some of Russia's most famous composers and finest music emerged. The so-called Group of Five, which included Modest Mussorgsky (1839–81) and Nikolai Rimsky-Korsakov (1844–1908), believed that a radical departure from Europe was necessary, and they looked to *byliny* (folk music) for themes. Mussorgsky penned *Pictures at an Exhibition* and the opera *Boris Godunov;* Rimsky-Korsakov is best known for *Scheherazade.*

Classical Music Venues

....

Tchaikovsky Concert Hall

....

Moscow Tchaikovsky Conservatory

....

Moscow International House of Music

Pyotr Tchaikovsky (1840–93) also embraced Russian folklore and music, as well as the disciplines of Western European composers. Tchaikovsky is widely regarded as the father of Russian national composers. His output – which includes the magnificent *1812 Overture;* concertos and symphonies; ballets *Swan Lake, Sleeping Beauty* and *The Nutcracker;* and the opera *Yevgeny Onegin* – are among the world's most popular classical works. They are certainly the shows that are staged most often at the Bolshoi and other theatres around Moscow.

Following in Tchaikovsky's romantic footsteps was Sergei Rachmaninov (1873–1943) and the innovative Igor Stravinsky (1882–1971). Both fled Russia after the revolution. Stravinsky's *The Rite of Spring,* which created a furore at its first performance in Paris, and *The Firebird* were influenced by Russian folk music. Sergei Prokofiev (1891–1953), who also left Soviet Russia but returned in 1934, wrote the scores for Sergei Eisenstein's films *Alexander Nevsky* and *Ivan the Terrible,* the ballet *Romeo and Juliet,* and *Peter and the Wolf,* so beloved by music teachers of young children. His work, however, was condemned for 'formalism' towards the end of his life.

Similarly, Dmitry Shostakovich (1906–75) was alternately praised and condemned by the Soviet government. He wrote brooding, bizarrely dissonant works, in addition to more accessible traditional classical music. After official condemnation by Stalin, Shostakovich's *7th Symphony* (also known as the *Leningrad Symphony*) brought him honour and international standing when it was performed by the Leningrad Philharmonic during the Siege of Leningrad. The authorities changed their minds again and banned his formalist music in 1948, then 'rehabilitated' him after Stalin's death.

Classical opera was performed regularly during the Soviet period, and continues to be popular. Nowadays, the top theatres – especially the Bolshoi – are attempting to showcase new works by contemporary composers, as well as unknown works that were censored or banned in the past.

Contemporary

Russian music is not all about classical composers. Ever since the 'bourgeois' Beatles filtered through in the 1960s, Russians both young and old have been keen to sign up for the pop revolution. Starved of decent equipment and the chance to record or perform in front of big audiences, Russian rock groups initially developed underground. All music was circulated by illegal tapes known as *magizdat,* passed from listener to listener; concerts were held in remote halls in city suburbs. By the 1970s – the Soviet hippie era – such music had developed a huge following among the disaffected, distrustful youth.

Andrei Makarevich was the leader of Mashina Vremeni (Time Machine), now considered one of the patriarch groups of Soviet rock. Inspired by the Beatles, the band formed in 1968, playing simple guitar riffs and singable melodies. Even today, Mashina Vremeni remains popular across generations.

The god of *russky rok,* though, was Viktor Tsoy, front person of the group Kino; the band's classic album is 1988's *Gruppa Krovi (Blood Group).* Tsoy's early death in a 1990 car crash sealed his legendary

Contemporary Music Venues
....
Masterskaya
....
Sixteen Tons
....
Rhythm Blues Cafe

MOSCOW ALBUMS

200km/h in the Wrong Lane The English-language debut of the sexy, pseudo-lesbian duo tATu earned the Moscow natives the devotion of sugar-sweet pop lovers around the world.

Best of the Red Army Choir The two-disc album uses classic folk songs and a few Soviet gems to show off the impressive vocals of Russia's celebrated choral group.

Eto bylo tak davno (That was so long ago) The first studio recording of Moscow musicians Mashina Vremeni (Time Machine) made the legendary group the tsars of *'russky rok'.*

Horowitz in Moscow Both emotionally moving and musically magnificent, this live recording showcases the performance of world-renowned pianist Vladimir Horowitz when he returned to his homeland after almost 60 years away.

Mergers & Acquisitions The insightful Ilya Lagushenko leads Moscow band Mumiy Troll in this album, providing sharp commentary and social criticism.

Moscow The live album of heavy-metal rocker Valery Kipelov, who once fronted the group Aria, known as the 'Russian Iron Maiden'.

Peter & the Wolf Each character in this children's classic is represented by a particular instrument and musical theme. Sergei Prokofiev wrote the masterpiece in 1936, after he returned to Moscow to live out his final years.

status. To this day, there is a graffiti-covered wall on ul Arbat that is dedicated to Tsoy, and fans gather on the anniversary of his death (15 August) to play his music.

Many contemporary favourites on the Russian rock scene have been playing together since the early days. One of the most notable Moscow bands (originally from Vladivostok) is Mumiy Troll, led by the androgynous Ilya Lagushenko. After 25 years, the band continues to produce innovative stuff. Its latest studio album, *SOS Matrosu,* was released in 2013.

Gaining worldwide renown is Bi-2, whose members Shura and Leva have lived in Israel and Australia. Their popularity soared with the release of their namesake album in 2000. The duo is famed for their collaborations with other Russian rock stars. Several years and several records later, this 'postpunk' duo often appears at Moscow rock festivals.

Making a name for herself in the folk scene, art-rock-folk vocalist Pelageya is apparently Putin's favourite. She sings rock arrangements of folk songs from around the world. Arkona represent the incongruous pagan metal movement – heavy metal music that incorporates Russian folklore, Slavic mythology and other pre-Christian rites. Arkona employs traditional Russian instruments and their lead singer is renowned for her death-growl singing style.

The likes of techno-pop girl duo tATu and pretty-boy singer Dima Bilan (winner of 2008's Eurovision Song Contest) are the tame international faces of Russia's contemporary music scene. tATu has been mostly on the fritz since 2011, although they did reunite long enough to perform at the Sochi Olympics.

At the other end of the spectrum, today's most renowned Moscow rockers are Pussy Riot, a feminist punk rock band, who famously staged a performance in the Cathedral of Christ the Saviour in protest of Putin's election in 2012. The one-minute performance was used in their music video *Punk Prayer,* and led to the arrest of three members of the band.

The women were sentenced to two years in prison, which was widely considered to harsh for the crime, but they were released on amnesty after about six months.

Ballet & Dance

Ballet in Russia evolved as an offshoot of French dance combined with Russian folk and peasant dance techniques. As a part of his efforts towards Westernisation, Peter the Great invited artists from France to perform this new form of dance. In 1738 French dance master Jean Baptiste Lande established a school of dance in St Petersburg's Winter Palace, the precursor to the famed Vaganova School of Choreography. The Bolshoi Opera & Ballet Company was founded a few years later in 1776.

The father of Russian ballet is considered to be the French dancer and choreographer Marius Petipa (1819–1910), who acted as principal dancer and premier ballet master of the Imperial Theatre. All told he produced more than 60 full ballets, including the classics *Sleeping Beauty* and *Swan Lake.*

At the turn of the 20th century, Sergei Diaghilev's Ballets Russes took Europe by storm. The stage decor was unlike anything seen before. Painted by artists such as Alexander Benois, Mikhail Larianov, Natalia Goncharova and Leon Bakst, it suspended disbelief and shattered the audience's sense of illusion.

Dance Venues
....
Bolshoi Theatre
....
Stanislavsky & Nemirovich-Danchenko Musical Theatre
....
New Ballet
....
Kremlin Ballet

Bolshoi Ballet

During Soviet rule ballet enjoyed a privileged status, which allowed companies such as the Bolshoi to maintain a level of lavish production and high performance standards. In the 1960s, Yury Grigorovich emerged as a bright, new choreographer, with *Spartacus, Ivan the Terrible* and other successes.

Grigorovich directed the company for over 30 years, but not without controversy. In the late 1980s he came to loggerheads with some of his leading dancers. Many stars resigned, accusing him of being 'brutal' and 'Stalinist'. With encouragement from President Yeltsin, Grigorovich finally resigned in 1995, prompting his loyal dancers to stage the Bolshoi's first-ever strike.

In the next decade, the Bolshoi would go through three different artistic directors, all of them promising, but none able to pry Grigorovich's grasp from the company. Finally, in 2004, rising star Alexey Ratmansky was appointed artistic director. Born in 1968 in Ukraine, Ratmansky was young but accomplished. Most notably, *The Bright Stream* – which received a National Dance Award in 2003 – earned him the promotion.

Ratmansky's productions were well received, even when he stretched the traditionally narrow focus of the Bolshoi. In 2006, in honour of the 100th anniversary of Dmitry Shostakovich's birthday, the Bolshoi ballet premiered the composer's ballet *Bolt*. Prior to that, the ballet was performed exactly once – in 1931 – before it was banned for its 'most serious formalist errors'. Ratmansky earned the Golden Mask in 2007 for his staging of *Jeu de Cartes*. In 2008 he re-created the revolutionary ballet *Flames of Paris,* which was originally performed in the 1930s. At the end of the 2008 season Ratmansky resigned.

Ratmansky was succeeded by Yury Burlaka, who is known for reconstructing classical ballets. The Bolshoi administration also appointed Yury Grigorovich as staff ballet master. Burlaka was a discreet presence in the Bolshoi, but he succeeded in carrying on Ratmansky's legacy, promoting promising young dancers and directing innovative programming. Prima ballerina Svetlana Zakharova starred in the 2009 one-act ballet *Zakharova Supergame*. The unusual piece was an on-stage video game by Italian choreographer Francesco Ventriglia.

The 2010 season opened with a ballet by French choreographer Angolin Preljocaj. Entitled *And then, 1000 Years Peace – Creation 2010,* the abstract piece was composed specially for the Bolshoi dancers. It was not your traditional ballet, as there is no storyline, but it was a cool, contemporary creation, with music by Laurent Garnier and costumes by Igor Chapurin.

Burlaka's contract expired in 2011. Around the same time, the director of the company, Gennady Yanin, also resigned suddenly amid scandal, when a website full of erotic photos (featuring Yanin) became public knowledge. Without a director or an artistic director, the Bolshoi administration acted quickly: soloist Yan Godovsky was named director, while Sergei Filin – previously director of the Stanislavsky and Nemirovich-Danchenko dance company – was appointed artistic director. Two years later, Filin was attacked with sulphuric acid, causing severe disfiguration and loss of eyesight. Three dancers were charged with the crime.

Despite these devastating developments, Filin has stayed on as artistic director at the Bolshoi, emphasising the artistry of the ballet and the importance of preserving the work of Grigorovich and Ratmansky. The show must go on. And the world awaits to see if this most celebrated theatre can recover from this latest, most horrific incident.

PERFORMING ARTS BALLET & DANCE

BOLSHOI THEATRE

After six years and a US$1-billion-plus renovation, the main stage of the Bolshoi Theatre reopened to much acclaim in the autumn of 2011.

Other Dance Companies

The Bolshoi is Moscow's best known (and therefore most political) ballet company, but other companies in the city have equally talented dancers and directors. Both the Kremlin Ballet and the Stanislavsky & Nemirovich-Danchenko Musical Theatre stage excellent performances of the Russian classics.

The New Ballet, directed by Pavel Nestratov, stages a completely different kind of dance. Dubbed 'plastic ballet', it combines dance with pantomime and drama. Productions vary widely, incorporating elements such as folk tales, poetry and improvised jazz. This bizarre, playful performance art is a refreshing addition to Moscow's dance scene.

Drama Theatres

Moscow Art Theatre

Moscow English Theatre

Taganka Theatre

Theatre

Moscow's oldest theatre, the Maly Theatre, was established in 1756 upon the decree of Empress Elizabeth. But Russia's theatre scene flourished under the patronage of drama-lover Catherine the Great, who set up the Imperial Theatre Administration and herself penned several plays. During her reign Moscow playwright Denis Fonvizin wrote *The Brigadier* (1769) and *The Minor* (1791), satirical comedies that are still performed today.

Alexander Ostrovsky (1823–86) was a prominent playwright who lived in Zamoskvorechie and based many of his plays on the merchants and nobles who were his neighbours. As the director of the Maly Theatre, he is credited with raising the reputation of that institution as a respected drama theatre and school. Other 19th-century dramatists included Alexander Pushkin, whose drama *Boris Godunov* (1830) was later used as the libretto for the Mussorgsky opera; Nikolai Gogol, whose tragic farce *The Government Inspector* (1836) was said to be a favourite play of Nicholas I; and Ivan Turgenev, whose languid *A Month in the Country* (1849) paved the way for the most famous Russian playwright of all: Anton Chekhov (1860–1904).

Chekhov lived on the Garden Ring in Presnya, though he spent much of his time at his country estate in Melikhovo. In 1898 Konstantin Stanislavsky implemented his innovative approach of method acting and made Chekhov a success. Chekhov's *The Seagull, The Three Sisters, The Cherry Orchard* and *Uncle Vanya,* all of which take the angst of the provincial middle class as their theme, owed much of their success to their 'realist' productions at the Moscow Art Theatre.

Through the Soviet period theatre remained popular, not least because it was one of the few areas of artistic life where a modicum of freedom of expression was permitted. Stalin famously said of Mikhail Bulgakov's play *White Guard* that, although it had been written by an enemy, it still deserved to be staged because of the author's outstanding talent. Bulgakov is perhaps the only person dubbed an 'enemy' by Stalin who was never persecuted.

Others were not so fortunate. The rebellious director of the Taganka Theatre, Yury Lyubimov, was sent into exile as a result of his controversial plays. The avant-garde actor-director Vsevolod Meyerhold suffered an even worse fate. Not only was his Moscow theatre closed down but he was imprisoned and later tortured and executed as a traitor.

Throughout the 1980s and 1990s, Pyotr Fomenko was unable to find permanent work until he set up his own theatre company, which became wildly popular almost immediately. The Pyotr Fomenko Studio Theatre moved into a proper (beautiful) home theatre in 2008, just a few short years before the beloved director died in 2012.

Today, Moscow's theatre scene is as lively as those in London and New York. The capital hosts over 40 theatres, which continue to en-

CHEKHOV

Anton Chekhov describes his style: 'All I wanted was to say honestly to people: have a look at yourselves and see how bad and dreary your lives are! The important thing is that people should realise that, for when they do, they will most certainly create another and better life for themselves.'

tertain and provoke audiences. Notable directors include Kama Ginkas, who works with the Moscow Art Theatre and the New Generation Theater; and Oleg and Vladimir Presnyakov, who cowrite and direct their plays under the joint name Presnyakov Brothers.

Circus

While Western circuses grow smaller and scarcer, the Russian versions are like those from childhood stories – prancing horses with acrobats on their backs, snarling lions and tigers, heart-stopping high-wire artists and hilarious clowns. No wonder the circus remains highly popular, with around half the population attending a performance once a year.

The Russian circus has its roots in the medieval travelling minstrels *(skomorokhi),* and circus performers today still have a similar lifestyle. The Russian State Circus company, RosGosTsirk, assigns its members to a particular circus for a performance season, then rotates them around to other locations. What the members give up in stability they gain in job security. RosGosTsirk ensures them employment throughout their circus career.

Many circus performers find their calling not by chance but by ancestry. It is not unusual for generations of one family to practise the same circus skill, be it tightrope walking or lion taming. As one acrobat explained quite matter of factly: 'We can't live without the circus. There are very few who leave.'

Moscow is home to several circuses, including the acclaimed Nikulin Circus on Tsvetnoy bulvar. Its namesake is the beloved clown Yury Nikulin, who is described as 'the honour and conscience of the Russian circus'.

Speaking of honour and conscience, most of the major troupes have cleaned up their act with regard to the treatment of animals. In Moscow circuses, it is unlikely you will see animals treated cruelly, though their very presence in the ring is controversial.

Circus

....

Nikulin Circus on Tsvetnoy Bulvar

....

Bolshoi Circus on Vernadskogo

Art & Architecture

The Russian capital is an endless source of amusement and amazement for the art and architecture aficionado. Moscow has great visual appeal, from the incredible Moscow baroque and Russian revival architecture to the world-famous collections of Russian and Impressionist art. Now the capital is experiencing a burst of creative energy as artists and architects experiment with integrating old and new forms in this timeless city.

Visual Arts

Art is busting out all over Moscow, with the ongoing expansion of the Pushkin Museum of Fine Arts and the countless new contemporary art galleries that are taking over the city's former industrial spaces.

Icons

Up until the 17th century, religious icons were Russia's key art form. Originally painted by monks as a spiritual exercise, icons are images intended to aid the veneration of the holy subjects they depict, and are sometimes believed able to grant luck, wishes or even miracles. They're most commonly found on the iconostasis (screen) of a church.

Traditional rules decreed that only Christ, the Virgin, angels, saints and scriptural events could be depicted by icons – with all meant to be copies of approved prototype images. Christ images include the Pantokrator (All-Ruler) and the Mandilion, the latter called 'not made by hand' because it was allegedly developed from the imprint of Christ's face on St Veronica's handkerchief. Icons were traditionally painted in tempera (pigment mixed with a binder such as egg yolk) on wood.

The beginning of a distinct Russian icon tradition came when artists in Novgorod started to draw on local folk art in their representation of people, producing sharply outlined figures with softer faces and introducing lighter colours, including pale yellows and greens. The earliest outstanding painter was Theophanes the Greek (1340–1405), or Feofan Grek in Russian. Working in Byzantium, Novgorod and Moscow, Theophanes brought a new delicacy and grace to the form. His finest works are in the Annunciation Cathedral of the Moscow Kremlin.

Andrei Rublyov (1370–1430), a monk at the Trinity Monastery of St Sergius and Andronikov Monastery, was the greatest Russian icon painter. His most famous work is the dreamy *Old Testament Trinity*, in Moscow's Tretyakov Gallery. The layperson Dionysius, the leading late-15th-century icon painter, elongated his figures and refined the use of colour. Sixteenth-century icons were smaller and more crowded, their figures more realistic and Russian-looking. In 17th-century Moscow, Simon Ushakov (1626–86) moved towards Western religious painting with the use of perspective and architectural backgrounds.

Besides the outstanding collection at the Tretyakov Gallery and the Rublyov Museum of Early Russian Culture & Art, there is an impressive private collection on display at the Museum of the Russian Icon, not to mention the many churches around town.

Andrei Tarkovsky's 1966 film *Andrei Rublev* interpreted the life of the icon painter amid the harsh realities of medieval Russia. Addressing themes such as religious faith and artistic freedom, the film was heavily censored in the Soviet Union, but was awarded a prize at the Cannes Film Festival in 1969.

Peredvizhniki & Russian Revival

The major artistic force of the 19th century was the Peredvizhniki (Society of Wanderers) movement, in which art was seen as a vehicle for promoting national awareness and social change. The movement gained its name from the touring exhibitions with which it widened its audience. These artists were patronised by the brothers Pavel and Sergei Tretyakov (after whom the Tretyakov Gallery is named). Peredvizhniki artists included Vasily Surikov (1848–1916), who painted vivid Russian historical scenes; Nikolai Ghe (1831–94), who depicted Biblical and historical scenes; and Ilya Repin (1884–1930), perhaps the best loved of all Russian artists, whose works ranged from social criticism (*Barge Haulers on the Volga*) to history (*Zaporozhie Cossacks Writing a Letter to the Turkish Sultan*) to portraits. Many Peredvizhniki masterpieces are on display at the Tretyakov Gallery.

Later in the century, industrialist Savva Mamontov was a significant patron of the arts, promoting a Russian revivalist movement. His Abramtsevo estate near Moscow became an artists' colony. One frequent resident was Viktor Vasnetsov (1848–1926), a Russian-revivalist painter and architect famous for his historical paintings with fairy-tale subjects. In 1894, Vasnetsov designed his own house in Moscow, which is now a small museum. He also designed the original building for the Tretyakov Gallery, as well as the chapel at Abramtsevo.

Nikolai Rerikh (1874–1947) – known internationally as Nicholas Roerich – was an artist whose fantastical artwork is characterised by rich, bold colours, primitive style and mystical themes. In 2013, Rerikh's mesmerising painting *Madonna Laboris* sold at auction in London for some £7.9, topping the ever-changing list of most expensive Russian paintings. In Moscow, Rerikh's paintings are on display at the Rerikh Museum and the Museum of Oriental Art.

The work of late-19th-century genius Mikhail Vrubel (1856–1910) is unique in form and style. He was inspired by sparkling Byzantine and Venetian mosaics. His panels on the sides of Hotel Metropol are some of his best work.

Avant-Garde

In the 20th century, Russian art became a mishmash of groups, styles and 'isms', as it absorbed decades of European change in a few years. It finally gave birth to its own avant-garde futurist movements.

Mikhail Larionov (1881–1964) and Natalya Goncharova (1881–1962) developed neoprimitivism, a movement based on popular arts and primitive icons. Just a few years later, Kazimir Malevich (1878–1935) announced the arrival of suprematism. His utterly abstract geometrical shapes (with the black square representing the ultimate 'zero form') freed art from having to depict the material world and made it a doorway to

RUSSIAN ART & ARCHITECTURE

ART & ARCHITECTURE VISUAL ARTS

1405

Andrei Rublyov paints the icons in the Annunciation Cathedral in the Kremlin and in the Assumption Cathedral in Vladimir, representing the peak of Moscow iconography.

1555

Churches with tent-roofs and onion domes represent a uniquely Russian architectural style, the pinnacle of which is St Basil's Cathedral on Red Square.

1757

The Imperial Academy of Art is established to support romantic and classical painting and sculpture.

1870

After boycotting the Imperial Academy of Arts, a group of rebellious art students form the Peredvizhniki (Society of Wanderers), whose work focuses on social and political issues.

1900–03

Fyodor Shekhtel fuses Russian revival and art nouveau to create architectural masterpieces such as Yaroslavsky station and Ryabushinksy Mansion.

1915–20

Kazimir Malevich publishes a treatise on suprematism, as exemplified by his iconic painting *The Black Square*. Constructivist artists and architects explore the idea of art with a social purpose.

higher realities. Another famed futurist, who managed to escape subordinate 'isms', was Vladimir Mayakovsky, who was also a poet. Works by all of these artists are on display at the New Tretyakov Gallery, as well as the Moscow Museum of Modern Art.

An admirer of Malevich, Alexander Rodchenko (1891–1956) was one of the founders of the constructivist movement. He was a graphic designer, sculptor and painter, but he is best known for his innovative photography. Rodchenko's influence on graphic design is immeasurable, as many of his techniques were used widely later in the 20th century.

Soviet-Era Art

Futurists turned to the needs of the revolution – education, posters and banners – with enthusiasm. They had a chance to enact their theories of how art shapes society. But, at the end of the 1920s, abstract art fell out of favour and was branded 'formalist'. The Communist Party wanted 'socialist realism', or realist art that advanced the goals of the glorious socialist revolution. Images of striving workers, heroic soldiers and inspiring leaders took over from abstraction. Plenty of examples of this realism are on display at the New Tretyakov Gallery. Two million sculptures of Lenin and Stalin dotted the country. Malevich ended up painting penetrating portraits and doing designs for Red Square parades; Mayakovsky committed suicide.

After Stalin, an avant-garde 'conceptualist' underground was allowed to form. Ilya Kabakov (b 1933) painted, or sometimes just arranged the debris of everyday life, to show the gap between the promises and realities of Soviet existence. The 'Sots art' style of Erik Bulatov (b 1933) pointed to the devaluation of language by ironically reproducing Soviet slogans and depicting words disappearing over the horizon.

In 1962 the Moscow artist union celebrated the post-Stalin thaw with an exhibit of previously banned 'unofficial' art. Cautious reformer Khrushchev was aghast by what he saw, declaring the artwork to be 'dog shit'. The artists returned to the underground.

Contemporary Art

In the immediate post-Soviet years contemporary painters of note abandoned Russia for the riches of the West. Today, with increased economic prosperity, many of the most promising young artists are choosing to stay put. There is unprecedented interest in contemporary art, as entrepreneurs are investing their new-found wealth in established and up-and-coming artists. Industrial space is being converted into art galleries such as Winzavod Center for Contemporary Art. The former Red October chocolate factory is packed with galleries and studio space.

BOGATYRS

Among the most beloved of Russian paintings is the evocative *Bogatyrs,* by Viktor Vasnetsov (on display at the Tretyakov). The oil painting depicts three characters from Russian folklore, or *bylina*. Heroic Ilya Muromets is supposedly based on an actual historic medieval warrior and monk; Dobrynya Nikitich is a noble warrior best known for defeating a dragon; and the cunning and crafty Alyosha Popovich often outsmarts his foes. *Bylina* was originally an oral tradition – a narrative song – that passed down legends of Kyivan Rus. The stories were published in written form starting in the 18th century. Vasnetsov's Russian revival paintings are yet another recasting of these ancient tales.

The best-known artists in Russia today are individuals who have been favoured by politicians in power, meaning that their work appears in public places. You might not know the name Alexander Burganov (b 1935), but you will certainly recognise his sculptures, which grace the Arbat and other locales. More notorious than popular is the artist and architect Zurab Tsereteli (b 1934), whose monumental buildings and statues are ubiquitous in Moscow.

Religious painter Ilya Glazunov (b 1930) has been a staunch defender of the Russian Orthodox cultural tradition, while Alexander Shilov (b 1943) is famous for his insightful portraits of contemporary movers and shakers.

The most intriguing aspect of Moscow's contemporary art scene is not the established artists with their own named galleries, but rather the up-and-coming creatives who are stashed at the city's art centres. Artists now have more freedom than they ever did in the past to depict all aspects of Russian life, with even the government pitching in to fund prestigious events such as the Moscow Biennale of Contemporary Art. That said, contemporary artists and curators risk prosecution, especially if they tackle such sensitive topics as the war in Chechnya, the Russian Orthodox Church or the Russian government.

1934

Avant-garde ideas are officially out of favour with the institution of socialist realism. Architecture tends toward bombastic neoclassicism.

1985

The policy of *glasnost*, or openness, gradually allows for more freedom of expression by artists and architects, who begin to explore diverse styles and themes.

Architecture

Moscow's streets are a textbook of Russian history, with churches, mansions, theatres and hotels standing as testament to the most definitive periods. Despite the tendency to demolish and rebuild (exhibited both in the past and in the present), Moscow has managed to preserve an impressive array of architectural gems.

Medieval Moscow

Moscow's oldest architecture has its roots in Kyivan Rus. The quintessential structure is the Byzantine cross-shaped church, topped with vaulted roofs and a central dome. In the 11th and 12th centuries, Russian culture moved from Kyiv to principalities further northeast. These towns – now comprising the so-called 'Golden Ring' – copied the Kyivan architectural design, developing their own variations on the pattern. Roofs grew steeper to prevent the crush of heavy snow; windows grew narrower to keep out the cold.

In many cases, stone replaced brick as the traditional building material. For example the white stone Assumption Cathedral and Golden Gate, both in Vladimir, are close copies of similar brick structures in Kyiv. In some cases, the stone facade became a tableau for a glorious kaleidoscope of carved images, such as the Cathedral of St Dmitry in Vladimir and the Church of the Intercession on the Nerl in Bogolyubovo.

Early church-citadel complexes required protection, so all of these settlements had sturdy, fortress-style walls replete with fairy-tale towers – Russia's archetypal kremlins. They are still visible in Suzdal and, of course, Moscow.

At the end of the 15th century, Ivan III imported architects from Italy to build two of the three great cathedrals in the Moscow Kremlin: Assumption Cathedral and Archangel Cathedral. Nonetheless, the outsider architects looked to Kyiv for their inspiration, again copying the Byzantine design.

Moscow's Art & Architecture

From icons and onion domes to skyscrapers and socialist realism, Russia has always invented its own forms of art and architecture – incorporating European influences but remaining true to its Slavic heart. There is no better place than Moscow to witness the dramatic and divergent visual expressions of Russian culture.

4

1. Kotelnicheskaya apartment block (p219)
One of Stalin's 'seven sisters' that dot the city's skyline.

2. Hotel Metropol (p81)
A beautiful example of Style Moderne, Russia's take on art nouveau.

3. Art Muzeon (p137)
Home to an array of sculpture and monuments torn down in the post-1991 wave of anti-Soviet sentiment.

4. Icons (p212)
Developed from a folk art tradition and now Russia's signature art form.

3

It was not until the 16th century that architects found inspiration in the tent roofs and onion domes on the wooden churches in the north of Russia. Their innovation was to construct these features out of brick, which contributed to a new, uniquely Russian style of architecture. The whitewashed Church of the Ascension at Kolomenskoe is said to be the earliest example of this innovative style, featuring open galleries at its base, tiers of *kokoshniki* (gables) in the centre, and the pronounced tent roof up top. Of course, St Basil's Cathedral is the ultimate example of the Russian style, but there are plenty of other examples around Moscow.

In the 17th century, merchants financed smaller churches bedecked with tiers of *kokoshniki* (gables), colourful tiles and brick patterning. The Church of St Nicholas in Khamovniki and the Church of the Trinity in Nikitniki are excellent examples, as are most of the churches in Suzdal. Patriarch Nikon outlawed such frippery shortly after the construction of the Church of the Nativity of the Virgin in Putinki.

Iconic Moscow Architecture

....

Ascension Church at Kolomenskoe

....

Church of the Intercession at Fili

....

Hotel Metropol

....

Narkomfin

Imperial Moscow

Embellishments returned at the end of the 17th century with the Western-influenced Moscow baroque. This style is sometimes called Naryshkin baroque, named after the boyar family that inhabited the western suburbs of Fili in the 17th century. There, in honour of his brothers' deaths, Lev Naryshkin commissioned the Church of the Intercession, the ornate beauty that would define the city's style for years to come. It featured exquisite white detailing against red-brick walls. Another example is the Epiphany Cathedral in the monastery of the same name in Kitay Gorod. Zamoskvorechie is a treasure chest of Moscow baroque churches.

Tsar Alexander I favoured the grandiose Russian Empire style, commissioning it almost exclusively. Moscow abounds with Empire-style buildings, since much of the city had to be rebuilt after the fire of 1812. The flamboyant decorations of earlier times were used on the huge new buildings erected to proclaim Russia's importance, such as the Triumphal Arch and the Bolshoi Theatre.

The Russian revival of the end of the 19th century extended to architecture. The Cathedral of Christ the Saviour was inspired by Byzantine Russian architecture. The State History Museum and the Leningradsky vokzal (Leningrad station) were inspired by medieval Russian styles. The extraordinary Kazansky vokzal (Kazan station) embraces no fewer than seven earlier styles.

Meanwhile, Russia's take on art nouveau – Style Moderne – added wonderful curvaceous flourishes to many buildings across Moscow. Splendid examples include Yaroslavsky vokzal and the Hotel Metropol.

Soviet Moscow

The revolution gave rise to young constructivist architects, who rejected superficial decoration; they designed buildings whose appearance was a direct function of their uses and materials – a new architecture for a new society. They used lots of glass and concrete in uncompromising geometric forms.

Konstantin Melnikov was probably the most famous constructivist, and his own house off ul Arbat is one of the most interesting and unusual examples of the style. The former bus depot that now houses the Jewish Museum & Centre of Tolerance is a more utilitarian example. In the 1930s, constructivism was denounced, as Stalin had much grander predilections.

Stalin favoured neoclassical architecture, which echoed ancient Athens ('the only culture of the past to approach the ideal', according to

Anatoly Lunacharsky, the first Soviet Commissar of Education). Stalin also favoured building on a gigantic scale to underline the might of the Soviet state. Monumental classicism inspired a 400m-high design for Stalin's pet project, a Palace of Soviets, which (mercifully) never got off the ground. Stalin's architectural excesses reached their apogee in the seven wedding-cake-style skyscrapers that adorn the Moscow skyline, also known as the 'Seven Sisters'.

In 1955 a decree ordered architects to avoid 'excesses'. A bland modern style was introduced, stressing function over form. The State Kremlin Palace is representative of this period. The White House was built later, but harks back to this style.

Contemporary Planning & Development

At the end of the Soviet Union, architectural energies and civic funds were initially funnelled into the restoration of decayed churches and monasteries, as well as the rebuilding of structures such as the Cathedral of Christ the Saviour and Kazan Cathedral.

In the 2000s, Moscow was a hotbed of development. Skyscrapers and steeples changed the city skyline; the metro expanded in all directions; and office buildings, luxury hotels and shopping centres went up all over the city. The most visible urban development is in Moscow-City, the flashy new International Business Centre that is sprouting up along the Moscow River in Presnya. The complex is impressive, with shiny glass-and-metal buildings on either side of the Moscow River and a cool pedestrian bridge connecting them. It includes two of Europe's tallest skyscrapers: the Moscow Tower of the double-pronged City of Capitals, and neighbouring Mercury City Tower, a 75-storey building that topped out at nearly 340m high.

STALIN'S SEVEN SISTERS

The foundations for seven large skyscrapers were laid in 1947 to mark Moscow's 800th anniversary. Stalin had decided that Moscow suffered from a 'skyscraper gap' when compared with the USA, and ordered the construction of these seven behemoths to jump-start the city's skyline.

One of the main architects, Vyacheslav Oltarzhevsky, had worked in New York during the skyscraper boom of the 1930s, and his experience proved essential. (Fortunately, he'd been released from a Gulag in time to help.)

In addition to the 'Seven Sisters' listed here, there were plans in place to build an eighth Stalinist skyscraper in Zaryadie (near Kitay Gorod). The historic district was razed in 1947 and a foundation was laid for a 32-storey tower. It did not get any further than that – for better and for worse – and the foundation was later used for the gargantuan Hotel Rossiya (demolished in 2006).

With their widely scattered locations, the towers provide a unique visual reference for Moscow. Their official name in Russia is *vysotky* (high-rise) as opposed to *neboskryob* (foreign skyscraper). They have been nicknamed variously the 'Seven Sisters', the 'wedding cakes', 'Stalin's sisters' and more.

Foreign Affairs Ministry (Map p260; Smolenskaya-Sennaya pl 32/34; Ⓜ Smolenskaya)

Hilton Moscow Leningradskaya (Kalanchevskaya ul 21/40; Ⓜ Komsomolskaya)

Kotelnicheskaya apartment block (Kotelnicheskaya nab 17/1; Ⓜ Taganskaya)

Kudrinskaya apartment block (Kudrinskaya pl 1; Ⓜ Barrikadnaya)

Moscow State University (Universitetskaya pl; Ⓜ Universitet)

Radisson Royal (Hotel Ukraine; Kutuzovsky pr 2/1; Ⓜ Kievskaya)

Transport Ministry (ul Sadovaya-Spasskaya; Ⓜ Krasnye Vorota)

With the appointment of Sergei Sobyanin as mayor, the pace of construction has slowed dramatically. Several large-scale shopping malls and other projects were called off, in favour of more enlightened endeavours. Recent urban planning has focused on the redevelopment of parks such as Gorky Park, as well as increasing and improving pedestrian routes, such as the fountain- and art-filled Krymskaya nab. Sobyanin's focus on public places emphasising usability and liveability is a radical departure from the policies of his predecessor.

The highest profile example, perhaps, is the site of the former Hotel Rossiya in Zaryadie near Kitay Gorod. The Soviet behemoth was destroyed in 2006, in anticipation of a new luxury hotel and commercial complex. When the recession hit two years later, investors pulled out and construction came to a halt. After six years, the city administration finally reached some conclusion about what to do with the prime real estate: turn it into a park. The green space will re-create Russia's four microclimates – taiga, steppe, forest and marsh – each with a different view to the Kremlin.

The centrepiece of the former Red October chocolate factory is the Strelka Institute for Media, Architecture and Design (www.strelkainstitute.com), an exciting and innovative organisation that hosts all kinds of cultural events and activities for public consumption.

Endangered Architecture

The urban development taking place in Moscow is an exciting sign of the city's prosperity and possibility. It is also a source of contention among architects, historians and other critics, who claim that Moscow is losing its architectural heritage.

The nonprofit **Moscow Architectural Preservation Society** (MAPS; www.maps-moscow.com) estimates that more than 1000 buildings have been razed since the collapse of communism, including as many as 200 buildings of historical interest. The latter are protected by federal law, but critics claim the laws are useless in the face of corruption and cash.

Preservationists are distressed by the tendency to tear down and build up, rather than preserve. Many buildings might look old, but they are in fact replicas, such as some of the buildings along the Arbat. In other cases, developers maintain the historic facade, but destroy the building behind it, such as the complex that houses Café Pushkin and Turandot.

More recently, there is a sense – or at least a hope – that the tide is turning. The city's artists and architects have started to explore the possibilities of recycling instead of rebuilding. As industry moves away from the city centre, a slew of former factories and warehouses are being converted into centres for art and design. Most prominently, the Red October chocolate factory – occupying a prime spot opposite the Kremlin – has been revamped into a vibrant space for art, entertainment and nightlife, with an emphasis on preserving the historic building. And that's just one in a long list.

When Mayor Sobyanin was appointed in 2010, he promised to halt all construction in the centre and stop all demolition of historic buildings. Preservationists lauded his efforts to clear the kiosks and billboards from the city streets. Since then, he has simplified the process of issuing preservation orders.

Buildings under Threat

Melnikov House

Narkomfin

Shukhov Tower

'konsky House

Unfortunately, critics claim that under Sobyanin's watch, several historic buildings have been lost to developers. Others are in danger, deteriorating while they languish in red-tape limbo, unable to overcome the legal and administrative barriers to protection. Some wonder if the new mayor has the power to defy the cycle of destruction and construction.

Literature & Cinema

Of Russia's rich cultural offerings, none is more widely appreciated than her traditions of literature and cinema, much of which originates in Moscow. The classics (think *War and Peace* by Leo Tolstoy and *Battleship Potemkin* by Sergei Eisenstein) are masterpieces that have earned the admiration of international audiences across the ages. Contemporary Russian culture may be lesser known, but the electric atmosphere in the creative capital continues to stimulate the creation of innovative and insightful literature and film.

Literature

A love of literature is an integral part of Russian culture, and Ivans and Olgas will wax rhapsodic on the Russian classics without hesitation. With the end of Soviet censorship, the literati have figured out what to do with their new-found freedom and new authors have emerged, exploring literary genres from historical fiction to science fiction.

Romanticism in the Golden Age

Among the many ways that Peter the Great and Catherine the Great Westernised and modernised Russia was through the introduction of a modern alphabet. As a result it became increasingly acceptable during the Petrine era to use popular language in literature. This development paved the way for two centuries of Russian literary prolificacy.

Romanticism was a reaction against the strict social rules and scientific rationalisation of previous periods, typically exalting emotion and aesthetics. Nobody embraced Russian romanticism more than the national bard, Alexander Pushkin (1799–1837). Pushkin was born in Moscow and it was here that he met his wife, Natalia Goncharova. The two were wed at the Church of Grand Ascension and lived for a time on ul Arbat.

Pushkin's most celebrated drama, *Boris Godunov*, takes place in medieval Muscovy. The plot centres on the historical events leading up to the Time of Troubles and its resolution with the election of Mikhail Romanov as tsar. The epic poem *Yevgeny Onegin* is set, in part, in imperial Moscow. Pushkin savagely ridicules its foppish, aristocratic society, despite being a fairly consistent fixture of it himself.

Leo Tolstoy is one of the most celebrated novelists, not only in Russia but in the world. The depth of his characters and the vividness of his descriptions evoke 19th-century Russia. His novels *War and Peace* and *Anna Karenina,* both of which are set in Moscow, express his scepticism with rationalism, espousing the idea that history is the sum of an infinite number of individual actions.

Tolstoy spent most of his time at his estate in Yasnaya Polyana, but he also had property in Moscow, and he was a regular parishioner at the Church of St Nicholas of Khamovniki.

Although Fyodor Dostoevsky (1821–81) is more closely associated with St Petersburg, he was actually born in Moscow. He was among the first writers to navigate the murky waters of the human subconscious,

Explore Moscow alongside Professor Woland, Bohemoth and Margarita using the interactive map at www.masterand margarita.eu.

blending powerful prose with psychology, philosophy and spirituality. Dostoevsky's best-known works, such as *Crime and Punishment,* were all written (and to a large degree set) in his adopted city of St Petersburg. But bibliophiles assert that his early years in Moscow profoundly influenced his philosophical development.

Amid the epic works of Pushkin, Tolstoy and Dostoevsky, an absurdist short-story writer such as Nikolai Gogol (1809–52) can get lost in the annals of Russian literature. But his troubled genius created some of Russian literature's most memorable characters, including Akaki Akakievich, tragicomic hero of *The Overcoat.*

Gogol spent most of his years living abroad, but it was his hilarious satire of life in Russia that earned him the respect of his contemporaries. *Dead Souls* is his masterpiece. This 'novel in verse' follows the scoundrel Chichikov as he attempts to buy and sell deceased serfs, or 'dead souls', in an absurd money-making scam.

After the novel's highly lauded publication in 1841, Gogol suffered from poor physical and mental health. While staying at the Gogol House, in a fit of depression, he threw some of his manuscripts into the fire, including the second part of *Dead Souls,* which was not recovered in its entirety (the novel ends midsentence). The celebrated satirist died shortly thereafter and he is buried at Novodevichy Cemetery.

Literary Sights

Tolstoy Estate-Museum

Bulgakov House-Museum

Gogol House

Dostoevsky House-Museum

Chekhov House-Museum

Symbolism in the Silver Age

The late 19th century saw the rise of the symbolist movement, which emphasised individualism and creativity, and maintained that artistic endeavours were exempt from the rules that bound other parts of society. The outstanding figures of this time were novelists Vladimir Solovyov (1853–1900), Andrei Bely (1880–1934) and Alexander Blok (1880–1921), as well as poets Sergei Yesenin (1895–1925) and Vladimir Mayakovsky (1893–1930).

Although Bely lived in Moscow for a time, he is remembered for his mysterious novel *Petersburg.* His essays and philosophical discourses were also respected, making him one of the most important writers of the symbolist movement.

Mayakovsky was a futurist playwright and poet, and he acted as the revolution's official bard. He lived near Lyubyanskaya pl, where his flat has been converted into a museum. He devoted his creative energy to social activism and propaganda on behalf of the new regime, but the romantic soul was unlucky in love and life. As is wont to happen, he became disillusioned with the Soviet Union, as reflected in his satirical plays. In one of his last letters, he wrote, 'She did devour me, lousy, snuffling dear Mother Russia, like a sow devouring her piglet.'

He shot himself in 1930 and is buried at Novodevichy Cemetery. He is memorialised at Triumfalnaya pl, site of Mayakovskaya metro.

Revolutionary Literature

The immediate aftermath of 1917 saw a creative upswing in Russia. Inspired by social change, writers carried over these principles into their work, pushing revolutionary ideas and ground-breaking styles.

The trend was temporary, of course. The Bolsheviks were no connoisseurs of culture, and the new leadership did not appreciate literature unless it directly supported the goals of communism. Some writers managed to write within the system, penning some excellent poetry and plays in the 1920s; however, most found little inspiration in the prevailing climate of art 'serving the people'. Stalin announced that writers were 'engineers of the human soul' and as such had a responsibility to write in a partisan direction.

The clampdown on diverse literary styles culminated in the late 1930s with the creation of socialist realism, a literary form created to promote the needs of the state, praise industrialisation and demonise social misfits. Alexey Tolstoy (1883–1945), for example, wrote historical novels comparing Stalin to Peter the Great and recounting the glories of the Russian civil war.

Literature of Dissent

While Stalin's propaganda machine was churning out novels with titles such as *How the Steel Was Tempered,* the literary community was secretly writing about life under a tyranny. Many accounts of Soviet life were printed in samizdat (underground) publications and secretly circulated among the literary community. Now-famous novels such as Anatoly Rybakov's *Children of the Arbat* were published in Russia only with the loosening of censorship under *glasnost* (openess). Meanwhile, some of the Soviet Union's most celebrated writers were silenced in their own country, while their works received international acclaim. *Dr Zhivago,* for example, was published in 1956, but it was officially printed in the Soviet Union only 30 years later.

Boris Pasternak (1890–1960) lived in a country estate on the outskirts of Moscow. *Dr Zhivago's* title character is torn between two lovers, as his life is ravaged by the revolution and the civil war. The novel was unacceptable to the Soviet regime, not because the characters were anti-revolutionary but because they were apolitical, valuing their individual lives over social transformation. The novel was awarded the Nobel Prize for Literature in 1958, but Pasternak was forced to reject it.

Mikhail Bulgakov (1890–1940) was a prolific playwright and novelist who lived near Patriarch's Ponds. He wrote many plays that were performed at the Moscow Art Theatre, some of which were apparently enjoyed by Stalin. But later his plays were banned, and he had difficulty finding work. Most of his novels take place in Moscow, including *Fatal Eggs, Heart of a Dog* and, most famously, *The Master and Margarita.*

The post-*glasnost* era of the 1980s and 1990s uncovered a huge library of work that had been suppressed during the Soviet period. Authors such as Yevgeny Zamyatin, Daniil Kharms, Anatoly Rybakov, Venedict Erofeev and Andrei Bitov – banned in the Soviet Union – are now recognised for their cutting-edge commentary and significant contributions to world literature.

Written in 1970 by Venedict Erofeev, *Moscow to the End of the Line* recounts a drunken man's train trip to visit his lover and child on the outskirts of the capital. As the journey progresses, the tale becomes darker and more hallucinogenic. *Moscow Stations,* by the same author, is another bleakly funny novella recounting alcohol-induced adventures.

Contemporary Literature

Russia's contemporary literary scene is largely based in Moscow and, to some degree, abroad, as émigré writers continue to be inspired and disheartened by their motherland.

Check out what your neighbour is reading as she rides the metro: more than likely, it's a celebrity rag or a murder mystery. Action-packed thrillers and detective stories have become wildly popular in the 21st century, with Polina Dashkova, Darya Dontsova, Alexandra Marinina and Boris Akunin ranking among the best-selling and most widely translated authors. *The Winter Queen,* by Akunin, is just one in the series of popular detective novels featuring the foppish Erast Fandorin as a member of the 19th-century Moscow police force. Several of these are now being made into movies.

TATYANA TOLSTAYA

Besides being an accomplished writer of fiction, Tatyana Tolstaya co-hosted the popular TV talk show *The School for Scandal.* Her son is the founder and owner of Art Lebedev Cafe Studio in Presnya.

Realist writers such Ludmilla Petrushevskaya engage readers with their moving portraits of everyday people living their everyday lives. Tatyana Tolstaya has been celebrated for her collection of short stories *On the Golden Porch*. Her lesser-known novel *The Slynx* is set in a post-nuclear-war Moscow that seems strangely similar to Moscow in the 1990s. In this dystopia, an uneducated scribe learns enough history to start his own revolution.

Multiple award-winning author Mikhail Shishkin is not bound by traditional literary devices. According to *The Economist*, his novel *Taking of Izmael* 'has no plot, no chapters and no characters...' yet it won the Booker Prize in 2001. His 2014 novel, *The Light & the Dark,* is a letter-book, comprised of the intimate correspondence between two lovers who are separated by thousands of miles but also by centuries.

Meanwhile, social critics continue the Soviet literary tradition of using dark humour and fantastical storylines to provide scathing social commentary. In *Homo Zapiens,* Viktor Pelevin tells the tale of a literature student who takes a job as a copywriter for New Russian gangsters, offering a darkly comic commentary on contemporary Russia. Pelevin won the 1993 Russian 'Little Booker' Prize for short stories. *Russian Beauty*, by Viktor Erofeyev, is the tale of a wily beauty from the provinces who sleeps her way to the top of the Moscow social scene. She finds herself pregnant just about the same time she finds God. Caustically funny and overtly bawdy, this best seller in Russia has been translated into 27 languages. *Day of the Oprichnik,* by Vladimir Sorokin, describes Russia in the year 2028 as a nationalist country ruled with an iron fist that has shut itself off from the West by building a wall.

Irony of Fate (1975) is a classic that is still screened on TV every New Year's Eve. After a mind-bending party in Moscow, the protagonist wakes up in St Petersburg, where his key fits into the lock of an identical building at the same address in a different town. Comedy ensues.

Cinema

In the Hollywood hills they have Leo the MGM lion, and in Sparrow Hills they have the iconic socialist sculpture, *Worker and Peasant Woman,* the instantly recognisable logo of Mosfilm. Russia's largest film studio has played a defining role in the development of Soviet and Russian cinema.

Revolutionary Cinema

During the Soviet period, politics and cinema were always closely connected. The nascent film industry received a big boost from the Bolshevik Revolution, as the proletarian culture needed a different kind of canvas. Comrade Lenin recognised that motion pictures would become the new mass medium for the new mass politics. By government decree, the film studio Mosfilm was officially founded in 1923, under the leadership of Alexander Khanzhokov, the pioneer of Russian cinema.

In this golden age, Soviet film earned an international reputation for its artistic experimentation and propaganda techniques. Legendary director Sergei Eisentein, a socialist true believer, popularised a series of innovations, such as fast-paced montage editing and mounted tracking

---

MOSCOW DOESN'T BELIEVE IN TEARS

˙hree young women arrive in the capital in 1958, starting new careers and looking for
e. They become friends. This is the simple premise of one of the most iconic films
˙me out of the Soviet Union, *Moscow Doesn't Believe in Tears,* which won the Academy
ward for Best Foreign Film in 1980. The three friends follow different paths, of
and the film then flashes forward 20 years to show us how things turn out.
e way, we get insights into class consciousness (yes, even in the Soviet Union)
tic relationships – with plenty of shots of 1970s Moscow as a backdrop.

cameras, to arouse emotional response from the audience that could be used to shape political views. His *Battleship Potemkin* (1925) remains one of film history's most admired and most studied silent classics.

Socialist Realism

Under Stalin, the cinematic avant-garde was kept on a tight leash. Stylistic experimentation was repressed, and socialist realism was promoted. There was no mistaking the preferred social values of the political regime. Characters and plot lines were simple; the future looked bright.

Some directors were assigned 'partners' to ensure that they did not get too creative and stray into formalism. During this period, Sergei Eisenstein produced award-winning historical dramas such as *Alexander Nevsky* (1938) and *Ivan the Terrible* (1946).

When Stalin departed the scene, directors responded with more honest depictions of Soviet daily life and more creative styles. Russian productions again received international acclaim, earning top honours at all the most prestigious cinematic venues. During this period, the Academy Award for Best Foreign Language Film went to Mosfilm works multiple times, for films such as *War and Peace* (1968), *The Brothers Karamazov* (1969), *Tchaikovsky* (1971), *Dersu Ozala* (1975) and *Moscow Doesn't Believe in Tears* (1980).

However, getting past the censors at home still posed challenges. The fate of any movie was decided by the risk-averse Goskino, the vast Moscow-based bureaucracy that funded and distributed films.

Elem Klimov's comedies were thinly veiled critiques of contemporary society. They were not exactly banned, but they were not exactly promoted. The dark and rather disturbing *Adventures of a Dentist* (1965) was shown in less than 100 theatres. Klimov's war drama *Come and See* was on the shelf for eight years before it was finally released in 1985 to commemorate the 40th anniversary of the Soviet victory in WWII.

Andrei Tarkovsky earned worldwide recognition for his films, including his first feature film *Ivan's Childhood* (1962), which won in Venice, and *Andrei Rublyov* (1965), which won in Cannes. The latter film was cut several times before a truncated version was finally released in the Soviet Union in 1971.

Glasnost & Transition

During a 1986 congress of Soviet filmmakers held in Moscow, *glasnost* touched the USSR's film industry. By a large vote the old conservative directors were booted out of the leadership and renegades demanding more freedom were put in their place.

Over 250 previously banned films were released. As such, some of the most politically daring and artistically innovative works finally made it off the shelf and onto the big screen for audiences to see for the first time. By the end of the Soviet regime, Mosfilm was one of Europe's largest and most prolific film studios, with over 2500 films to its credit.

With the collapse of the Soviet Union, the film industry fell on hard times. Funding had dried up during the economic chaos of the early 1990s and audiences couldn't afford to go to the cinema anyway. Mosfilm was finally reorganised into a quasi-private concern, although it continued to receive significant state patronage.

At this low point, ironically, Mosfilm produced one of its crowning achievements – the Cannes Grand Prize and Academy Award–winning film *Burnt by the Sun* (1994), featuring the work of actor and director Nikita Mikhailkov. The story of a loyal apparatchik who becomes a victim of Stalin's purges, the film demonstrated that politics and cinema were still inextricably linked.

Every year in June, the Moscow International Film Festival offers a venue for directors of independent films from Russia and abroad to compete for international recognition.

Vasily Pichul's ground-breaking film *Little Vera* (1988), produced by the Gorky Film Studio, caused a sensation with its frank portrayal of a family in chaos (exhausted wife, drunken husband, rebellious daughter) and with its sexual frankness – mild by West standards startling t audie

INDIE

In this age of corporate-sponsored cinema, some Russian directors are still turning out stimulating art-house films.

In 2003 Moscow director Andrei Zvyagintsev came home from Venice with the Golden Lion, awarded for his moody thriller *The Return*. His follow-up film, *The Banishment*, refers to the end of paradise for a couple whose marriage is falling apart. Zvyagintsev continues to earn accolades at Venice and in Cannes. *Elena* (2011) is an evocative, if disheartening portrait of relationships in modern Moscow. *Leviathan* (2014) is another starkly realistic drama about an everyday guy who tries to seek justice and take on the system – with a tragic outcome.

In 2006 stage director Ivan Vyrypaev won the small Golden Lion for his cinematic debut, the tragic love story *Euphoria*. Meanwhile, Alexey Popogrebsky has won a slew of lesser awards for *How I Ended this Summer* (2010), a compelling drama set at a remote Arctic research station. *Silent Souls* (2011) by Igor Mishin was called *The Buntings* (Овсянки) in Russian. Nominated for the Golden Lion in Venice, it's a beautiful, moving film about ties to the ancient in modern-day, rural Russia.

Contemporary Cinema

Moscow's film industry has made a remarkable comeback since the lull in the 1990s. Mosfilm is one of the largest production companies in the world, producing almost all of Russia's film, TV and video programming. Moscow is indeed the Russian Hollywood. Unfortunately, just like its American counterpart, the industry does not leave much room for artsy, independent films that are not likely to be blockbusters.

But there is no shortage of blockbusters. *The Turkish Gambit,* a drama set during the Russo-Turkish War, broke all post-Soviet box-office records in 2005. In 2007, the prolific Mikhailkov directed *12*, a film based on Sidney Lumet's *12 Angry Men*. The Oscar-nominated film follows a jury deliberating over the trial of a Chechen teenager accused of murdering his father, who was an officer in the Russian army. Vladimir Putin is quoted as saying that it 'brought a tear to the eye'.

The glossy vampire thriller *Night Watch* (2004) struck box-office gold both at home and abroad, leading to an equally successful sequel, *Day Watch* (2006) – and to Kazakhstan-born director Timur Bekmambetov being lured to Hollywood. Bekmambetov's most successful effort since the *Night Watch* series is undoubtedly his direction of *Irony of Fate: Continuation* (2007), a follow-up to the classic 1970s comedy. Simultaneously released on 1000 screens across the nation, the movie was poorly reviewed but widely watched. It is still one of the highest grossing films of the era.

In 2013, Fedor Bondarchuk directed Russia's first IMAX production, a historical war film called *Stalingrad*. It was acclaimed for stunning visuals but derided for melodramatic plot line. Nonetheless, the film shattered all box-office records. Another 3D film was a huge hit in 2014: *Viy,* directed by Oleg Stepchenko, was based on a horror story by Gogol.

In 2010 Nikita Mikhailkov used the largest production budget ever seen in Russian cinema to make the sequel to his 1994 masterpiece, *Burnt by the Sun II* received universally negative reviews and was a box-office flop.

Survival Guide

Transport

ARRIVING IN MOSCOW

Air

Most travellers arrive in Moscow by air, flying into one of the city's three airports: Domodedovo, Sheremetyevo or Vnukovo International Airport. The vast majority of international flights go in and out of Domodedovo and Sheremetyevo, both of which are about an hour from the city centre by car or train.

All three airports are accessible by the convenient **Aeroexpress train** (☑8-800-700 3377; www. aeroexpress.ru; ₽340-400; ☺6am-midnight) from the city centre; reduced rate is available for online purchase. Alternatively, order an official airport taxi from the dispatcher's desk in the terminal (₽2000 to ₽2200 to the city centre). You can save some cash by booking in advance to take advantage of the fixed rates offered by most companies (usually from ₽1500 to ₽1800 to/ from any airport). Driving times vary wildly depending on traffic.

Domodedovo International Airport

Since 2003, **Domodedovo** (Домодедово; www.domode dovo.ru), located about 48km south of the city, has undergone extensive upgrades and has become the city's largest and most efficient international airport. The Aeroexpress train leaves Paveletsky vokzal (station) every half-hour between 6am and midnight for the 45-minute trip to Domodedovo.

Sheremetyevo International Airport

Sheremetyevo (Шереметьево; http://svo. aero) is 30km northwest of the city centre. The Aeroexpress train makes the 35-minute trip between Sheremetyevo (located next to Terminal E) and Belorussky vokzal every half-hour from 5.30am to 12.30am.

Vnukovo International Airport

About 30km southwest of the city centre, **Vnukovo** (Внуково; www.vnukovo.ru) serves most flights to/from the Caucasus, Moldova and Kaliningrad, as well as domestic flights and a smattering of flights to Europe. The Aeroexpress train makes the 35-minute run from Kievsky vokzal to Vnukovo airport every hour from 6am to 11pm.

Train

Rail riders will arrive at one of Moscow's central train stations: Kievsky or Belorussky vokzal if you're

---

CLIMATE CHANGE & TRAVEL

Every form of transport that relies on carbon-based fuel generates CO_2, the main ~~c~~ause of human-induced climate change. Modern travel is dependent on aeroplanes, ~~wh~~ich might use less fuel per kilometre per person than most cars but travel much ~~grea~~ter distances. The altitude at which aircraft emit gases (including CO_2) and par~~ticles~~ also contributes to their climate change impact. Many websites offer 'carbon ~~calcula~~tors' that allow people to estimate the carbon emissions generated by their ~~journey a~~nd, for those who wish to do so, to offset the impact of the greenhouse gases ~~wit~~h contributions to portfolios of climate-friendly initiatives throughout the ~~world. Lonel~~y Planet offsets the carbon footprint of all staff and author travel.

coming from Europe; Leningradsky vokzal if you're coming from St Petersburg; and Yaroslavsky or Kazansky vokzal if you're coming from the east.

All of the train stations are located in the city centre, and have easy access to the metro.

Alternatively, most taxi companies offer a fixed rate of ₽400 to ₽600 for a train station transfer.

Leningradsky vokzal

Located at busy Komsomolskaya pl, **Leningrad Station** (Ленинградский вокзал; http://leningradsky.dzvr.ru/en/; Komsomolskaya pl; 🚇; Ⓜ Komsomolskaya) serves Tver, Novgorod, Pskov, St Petersburg, Vyborg, Murmansk, Estonia and Helsinki. Note that sometimes this station is referred to on timetables and tickets by its former name, Oktyabrsky (Октябрский).

Belorussky vokzal

At the top of Tverskaya ul, **Belarus Station** (Белорусский вокзал; www.belorusskiy.info; Tverskaya Zastava pl; 🚇; Ⓜ Belorusskaya) serves trains to/from northern and central Europe, as well as suburban trains to/from the west, including Mozhaysk and Borodino. This is also where you'll catch the Aeroexpress to Sheremetyevo International Airport.

Kievsky vokzal

Located in Dorogomilovo, **Kyiv Station** (Киевский вокзал; www.kievsky-vokzal.ru; Kievskaya pl; 🚇; Ⓜ Kievskaya) serves Kyiv and western Ukraine, as well as points further west, including Moldova, Slovakia, Hungary, Austria, the Czech Republic, Romania, Bulgaria, Croatia, Serbia and Greece. This is also where you'll catch the Aeroexpress to Vnukovo International Airport.

Yaroslavsky vokzal

The main station for Trans-Siberian trains, **Yaroslav Station** (Ярославский вокзал; http://yaroslavsky.dzvr.ru; Komsomolskaya pl; 🚇; Ⓜ Komsomolskaya) serves Yaroslavl, Arkhangelsk, Vorkuta, the Russian Far East, Mongolia, China and North Korea; some trains to/from Vladimir, Nizhny Novgorod, Kostroma, Vologda, Perm, the Urals and Siberia; and suburban trains to/from the northeast, including Abramtsevo and Sergiev Posad.

Kazansky vokzal

Kazan Station (Казанский вокзал; http://kazansky.dzvr.ru; Komsomolskaya pl; 🚇; Ⓜ Komsomolskaya), at Komsomolskaya pl, serves trains to/from Kazan and points southeast, as well as some trains to/from Vladimir, Nizhny Novgorod, the Ural Mountains and Siberia.

GETTING AROUND MOSCOW

Metro

The **Moscow metro** (www.mosmetro.ru) is by far the easiest, quickest and cheapest way of getting around Moscow. Plus, many of the elegant stations are marble-faced, frescoed, gilded works of art. The 150-plus stations are marked outside by large 'M' signs.

Reliability The trains are generally reliable: you will rarely wait on a platform for more than three minutes. Nonetheless, they do get packed, especially during the city's rush hour.

Ticket Magnetic tickets (₽40) are sold at ticket booths. Queues can be long, so it's useful (and slightly cheaper) to buy a multiple-ride ticket (11 rides for ₽320 or 20 rides for ₽520). The ticket is actually a contactless smart card, which you must tap on the reader before going through the turnstile.

Maps & Signage Stations have maps of the system at the entrance and signs on each platform showing the destinations. The maps are generally in Cyrillic and Roman script, although the signs are usually only in Cyrillic. The carriages also have maps inside that show the stops for that line in both Roman and Cyrillic letters.

Transfers Interchange stations are linked by underground passages, indicated by *perekhod* signs, usually blue with a stick figure running up the stairs. Be aware that when two or more lines meet, the intersecting stations often (but not always) have different names.

Taxi

Taxi cabs are relatively affordable, but not that easy for casual visitors to use. Most taxi drivers and dispatchers don't speak English.

Official Taxis

The safest and most reliable way to get a taxi is to order an official taxi by phone or book it online. Normally, the dispatcher will ring you back within a few minutes to provide a description and licence number of the car. Most companies will send a car within 60 minutes of your call. Some reliable companies offer online scheduling.

Central Taxi Reservation Office (Центральное бюро заказов такси; ☎495-627 0000; www.6270000.ru; 30min for ₽400)

Detskoe Taxi (Детское Такси; ☎495-765 1180; www.detskoetaxi.ru; ₽500) 'Children's Taxi; smoke-free cars a[...] for your children[...]

Diligence Taxi Service
(Дилижанс; ☑495-419 3524; www.the-taxi.ru; 40min for ₽500)

New Yellow Taxi (Новое жёлтое такси; ☑495-940 8888; www.nyt.ru; per 1km ₽30, min ₽400)

Taxi Bistro (Такси Бистро; ☑495-685 1300; www.taxo park.ru; per 20min ₽320-420)

Woman Taxi (Женское Такси; ☑495-662 0033; www. womantaxi.ru; 30min for ₽600-650) Offers female drivers and child car seats (and pink cars).

Unofficial Taxis

Almost any car in Moscow could be a taxi if the price is right, so if you're stuck, get on the street and stick your arm out.

➡ Many private cars cruise around as unofficial taxis, and other drivers will often take you if they're going in roughly the same direction.

➡ Expect to pay ₽200 to ₽400 for a ride around the city centre.

➡ Don't hesitate to wave on a car if you don't like the look of its occupants. As a general rule, it's best to avoid riding in cars that already have a passenger. Be particularly careful taking a taxi that is waiting outside a nightclub or bar.

Bus

Buses, trolleybuses and trams might be necessary for reaching some sights away from the city centre. They can also be useful for a few cross-town or radial routes that the metro miss-s. Tickets (₽40) are usually ʲd on the vehicle by a con- ᵗor or by the driver.

rspectives on ᵉighbourhoods, he Kremlin,

or just good, old-fashioned transport, a boat ride on the Moscow River is one of the city's highlights. The main route runs between the boat landings at Kievsky vokzal and Novospassky most, near the Novospassky Monastery, with six intermediate stops. **Capital Shipping Co** (ССК, Столичная Судоходная Компания; ☑495-225 6070; www.cck-ship.ru; 90-min tour adult/child ₽500/300, 24hr pass ₽800/400) offers a one-day pass, so you can get on and off wherever you wish.

Car & Motorcycle

There's little reason for travellers to rent a car to get around Moscow, as public transport is quite adequate. However, you might want to consider car rental for trips out of the city. Be aware that driving in Russia is an unfiltered Russian experience, mainly due to poor signage and ridiculous traffic.

Requirements

➡ To drive in Russia, you must be at least 18 years old and have a full driving licence.

➡ In addition, you may be asked to present an International Driving Permit with a Russian translation of your licence, or a certified Russian translation of your full licence (you can certify translations at a Russian embassy or consulate) – though this is unlikely.

➡ For your own vehicle, you will also need registration papers and proof of insurance. Be sure your insurance covers you in Russia.

➡ Finally, a customs declaration, promising that you will take your vehicle with you when you leave, is also required.

Safety

Drinking & Driving As of 2013, the maximum legal blood-alcohol content is 0.0356%.

Prior to this change it was practically illegal to drive after consuming any alcohol at all, and this rule was strictly enforced. In any case, it is not advisable to drink and drive in Russia, even a small amount.

Road Patrol Officers of the Road Patrol Service (Dorozhno-Patrulnaya Sluzhba), better known as DPS, skulk about on the roadsides all around Moscow waiting for miscreant drivers. They are authorised to stop you (by pointing their striped stick at you and waving you towards the side), and the DPS also hosts the occasional speed trap. Fines are *not* payable on the spot: you'll have a set amount of time to pay at a local bank; make sure you keep your receipt.

Fuel

Moscow has no shortage of petrol stations that sell all grades of petrol. Most are open 24 hours and can be found on the major roads in and out of town.

Hire

While driving around Moscow is an unnecessary hassle, renting a car may be a reasonable option for trips out of the city. Be aware that some firms won't let you take their cars out of the Moscow Oblast (Moscow Region).

The major international car-rental firms have outlets in Moscow (at either Sheremetyevo or Domodedovo airports, as well as in the city centre). Prices start at ₽2000 per day, although you may be able to cut this price by reserving in advance. The major car-rental agencies will usually pick up or drop off the car at your hotel for an extra fee.

Avis (Авис-Москва; www.avis.com) Leningradsky vokzal (☑495-988 6216; Komsomolskaya pl 3; ☺10am-8pm; Ⓜ Komsomolskaya);

Zamoskvorechie (Map p266; ☑495-988 6216; 4-y Dobryninsky per 8; ◎9am-9pm; ⓂOktyabrskaya)

Europcar (Map p266; ☑495-926 6373; www.europ car.ru; 4-y Dobryninsky per 8; ◎9am-6pm; ⓂOktyabrskaya) From Oktyabrskaya metro station, walk two blocks south on Mytnaya ul and turn left on 4-y Dobryninsky per. Hire cars are prohibited from leaving Moscow Oblast.

Hertz (Map p264;☑495-232 0889; www.hertz.ru; 1-ya Brestskaya ul 34; ◎9am-9pm; ⓂBelorusskaya)

Thrifty (☑495-788-6888; www.thrifty.ru) Outer North (Yaroslavskoe sh 31; ◎9am-6pm; ⓂBabushinskaya); Outer South (Profsoyuznaya ul 65; ◎9am-9pm; ⓂKaluzhskaya) Mileage limited to 200km per day.

Bicycle

There are more and more bicycles on the streets and sidewalks of Moscow. Cycling in the centre of Moscow is still a dangerous prospect, as the streets are overcrowded with fast-moving cars, whose drivers probably do not expect bikes on the road. That said, there are a few parks and other off-road areas that are suitable for pleasure riding, including Gorky Park, Vorobyovy Gory Nature Preserve, Ostankino Park

> ## GETTING OUT OF TOWN ON YOUR BIKE
>
> ➡ Bicycles are not allowed on the metro (with the exception of folding bikes).
>
> ➡ They are permitted on long-distance trains, but you must buy a special ticket to bring your bike on the *elektrichka* (suburban commuter train).
>
> ➡ Bicycles are allowed on intercity passenger trains as long as your total luggage does not exceed the weight limit (36kg). You should disassemble and package the bike to ensure that you will be able to find space to store it.
>
> ➡ The **Russian Cycle Touring Club** (www.rctc.ru) organises weekend rides around Moscow and longer-distance bicycle tours around Russia, including a popular tour of the Golden Ring.

and the All-Russia Exhibition Centre.

Hire

Rent bikes for park riding in Gorky Park, Vorobyovy Gory Nature Preserve or Ostankino Park. For a wide variety of excellently maintained bicycles, visit **Oliver Bikes** (Оливер Байкс; Map p266; ☑499-340 2609; www. bikerentalmoscow.com; Pyatnitskaya ul 2; per hour/day from ₽100/500, tours ₽900; ◎2-10pm Tue-Fri, 11am-10pm Sat & Sun; ⓂNovokuznetskaya) in Zamoskvorechie.

Bike Share

Moscow's new bike share is **Velobike** (Велобайк; www. velobike.ru), an innovative program designed to cut down on traffic and encourage healthier living in the

capital. It started in 2013 with 30 bike stations and a few hundred bikes, with plans to expand exponentially in coming years.

➡ Go online to purchase a membership (₽150 for a day, ₽400 for a week, ₽600 for a month, plus deposit). Now you are ready to roll!

➡ Use your credit card to unlock a bike at any station, go for a ride, and return your bike to any station. The first 30 minutes incurs no additional charge, but after that you'll pay for use.

➡ The system is designed for transportation rather than recreation, so it's a good deal for short rides from point A to point B. For longer rides, however, you're better off renting from outfits like Oliver Bikes.

Directory A–Z

Customs Regulations

➡ Searches beyond the perfunctory are quite rare, but clearing customs when you leave Russia by a land border can be lengthy.

➡ Visitors are allowed to bring in and take out up to US$10,000 (or its equivalent) in currency, as well as goods up to the value of €10,000, weighing less than 50kg, without making a customs declaration.

➡ Fill in a customs declaration form if you're bringing into Russia major equipment, antiques, art works or musical instruments (including a guitar) that you plan to take out with you – get it stamped in the red channel of customs to avoid any problems leaving with the same goods.

➡ If you plan to export anything vaguely 'arty' – instruments, coins, jewellery, antiques, antiquarian manuscripts and books (older than 50 years), or art (also older than 50 years) – it should first be assessed by the **Expert Collegium** (Коллегия экспертизы; ☑499-391 4212; ul Akademika Korolyova 21, Bldg 1, office 505, 5th fl; price ₽350; ☺11am-5pm Mon-Fri; ⓂVDNKh). It is very difficult to export anything over 100 years old.

➡ If you do have an item to export, bring two photographs of your item, your receipt and your passport. If export is allowed, you'll be issued a receipt for the tax paid, which you need to show to customs officers on your way out of the country.

Electricity

Access electricity (220V, 50Hz AC) with a European plug with two round pins. A few places still have the old 127V system.

PRACTICALITIES

Smoking Smoking is widespread, though restrictions are increasingly strict and enforced. Nowadays, all hotels must offer nonsmoking rooms. As of 2014, all restaurants are required to offer nonsmoking areas with separate ventilation systems to protect guests from second-hand smoke.

Newspapers *The Moscow Times* (www.themoscowtimes.com) is a first-rate daily that is the last remaining publication for English-language news. It covers Russian and international issues, as well as sport and entertainment. The Friday edition is a great source for information about what's happening at the weekend. Find it at hotels and restaurants around town.

Television TV channels include Channel 1 (Pervy Kanal; www.1tv.ru); NTV (www.ntv.ru); Rossiya (www.russia.tv); Rossiya-2 (www.2.russia.tv); Kultura (www.tvkultura.ru); RenTV (www.ren-tv.com); and RT (http://rt.com), offering the 'Russian perspective' to overseas audiences in English, Arabic and Spanish.

Weights & Measures Russia uses the metric system. Menus often list food and drink servings in grams: a teacup is about 200g, a shot-glass 50g. The unit for items sold by the piece, such as eggs, is *shtuka* ('thing' or 'piece') or *sht*.

220V/50Hz

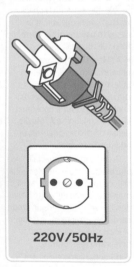

220V/50Hz

Embassies

It's wise to register with your embassy, especially if you'll be in Russia for a long stay.

Australian Embassy
(Посольство Австралии; Map p270; ☑495-956 6070; www.russia.embassy.gov.au; Podkolokolny per 10a/2, Moscow; MKitay-Gorod)

Belarusian Embassy
(Посольство Беларусии; Map p270; ☑495-777 6644; www.embassybel.ru; ul Maroseyka 17/6, Moscow; MKitay-Gorod)

Canadian Embassy
(Посольство Канады; Map p260; ☑495-925 6000; http://russia.gc.ca; Starokonyushenny per 23, Moscow; MKropotkinskaya)

Chinese Embassy
(Посольство Китая; ☑consular 499-951 8435; http://ru.chineseembassy.org/rus; ul Druzhby 6, Moscow; MUniversitet)

French Embassy
(Посольство Франции; Map p266; ☑495-937 1500; www.ambafrance-ru.org; ul Bolshaya Yakimanka 45, Moscow; MOktyabrskaya)

German Embassy
(Посольство Германии; ☑495-937 9500; www.germania.diplo.de; Mosfilmovskaya ul 56, Moscow; ☐119, MUniversitet)

Irish Embassy (Посольство Ирландии; ☑495-937 5911; www.embassyofireland.ru; Grokholsky per 5, Moscow; MProspekt Mira)

Mongolian Embassy
(Посольство Визовый отдел; Map p264; ☑495-690 6792; Borisoglebsky per 11, Moscow; MArbartskaya); Consular section (Посольство Монголии (Визовая отдель); Map p260; ☑499-241 1548; Spasopeskovsky per 7/1; MSmolenskaya).

Netherlands Embassy
(Посольство Королевства Нидерландов; Map p264; ☑495-797 2900; www.netherlands-embassy.ru; Kalashny per 6, Moscow; MArbatskaya)

UK Embassy (Посольство Великобритании; Map p260; ☑495-956 7200; www.gov.uk/government/world/russia; Smolenskaya nab 10, Moscow; MSmolenskaya)

Ukrainian Embassy
(Посольство Украины; Map p264;☑495-629 9742; http://russia.mfa.gov.ua; Leontevsky per 18, Moscow; MPushkinskaya)

US Embassy (Посольство США; Map p264; ☑495-728 5000; http://moscow.usembassy.gov; Bol Devyatinsky per 8, Moscow; MBarrikadnaya)

Emergency

Ambulance (☑03)
Fire (☑01)
Police (☑02)
Tourist Helpline (☑800-220 0002)
Universal Emergency Number (☑112) Currently functional from mobile phones, this universal number will eventually replace the separate numbers for ambulance, fire and police.

Gay & Lesbian Travellers

➡ Russia is a conservative country and being gay is generally frowned upon. LGBT people face stigma, harassment, and violence in their everyday lives.

➡ Homosexuality isn't illegal, but promoting it (and other LGBT lifestyles) is. What constitutes promotion is at the discretion of the authorities.

➡ Moscow Pride takes place in May or June, but in recent years city officials have refused to grant permission to assemble (despite fines from the European Court of Human Rights in 2010). Activists have been violently attacked by extremists when they attempt to carry out their event as planned.

Gay Russia (www.gayrussia.eu) is an advocacy group that has been involved with the organisation of Moscow and other campaigns.

➡ That said, Moscow most cosmopolita cities, and the a

lesbian scene reflects this attitude. Newspapers such as *The Moscow Times* feature articles about gay and lesbian issues, as well as listings of gay and lesbian clubs.

➡ Visit Gay.ru (http://english.gay.ru) for up-to-date information, good links and a resource for putting you in touch with personal guides.

➡ See p47 for Gay & Lesbian bars and clubs. See also p15 for more information.

Internet Access

➡ Almost all hotels and hostels offer wi-fi, as do many bars, restaurants and cafes. It isn't always free, but it is ubiquitous.

➡ Also popular is shared work space, which offers a comfortable work space, functional wi-fi, and sometimes drinks and snacks, for a per-minute or per-hour fee.

➡ Most hostels and hotels offer internet access for guests who are not travelling with their own computers. Internet cafes are a thing of the past.

Ziferblat (Циферблат; www.ziferblat.net; per min ₽2); Tverskaya (Map p258; Tverskaya ul 12c1; ⏱11am-midnight; ⓂPushkinskaya); Pokrovka (Map p270; ul Pokrovka 12 c 1; ⏱11am-midnight Sun-Thu, 11am-7pm Fri-Sat; ⓂChistye Prudy).

Legal Matters

It's not unusual to see police officers (*politsiya*) randomly stopping people on the street to check their documents. Often, the *politsiya* stop individuals who they come from the Caucasus, and other with darkish skin. have the right ne, and they do

Technically, everyone is required to carry a passport (*dokumenty*) at all times. Such reports have declined, but in the past travellers have complained about police pocketing their passports and demanding bribes.

The best way to avoid such unpleasantness is to carry a photocopy of your passport, visa and registration, and present them when an officer demands to see your *dokumenty*. A photocopy is sufficient, despite what the officer may argue.

Medical Services

Hospitals

Both the American Medical Centre and the European Medical Centre accept health insurance from major international providers.

American Medical Centre (☑495-933 7700; www.amcenter.ru; Grokholsky per 1; ⏱24hr; ⓂProspekt Mira) Offers 24-hour emergency service, consultations and a range of medical specialists, including paediatricians and dentists. There is also a pharmacy with English-speaking staff.

Botkin Hospital (☑495-945 0045; www.mosgorzdrav.ru; 2-y Botkinsky proezd 5; ⏱24hr; ⓂBegovaya) The best Russian facility. From Begovaya metro station, walk 1km northeast on Khoroshevskoe sh and Begovoy pr. Turn left on Begovaya ul and continue to 2-y Botkinsky proezd.

European Medical Centre (Map p264; ☑495-933 6655; www.emcmos.ru; Spirodonevsky per 5; ⏱24hr; ⓂMayakovskaya) Includes medical and dental facilities, which are open around the clock for emergencies. Staff speak 10 languages.

Pharmacies

A chain of pharmacies called **36.6** (Аптека 36.6; ☑495-797

6366; www.366.ru) has many branches all around the city.

36.6 Arbat (Map p260; ul Novy Arbat 15; ⏱9am-10pm; ⓂArbatskaya)

36.6 Pokrovka (Map p270; ul Pokrovka 1/13; ⏱9am-9pm; ⓂKitay-Gorod)

36.6 Tverskaya (Map p258; Tverskaya ul 25/9; ⏱24hr; ⓂMayakovskaya)

36.6 Zamoskvorechie (Map p266; Klimentovsky per 12; ⏱8am-10pm; ⓂTretyakovskaya)

Money

➡ Russian currency is the rouble (₽), written as рубль or abbreviated as руб. In one rouble, there are 100 *kopecks*, written копеек or коп. It is illegal to use any other currency than the rouble.

➡ ATMs on international networks are widely available, though they sometimes run out of cash on weekends. Look for signs for a bankomat (Банкомат). Some ATMs dispense US dollars or euros, in addition to roubles.

➡ Credit cards -- especially Visa and Mastercard – are also widely accepted. American travellers may have some difficulty if they don't have a chip-and-pin credit card. This is more of an issue at local shops, as opposed to hotels and restaurants.

➡ US dollars and euros are now widely accepted at exchange bureaus around Moscow. (Bring your passport.) Travellers cheques are not recommended.

Opening Hours

Government offices Open at 9am or 10am and close at 5pm or 6pm on weekdays.

Banks and other services Hours vary. Large branches

in busy commercial areas are usually open from 9am to 6pm weekdays, with shorter hours on Saturday; smaller bank branches have shorter hours, and will often close for a one-hour break (pereriv) in the middle of the day.

Shops Most are open daily, often from 10am to 8pm. Department stores and food shops are usually open from 8am to 8pm or 10pm daily. These days, some larger food shops stay open kruglosutochno (around the clock).

Restaurants Typically open from noon to midnight, although – again – it is not unusual for them to stay open for 24 hours a day. Bars may stay open until 2am, while some restaurants, bars and clubs are open until 5am or 6am on weekends.

Museums Opening hours change often, as do their weekly days off. Recently, many museums have instituted evening hours one day a week, usually until 8pm or 9pm. Most museums shut their entrance doors one hour before closing time. Many also close for a 'sanitary day' during the last week of every month.

Post

While things have improved dramatically in recent years, the usual warnings about delays and disappearances of incoming and outgoing mail apply to Moscow. Airmail letters take at least two weeks from Moscow to Europe, and longer to the USA or Australasia. DHL, UPS and FedEx are all active in Moscow.

Should you decide to send mail to Moscow, or try to receive it, addresses should be written in reverse order: Russia, postal code, city, street address and then name.

Central Telegraph (Map p264; Tverskaya ul 7; ⊙post

8am-10pm, telephone 24hr; ⓂOkhotny Ryad)

Main Post Office (Map p270; Myasnitskaya ul 26; ⊙24hr; ⓂChistye Prudy)

Public Holidays

New Year's Day 1 January

Russian Orthodox Christmas 7 January

International Women's Day 8 March

International Labour Day/ Spring Festival 1 and 2 May

Victory (1945) Day 9 May

Russian Independence 12 June

Day of Reconciliation and Accord (formerly Revolution Day) 7 November

Safe Travel

Although street crime is on the rise, Moscow is a mostly safe city with few dangerous areas.

➡ As in any big city, be on your guard against pickpockets and muggers, especially around train stations and in crowded metro cars.

➡ Always be cautious about taking taxis late at night, especially near bars and clubs that are in isolated areas. Never get into a car that already has two or more people in it.

➡ Always carry a photocopy of your passport, visa and registration stamp. If stopped by a member of the police force, do not hand over your passport! It is perfectly acceptable to show a photocopy instead.

➡ Your biggest threat in Moscow is xenophobic or overly friendly drunks.

Taxes & Refunds

The value-added tax (VAT, in Russian NDS) is 18% and is usually included in the price listed for purchases. Moscow

also has a 5% sales tax that is usually only encountered in top hotels.

Telephone

Mobile Phones

Local SIM cards can be used in European and Australian phones; other phones must be set to roaming.

Beeline (www.beeline.ru)

Megafon (Map p258; www.megafon.ru)

MTS (Map p270; www.mts.ru)

Phone Codes

➡ Russia's country code is ⊡7.

➡ There are now three area codes operating within Moscow. The most common code is ⊡495, while some numbers – especially on the outskirts – use ⊡498 or ⊡499.

➡ For all calls within Moscow (from land line or mobile phone), you must dial ⊡8 + the 10-digit number including the area code.

➡ To make an intercity call from Moscow, dial ⊡8 plus the area code and number. To call internationally from Moscow, dial ⊡810 plus the country code, city code and phone number.

➡ The method of placing calls is expected to change in the near future (⊡0 for intercity and ⊡00 for international).

Phonecards

➡ Payphones (таксофон) are increasingly rare in Moscow. Where they do exist, they require prepaid phonecards, available from metro token booths and from kiosks.

➡ Cards can be used for loc and domestic or internatio long-distance calls and a available in a range of international calls re least 100 units.

➡ Remember to r with the speake your party an

Time

Russians use the 12-hour clock and the 24-hour clock interchangeably. Moscow time is GMT/UTC plus three hours. So when it is noon in Moscow, it is 9am in London, 4am in New York, 1am in San Francisco and 6pm in Vladivostok. Daylight Savings Time is not observed in Moscow.

Toilets

Pay toilets are identified by the words платный туалет (platny tualet). In any toilet Женский or Ж stands for women's (zhensky), while Мужской or М stands for men's (muzhskoy). Portable loos are scattered around Moscow in public places, but other public toilets are rare. In any case, toilets in hotels, restaurants and cafes are usually modern and clean, so public toilets need only be used for emergencies. Toilet paper is not the rarity it once was, but it's still wise to carry your own supply.

Travellers with Disabilities

Inaccessible transport, lack of ramps and lifts, and no centralised policy for people with physical limitations make Russia a challenging destination for wheelchair-bound visitors. More mobile travellers will have an easier time, but keep in mind that there are obstacles along the way.

Toilets are frequently accessed from stairs in restaurants and museums; distances are great; public transport is extremely crowded; and many footpaths are in a poor condition.

This situation is changing (albeit very slowly) as buildings undergo renovations and become more accessible. Many hotels offer accessible rooms.

All-Russian Society for the Blind (Всероссийское общество слепых; Map p255; www.vos.org.ru) Provides info and services for visually impaired people, including operating holiday and recre-ation centres.

All-Russian Society for the Deaf (Всероссийское общество глухих; http://vog. deafnet.ru) Organises cultural activities and recreational facilities for its members.

All-Russian Society of Disabled People (Всероссийское общество инвалидов; www.voi.ru; ⓂUniversitet) Does not offer any services to travellers, but may provide publications (in Russian) on legal issues or local resources.

Women Travellers

➡ Although sexual harassment on the streets is rare, it is common in the workplace, in the home and in personal relations. Discrimination and domestic violence are hard facts of life for many Russian women. Alcoholism and unemployment are related problems.

➡ Activists ridicule as hypocritical the Women's Day celebrations (8 March) in Russia while such problems continue. Others say it is the one day in the year that men have to be nice to their mates.

➡ Russian women dress up and wear lots of make-up on nights out. If you are wearing casual gear, you might feel uncomfortable in an upmarket restaurant, club or theatre (or you may not even be allowed to enter).

➡ The **International Women's Club** (www.iwcmoscow.ru) is an active group of expat women. It is involved in organising social and charity events.

Language

Russian belongs to the Slavonic language family and is closely related to Belarusian and Ukrainian. It has more than 150 million speakers within the Russian Federation and is used as a second language in the former republics of the USSR, with a total number of speakers of more than 270 million people.

Russian is written in the Cyrillic alphabet (see the opposite page), and it's well worth the effort familiarising yourself with it so that you can read maps, timetables, menus and street signs. Otherwise, just read the coloured pronunciation guides given next to each Russian phrase in this chapter as if they were English, and you'll be understood. Most sounds are the same as in English, and the few differences in pronunciation are explained in the alphabet table. The stressed syllables are indicated with italics.

BASICS

Hello.	Здравствуйте.	zdrast·vuy·tye
Hi.	Привет.	priv·yet
Goodbye.	До свидания.	da svi·da·nya
Excuse me.	Простите.	pras·ti·tye
Sorry.	Извините.	iz·vi·ni·tye
Please.	Пожалуйста.	pa·zhal·sta
Thank you.	Спасибо.	spa·si·ba
You're welcome.	Пожалуйста.	pa·zhal·sta
Yes.	Да.	da
No.	Нет.	nyet

WANT MORE?

For in-depth language information and handy phrases, check out Lonely Planet's *Russian phrasebook*. You'll find it at **shop.lonelyplanet.com**, or you can buy Lonely Planet's iPhone phrasebooks at the Apple App Store.

How are you?
Как дела? — kak di·la

Fine, thank you. And you?
Хорошо, спасибо. А у вас? — kha·ra·sho spa·si·ba a u vas

What's your name?
Как вас зовут? — kak vas za·vut

My name is ...
Меня зовут ... — mi·nya za·vut ...

Do you speak English?
Вы говорите по-английски? — vi ga·va·ri·tye pa·an·gli·ski

I don't understand.
Я не понимаю. — ya nye pa·ni·ma·yu

ACCOMMODATION

Where's a ...?	Где ...?	gdye ...
boarding house	пансионат	pan·si·a·nat
campsite	кемпинг	kyem·ping
hotel	гостиница	ga·sti·ni·tsa
youth hostel	общежитие	ap·shi·zhih·ti·ye

Do you have a ... room?	У вас есть ...?	u vas yest' ...
single	одноместный номер	ad·na·myest·nih no·mir
double	номер с двуспальней кроватью	no·mir z dvu·spal'·n kra·va·ty

How much is it for ...?	Сколько стоит за ...?	skol'·k sto·i
a night	ночь	n
two people	двоих	

The ... isn't working.	... не работает.	... ne ra·bo·ta·yit
heating	Отопление	a·ta·plye·ni·ye
hot water	Горячая вода	ga·rya·cha·ya va·da
light	Свет	svyet

I don't eat ...	Я не ем ...	ya nye yem ...
eggs	яиц	ya·its
fish	рыбы	rih·bih
poultry	птицы	ptit·sih
red meat	мяса	mya·sa

DIRECTIONS

Where is ...?
Где ...? gdye ...

What's the address?
Какой адрес? ka·koy a·dris

Could you write it down, please?
Запишите, za·pi·shih·tye
пожалуйста. pa·zhal·sta

Can you show me (on the map)?
Покажите мне, pa·ka·zhih·tye mnye
пожалуйста pa·zhal·sta
(на карте). (na kar·tye)

Turn ...	Поверните ...	pa·vir·ni·tye ...
at the corner	за угол	za u·gal
at the traffic lights	на светофоре	na svi·ta·fo·rye
left	налево	na·lye·va
right	направо	na·pra·va

behind ...	за ...	za ...
far	далеко	da·li·ko
in front of ...	перед ...	pye·rit ...
near	близко	blis·ka
next to ...	рядом с ...	rya·dam s ...
opposite ...	напротив ...	na·pro·tif ...
straight ahead	прямо	prya·ma

EATING & DRINKING

I'd like to reserve a table for ...	Я бы хотел/ хотела заказать столик на ... (m/f)	ya bih khat·yel/ khat·ye·la za·ka·zat' sto·lik na ...
two people	двоих	dva·ikh
eight o'clock	восемь часов	vo·sim' chi·sof

What would you recommend?
Что вы рекомендуете? shto vih ri·ka·min·du·it·ye

What's in that dish?
Что входит в это shto fkho·dit v e·ta
блюдо? blyu·da

It's delicious!
Очень вкусно! bih·la o·chin' fkus·na

Bring the bill.
Принесите pri·ni·sit·ye
счёт. pa·zhal·sta shot

Cyrillic	Sound	
А, а	a	as in 'father' (in a stressed syllable); as in 'ago' (in an unstressed syllable)
Б, б	b	as in 'but'
В, в	v	as in 'van'
Г, г	g	as in 'god'
Д, д	d	as in 'dog'
Е, е	ye	as in 'yet' (in a stressed syllable and at the end of a word);
	i	as in 'tin' (in an unstressed syllable)
Ё, ё	yo	as in 'yore' (often printed without dots)
Ж, ж	zh	as the 's' in 'measure'
З, з	z	as in 'zoo'
И, и	i	as the 'ee' in 'meet'
Й, й	y	as in 'boy' (not transliterated after ы or и)
К, к	k	as in 'kind'
Л, л	l	as in 'lamp'
М, м	m	as in 'mad'
Н, н	n	as in 'not'
О, о	o	as in 'more' (in a stressed syllable);
	a	as in 'hard' (in an unstressed syllable)
П, п	p	as in 'pig'
Р, р	r	as in 'rub' (rolled)
С, с	s	as in 'sing'
Т, т	t	as in 'ten'
У, у	u	as the 'oo' in 'fool'
Ф, ф	f	as in 'fan'
Х, х	kh	as the 'ch' in 'Bach'
Ц, ц	ts	as in 'bits'
Ч, ч	ch	as in 'chin'
Ш, ш	sh	as in 'shop'
Щ, щ	shch	as 'sh-ch' in 'fresh chips'
Ъ, ъ	–	'hard sign' meaning the preceding consonant is pronounced as it's written
Ы, ы	ih	as the 'y' in 'any'
Ь, ь	'	'soft sign' meaning the preceding consonant is pronounced like a faint y
Э, э	e	as in 'end'
Ю, ю	yu	as the 'u' in 'use'
Я, я	ya	as in 'yard' (in a stressed syllable);
	ye	as in 'yearn' (in an unstressed syllable)

Key Words

bottle	бутылка	bu·*tihl*·ka
bowl	миска	*mis*·ka
breakfast	завтрак	*zaf*·trak
cold	холодный	kha·*lod*·nih
dinner	ужин	*u*·zhihn
dish	блюдо	*blyu*·da
fork	вилка	*vil*·ka
glass	стакан	sta·*kan*
hot (warm)	жаркий	*zhar*·ki
knife	нож	nosh
lunch	обед	ab·*yet*
menu	меню	min·*yu*
plate	тарелка	tar·*yel*·ka
restaurant	ресторан	ris·ta·*ran*
spoon	ложка	*losh*·ka
with	с	s
without	без	byez

Meat & Fish

beef	говядина	gav·*ya*·di·na
caviar	икра	i·*kra*
chicken	курица	*ku*·rit·sa
duck	утка	*ut*·ka
fish	рыба	*rih*·ba
herring	сельдь	syelt'
lamb	баранина	ba·*ra*·ni·na
meat	мясо	*mya*·sa
oyster	устрица	*ust*·rit·sa
pork	свинина	svi·*ni*·na
prawn	креветка	kriv·*yet*·ka
salmon	лососина	la·sa·*si*·na
turkey	индейка	ind·*yey*·ka
veal	телятина	til·*ya*·ti·na

Fruit & Vegetables

apple	яблоко	*yab*·la·ka
bean	фасоль	fa·*sol'*
cabbage	капуста	ka·*pu*·sta
capsicum	перец	*pye*·rits
carrot	морковь	mar·*kof'*
cauliflower	цветная капуста	tsvit·*na*·ya ka·*pu*·sta
cucumber	огурец	a·gur·*yets*
fruit	фрукты	*fruk*·tih
mushroom	гриб	grip
nut	орех	ar·*yekh*
onion	лук	luk
orange	апельсин	a·pil'·*sin*
peach	персик	*pyer*·sik
pear	груша	*gru*·sha
plum	слива	*sli*·va
potato	картошка	kar·*tosh*·ka
spinach	шпинат	shpi·*nat*
tomato	помидор	pa·mi·*dor*
vegetable	овощ	*o*·vash

Other

bread	хлеб	khlyep
cheese	сыр	sihr
egg	яйцо	yeyt·*so*
honey	мёд	myot
oil	масло	*mas*·la
pasta	паста	*pa*·sta
pepper	перец	*pye*·rits
rice	рис	ris
salt	соль	sol'
sugar	сахар	*sa*·khar
vinegar	уксус	*uk*·sus

Drinks

beer	пиво	*pi*·va
coffee	кофе	*kof*·ye
champagne	шампанское	sham·*pan*·ska·ye
(orange) juice	(апельсиновый) сок	(a·pil'·*si*·na·vih) sok
milk	молоко	ma·la·*ko*
tea	чай	chey
(mineral) water	(минеральная) вода	(mi·ni·*ral'*·r va·*da*
wine	вино	vi·*no*

EMERGENCIES

Help!	Помогите!	pa·ma·gi·tye

Call ...!	Вызовите ...!	vih·za·vi·tye ...
a doctor	врача	vra·cha
the police	милицию	mi·li·tsih·yu

Leave me alone!
Приваливай! — pri·va·li·vai
There's been an accident.
Произошёл — pra·i·za·shol
несчастный случай. — ne·shas·nih slu·chai
I'm lost.
Я заблудился/ — ya za·blu·dil·sa/
заблудилась. (m/f) — za·blu·di·las'
Where are the toilets?
Где здесь туалет? — gdye zdyes' tu·al·yet
I'm ill.
Я болен/больна. (m/f) — ya bo·lin/bal'·na
It hurts here.
Здесь болит. — zdyes' ba·lit
I'm allergic to (antibiotics).
У меня алергия — u min·ya a·lir·gi·ya
на (антибиотики). — na (an·ti·bi·o·ti·ki)

SHOPPING & SERVICES

I need ...
Мне нужно ... — mnye nuzh·na ...
I'm just looking.
Я просто смотрю. — ya pros·ta smat·ryu
Can I look at it?
Покажите, — pa·ka·zhih·tye
пожалуйста. — pa·zhal·sta
How much is it?
Сколько стоит? — skol'·ka sto·it
That's too expensive.
Это очень дорого. — e·ta o·chen' do·ra·ga
There's a mistake in the bill.
Меня обсчитали. — min·ya ap·shi·ta·li

bank	банк	bank
market	рынок	rih·nak
post office	почта	poch·ta
telephone office	телефонный пункт	ti·li·fo·nih punkt

QUESTION WORDS

What?	Что?	shto
When?	Когда?	kag·da
Where?	Где?	gdye
Which?	Какой?	ka·koy
Who?	Кто?	kto
	Почему?	pa·chi·mu

TIME, DATES & NUMBERS

What time is it?
Который час? — ka·to·rih chas
It's (10) o'clock.
(Десять) часов. — (dye·sit') chi·sof

morning	утро	ut·ra
afternoon	после обеда	pos·lye ab·ye·da
evening	вечер	vye·chir
yesterday	вчера	vchi·ra
today	сегодня	si·vod·nya
tomorrow	завтра	zaft·ra

Monday	понедельник	pa·ni·dyel'·nik
Tuesday	вторник	ftor·nik
Wednesday	среда	sri·da
Thursday	четверг	chit·vyerk
Friday	пятница	pyat·ni·tsa
Saturday	суббота	su·bo·ta
Sunday	воскресенье	vas·kri·syen·ye

January	январь	yan·var'
February	февраль	fiv·ral'
March	март	mart
April	апрель	ap·ryel'
May	май	mai
June	июнь	i·yun'
July	июль	i·yul'
August	август	av·gust
September	сентябрь	sin·tyabr'
October	октябрь	ak·tyabr'
November	ноябрь	na·yabr'
December	декабрь	di·kabr'

1	один	a·din
2	два	dva
3	три	tri
4	четыре	chi·tih·ri
5	пять	pyat'
6	шесть	shest'
7	семь	syem'
8	восемь	vo·sim'
9	девять	dye·vyat'
10	десять	dye·syat'
20	двадцать	dva·tsat'
30	тридцать	tri·tsat'
40	сорок	so·rak
50	пятьдесят	pi·dis·yat
60	шестдесят	shihs·dis·yat
70	семьдесят	syem'·dis·yat

80	восемьдесят	vo·sim'·di·sit
90	девяносто	di·vi·no·sta
100	сто	sto
1000	тысяча	tih·si·cha

TRANSPORT

Public Transport

A ... ticket (to Novgorod).	Билет ... (на Новгород).	bil·yet ... (na nov·ga·rat)
one-way	в один конец	v a·din kan·yets
return	в оба конца	v o·ba kan·tsa
bus	автобус	af·to·bus
train	поезд	po·ist
tram	трамвай	tram·vai
trolleybus	троллейбус	tra·lyey·bus
first	первый	pyer·vih
last	последний	pas·lyed·ni
metro token	жетон	zhi·ton
platform	платформа	plat·for·ma
(bus) stop	остановка	a·sta·nof·ka
ticket	билет	bil·yet
ticket office	билетная касса	bil·yet·na·ya ka·sa
timetable	расписание	ras·pi·sa·ni·ye

When does it leave?
Когда отправляется? kag·da at·prav·lya·it·sa

How long does it take to get to ...?
Сколько времени skol'·ka vrye·mi·ni
нужно ехать до ...? nuzh·na ye·khat' da ...

Does it stop at ...?
Поезд останав- po·yist a·sta·nav·
ливается в ...? li·va·yit·sa v ...

Please stop here.
Остановитесь здесь, a·sta·na·vit·yes' zdyes'
пожалуйста! pa·zhal·sta

Driving & Cycling

I'd like to hire a ...	Я бы хотел/ хотела взять ... на прокат. (m/f)	ya bih kha·tyel/ kha·tye·la vzyat' ... na pra·kat
4WD	машину с полным приводом	ma·shih·nu s pol·nihm pri·vo·dam
bicycle	велосипед	vi·la·si·pyet
car	машину	ma·shih·nu
motorbike	мотоцикл	ma·ta·tsikl

KEY PATTERNS

To get by in Russian, mix and match these simple patterns with words of your choice:

When's (the next bus)?
Когда (будет kag·da (bu·dit
следующий slye·du·yu·shi
автобус)? af·to·bus)

Where's (the station)?
Где (станция)? gdye (stant·sih·ya)

Where can I (buy a padlock)?
Где можно (купить gdye mozh·na (ku·pit'
нависной замок)? na·vis·noy za·mok)

Do you have (a map)?
Здесь есть (карте)? zdyes' yest' (kart·ye)

I'd like (the menu).
Я бы хотел/ ya bih khat·yel/
хотела (меню). (m/f) khat·ye·la (min·yu)

I'd like to (hire a car).
Я бы хотел/ ya bih khat·yel/
хотела (взять khat·ye·la (vzyat'
машину). (m/f) ma·shih·nu)

Can I (come in)?
Можно (войти)? mozh·na (vey·ti)

Could you please (write it down)?
(Запишите), (za·pi·shiht·ye)
пожалуйста. pa·zhal·sta

Do I need (a visa)?
Нужна ли (виза)? nuzh·na li (vi·za)

I need (assistance).
Мне нужна mnye nuzh·na
(помощь). (po·mash)

diesel	дизельное топливо	di·zil'·na·ye to·pli·va
regular	бензин номер 93	ben·zin no·mir di·vi·no·sta tri
unleaded	очищенный бензин	a·chi·shi·nih bin·zin

Is this the road to ...?
Эта дорога ведёт в ...? e·ta da·ro·ga vid·yot f ...

Where's a petrol station?
Где заправка? gdye za·praf·ka

Can I park here?
Здесь можно стоять? zdyes' mozh·na sta·yat'

I need a mechanic.
Мне нужен mnye nu·zhihn
автомеханик. af·ta·mi·kha·nik

The car has broken down.
Машина сломалась. ma·shih·na sla·ma·las

I have a flat tyre.
У меня лопнула шина. u min·ya lop·nu·la

I've run out of petrol.
У меня кончился u min·ya kon·
бензин. bin·zin

GLOSSARY

avtovokzal – bus terminal

bankomat – ATM
banya – Russian bathhouse, similar to a sauna
bilet, bilety – ticket, tickets
boyar – high-ranking noble
bufet – snack bar
bulvar – boulevard

dacha – country cottage or summer house
devushka or **devushki** (pl) – young woman
dom – house, building
DPS (Dorozhno-Patrulnaya Sluzhba) – Road Patrol Service
duma – parliament

elektrichka – slow, suburban train

firmeny poezd – a fancy, fast train, often with a special name

glasnost – literally 'openness'; used in reference to the free-expression aspect of the Gorbachev reforms in the 1980s
gostinitsa – hotel

kamera khraneniya – left-luggage
kassa – cash register or ticket office
kremlin – fort, usually a town's foundation
kruglosutochno – around the

clock, 24 hours a day, usually used in reference to opening hours
kupeyny or **kupe** – 2nd class on a train; usually four-person couchettes

lyux – luxury or 1st class; often refers to a sleeping car on a train or rooms in a hotel

magazin – shop
maly – small
matryoshka – painted wooden nesting doll
mesto – place, as in seat on a train
MKAD (Moskovskaya Koltsevaya Avtomobilnaya Doroga) – Moscow Automobile Ring Road; refers to the outermost highway around the city
most – bridge
muzey – museum

naberezhnaya – embankment

passazhirsky poezd – slow, intercity passenger train
perekhod – cross walk, often underground
pereriv – break period, often in the middle of the day, when stores close
perestroika – literally 'restructuring'; refers to Gorbachev's economic reforms of the 1980s
pereulok – lane or side street
platskartny – 3rd class, general seating on an intercity train

ploshchad – square
prigorodny poezd – slow, suburban train
proezd – passage
prospekt – avenue

rynok – market
ryumochnaya – bar

sad – garden
samizdat – underground publishing during the Soviet period
shampanskoye – Russian sparkling wine
shapka – fur hat
shosse – highway
skory poezd – fast train
spalny vagon (SV) – sleeping car
stolovaya – canteen or cafeteria

tsarevitch – son of the tsar, successor to the throne
tsarina – wife of the tsar
tserkov – church

ulitsa – street
uslovie yedenitsiy (y.e.) – standard unit that usually equates to €s or US dollars; sometimes used to quote prices in upmarket restaurants and hotels

vagon – train carriage
val – rampart
vokzal – train station

MENU DECODER

y – crêpes блины
h – beetroot soup борщ
od – open-faced sandерброд

nish, or side dish

ikra (chyornaya, krasnaya) – caviar (black, red) икра (чёрная, красная)

kartoshki – potatoes картошки
kasha – porridge каша

kefir – sour yogurt-like drink кефир
khleb – bread хлеб
kvas – mildly alcoholic fermented-rye-bread drink квас
lapsha – noodle soup лапша

losos – salmon лосось

mineralnaya voda (gazirovannaya, negazirovannaya) – water (sparkling, still) минеральная вода (газированная, негазированная)

moloko – milk молоко

morozhenoye – ice cream мороженое

myaso – meat мясо

obed – midday meal обедь

okroshka – cold cucumber soup with a *kvas* base окрошка

ovoshchi – vegetables овощи

ovoshnoy salat – tomato and cucumber salad, literally 'vegetable salad' овошной салат

pelmeni – dumplings filled with meat or vegetables пельмени

pirog or pirogi (pl) – pie пирог, пироги

pivo (svetloe, tyomnoe) – beer (light, dark) пиво (светлое, тёмное)

ptitsa – poultry птица

ris – rice рис

ryba – fish рыба

salat olivier – see *stolichny salat* салат Оливье

seld pod shuboy – salad with herring, potatoes, beets and carrots, literally 'herring in a fur coat' сельдь под шубой

shashlyk (myasnoy, kuriny, rybnoy) – kebab (meat, chicken, fish) шашлык (мясной, куриный, рыбной)

shchi – cabbage soup щи

solyanka – a tasty meat soup with salty vegetables and hint of lemon солянка

svekolnik – cold beet soup свекольник

sok – juice сок

stolichny salat – 'capital salad', which contains beef, potatoes and eggs in mayonnaise; also called *salat olivier* столичный салат

tvorog – soft sweet cheese similar to ricotta творог

uzhin – dinner ужин

zavtrak – breakfast завтрак

zakuski – appetisers закуски

Behind the Scenes

SEND US YOUR FEEDBACK

We love to hear from travellers – your comments keep us on our toes and help make our books better. Our well-travelled team reads every word on what you loved or loathed about this book. Although we cannot reply individually to your submissions, we always guarantee that your feedback goes straight to the appropriate authors, in time for the next edition. Each person who sends us information is thanked in the next edition – the most useful submissions are rewarded with a selection of digital PDF chapters.

Visit **lonelyplanet.com/contact** to submit your updates and suggestions or to ask for help. Our award-winning website also features inspirational travel stories, news and discussions.

Note: We may edit, reproduce and incorporate your comments in Lonely Planet products such as guidebooks, websites and digital products, so let us know if you don't want your comments reproduced or your name acknowledged. For a copy of our privacy policy visit lonelyplanet.com/privacy.

OUR READERS

Many thanks to the travellers who used the last edition and wrote to us with helpful hints, useful advice and interesting anecdotes:

Anna Forsberg, Anna Roberts, Barbara Hofmann, Chiara Tosi, Ines Biemmi, Karen Hamilton, Maggie Mancktelow, Martin Gruber, Mikhail Kochikov, Moritz Classen, Oli Somenzi, Sain Alizada, Uvo Lancing.

AUTHOR THANKS

Mara Vorhees

Самое большое спасибо to my friend and co-author, Leonid Ragozin, who is a pleasure to work with and *fontanka* of information about his home town. Thanks to Tim O'Brien (of course), Marc Bennetts, Simon Richmond and Andrei Muchnik for lots of ideas. And finally, what a treat to spend time (not enough) with two dear friends from my past: 'Nasha Pasha' Yesin and Lyonya Klyuev. As always, thanks to my little guys, S&V, for challenging me to see familiar destinations from new perspectives, and to Daddio for, well, everything.

Leonid Ragozin

On this occasion I need to thank God for the fact that I was born and lived all my life in Moscow, which is why this LP title was particularly important to me. Of human beings, I would like to thank my wife, Masha Makeyeva, and my friend Dmitry Zhuravlev for all their invaluable advice. Also huge thanks to my LP colleagues Mara Vorhees and Brana Vladisavljevic for their great, friendly attitudes and help dealing with the complexities of LP authoring.

ACKNOWLEDGEMENTS

Cover photo: St Basil's Cathedral. Dallas and John Heaton/Alamy.

THIS BOOK

This 6th edition of Lonely Planet's *Moscow* guidebook was researched and written by Mara Vorhees and Leonid Ragozin. The 5th edition was written by Mara Vorhees and Leonid Ragozin, and the 4th edition by Mara Vorhees. This guidebook was commissioned in Lonely Planet's London office, and produced by the following:

Destination Editor Brana Vladisavljevic

Coordinating Editor Lauren O'Connell

Product Editor Pete Cruttenden

Assisting Editors Kate Evans, Victoria Harrison

Senior Cartographer Valentina Kremenchutskaya

Assisting cartographer Laura Matthewman

Book Designer Jessica Rose

Assisting Book Designer Clara Monitto

Cover Researcher Naomi Parker

Illustrator Javier Zarracina

Thanks to Sasha Baskett, Elin Berglund, Ljubomir Ceranic, Brendan Dempsey, Ryan Evans, Larissa Frost, James Hardy, Jouve India, Wayne Murphy, Claire Naylor, Karyn Noble, Angela Tinson, Samantha Russell-Tulip, Anna Tyler

Index

Moscow Maps

Sights

- Beach
- Bird Sanctuary
- Buddhist
- Castle/Palace
- Christian
- Confucian
- Hindu
- Islamic
- Jain
- Jewish
- Monument
- Museum/Gallery/Historic Building
- Ruin
- Sento Hot Baths/Onsen
- Shinto
- Sikh
- Taoist
- Winery/Vineyard
- Zoo/Wildlife Sanctuary
- Other Sight

Activities, Courses & Tours

- Bodysurfing
- Diving
- Canoeing/Kayaking
- Course/Tour
- Skiing
- Snorkelling
- Surfing
- Swimming/Pool
- Walking
- Windsurfing
- Other Activity

Sleeping

- Sleeping
- Camping

Eating

- Eating

Drinking & Nightlife

- Drinking & Nightlife
- Cafe

Entertainment

- Entertainment

Shopping

- Shopping

Information

- Bank
- Embassy/Consulate
- Hospital/Medical
- Internet
- Police
- Post Office
- Telephone
- Toilet
- Tourist Information
- Other Information

Geographic

- Beach
- Hut/Shelter
- Lighthouse
- Lookout
- Mountain/Volcano
- Oasis
- Park
- Pass
- Picnic Area
- Waterfall

Population

- Capital (National)
- Capital (State/Province)
- City/Large Town
- Town/Village

Transport

- Airport
- Border crossing
- Bus
- Cable car/Funicular
- Cycling
- Ferry
- Metro station
- Monorail
- Parking
- Petrol station
- S-Bahn/Subway station
- Taxi
- T-bane/Tunnelbana station
- Train station/Railway
- Tram
- Tube station
- U-Bahn/Underground station
- Other Transport

Note: Not all symbols displayed above appear on the maps in this book

Routes

- Tollway
- Freeway
- Primary
- Secondary
- Tertiary
- Lane
- Unsealed road
- Road under construction
- Plaza/Mall
- Steps
- Tunnel
- Pedestrian overpass
- Walking Tour
- Walking Tour detour
- Path/Walking Trail

Boundaries

- International
- State/Province
- Disputed
- Regional/Suburb
- Marine Park
- Cliff
- Wall

Hydrography

- River, Creek
- Intermittent River
- Canal
- Water
- Dry/Salt/Intermittent Lake
- Reef

Areas

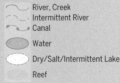

- Airport/Runway
- Beach/Desert
- Cemetery (Christian)
- Cemetery (Other)
- Glacier
- Mudflat
- Park/Forest
- Sight (Building)
- Sportsground
- Swamp/Mangrove

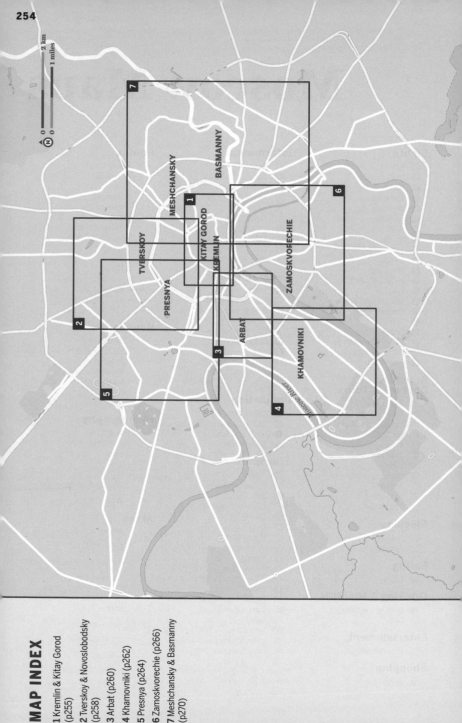

254

MAP INDEX

MESHCHANSKY

BASMANNY

TVERSKOY

KITAY GOROD

KREMLIN

PRESNYA

ZAMOSKVORECHIE

ARBAT

KHAMOVNIKI

Moskva River

2 km

1 miles

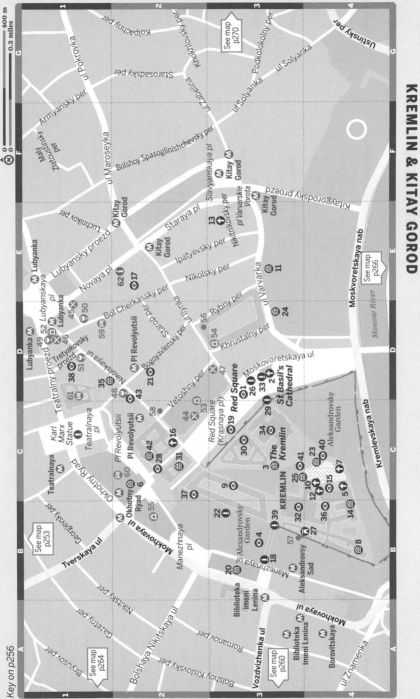

Key on p256

TVERSKOY & NOVOSLOBODSKY Map on p258

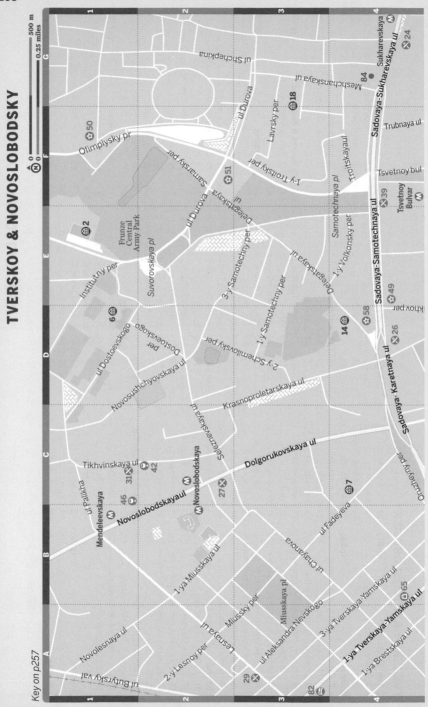

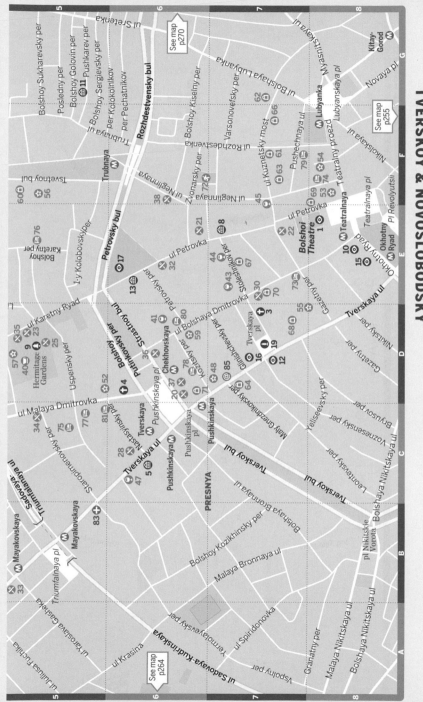

See map p270

See map p255

See map p264

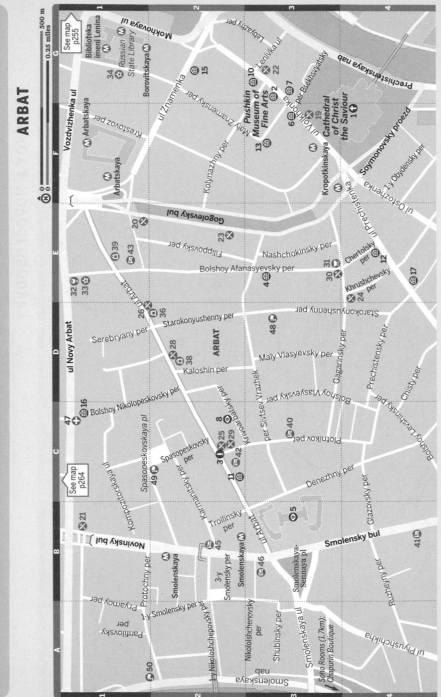

ARBAT

See map p270

Krasny Oktabr

Moscow River

Prechistenskaya nab

Kursovoy per

2-y Obydensky per

Pozharsky per

1-y Zachatyevsky per

Barykovsky per

Sechenovsky per

ul Ostozhenka

Mansurovsky per

Evropkinsky per

Maly Levshinsky per

ul Prechistenka

Kropotkinsky per

See map p262

Zubovsky bul

KHAMOVNIKI

1-y Neopalimovsky per

Serpov per

Zemledelchesky per

◎ Top Sights   (p117)
1 Cathedral of Christ the Saviour F4
2 Pushkin Museum of Fine Arts G3

◎ Sights   (p122)
3 Bulat Okudzhava Statue C2
4 Burganov House B3
5 Foreign Affairs Ministry E3
6 Gallery of European & American
  Art of the 19th & 20th
  Centuries F3
7 Glazunov Gallery G3
8 Melnikov House C2
9 Multimedia Art Museum E5
10 Museum of Private Collections G3
11 Pushkin House-Museum C2
12 Pushkin Literary Museum E4
13 Rerikh Museum F3

14 Russian Academy of Arts D5
15 Shilov Gallery G2
16 Tochka-G Museum of Erotic Art.... C1
17 Tolstoy Literary Museum E4
18 Tsereteli Gallery D5

⊗ Eating   (p126)
19 Akademiya F3
20 Akademiya E1
21 Balkon B1
22 Cafe Schislva G3
23 Chemodan E2
24 Elardzhi E4
Galereya Khudozhnikov .... (see 18)
25 Moo-Moo C2
26 Rukkola D1
27 Tiflis D5
28 Varenichnaya No 1 .... D2

29 Vostochny Kvartal C2
30 Zhurfak Cafe E3

◎ Drinking & Nightlife   (p128)
31 Gogol-Mogol E3
32 Zhiguli Beer Hall E1

✪ Entertainment   (p129)
33 Gelikon Opera E1
34 Rhythm Blues Cafe G1

◎ Shopping   (p130)
35 Artefact Gallery Centre D5
36 Association of Artists of the
  Decorative Arts (AHDI) C2
37 Buro Nahodok B5
38 Russian Embroidery & Lace D2
39 Russkie Chasovye Traditsii D2

⊜ Sleeping   (p180)
40 Arbat Hotel C3
41 Bear Hostel on Smolenskaya B4
42 Bulgakov Mini-Hotel C2
43 Dal Hostel E1
44 Kebur Palace E5
45 Mercure Arbat Hotel B2
46 People Hotel B3

⊙ Information   (p232)
47 36.6 Arbat C1
48 Canadian Embassy D3
49 Mongolian Embassy (Visa
  Section) C2
50 UK Embassy A1

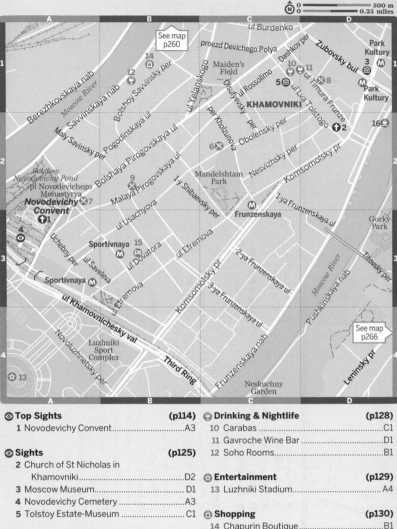

PRESNYA *Map on p264*

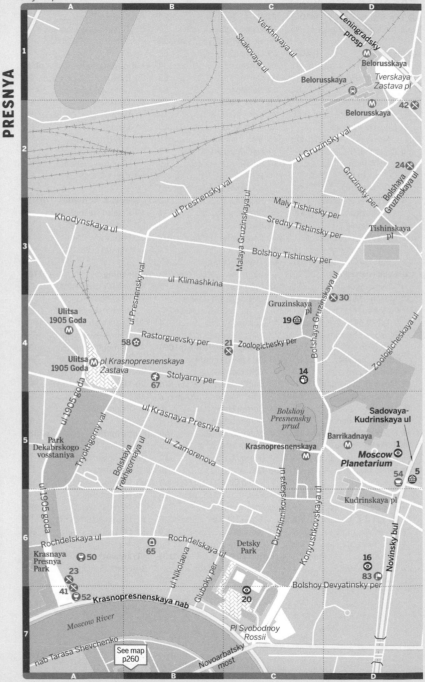

Key on p263

PRESNYA

A **B** **C** **D**

Leningradsky prosp

Verkhnyaya ul

Skakovaya ul

Belorusskaya

M Belorusskaya

Tverskaya Zastava pl

Belorusskaya

42 ✕

ul Gruzinsky val

Gruzinsky per

Bolshaya Gruzinskaya ul

24 ✕

ul Presnensky val

Maly Tishinsky per

Sredny Tishinsky per

Tishinskaya pl

Khodynskaya ul

Malaya Gruzinskaya ul

Bolshoy Tishinsky per

ul Klimashkina

Bolshaya Gruzinskaya ul

Zoologichesky ul

ul Presnensky val

Gruzinskaya pl

19 🏛

30 ✕

Ulitsa 1905 Goda

M

58 ✪

Rastorguevsky per

21 ✕

Zoologichesky per

14 ✿

Ulitsa 1905 Goda M

pl Krasnopresnenskaya Zastava

67 ✦

Stolyarny per

ul Krasnaya Presnya

Bolshoy Presnensky prud

Sadovaya-Kudrinskaya ul

ul 1905 goda

Tryokhgorny val

Bolshaya Trekhgornaya ul

ul Zamorenova

Krasnopresnenskaya M

Barrikadnaya M

1 ◎ Moscow Planetarium

54 🏛 5

Park Dekabrskogo vosstaniya

Kudrinskaya pl

ul 1905 goda

Druzhinnikovskaya ul

Konyushkovskaya ul

Novinsky bul

Rochdelskaya ul

65 🔒

Rochdelskaya ul

Detsky Park

16 ◎

Krasnaya Presnya Park

50 ◉

ul Nikolaeva

Gluboky per

83 ◉

Bolshoy Devyatinsky per

23 ✕

41 ✕

52 ◉

Krasnopresnenskaya nab

20 ◎

Moscow River

Pl Svobodnoy Rossii

nab Tarasa Shevchenko

See map p260

Novoarbatsky most

A **B** **C** **D**

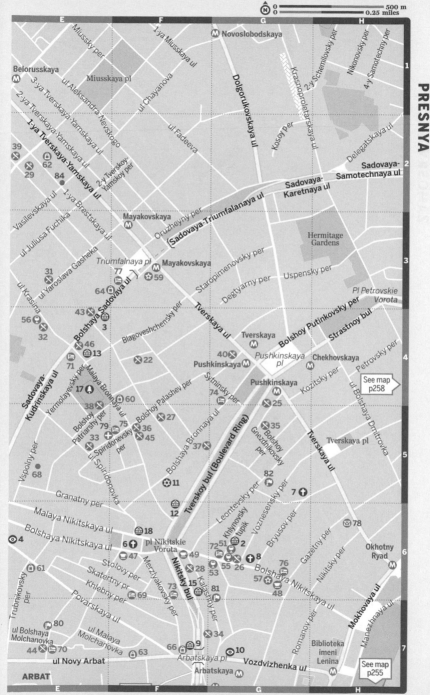

ZAMOSKVORECHIE

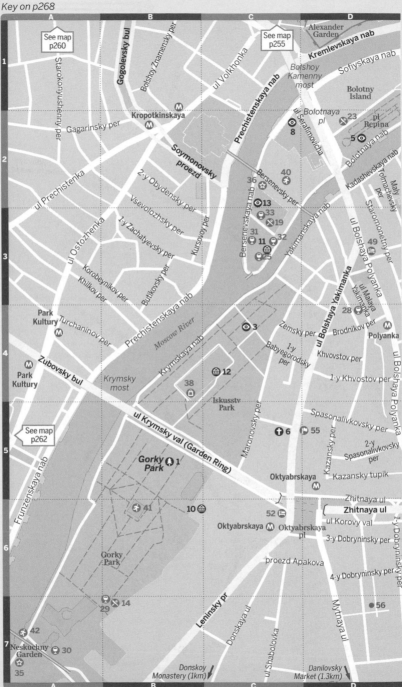

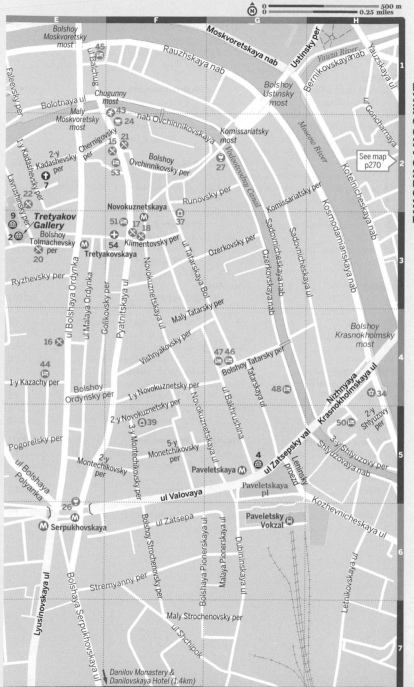

0 —— 500 m
0 —— 0.25 miles

Bolshoy
Moskvoretsky
most

ul Balchug

45

Moskvoretskaya nab

Rauzhskaya nab

Ustinsky per

Yauza River
Bernikovskaya nab

Yauzskaya ul

Bolshoy
Ustinsky
most

Bolotnaya ul

Chugunny
most

Maly
Moskvoretsky
most

43

24

nab Ovchinnikovskaya

Komissariatsky
most

ul Goncharnaya

See map
p270

Faleevsky per

2-y
Kadashevsky
per

15

Chernigovsky per

21

Bolshoy
Ovchinnikovsky per

Vodootvodny Canal

Komissariatsky per

Moscow River

Kotelnicheskaya nab

Kosmodamianskaya nab

1-y Kadashevsky per

7

53

Runovsky per

27

Sadovnicheskaya nab

Lavrushinsky per

22

9

Tretyakov
Gallery

2

Bolshoy
Tolmachevsky
per

20

Novokuznetskaya

51

17 18

37

Ozerkovsky per

Sadovnicheskaya ul

Ozerkovskaya nab

54

Klimentovsky per

Tretyakovskaya

Ryzhevsky per

ul Bolshaya Ordynka

ul Malaya Ordynka

Golikovsky per

Pyatnitskaya ul

Novokuznetskaya ul

ul Tatarskaya Bol

Maly Tatarsky per

Bolshoy
Krasnokholmsky
most

16

44

1-y Kazachy per

Bolshoy
Ordynsky per

1-y Novokuznetsky per

Vishnyakovsky per

47 46

Bolshoy Tatarsky per

48

Nizhnyaya
Krasnokholmskaya ul

34

Pogorelsky per

2-y
Montechikovsky
per

2-y Novokuznetsky per

3-y Montechikovsky per

39

Novokuznetskaya ul

ul Bakhrushina

50

2-y
Shlyuzovy
per

3-y Shlyuzovy per

Shlyuzovaya nab

ul Bolshaya
Polyanka

5-y
Monetchikovsky
per

4

Paveletskaya

ul Zatsepsky val

Leninsky
proezd

26

ul Valovaya

Paveletskaya
pl

Kozhevnicheskaya ul

Serpukhovskaya

ul Zatsepa

Paveletsky
Vokzal

Lyusinovskaya ul

Bolshaya Serpukhovskaya ul

Stremyanny per

Bolshoy Strochenovsky per

Bolshaya Pionerskaya ul

Malaya Pionerskaya ul

Dubininskaya ul

Letnikovskaya ul

Maly Strochenovsky per

ul Shchipok

Danilov Monastery &
Danilovskaya Hotel (1.4km)

ZAMOSKVORECHIE *Map on p266*

MESHCHANSKY & BASMANNY

Key on p269

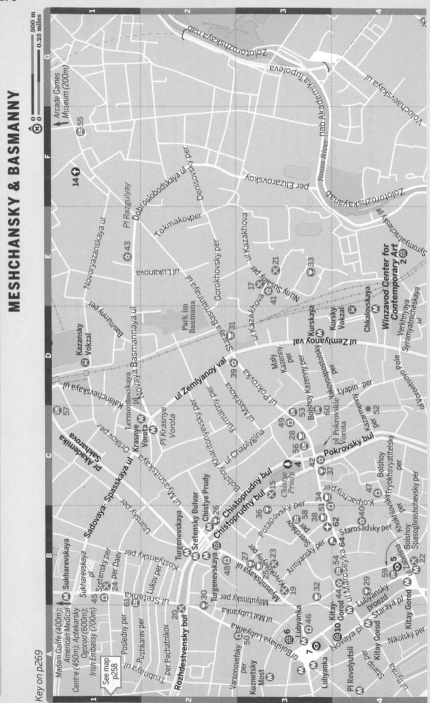

0
0

N

500 m
0.25 miles

Arcade Games
Museum (200m)

Madam Galife (400m);
American Medical
Centre (450m); Aptekarsky
Ogorod (600m);
Irish Embassy (700m)

See map
p258

See map
p258

Winzavod Center for
Contemporary Art